Making History

Making History offers a fresh perspective on the study of history. It is a detailed exploration of the practice of history, of historical traditions and of the theories that surround them. Discussing the development and growth of history as a discipline and of the profession of the historian, the book encompasses a huge diversity of influences, and is organised around the following themes:

- The professionalisation of the discipline, its methodology, the nature of 'scientific' history and the problem of objectivity
- the most significant movements in historical scholarship in the last century, including the *Annales* School, and other variants of social and economic history
- the increasingly interdisciplinary trends in scholarship, showing interconnections between history and a range of disciplines from psychoanalysis to anthropology.
- theory in historical practice, looking at the social movements and ideologies that carried them, including Marxism, post-modernism and gender history
- historical practice outside the academy with reference to 'amateur' history, heritage, film, and popular culture.

The volume offers a coherent and carefully considered set of chapters that will support undergraduates, postgraduates and others interested in the historical processes that have shaped the discipline of history.

Peter Lambert is Lecturer in History at the University of Wales, Aberystwyth, and has published on historiography. **Phillip Schofield** is Senior Lecturer in History at the University of Wales, Aberystwyth, and is the author of *Peasant and Community in Medieval England, 1200–1500*.

Making History

Making History offers a fresh perspective on the study of history. It is a detailed exploration of the practice of history, of historical traditions and of the theories that surround them. Discussing the development and growth of history as a discipline and of the profession of the historian, the book encompasses a huge diversity of influences, and is organised around the following themes:

- The professionalisation of the discipline, its methodology, the nature of 'scientific' history and the problem of objectivity
- the most significant movements in historical scholarship in the last century, including the *Annales* School, and other variants of social and economic history
- the increasingly interdisciplinary trends in scholarship, showing interconnections between history and a range of disciplines from psychoanalysis to anthropology.
- theory in historical practice, looking at the social movements and ideologies that carried them, including Marxism, post-modernism and gender history
- historical practice outside the academy with reference to 'amateur' history, heritage, film, and popular culture.

The volume offers a coherent and carefully considered set of chapters that will support undergraduates, postgraduates and others interested in the historical processes that have shaped the discipline of history.

Peter Lambert is Lecturer in History at the University of Wales, Aberystwyth, and has published on historiography. **Phillip Schofield** is Senior Lecturer in History at the University of Wales, Aberystwyth, and is the author of *Peasant and Community in Medieval England, 1200–1500*.

Making History

An introduction to the history and practices of a discipline

Edited by Peter Lambert
and Phillipp Schofield

Routledge
Taylor & Francis Group

LONDON AND NEW YORK

First published 2004
by Routledge
2 Park Square, Milton Park, Abingdon, Oxon OX14 4RN

Simultaneously published in the USA and Canada
by Routledge
270 Madison Ave, New York, NY 10016

Routledge is an imprint of the Taylor & Francis Group

Transferred to Digital Printing 2005

© 2004 selection and editorial matter Peter Lambert and Phillipp
Schofield; individual chapters © the contributors

Typeset in Gill Sans and Galliard by Taylor & Francis Books Ltd

British Library Cataloguing in Publication Data
A catalogue record for this book is available from the British
Library

Library of Congress Cataloging in Publication Data
Making history: an introduction to the history and practices of a
discipline / [edited by] Peter Lambert and Phillipp Schofield.
p. cm.
Includes bibliographical references and index.
1. Historiography. I. Lambert, Peter, 1956– II. Schofield, Phillipp R.,
1964–
D13.M2655 2004
907'.2—dc22

                              2004007116

ISBN 0–415–24254–1 (hbk)
ISBN 0–415–24255–X (pbk)

Printed and bound by Antony Rowe Ltd, Eastbourne

Contents

Contributors

John Davidson retired, in 1998, as Senior Lecturer in African and South Asian History in the Department of History and Welsh History, University of Wales, Aberystwyth. His early research was in the history of southern Sierra Leone. His current research interest is the history of Edinburgh in the mid-nineteenth century.

Susan Davies is Lecturer in Palaeography and Archive Studies, Department of History and Welsh History, University of Wales, Aberystwyth. Her research interests include medieval records, editorial methods and archival and heritage issues. She has served as a member of the Royal Commission on Historical Manuscripts and is currently Vice-president of the National Museum and Galleries of Wales (2002–).

Robert Harrison teaches American History at the University of Wales, Aberystwyth. His research interests cover various aspects of late nineteenth- and early twentieth-century American social and political history, and his recent publications include *State and Society in Twentieth-Century America*, London, Longman, 1997; and *Congress, Progressive Reform, and the New American State*, Cambridge, Cambridge University Press, 2004.

Aled Jones is Professor of Welsh History at the University of Wales, Aberystwyth. He specialises in the history of communications, and his publications include *Press, Politics and Society: A History of Journalism in Wales*, Cardiff, University of Wales Press, 1993; *Powers of the Press: Newspapers, Power and the Public in Nineteenth-century England*, Aldershot, Scolar Press, 1996; and, with Bill Jones, *Welsh Reflections. Y Drych and America 1851–2001*, Llandysul, Gomer Press, 2001.

Peter Lambert lectures in Modern European History at the University of Wales, Aberystwyth, and has published widely on German historiography. He is editor (with Stefan Berger and Peter Schumann) of *Historikerdialoge*, Göttingen, Vandenhoeck & Ruprecht, 2003, a collection of essays on Anglo-German historiographical relations (2003), and is currently working on a book about the Weimar Republic.

Peter Miskell is a lecturer in Business History at the University of Reading Business School. His primary research interest is in the growth of the film industry in the twentieth century and its social/cultural influence. He is currently working on a British Academy funded project entitled 'Movies and Multinationals: US Film Companies in Britain, 1918–1939'.

Siân Nicholas is Lecturer in Modern British History, Department of History and Welsh History, University of Wales, Aberystwyth. Her research focuses upon the role of the mass media in modern British politics and society, and her publications include *The Echo of War: Home Front Propaganda and the Wartime BBC*, Manchester, Manchester University Press, 1996.

Paul O'Leary is Senior Lecturer in Welsh History in the Department of History and Welsh History, University of Wales, Aberystwyth. His research focuses on issues relating to migration, ethnicity and popular politics in nine-teenth- and twentieth-century Wales, and his publications include *Immigration and Integration: The Irish in Wales, 1798–1922*, Cardiff, University of Wales Press, 2000.

Michael Roberts teaches History at the University of Wales, Aberystwyth. His research interests include the histories of women, work and gender, the cultural formation of the British Isles, and historiography. He edited (with Simone Clarke), *Women and Gender in Early Modern Wales*, Cardiff, University of Wales Press, 2000.

William D. Rubinstein is Professor of Modern History at the University of Wales, Aberystwyth. Born and educated in the United States, he lived for many years in Australia, and was Professor of Social and Economic History at Deakin University in Victoria before taking up his present post in 1995. He has written widely on many aspects of history, his two most recent books being *Twentieth Century Britain: A Political History*, Basingstoke, Palgrave, 2003; and *Genocide: A History*, London, Longman, 2004.

Phillipp Schofield is Senior Lecturer in Medieval History, Department of History and Welsh History, University of Wales, Aberystwyth. His research focuses upon the nature of rural society in the high and late Middle Ages and his publications include *Peasant and Community in Medieval England, 1200–1500*, Basingstoke, Palgrave, 2002.

Gareth Williams is Professor of History in the Centre for Modern and Contemporary Wales at the University of Glamorgan. He was previously Professor of History at the University of Wales, Aberystwyth. He has written extensively on popular culture in Wales and has co-authored and co-edited several books on the social history of sport and music. His own publications include *1905 and All That: Essays on Rugby Football and Welsh Society*, Llandysul, Gomer Press, 1991; *George Ewart Evans*, Cardiff, University of

Wales Press, 1991; and *Valleys of Song: Music and Society in Wales 1840–1914*, Cardiff, University of Wales Press, 1998, repr. 2003.

Tim Woods is Professor of English and American Studies, Department of English, University of Wales, Aberystwyth. His research focuses principally upon contemporary American and British literature and literary theory, and his publications include *Beginning Postmodernism*, Manchester, Manchester University Press, 1999; *Literatures of Memory* (co-authored with Peter Middleton), Manchester, Manchester University Press, 2000; and *The Poetics of the Limit: Ethics and Politics in Modern and Contemporary American Poetry*, Basingstoke, Palgrave Macmillan, 2002.

Acknowledgements

This volume has grown out of a course on historiography taught in the Department of History and Welsh History at the University of Wales, Aberystwyth. Our first debt is to those of our current and former colleagues who helped mould the course. Among the latter, thanks especially to R. R. Davies, who initiated the course, and who liberated subsequent generations of students from the suffocating fixation with long lines of 'great' historians; and to John Watts, who played a pivotal part in giving it its current shape. We have been fortunate in being able to include four chapters by scholars working outside our department. Tim Woods is a member of Aberystwyth's Department of English, and provided us with a refreshing perspective from his own discipline. Peter Miskell, who is now a lecturer in the School of Management at the University of Reading, had studied history at Aberystwyth and taught on the course while a postgraduate. Gareth Williams moved from our department to take up a chair at the Centre for Modern and Contemporary Wales, University of Glamorgan. John Davidson retired from his post at Aberystwyth. All their contributions were beyond any imaginable call of duty.

Second, we owe a great deal to the successive cohorts of students who have taken the course, to their comments and to their suggestions for its development. We were able to recommend many excellent set texts to them, but not to suggest one text which covered the same ground as our course, and did so in similar ways. Finally, our thanks go to Chris Wickham and David Carpenter, who acted as external examiners for the course over the last four years. Their warm remarks on its outcomes encouraged us to believe that a 'book of the course' might be worthwhile.

P.A.L.
P.R.S.
Aberystwyth
August 2003

Introduction

Peter Lambert and Phillipp Schofield

This book is about how, when and why particular approaches to making history have emerged, established themselves, changed and even collapsed. Our focus is on the 'history' produced as an academic discipline, that is, very largely in university history departments. We first explore the beginnings of professional, academic historical research and writing in the late eighteenth and nineteenth centuries. A good deal of what we describe there will be perfectly recognisable to an undergraduate history student or to any reader of academic history books. Ways of teaching historians, through seminars and workshops dedicated to dissecting documents, which continue to occupy a pivotal position in the delivery of history degree schemes today, had evolved in the era of professionalisation. Results of these training regimes showed through in books displaying a rigorous use of primary sources. But much else that was characteristic of the nascent profession will seem alien. Above all, it will seem narrow – in its social composition and its work. Elitism and nationalism were definitive of both.

The bulk of the volume concerns subsequent developments within academic history, tracing the intellectual fashions and movements through which academic history acquired new identities. Historians drew eclectically on the questions, methods and sensibilities of other academic disciplines. They forged sub-disciplines, like economic and social history. Many tried to show what theory could offer history. Sometimes, self-consciously 'progressive' historians bunched themselves into schools. Even where links were looser than that, historians could share distinctive perspectives. Some sought (and still seek) to interpret the past 'from below' or in ways informed by feminism; others, to comprehend a past culture in its totality.

We do not just document and try to explain these innovations and shifts. We also draw on them. That is, we use a broad range of tried and tested historical methods, perspectives and approaches to understanding causes. Studying the history of historiography (i.e. the history of historical writing) and of other stages in the process of making history, or other ways of making history, demands no special skills. Rather, the challenge is to see how far historians can get in understanding the history of their own discipline by using the skills and methods that discipline has supplied and which they would apply to any comparable historical problem. In that sense, we recognise a collective debt to our own subject-matter.

Until quite recently, a book of this sort would have begun and ended with outlines of the careers and influence of a handful of 'great' historians. It might have recognised commonalities among some of them, distinguishing particular schools of historians or distinctive national traditions of historical scholarship, for instance. But the individual historian would still have been the focus of attention – whether as the charismatic intellectual leader around whom admirers and imitators clustered to form a school, or as the pre-eminent exponent of a national culture. There is much to be said for that approach. It allows one to try to do justice to the researcher bringing new evidence to light, or to the author of magisterial overviews, presenting new ways of connecting familiar bodies of evidence.

These, of course, are objectives which no sensible attempt at explaining developments in historical research and writing should neglect. However, just as academic historians have long since jettisoned the view that 'great men' (and occasionally women) make history, so they have generally accepted that there is a great deal more to the history of historiography than just the work of great historians. Broad trends in scholarship are not reducible to models provided by this or that individual historian. And it is broad trends that this book is about. Emphatically, the authors of the essays below do not imagine these trends in terms of the straightforward accumulation of knowledge. Nor do they necessarily equate changes in how history has been practised with progress. In both respects, this volume is indebted to the work of a trained physicist, and historian and philosopher of science, Thomas Kuhn. And it is with Kuhn's contentions as to how science changes that we begin.

Kuhn argued that science is produced by a community of scholars. They enjoy a collective identity founded on a shared definition of the problems confronting them, and of the methods appropriate to their solution. So long as the solutions keep coming – smoothly, according to a pattern and in conformity to the conceptual framework common to the community of scholars – 'normal science' prevails. Kuhn identified the constitutive elements of 'normal science' as comprising a nexus of collectively identified problems, tools for tackling them, and answers to them. He called this a 'paradigm'. A paradigm can be robust, durable and above all useful – but only for as long as the outcomes of research or experiment remain predictable. Unpredicted, anomalous answers may imply that something is amiss with the way a problem has been presented. Fundamental change occurs when anomalies proliferate to such a degree that the over-arching claims of the paradigm collapse. At that point, the community of scholars fragments, and their formerly cohesive approach gives way to an interlude of turmoil in which scholarship has no core. Divergent approaches now compete until the power/knowledge vacuum is filled with the emergence of a new paradigm. Thus, a long period of stability and security in the practical, problem-solving potential of a 'normal science' ends in the sudden collapse of an old order of knowledge and finally, through a 'scientific revolution', in the arrival of a new. Next, the whole cycle will simply be repeated.[1]

Kuhn was ambiguous about the applicability of his thesis beyond the history of science, but historians have sought to apply it to their own discipline. They have seldom done so rigidly.[2] It is in this spirit that the contributors to this volume have set themselves questions provoked at least in part by Kuhn. Were one to substitute 'historical scholarship' for 'science', would his model work? Has there ever been such a thing as 'normal science' in the pursuit of history? If so, have the great changes in historical practice been revolutionary, or has the 'normal science' of historians been capable of adapting itself to meet challenges, so that the development of the discipline has been evolutionary, not revolutionary? How far can the history of historiography be written 'from the inside' of the discipline, and how far is the shaping of scholarship dictated by wider political, social, economic or cultural forces or by events? These forces and events are the subject of historians' work; to what extent are historians simultaneously subject to their influence?

Approaches that essentially concern themselves with the internal dynamics and development of the discipline of history can tend to an architectural interpretation. Each successive generation of historians will appear to build on the work of its predecessor, so that layers of historical knowledge accumulate on top of each other and the discipline makes steady progress through a phase in which 'normal science' predominates. A paradigm, at this point, can have a Janus-faced quality. It may function simultaneously as a safe-haven, defending and promoting a particular approach to advancing historical inquiry, *and* as a sort of intellectual prison, with inmates bound by rules and regulations. Early on in the establishment of history as a profession, which is the point of departure for this book, it clearly exhibited both these characteristics to a high degree. Professionalisation entailed the creation of hierarchies, qualifications and bureaucratic mechanisms of control. On the one hand, these sought to immunise the scholarly community from the unwanted attentions of governments or of other powerful forces with dilettante or partisan interests in the past. This entailed a more or less explicit assumption that, even while it was impossible for professional historians to acquire a monopoly over interpretation of the past, their interpretation was nevertheless superior to that of amateurs. Thus historians first proclaimed an ideal of 'academic liberty' as a justification for allowing the scholarly community to regulate itself. It was, on the other hand, emphatically not a license to write whatever history one pleased. In relation to what constituted an acceptable source, interpretation, and field of inquiry, founder-generations of historians imposed limits and tried hard to constrain entrants into their profession to adhere to them. History, for them, was coterminous with *political* history, and even that was narrowly defined. Ultimately, however, their attempts at maintaining an exclusive concept of the discipline failed.

Challenges to it proliferated. The essays in Part II explore some of the most significant innovatory movements within the discipline, and the conditions under which they broke the shackles of 'normal science', especially around the middle of the twentieth century. Ideas, perspectives, methodologies and questions promoted in this period were seldom wholly new. Many of them had their roots in the work of aberrant historians, mavericks whose work had been dismissed by the academic community in earlier decades but now found a new resonance. So it was not simply the accumulation of 'anomalies' which 'normal science' could not readily accommodate that resulted in crisis. Rather, the impact of change in the social and political *context* within which historians worked was crucial in forcing the disintegration of the established paradigm. The particular generational experiences of historians – experiences of two world wars, of the Holocaust, of the break-up of empires – played their part in the collapse of old certainties about what history was and how it should be done. So, too, did social transformations which deeply affected the functions universities and university-based disciplines were expected to fulfil. In terms of its members' ethnic origins, class backgrounds and gender, the community of historians itself became more varied, and reconfigurations of historians' agendas reflected the loss of the profession's early social homogeneity.

As well as responding generally to social change, historians have been open to highly specific influences clearly traceable to the dynamism of other academic disciplines, to ideologies and to the movements which have adopted them. Throughout the era of professionalisation, historians intent on staking out a distinctive intellectual territory which they could call their own had been wary of neighbouring disciplines. The closer to history the latter might seem, the greater the likelihood that they would be treated as rivals. This was especially true of newly emerging disciplines, like sociology, from the late nineteenth century onward. They were feared not only because they might draw resources, students and readers away from history, but also because they dealt in the coin of theory and generalisation where history was empiricist and dedicated to the particular. Yet, if the intellectual economy of history was at first autarchic, with borders closely patrolled to stop anyone smuggling in cultural imports from other disciplines, it became far more open in the course of the next century. Its borders became not barriers, but sites of interchange. The contributions to Part III look at the conditions under which disciplinary insularity could be overcome, and how much historians owe to theories generated within other disciplines. Historians have been notorious under-achievers in the construction of grand theories, but adept and eclectic in adopting, testing and adapting theories produced by others. We return to this theme from a different angle in Part IV. Here, contributors focus on examples of the adoption of perspectives on the past informed by ideologies. This simultaneously involves part of a wider story: the relationship between history as it is pursued inside academe and beyond it.

Finally, we turn from theoretical to practical influences on the making of history. The chapters in Part V focus on the uses of history in the recent past. They reflect on a fact we have already noted: at no point have academic historians been the *sole* interpreters of the past. They can ill afford to ignore perceptions and manipulations of the past generated from innumerable locations beyond the academy. How should professional historians respond? And how successful, and above all intellectually persuasive, have they been where they have attempted to realign their work to take account of commercial, technological or political initiatives and opportunities?

Receptive to so wide a variety of positive impulses, yet vulnerable to an equally diverse range of pressures and constraints, history has become very catholic in its range of questions, perspectives, and techniques of research and writing. So much so, indeed, that it seems doubtful whether such a phenomenon as 'normal science' is discernable, or has been for more than half a century. Seen in one light, the result is often seen as unhealthy fragmentation, and a sense of crisis has frequently overtaken fractious members of a scholarly 'community' in an apparently permanent state of flux bordering on disintegration. Not only have different historians reacted to the same influences in different ways, but they have experienced pulls and pushes affecting their practices in ways which vary with time and place. Radically dissimilar assumptions about what history is and how it should be done have proliferated. In some contexts, they have contrived to co-exist with a measure of mutual toleration and even communication and respect. In others, relations between them have been characterised by intense rivalry and mutual hostility. No over-arching claim on behalf of any new approach to history has proved so uniformly persuasive as to have transformed the *whole* of the discipline. However, if we re-cast Kuhn's concept of paradigms and paradigm shifts a little less ambitiously, his approach seems as relevant as ever. If not for academic history in general – internationally and irrespective of historians' period and other specialisms – may not Kuhn's ideas be applicable to *parts* of the discipline? Whether at a national level or with reference to the understanding of a particular historical period, problem, event or other subject, paradigm shifts may prove easier to detect. Some scholars have used a conceptual vocabulary that Kuhn had inserted as an addendum to his work in order to describe intellectual movements of this sort. Thus the term 'disciplinary matrix' is employed to describe a cohesive network of scholars, united by the promulgation of a shared methodology.[3] Generic characteristics of a 'disciplinary matrix' include the sustained application of the agreed methodology to a clearly delimited field of historical inquiry, the resultant development of a thesis claiming adequately to address the problems thrown up within that field, and an understanding of the function of history common to the group. To establish itself, a 'disciplinary nexus' further requires a secure institutional base in university departments (and sometimes research institutes) and such means of communicating within and beyond the group as journals, publication series and conferences under its control. A given 'disciplinary matrix' may intend, but in fact fail, to force through what Kuhn would recognise as a paradigm shift. It may nevertheless achieve enduring significance even while falling short of its own targets. In the absence of an all-embracing paradigm shift, the bulk of the essays here engage with this scale of change. Our choice of examples is not, and is not intended to be, in any sense exhaustive. It has been determined partly because of their intrinsic importance, but also because of the ways in which they illuminate the *kinds* of process that have occasioned change in the making of history.

Notes

1   T. S. Kuhn, *The Structure of Scientific Revolutions*, Chicago, University of Chicago Press, 1962; revised edn 1970.
2   Cf. D. Hollinger, 'T. S. Kuhn's Theory of Science and Its Implications for History', *American Historical Review*, 1973, vol. 78, pp. 370–93; G. Iggers, *Historiography in the Twentieth Century: From Scientific Objectivity to the Postmodern Challenge*, Hanover and London, Wesleyan University Press, 1997, p. 18.
3   See the 'Postscript – 1969' to Kuhn, *Structure of Scientific Revolutions*. It occurs perhaps most frequently in the work of German experts on historiography. See e.g. J. Rüsen, *Rekonstruktion der Vergangenheit*, Göttingen, Vandenhoeck & Ruprecht, 1986; H. W. Blanke, *Historiographiegeschichte als Historik*, Stuttgart, Frommann, 1991.

Part I

The professionalisation of history

The subject of Part I is the development of professional historical research and writing. We focus in particular on Germany from the late eighteenth century to 1933 (Peter Lambert's contribution), the United States of America between the 1870s and the 1930s (discussed by Robert Harrison), and Great Britain from c.1850 to c.1930 (addressed by Aled Jones). If Thomas Kuhn's postulation of the existence of paradigms is applicable at all to historiography, it should be applicable to the early decades of professionalisation. During this formative period, academic historians were in substantial agreement over what constituted their most important subject-matter: political history and the rise of the state. They shared a similarly clear consensus over the methods of source analysis and the attitude of scholarly detachment that together went to make up what they commonly characterised as 'scientific history'. At the same time, the process of professionalisation created a community of scholars, an 'invisible college' whose members considered themselves to be engaged in a common intellectual endeavour, as well as the institutional mechanisms through which its values and priorities could be imposed.

That moment of unity did not last. The paradigm of 'scientific history' turned out to be hopelessly flawed. A series of shocks, encountered at different points from the 1880s onward, loosened its foundations. The period from c.1880 to the 1930s, in which the professionalisation of history was completed in Europe and in the USA, but also expanded beyond its 'western' points of origin, was crisis-ridden. Intellectual transformations and challenges beyond the discipline of history, but also socio-economic change and the impact of cataclysmic events – the First World War, the Russian Revolution and Terror, the rise of Fascism and Nazism – all influenced academic history. The relationship between these very different kinds of impulse to change, however, is complex. It would be premature to accord primacy of importance in the reshaping of history to events, for example, however cataclysmic, since the 'fundamental processes at work in the history of ideas and of scholarship, and the corresponding disciplinary and interdisciplinary changes, transcend the limits of the actual historical upheaval'.[1] In Germany, statist history survived successive crises, but in doing so forfeited the primacy of place the discipline itself had come to occupy within the humanities. In the USA, by contrast, a somewhat later experience of crisis cleared the way for what might be termed a 'paradigm shift', the end-product of which was the 'Progressive History' of the interwar years.

The first aim of Part I, then, is to establish the extent to which history as practised in the era of professionalisation confirms the existence of a paradigm – of a named community of scholars engaged in essentially the same problem-solving activities according to agreed assumptions, questions and conventions. Its second aim is to ask *why* history became a professional activity, and why it acquired a set of highly specific characteristics. What promoted the rise of this foundation paradigm? Why was it first forged in Germany? How far did the German example serve as a model emulated in the USA and Britain? These are questions that are tackled in Chapter 1, which addresses processes of institutionalism and examines the ways in which the practice of history came to be organised in these three nations. Associated with issues of organisation in the ways set out here are also issues of chronology and timescale: what accounts for divergencies in the timescales over which the primacy of political history was accomplished, challenged and, depending on the time, place and nature of the challenge, either vindicated or destroyed? While the variance in the establishment of a 'normal science' is central to the discussion in the first chapter, and what that 'normal science' actually constituted and how it was practised, is central to the discussion of the second, it is the early indications of emergent challenge which inform the last of the three chapters here. One more question remains: did the various chronologies and nationally specific circumstances of professionalisation lead to any measure of historiographical diversity? Even where methodologies were agreed upon, and generically similar problems identified, it does not necessarily follow that there should have been a similar consensus as to the underlying *purposes* of historical scholarship.

Note

1   See W. Küttler, J. Rüsen and E. Schulin (eds) *Geschichtsdiskurs*, vol. 4: *Krisenbewußtsein, Katastrophenerfahrungen und Innovationen 1880–1945*, Frankfurt a.M., Fischer, 1997, 'Vorwort', p. 12.

Chapter 1

The institutionalisation and organisation of history

Robert Harrison, Aled Jones and Peter Lambert

The establishment of history as a discipline and a profession was predicated on its securing an institutional base and a career structure. History had to distinguish itself from older, neighbouring disciplines: only then could dedicated funding for historical work, and for appropriate training of future generations of historians be secured. In continental Europe, in Britain, and in the USA all this happened at differing points in the course of the nineteenth century, and with varying degrees of completeness and success. The importance of studying the history of the discipline itself – *including* that of the ways in which it was organised – is something that historians have recognised only relatively recently. Yet, as Theodor Schieder pointed out, all professional historians work within an organised system. University faculties and departments, seminars, institutes and societies, conferences and symposia, libraries and archives may be taken for granted by historians working today, but they are themselves outcomes of historical processes. Their existence was and is essential to the professional historian, but the precise ways in which they developed also helped shape the style and content of the histories produced. Schieder suggested that they impose a measure of uniformity on the practitioner of history: this 'powerful apparatus' (which he likened to an imposing building) 'often has about it something depressing, constraining the spontaneity of every individual' historian.[1] Such constraints, self-imposed by a founder-generation of professional historians and handed down to their successors, also made for shared experiences, for commonalities which facilitated the construction of a self-aware community.

Germany

To study or to write about the past is one thing. To be recognised – indeed, recognisable – as an historian is another. It requires definition and the formal trappings of recognition. Historians must first both see themselves, and be seen, as a discrete body of people engaged in a distinctive pursuit. If carrying the title of Professor of History or being enrolled at a university as a history student was, in the context of the nineteenth century, not a sufficient condition, it was certainly a necessary one for meeting these criteria. Although there had been practitioners of history at German universities in the eighteenth century, theirs was in general an identity without a name. It was not until 1804 that the first Chair of History was established, and it is in the first decades of the nineteenth century that the story of the professionalisation of history is conventionally begun. By the middle of the century, there were twenty-eight professors of history, distributed among nineteen universities. Sixty years later, there were no fewer than 185 professors of history, and their number continued to rise until the beginning of the 1930s, reaching a peak of 238 in 1931.

This professoriat contained within its ranks an elite of incumbents of full, established chairs, *Ordinarien*. These were the eminent master-craftsmen of what German historians came to refer to as 'the guild' (*die Zunft*), an imagined community of scholars which gradually developed rules and rituals of admission. The word 'guild' is itself suggestive of the past-mindedness of the men who created it. It gave a curiously pre-modern inflection to the highly modern processes of professionalisation and academic specialisation. The guild's apprentices were postgraduate students selected and finally judged by the *Ordinarien*. Admission to the guild generally required of them that they submit not one but two doctoral theses. The second of these, the *Habilitation*, was in effect the apprentice's masterpiece. If successfully defended, it qualified the student for an academic career. Since only *Ordinarien* had tenure (in other words, job security), and given that even Germany's greatest historians were generally appointed as *Ordinarien* between the ages of thirty and forty, the apprenticeships were long. They were also normally periods of financial hardship. For the fortunate few who did gain established chairs, however, the material rewards alone were considerable.[2] Around 1900, the lowest salary for an *Ordinarius* stood at four times that of an elementary school teacher. If that denoted comfort, then the fact that the average salary for an *Ordinarius* was twice, and the very highest salaries were nearly seven times as generous, suggests something closer to luxury. On top of their salaries, professors could add to their incomes very substantially not only through sales of their books, but via the fees they charged students who enrolled in their 'private' lectures. Grandee historians thus took their places among the wealthy elites of German society. Elite status was confirmed by the title of 'secret [state] councillor' (*Geheimrat*) awarded to historians whose academic stature was matched by their political trustworthiness, and sometimes by the acquisition of aristocratic titles. A few could pride themselves on proximity to the throne. Others – like the Berlin historian Friedrich Meinecke – presided with their wives over *salons*.

Why did the professionalisation of history occur in Germany first, why did the profession become so prestigious, and who were its members? What, in other words, caused the construction of the paradigmatic historical profession?

History in Germany in fact gained its identity in two distinct phases, separated by the French Revolution. That there was a first phase at all, one located in the late Enlightenment period and marked out by Enlightenment values, has only recently been recognised.[3] The propensity to see in the nineteenth-century

German historian Leopold von Ranke the 'father of history' long blinded historians to other, older impulses to the foundation of the discipline. Ranke had been masterly in his self-promotion as the inventor of a wholly new approach to history. For well over a century, his claims were taken at face value. Yet, at the University of Göttingen, founded in 1734, a group of historically minded German scholars (notably Johann Christoph Gatterer and August Ludwig Schlözer) had emerged from the middle of the eighteenth century onward. They were profoundly influenced by the Scottish Enlightenment. From Scottish thinkers, they adopted not only a belief in natural law and progress, hostility to absolutism and a commitment to building civil society, but a self-conscious determination to underscore this bundle of ideas and ideals historically. Elements of economic, social and cultural history are discernible in the work which resulted. Where the Scottish Enlightenment, however, had failed to leave much of a mark on the organisation and institutionalisation of historical practice in the universities, the job descriptions of some posts at Göttingen made specific reference to the study of history. This early acquisition of the beginnings of an institutional base facilitated the exchange of ideas. The very first historical journals, most notably Gatterer's *Allgemeine Historische Bibliothek*, provided space for reviews of historical literature. Furthermore, a specifically historical methodology was forged in this setting. Its chief characteristics were, first, rationally conducted research on historical sources and, second, an arrangement of the information gleaned from those sources which accorded with the view that history was a single process. A shared objective was the enlightenment of the reading public. The Göttingen historians confidently assumed that history could and should inform contemporary approaches to politics: history held lessons for life.

The second phase of professionalisation did not simply bring an Enlightenment project to completion, however. It took place in a radically altered intellectual climate and generated different replies to the questions of how historical work should be approached, and what its purpose and therefore also its content ought to be. All historians of professional German historiography are agreed that its origins are connected to the reaction to the Enlightenment, to the Terror unleashed by the French Revolution, and to the Revolutionary and Napoleonic Wars. They diverge in their understanding of exactly how this connection may be made. The earliest and most enduring interpretation, advanced by Max Lenz in a history of the University of Berlin published in 1910–18, emphasised the leading role of the Prussian reforms undertaken in the wake of Prussia's defeat by Napoleonic France in 1806–7. Alexander von Humboldt's reform of the Prussian universities, according to this account, constituted at once a dramatic contribution to the modernisation of the Prussian state and a vital first step along a path that was to lead to Germany's eventual unification in 1871. Humboldt's reforms were twofold. He erased the universities' institutional autonomy, and with it the pressures which local religious and secular interests could exert on academic teaching and research. Simultaneously, he established the principle of the autonomy of academics *within* each university – that is, the principle of 'academic liberty' – and so generated experimentation and innovation. Thus, Lenz argued, the conditions in which German scholarship could overtake that of all other nations were established. Equally, scholarly prowess infused the 'German spirit', and so secured the superiority of the German nation itself. However, as we will see, 'academic liberty' was far from complete, and the claims made for the innate intellectual superiority of German scholarship in general, and historical scholarship in particular, were overblown. One alternative interpretation has jettisoned these claims altogether, while stressing and giving a new inflection to the other strain in Lenz's reasoning: the significance of the institutional setting. It has drawn attention to the magnetic attraction to academic entrepreneurs of the career opportunities afforded by the expansion of the universities and the forging of new disciplines within them. Market forces thus dictated at least the rate of change in methods and ideas.[4] But this explanatory framework cannot account for the emergence and growth of any one academic discipline, and treats disciplines as if they acquired immunity to the impact of events outside academia, and to social forces.

A new approach to history was also a product of the confluence of three further developments: the emergence of Romanticism, the need of the German states to justify their existence, and the rise of a social class which placed a premium on educational attainment. The Enlightenment, confident that reason could ensure the perfectibility of society, had given rise to a judgmental approach to the past. History was explored in order to expose and denounce all those obstacles, embedded in past societies, to the triumph of reason. The detritus of the past was identified in order that it might be swept out. But when, in and after the latter stages of the French Revolution, the 'triumph of reason' appeared only to have resulted in terror, war, alienation and social dislocation, the past could appear to the Romantic imagination as a safe haven or an inspiration. Customs and traditions indicted by Enlightenment thinkers were now to be approached through empathetic 'understanding' (*Verstehen*) and celebrated. Where the Enlightenment invented universal, transhistorical, 'natural' laws, historians looked for individuality, for the particular and contingent. The new agenda was encapsulated in 1825 in Leopold von Ranke's programmatic statement of intent, to recover, comprehend, and above all to relate the past 'as it actually was' (*wie es eigentlich gewesen*). Past politics, its practitioners and its institutions, were to be understood in their own terms and specific contexts. This constituted an approach to the pursuit of history often called historism. Paradoxically, however, the creation of historism also indicated the limits of the Romantics' appeal, and a very real debt to the Enlightenment which survived in spite of the rejection of so much that Enlightenment thinkers had argued. Ranke had at first been inspired by Sir Walter Scott's romantic novel *Quentin Durward*, but not to emulate Scott and write novels himself.

Instead, he began to immerse himself in the history of the period about which Scott had written, in particular in the work of the chronicler Philippe de Commines, and rapidly concluded that Scott had not done justice to it. His critical engagement with historical evidence stood four-square within the tradition of the Enlightenment, even if it advanced technically beyond Enlightenment historians' work. And his research left him with the strong conviction of the superiority of history over romantic fiction.

Napoleon's eventual defeat did not result in a restoration of the map of Germany. Where 'Germany' had described hundreds of distinct polities, there were now just over thirty German states, almost all of which owed their expanded borders or their very existence to the Bonapartist reordering of Europe. In the reactionary climate of Europe after 1815, the debt to Napoleon was one which all the remaining German princes wished to deny. What they wanted was historical legitimacy. They invested in history and historians partly in order to furnish their territorial possessions with a validity that rested not on Napoleonic rationalisation, but on tradition. However, alongside their indebtedness to dynastic and court patronage, historians were shaped by, and considered the expectations of, the social class from which they came.

Historians were overwhelmingly drawn from the *Bildungsbürgertum*, the educated and cultivated middle class. Like the post-Napoleonic German states, this class was keenly interested in belying its own modernity. Its members looked to their history as a means of laying claim to social status, and constructed their family trees in order to supply themselves with surrogate roots. Through to (and beyond) the end of the century, a bare handful of historians were drawn from the ranks of the lower middle class or the entrepreneurial bourgeoisie. Fewer still came from either aristocratic or working-class backgrounds. The aristocrat Georg von Below had no less of a chip on his shoulder because of his class origins than did Dietrich Schäfer, the son of a manual worker. Both compensated by showing particular zeal in adopting the social, political and intellectual norms of a profession highly coloured by its cultivated bourgeois composition.

Close-knit clusters of students inspired by their teacher would form his 'school'. The forms of socialisation they generated – especially the drinking bouts which generally succeeded seminars – emphasised the male value-system of the discipline. Research was construed as a manly activity; seminar discussion was held to be beyond women. Indeed, the 'modernisation of scholarship was based on stringent gender differences'.[5] Before 1945, one lone woman qualified (by dint of passing her second doctorate) to take up a chair in history. Of course, she – Hedwig Hintze – was never appointed – though whether that was just because of her sex is open to doubt. She offended the sensibilities of her would-be colleagues by marrying a considerably older and highly respected historian; she was left wing; she was Jewish.[6] In the Weimar Republic, when she did qualify, any one of these would have been a sufficient ground for excluding her from the profession.

The vast majority of historians were also Protestant. The sons of Lutheran pastors formed an especially large group alongside the sons of middle- and higher-ranking state officials, teachers in the elite schools, the *Gymnasien*, and lawyers. This is a social profile which mirrors that of nineteenth-century German nationalism. In promoting the historical profession in particular and the *Bildungsbürgertum* in general, the individual states of Germany sowed seeds of their own ultimate dissolution into a single nation-state. Not content to write the histories of parochial principalities or of petty dynastic rivalries, and associating Germany's small states with small-minded, backward, and above all repressive politics, Liberal historians transferred their allegiance to an as yet imagined German nation. This was made easier by the fact that the Humboldtian model of the Prussian universities was widely copied in southern Germany, which meant that there was in effect a national job market for historians well before the political unification of Germany. In the mid-nineteenth century, historians, like other nationalists, forged links with one another across state boundaries to create, through mutual support, an effective counterweight to the intellectually constraining influence of reactionary governments. The historians' guild prefigured the nation, and the history it produced contributed to nation-building. According to Ranke (writing in 1863), the scholarly community conducted a 'single grand conversation', so that the very exercise of their academic freedom provided Germans with a vital moment of unity beyond ideological divides and functioned as a sort of substitute for still absent national political institutions.[7] Exchanges of letters between historians were one vital way in which this 'grand conversation' was conducted. The recipients carefully preserved their colleagues' correspondence: historians ordered their papers with a view to their finally being lodged in archives. In writing to one another about history and politics, they were also consciously generating primary sources for younger or future generations of historians to use. Nothing more pointedly illustrates the historian's confidence in the importance of his craft than this determination to contribute directly to the archival heritage. This is an aspect of professionalisation within the German tradition to which we will, of necessity, return in the next chapter.

United Kingdom

The process of professionalising the study of history in Britain during the second half of the nineteenth-century took place in a cultural environment in which public interest in the past was already intense, and had been so for a long time. The huge commercial success of novels and studies on historical themes by Edward Gibbon, Sir Walter Scott, Thomas Babington Macaulay, Thomas Carlyle, J. A. Froude and others indicates something of the vibrancy of history's popular appeal, and if treatments of the past found in other popular cultural forms are also taken into account, such as in paintings, popular songs and ballads, poetry, fiction, periodicals, broadsides and the design of buildings, it may be appreciated just how difficult it was for anyone in nineteenth-century Britain to escape the presence of history in their lives. But that public interest was not cultivated without discrimination, nor were the subjects that drew the greatest attention arbitrarily chosen. Two historical periods in particular, the seventeenth century and the Middle Ages, dominated public consciousness of the past in Victorian Britain. The importance attached to the Civil War was not only apparent in the 175 or so paintings alluding to the conflict and its principal figures exhibited in the Royal Academy between 1820 and 1900,[8] but also in the many ways in which the war continued to define the fault-lines within Victorian British political culture. The tensions that distinguished differing attitudes to the monarchy, the powers of parliament and the longer-term consequences of the constitutional 'revolution' of 1688, as well as the competing political idioms of Liberalism and Conservatism, were often explicitly connected to the debate about the fundamental political and religious issues that underpinned the Civil War.[9]

The medieval past, too, was quarried for materials to build more contemporary arguments and movements. The belief that medieval Englishmen had lost vital political and social rights following the imposition of the 'Norman Yoke', for example, made a powerful return to British popular politics during the middle decades of the nineteenth century, and traces of its assumptions may be found in instances from William Cobbett's *Rural Rides* and the poetry of John Clare in the 1820s and 1830s, to the defence case in the Tichborne trial and the socialist writings of William Morris from the 1870s to the 1890s.[10] In addition, an aesthetic critique of industrial society, in which the search for the medieval became both a refuge from modernity and a means of mediating or camouflaging its impact on the present, became evident, for example, in the writings of such major cultural critics as John Ruskin. Medieval style assumed even more tangible forms in Victorian architecture, from Augustus Pugin's gothic design for the rebuilding of the Houses of Parliament to Manchester's Town Hall and the audacity of the St Pancras railway station. Significantly, Ruskin began the second volume of his *Stones of Venice* in 1851 on the day the Great Exhibition opened at the Crystal Palace in London, a building he excoriated as a 'greenhouse'.[11] The appeal to the gothic, however, was politically ambivalent, and could be pursued with equal enthusiasm by Tory organicists and early socialists.[12] The main issue which divided those who took an active interest in the past was whether, as the poet laureate Robert Southey believed, history was a repository of humanity's highest values and virtues, from which the present signified a fall from grace, or, as Macaulay famously argued, that the passage of time was also a process of improvement, of moral, constitutional and material progress that was especially discernible in the study of English history.[13] For much of the nineteenth century, then, history mattered to a broad spectrum of British people: it entertained them, helped them to shape the ways in which they defined themselves and others, and raised big issues, like popular rights and the responsibilities of those who governed them.

By the mid-1890s, however, history had less to do with popular politics, or the literary and visual arts, than it had with the activities of university professors engaged in what they defined as the scientific pursuit of the past, conducted primarily through the close study of documents, and carried out largely for its own sake. The turn towards the archive and the seminar, which were heavily influenced by new approaches to historical research pioneered in Germany, led also to the emergence of a new and professional group of historians with its own supporting apparatus of societies and publications. Many of these professional historians earned state-funded salaries and were responsible for teaching history as a new university degree subject as well as for undertaking and publishing research. The shift towards professional status, and a changing social role for historians, effectively began during the middle decades of the nineteenth century. Before this time, history was remarkably ill defined as what would later become known as an academic subject. Macaulay, writing in the *Edinburgh Review* in May 1828, confessed to finding it difficult to establish any underlying characteristics that might provide for it an autonomous identity as either a method of enquiry or a form of knowledge:

> we are acquainted with no history which approaches to our notion of what a history ought to be. ... This province of literature is a debatable land. It lies on the confines of two distinct territories. It is under the jurisdiction of two hostile powers; and, like other districts similarly situated, it is ill defined, ill cultivated, and ill regulated. Instead of being equally shared between its two rulers, the Reason and the Imagination, it falls alternatively under the sole and absolute dominion of each. It is sometimes fiction. It is sometimes theory.[14]

While in some important respects history has remained 'a debatable land', within fifty years of the publication of Macaulay's path-breaking exploration of its nature, history had become History, and had been furnished with a method, an epistemology, and a place in British educational institutions, especially in the universities.

From the 1830s onwards, then, historians began to acquire what Bonnie Smith has referred to as a 'sharper institutional profile' which identified them more clearly as historians. Unlike their predecessors, they were less likely to have been trained in theology and more likely to have had a more appropriate grounding in 'a distinct methodology, endowing them with expert knowledge, and providing them with credentials', especially through seminar and archival work.[15] At the core of this shift in the nature of the composition of the community of historians was the university, and its changing role in mid-Victorian society. A heated debate on the role of universities began in such periodicals as the *Edinburgh Review* during the early decades of the nineteenth century following some robust criticisms of Oxford's curriculum and the quality of its teaching by Sydney Smith and others.[16] Echoes of that debate reverberated in mid-century when, for example, John Henry Newman made a series of influential interventions in 1852 which insisted that universities were 'a place of *teaching* universal *knowledge*', their role being 'the diffusion and extension of knowledge', rather than its 'advancement'.[17] His was a strong defence of a university as a place where a liberal education, a 'turn of mind, a habit of thought',[18] was inculcated, rather than an opportunity to develop or transmit more specialised forms of knowledge. Universities, for Newman, were emphatically not research institutions. During the second half of the century, however, arguments continued to be made that such institutions poorly served the needs of a changing society, and the idea became implanted that universities were responsible for the nation's 'moral and political' welfare, as well as its cultural and religious life.[19] A Royal Commission on the universities, established in 1850, opened the way for the natural sciences to challenge the traditional dominance of mathematics and classics, and in their wake other disciplines such as history found their ways into the curriculum of higher education. This process coincided with the expansion of both Oxford and Cambridge Universities in the 1860s, the abolition of their religious tests, and the emergence of professional career tutors and a 'research endowment' movement.[20] But history's entrance to the charmed circle of university subjects was not by any means automatic, and a strong case needed to be made to overcome the considerable degree of scepticism that pervaded the older universities. John Kenyon has cited as reasons for the intellectual and political acceptance of history as a discipline at this time the international reputations of German historians Ranke and Mommsen, a genuine need to find historical explanations for such cataclysmic events as the French Revolution and the rise of nationalism, and the growing realisation among parliamentary reformers of the need to understand the origins and development of British constitutionalism. The impact of Darwinian science and the associated ideas of social evolution also evidently played their part in providing for history a fresh intellectual drive.[21] But the countervailing pressures that tended to marginalise history remained strong, and finding it a place in British academic curricula was effected only after historians in key positions had mounted some powerful and persuasive arguments in its favour.

History had been taught as an ancillary subject in the older universities at least since 1724, when George I had established the first Regius Professorships of History at both Oxford and Cambridge. However, their holders enjoyed no formal attachment to a college, nor involvement in university administration, and their lectures were at best marginal to undergraduate curricula. Many in the older established disciplines, such as classics, were sceptical of the modern history neophyte since it, and subjects like it, involved different concepts of education and assessment. Unlike the ancient past, medieval and more recent history was regarded as being an 'incomplete' and indeterminate form of knowledge. Since 'modern' history was still in progress, there was no canon of agreed set texts on which students' attention might be focused. Worse, it was not at all clear how historical knowledge might be examined. How, it was asked, could tutors possibly assess student opinions as opposed to demonstrable or accepted 'fact'?[22] All in all, history involved far too much controversy and pedagogical uncertainty. Fears were also expressed that history professors, being political appointments, might use their chairs to exert political influence and advocate ecclesiastical subversion. Often what lay behind the anxieties concerning history's 'undisciplined knowledge' was a deeper fear of political and social unrest.

However, two regius chairs at Oxford and Cambridge Universities at almost the same time began the process that led to the professionalisation of history throughout British higher education. William Stubbs, elected to the regius chair at Oxford in 1866, was, for John Kenyon, England's first 'professional historian', and the first holder of the chair in Oxford to make a 'serious contribution' to historical knowledge, largely through the publication in 1870 of the *Select Charters*.[23] Despite his aversion to the teaching of modern history in schools, his tenure at Oxford from 1866 to 1884 saw major strides in both history teaching and research at that university, including, in 1872, the introduction of England's first history degree scheme. However, as Peter Slee has demonstrated, a number of tendencies that would lead to the greater autonomy of history as an academic subject are clearly discernible in the years before Stubbs' appointment. History had made an appearance as part of the short-lived school of Law and Modern History in 1854, and the crucial shift from the study of texts to the study of periods and subject areas had already been advocated by Montagu Burrows, Stubbs' predecessor, in 1862. Furthermore, the growing body of specialist history teachers had benefited from the evolving corporate identity of university teachers as a whole from the 1840s,[24] and was further enhanced by the establishment of a Tutors' Association in 1854 and, more specifically, by the subsequent growth at Oxford of the Modern History Association.[25]

From 1848, history acquired a higher profile at Cambridge partly as a proactive measure to deflect parliamentary criticism of the university's curriculum, which many saw as being too narrowly defined. James Stephen, appointed to the regius chair at Cambridge in 1849, and then the only teacher of history in the entire university, was given the task of devising a new tripos in moral science, in which history was to comprise one of five cognate subjects.[26] Thus, from 1851, history was formally integrated into the Cambridge curriculum, though initially it was only believed to be suitable for poll, not reading, students.[27] Its lowly status as an academic subject at this time was similarly in evidence at other universities. E. S. Beesly, Chair of History at University College London between 1860 and 1893, recalled that in his earlier years history 'was the … most likely to be sacrificed in the competition of classes' in an overcrowded curriculum, and that it had been 'a very subordinate part' of the study of languages and literature.[28] Developments in the 1870s, however, were to challenge academe's long disdain for history as an academic subject. Ejected from the moral sciences tripos in 1867, history was unsuccessfully combined with law in the face of strong opposition from two directions: law students who found history so broad and difficult as to depress their examination marks and thus threaten their future legal careers, and a small group of historians who seized the moment to establish history as a separate university subject in its own right. John Seeley at Cambridge and A. W. Ward at Owen's College, Manchester, were the most critical and effective voices advocating this new policy. Ward challenged the dominant pedagogical tradition by arguing that history involved the acquisition of skills that were perfectly capable of being tested at different levels of proficiency, while Seeley in his inaugural lecture in 1869 argued that history was the key to understanding the modern world.

Like that of his contemporary, William Stubbs, at Oxford, J. R. Seeley's appointment to the regius chair at Cambridge broke the mould of the semi-detached history professors of the past. Unlike his predecessors, including Charles Kingsley, Seeley not only insisted on residing at the University, but also imbued the chair with a mission, which was no less than 'to explain the new industrial and democratic society, to establish principles of leadership in Church and state and to train a new intellectual aristocracy to take over the leadership functions once performed by a territorial aristocracy'.[29] Though not himself a historian, Seeley made a significant contribution to British historiography by emphasising the importance of Britain's colonies in the shaping of modern British history and the making of a British identity.[30] His clarion call for history to be acknowledged as 'the school of statesmanship', and for Cambridge to transform itself into 'a great seminary of politicians',[31] was made in his inaugural lecture at Cambridge in 1869. Everyone, he argued, 'who studies political institutions, whether in the past or in the present, studies history',[32] and what the student of history learns is

> not merely stored up for future use, but tells immediately upon his views and judgements of things around him. It sheds at once upon the political world, the world of states, nationalities, parliaments, armies, parties, and interests, an illumination like that which natural science sheds upon the world of physical and vital forces.[33]

In a stinging rebuke of romantic antiquarianism and the purveyors of nostalgia, Seeley pronounced on the need to see the past 'less drowsily' and as 'the best commentary on the present'.[34]

Though some historians remained sceptical of its crude instrumentality, as a 'rhetorical device',[35] Seeley's lecture undoubtedly helped to impel the study of history into the university curriculum at Cambridge. Cast out from the law tripos in 1872, modern history acquired under Seeley's guidance separate tripos status in 1873, a step which, though done with 'deep reluctance',[36] marked the establishment of history as an independent academic subject in both the ancient universities of England.[37] This feat was soon repeated in the 'new' Victorian universities, such as London (established in 1828), Durham (1832), and

Owen's College, Manchester (1851), which all featured chairs of history, although many remained as 'careless as to by whom, or whether, such posts were filled' as Oxford and Cambridge had been prior to the 1860s.[38] In Manchester, however, where a chair of history has been created in 1854, a distinctive school of history teaching was developed, particularly under the leadership of A. W. Ward in the 1870s and, from 1890, T. F. Tout.[39] The latter, described by John Kenyon as 'Stubbs's greatest pupil' had, since 1881, held the chair of history at the University of St David's, Lampeter,[40] and history had been taught at other Victorian universities such as the University College of Wales, Aberystwyth, since its foundation in 1872.[41] From this ferment of activity within both the older and the newer universities during the 1860s and 1870s, the outlines of a newly professionalised and salaried group of historians emerged with their own distinctive approach to the study of the past. That, together with a highly formalised means of transmitting the fruits of that learning by means of lectures and seminars, led to the targeting of a narrower and more selective audience of students and other professional historians than the one which Macaulay and Carlyle had once endeavoured to reach.

United States of America

In comparison with Britain at least, the process of institutionalisation in the United States was remarkably swift and remarkably complete. In mid-nineteenth-century America, as in mid-nineteenth-century Britain, historical writing was the province of amateurs. Historians were clergymen, lawyers, merchants and gentlemen of private means, drawn mostly from the patrician elites of the eastern seaboard. Works of history also emanated from the pens of some of the 'damned mob of scribbling women' whose prolific writing both impressed and alarmed Nathaniel Hawthorne. No history was written by professional historians because there were none. As late as 1880 there were only eleven professors of history in the United States. By 1895 the number had reached 100. In 1902, John Franklin Jameson, the editor of the *American Historical Review*, could say with some authority 'that in this age the leading influence upon historical writing is that of the university and the university professor'.[42] Of the thirty-four authors who contributed to Justin Winsor's *Narrative and Critical History of America*, published between 1884 and 1889, only two held chairs in history (although eight had chairs in other subjects). In contrast, of the twenty-four contributors to Harper's *American Nation* series, published between 1904 and 1907, twenty-one were university professors and all but two had carried out graduate work in history. In other words, the closing decades of the nineteenth century saw a significant change in the status and social position of the historian.

This change was, above all, an outcome of the growth and transformation of the American university in the decades around the turn of the century. Not only did student numbers increase dramatically, from 52,000 in 1870 to 1,100,000 in 1930. More significantly, the structure of the major public and private universities underwent a fundamental reorganisation in order to accommodate new disciplines and new modes of enquiry. In place of the traditional mixture of classics, mathematics and 'philosophy' that comprised the syllabus of the ante-bellum American college, the reformed university offered a range of 'elective' subjects, including history, from which students were asked to choose. Undergraduate courses became both more intensive and more specialised. They therefore required more specialised staff to teach them.

Where, then, were suitably qualified teachers of history to be found? American universities had offered few undergraduate courses in history before the 1870s and no postgraduate training at all. The first cohort of professional teachers of history consisted largely of men (and one or two women) who had studied for higher degrees in Germany. About half of those in post in 1895 had received graduate training at a German university. One of their number was Herbert Baxter Adams, who in 1876 at the newly-founded Johns Hopkins University established a research 'seminary' on the German model which attracted many able students, including Charles M. Andrews, Omer Haskins, John Franklin Jameson, Frederick Jackson Turner and Woodrow Wilson. Many of Adams' 'noble army of doctors' took posts at other universities, while a large wall-map in his seminar room traced their progress across the country, in effect as academic missionaries to darkest America.[43] Similar graduate programmes were established at Columbia, Harvard and elsewhere. By 1907, 250 doctorates in history had been awarded by American universities, and it appears that the overwhelming majority of recipients were employed in university teaching. Already by the 1890s completion of a doctorate was expected of the applicants for university posts; the Ph.D. had become, in effect, a certificate of entry to the historical profession (although it appears that the great majority of those admitted did not, and in view of their heavy teaching loads were not expected to, carry out much independent research once appointed). Thus in the course of not much over two decades academic history established itself as a brand-new profession.

The founding in 1884 of the American Historical Association (in which Herbert Baxter Adams played a founding role) was a key moment in this process. 'Scholars and students can no longer afford to live in isolation', argued a founder member.[44] The establishment of a learned society was an indication that academic historians regarded themselves as a community of scholars who shared a 'common universe of discourse'. The Association catered to a perceived need for contact and communication across the enormous distances of the continental United States. Its purpose, believed Adams, was 'the exchange of ideas and the widening of acquaintances, the dissemination of methods and original papers'.[45] The fact that historians believed themselves to be engaged in a cumulative process of investigation, in which individual endeavours contributed to a larger whole, made it all the more necessary to exchange information and avoid duplication of effort.

The AHA in its early years, like many local historical societies, included enthusiastic amateurs as well as academic professionals. Among its lay members were such luminaries as the once and future presidents Rutherford B. Hayes and Theodore Roosevelt and Senators George Frisbie Hoar and Henry Cabot Lodge. The Association conducted itself like a society of gentlemen; its meetings had some of the style of a gentlemen's club. Delegates at AHA conventions dined at clubs like the Cosmos in Washington, under the assumption that colleagues would be 'clubbable', an assumption that most blatantly excluded women members. Indeed, a 'Committee on Social Entertainment of the Ladies' was appointed to make separate arrangements. Over the years coexistence between the professional members and the 'patriarchs' became strained. The academic historians expressed irritation at the lightweight contributions of amateur historians, while the amateurs in turn were bored by the professionals' displays of erudition and offended by their ungentlemanly tendency to criticise each other's work. While the Association found it difficult to hold on to its lay members, it retained some of the social style of a gentlemen's club for a generation or more.

In fact, the first generation of professional historians was drawn from a fairly narrow social band. They were either the scions of high-status families or the children of middle-class households who took advantage of the opportunites presented by the expanding university system to attain the social standing that an academic career still afforded. Most were of older American stock, often of New England antecedents, and Protestant in religion. The profession contained no individuals of recent immigrant stock, relatively few Catholics, a small number of Jews (the genteel anti-Semitism that pervaded elite institutions in Gilded Age America extended into academic life), and almost no African-Americans. It also included very few women. As in other occupations, professionalisation was a distinctly gendered process. It entailed the replacement of casual, part-time endeavours by full-time salaried employment, the replacement of literary activity by 'scientific' historical research, and the displacement of 'low, unworthy and trivial' subjects by the 'serious' study of political institutions. There were few job opportunities for women outside the women's colleges, while the widespread application of marriage bars and anti-nepotism rules ensured that married women were virtually excluded altogether. Only a half of the female holders of Ph.D.s in 1939 held university posts, mostly in less prestigious institutions (for their male equivalents the proportion was nearer seven-eighths). The ethos of historical seminars and conferences, as well as many of their informal rules of behaviour, was essentially masculine. It engendered, argues Bonnie Smith, a fraternal spirit, a community of shared male endeavour in which differences of wealth and status were erased in pursuit of pure scholarship. Jameson, for example, referred to the 'professors of history in the principal universities' as 'this band of brothers'.[46] The Michigan historian Charles Kendall Adams barely tolerated the presence of women in his classroom. 'Of course', he claimed, 'the young women could not do seminary work'.[47] Women, then, were debarred from professional history as much by the spirit of the enterprise as by its formal rules.

Notes

1 T. Schieder, 'Organisation und Organisationen der Geschichtswissenschaft', *Historische Zeitschrift*, 1983, vol. 237, pp. 265–87; quotation p. 266.
2 F. K. Ringer, *The Decline of the German Mandarins. The German Academic Community, 1890–1933*, Cambridge MA, Harvard University Press, 1969, reprinted Hanover, University Press of New England, 1990, pp. 37ff.
3 Cf. G. G. Iggers, 'The University of Göttingen 1760–1800 and the Transformation of Historical Scholarship', *Storia della Storiographia*, 1982, vol. 2, pp. 11–37.
4 For a survey of the literature, see R. S. Turner, 'German Science, German Universities: Historiographical Perspectives from the 1980s', in Gert Schubring (ed.) *'Einsamkeit und Freiheit' neu besichtigt: Universitätsreformen und Disziplinenbildung in Preußen als Modell für Wissenschaftspolitik im Europa des 19. Jahrhunderts*, Stuttgart, Franz Steiner, 1989, pp. 24–36.
5 M. Grever, 'Die relative Geschichtslosigkeit der Frauen. Geschlecht und Geschichtswissenschaft', in W. Küttler, J. Rüsen and E. Schulin (eds) *Geschichtsdiskurs*, vol. 4: *Krisenbewußtsein, Katastrophenerfahrungen und Innovationen 1880–1945*, Frankfurt a. M., Fischer, 1997, pp. 108–23; quotation p. 114.
6 See H. Schleier, *Die bürgerliche Geschichtsschreibung der Weimarer Republik*, Berlin, Akademie Verlag, 1974, pp. 488ff.
7 P. Bahners, 'National Unification and Narrative Unity: The Case of Ranke's *German History*', in S. Berger, M. Donovan and K. Passmore (eds) *Writing National Histories: Western Europe since 1800*, London, Routledge, 1999, pp. 57–68; quotation p. 66.
8 R. Strong, *And When Did You Last See Your Father? The Victorian Painter and British History*, London, Thames and Hudson, 1978, p. 141. According to Strong, '(n)o other period could match this for intensity of public interest'. For Gibbon and his continuing influence in the nineteenth century, see R. Porter, *Edward Gibbon: Making History*, London, Weidenfeld and Nicolson, 1988.
9 J. W. Burrow, *A Liberal Descent. Victorian historians and the English past*, Cambridge, Cambridge University Press, 1981, p. 14. For Macaulay and Whig history, see pp. 11–93.
10 C. Hill, 'Lost Rights', in Dona Torr, *Tom Mann and His Times. Volume One: 1856–1890*, London, Lawrence and Wishart, 1956, especially pp. 120–31
11 M. J. Wiener, *English Culture and the Decline of the Industrial Spirit 1850–1980*, Cambridge, Cambridge University Press, 1981, p. 37.
12 E. P. Thompson, *William Morris. From Visionary to Revolutionary*, New York, Pantheon Books, 1977.
13 Wiener, *English Culture*, p. 29.
14 'History', repr. in Lord Macaulay, *The Miscellaneous Writings and Speeches of Lord Macaulay*, 1891, p. 133. Convinced of its morally improving nature, Macaulay was intent on extending historical knowledge to the widest possible popular audience, and considered writing a study of Stuart England for the Society for the Diffusion of Useful Knowledge, see O. D. Edwards, *Macaulay*, London, Weidenfeld and Nicolson, 1988, p. 17.
15 B. Smith, 'Gender and the Practices of Scientific History: the Seminar and Archival Research in the Nineteenth Century', *American Historical Review*, 1995, vol. 100, p. 1153.

16 The first major intervention came in a review of La Place's *Traité de Méchanique Céleste* by John Playfair in the *Edinburgh Review*, 1808, vol. 11, pp. 249–84, and was followed by a number of others, the most trenchant being by Sydney Smith, *Edinburgh Review*, 1809, vol. 15. This elicited a defence of Oxford by Edward Copleston, whose riposte assured the critics that the university's purpose was not to teach students 'useful' knowledge, or to turn them into 'professionals', but rather to prepare them for social leadership as 'gentlemen'; see M. McMackin Garland, 'Newman in His Own Day', in F. M. Turner (ed.) John Henry Newman, *The Idea of a University*, New Haven, Yale University Press, 1996, p. 271.

17 *Ibid.*, p. 3.

18 *Ibid.*, p. xv.

19 P. Levine, *The Amateur and the Professional: Antiquarians, Historians and Archaeologists in Victorian England, 1838–1886*, Cambridge, Cambridge University Press, 1986, p. 135.

20 John Wilkes, ' "A mist of prejudice": The Reluctant Acceptance of Modern History at Cambridge, 1845–1873', in J. Smith and C. Stray, *Teaching and Learning in Nineteenth-century Cambridge*, Woodbridge, Boydell, 2001, pp. 57–8.

21 J. Kenyon, *The History Men: The Historical Profession in England since the Renaissance*, London, Weidenfeld and Nicolson, 1983, pp. 149–50.

22 For the examinations controversy, see Burrow, *A Liberal Descent*, pp. 98–103, and P. H. Slee, *Learning and a Liberal Education. The Study of Modern History in the Universities of Oxford, Cambridge and Manchester 1800–1914*, Manchester, Manchester University Press, 1986, pp. 31–6.

23 Kenyon, *History Men*, p. 154.

24 Slee, *Learning and a Liberal Education*, pp. 87–8.

25 *Ibid.*, pp. 100–1.

26 *Ibid.*, p. 24.

27 Wilkes, ' "A mist of prejudice" ', pp. 46–51; R. N. Soffer, *Discipline and Power: The University, History and the Making of an English Elite, 1870–1930*, Stanford, Stanford University Press, 1994, p. 54.

28 *Notes and Materials for the History of University College, London, Faculties of Arts and Sciences*, 1898, pp. 36–7.

29 S. Rothblatt, *The Revolution of the Dons. Cambridge and Society in Victorian England*, Cambridge, Cambridge University Press, 1981, p. 179.

30 B. Schwarz, 'J. R. Seeley', in K. Boyd (ed.) *Encyclopedia of Historians and Historical Writing*, Chicago, Fitzroy Dearborn, vol. 2, 1999, p. 1079.

31 J. R. Seeley, 'The Teaching of Politics: An Inaugural Lecture Delivered at Cambridge', in J. R. Seeley, *Lectures and Essays*, London, Macmillan, 1870, p. 303.

32 *Ibid.*, p. 302.

33 *Ibid.*, p. 313.

34 *Ibid.*, p. 316.

35 Slee, *Learning and a Liberal Education*, p. 62.

36 Wilkes, ' "A mist of prejudice" ', p. 60. See, for the emergence of the 'endowment of research movement', A. J. Engel, *From Clergyman to Don: The Rise of the Academic Profession in Nineteenth-Century Oxford*, Oxford, Clarendon Press, 1983, pp. 129–55.

37 Soffer, *Discipline and Power*, p. 54.

38 Levine, *The Amateur and the Professional*, p. 136.

39 F. M. Powicke, *Modern Historians and the Study of History: Essays and Papers*, London, Oldhams Press, 1955, p. 19. See chapter on 'The Manchester History School', pp. 19–95

40 Kenyon, *History Men*, p. 189.

41 E. L. Ellis, *The University College of Wales, Aberystwyth 1872–1972*, Cardiff, University of Wales Press, 1972, p. 333.

42 J. F. Jameson, 'The Influence of the Universities upon Historical Writing', in M. Rothberg and J. Goggin (eds) *John Franklin Jameson and the Development of Humanistic Scholarship in America*, Athens GA, University of Georgia Press, 1993, p. 268.

43 E. Breisach, *Historiography. Ancient, Medieval and Modern*, Chicago, University of Chicago Press, 1983, p. 287.

44 J. Higham, *History: Professional Scholarship in America*, New York, Harpers, 1965, p. 6. See also below, pp. 33–6.

45 D. D. Van Tassel, 'From Learned Society to Professional Organization: The American Historical Association, 1884–1900', *American Historical Review*, 1984, vol. 89, p. 935.

46 Jameson, 'Influence of Universities', p. 272.

47 B. G. Smith, *The Gender of History: Men, Women, and Historical Practice*, Cambridge MA, Harvard University Press, 1998, p. 113.

Chapter 2

Methodology

'Scientific' history and the problem of objectivity

Robert Harrison, Aled Jones and Peter Lambert

Professional historical writing in Europe and the United States was not just history written by professionals; it was history written in a particular way. Few historians of the late nineteenth century would have taken exception to J. B. Bury's assertion that history was 'simply a science, no less and no more'. However, national historiographical traditions took science to mean rather different things.

Germany

In the first half of the nineteenth century, the 'science' (*Wissenschaft*) of the humanities in Germany enjoyed a higher reputation than did the natural sciences, and how much the former really owed to the latter is unclear. Accuracy was, of course, thought essential to the determination of facts, and by extension to the identification and authentication of primary sources. So far, the historian's claim to be able to fashion objective history seemed uncomplicated. But no German historian maintained that the sources spoke for themselves. In uncovering and verifying evidence, the historian had accomplished only the preliminaries. Now, his real work began. The main body of the historian's text was devoted to argument and persuasion while, as Anthony Grafton has pointed out, often copious footnotes provided the evidence and furnished the proofs.[1] And what marked the historian out from the antiquarian was his interpretative skill. Only through interpretation might historical truth be found. But interpretation, as historians readily accepted, generated views which varied especially according to when a historian was writing. The particular standpoint of the historian determined the sense he made of his evidence. Nevertheless, this realisation did not lead to a retreat from the claim to objectivity, leave alone a collapse into extreme relativism. The historian's standpoint was not a matter of arbitrary or individual choice. Rather, historians' perspectives were expressions of the epochs in which they wrote. While it was confidently held that Germany was actually advancing towards nation-statehood, and then to further accumulations of power for the nation-state, loyalty to the state and the nation constituted the historians' standpoint. Each generational cohort of historians was (as we will argue in the next chapter) able to assert that its standpoint was superior to that of the last. A stronger and more unified Germany should thus produce better, more objective history because it supplied a superior perspective on the past. In this way, historians identified might with right and conflated power and objectivity. According to their view, patriotic purpose and, in Imperial Germany, defence of the existing social and political order, did not conflict with the aim of achieving historical objectivity. On the contrary, they were a necessary condition for a real understanding of the past.

Thus, if the purely technical aspects of dealing with primary sources bore some kinship with the methods of natural scientists, the understanding of how those sources should be interpreted rested on a theory of knowledge which emphasised empathy and intuition. For Ranke, the essence of world history lay in 'spiritual [*geistige*], life-giving, creative forces'. These could 'neither be defined, nor reduced to abstractions. But they can be observed and distinguished; it is possible to create for oneself empathy for their being'.[2] Debates about whether history was (and for that matter is) a science have suffered ever since from a conceptual confusion. German *Wissenschaft* was mis-translated from the outset as 'science' by its would-be emulators abroad. In the context of the founding phase of professional history, the word 'scholarship' comes far closer to conveying the meaning of *Wissenschaft*. But bad translation is not the only explanation. By the end of the nineteenth century, as the seepage of Darwinian ideas even into German historiography indicates, the explanatory potential of the natural sciences was growing in historians' minds. To that point, historians had not needed to acknowledge any great debt to the natural sciences, and had laid claims of objectivity and truth-seeking which were independent of them.

The establishment and running of journals and periodicals, and historians' collaboration in large-scale editions of documents, provide further evidence of the sense of common purpose which drove historians, and of the increasing diversity and density of their organisational apparatus. The foundation of the *Historische Zeitschrift* in Munich in 1857 could draw on the experience of a variety of journals which had appeared for relatively brief periods since the latter part of the eighteenth century. It was to become *the* organ of the guild, and remains the most prestigious historical journal published in Germany today. In 1858, a 'Historical Commission' was also established in Bavaria, and provided both a forum in which research agendas could be collectively elaborated and resources to carry them out. The *Monumenta Germaniae Historica*, a massive collection of transcriptions of medieval German manuscripts, was founded on an initiative undertaken by the Freiherr vom Stein in 1819. The expectation that any edition of primary sources be supported with footnotes contextualising the documents through references to the secondary literature established itself rapidly. The first of the regular and avowedly 'national' German historians' conferences (*Historikertage*) may only have been held as relatively recently as 1892, but their gradual establishment as red-letter days on German historians' calendars merely added to an already impressive number of societies and institutions which supported work in the universities and made the guild remarkably multi-faceted.

The founding generation of historians 'arrived' equipped with a training from one or more of a group of already established disciplines. Each furnished them with some of the pieces of practical and intellectual equipment which, when put together, came close to filling up the historian's tool-box. From philology, they took the ability to read and accurately date their sources; from law, the capacity to use documents as a way in to understanding institutions; from ancient history, an already developed engagement with past societies.

Whereas earlier expositions of historical methods had focused on rhetorical devices and on ways of *writing* history which ensured that it had literary merit, in the period of professionalisation the emphasis shifted to a concern with how history should be *researched*. The two co-existed in the work of Ranke and his immediate successors but, by the end of the nineteenth century, literary merit had ceased to matter to many historians. In the work of Georg von Below, for instance, stylistic flourishes – metaphors, for instance – were abjured. His was the rhetoric of 'common sense'. Where he wished to underscore his arguments, or to paper over cracks in their logic, he prefaced them with words such as 'undoubtedly', 'of course' and 'naturally'. Research, not the production of aesthetically pleasing prose, was the 'calling' of the historian, and it was approached in the spirit of a markedly Protestant work ethic. While Ranke was in Rome on a research expedition in August 1829, he was 'naturally' not to be distracted by the pleasures of theatres and cafés which stayed open into the early hours: he hurried to bed in order to be back among the stacks of documents.[3] At least Ranke seems to have been foregoing one set of pleasures only for another – for one so much more alluring, indeed, that it could even interfere in his early-morning schedule: 'Yesterday I had a sweet, magnificent fling with the object of my love, a beautiful Italian, and I hope that we produce a beautiful Roman-German prodigy. I rose at noon, completely exhausted'. The object of his passion had been an archival repository.[4] Dour Lutheran pietism deprived later German historians of the ability to convey such joyousness. It was, as Hans Cymorek has pointed out, entirely appropriate that the hard grind which von Below's research had entailed should show through in his prose, so that the reader could feel the 'dust, sweat and toil' of the historian's everyday life.[5] Since the historian's labours had been so very gruelling, it was right that the reader should be made to work, too.

Research, according to von Below, was also the motor of historiographical change:

> Everywhere, our work proceeds as follows: we begin our research with particular conceptions, revise the latter according to the results obtained, then approach the issues anew with the findings we arrive at in order once again to approach a revision of our conceptions on the basis of new research work. This is how our work advances.[6]

Seminars were the 'workshops' within which the next, aspiring generations of historians learned the skills of their craft, thus securing the conditions for von Below's model of historiographical progress. The seminar supplemented the lecture, in which the student was passive. Seminars made students active participants. The very first seminars were held in the mid-1820s and conducted privately, in historians' own homes. Then in 1833, through a series of historical 'exercises' (*Übungen*) led by Leopold von Ranke at the University of Berlin, seminars had begun to migrate into an institutional setting. Ranke's enormously influential innovation centred first on its establishment of close contact between the professor and his students in order, second, to promote the collective discussion of primary sources in particular. Within a decade and a half, such exercises had become a ubiquitous element in history teaching throughout the German universities. However, the development of 'the seminar in the grand style' (Hermann Heimpel) was to take half a century, over which the component parts were manufactured and assembled. Making primary and secondary sources readily available to participants was vital to the process. Among the first dedicated seminar libraries was that established by Heinrich von Sybel at Bonn in 1865. It occupied a single book-case. Only later was the library space to become attached to the room in which the seminar was held. Over roughly the same period, seminars, strikingly informal in their earliest incarnations, came to be regulated by statutes.

It was this fully fledged model of the seminar which became a focal point in the attention of nascent professional history elsewhere. In France, the hard-headedness of German scholarship attracted admirers in the wake of her defeat in the Franco-Prussian War of 1870–1, and the emulation of German historiography was consciously intended as a contribution to the modernisation of France – the better to prepare for any future confrontation with Germany. When Camille Jullian visited Theodor Mommsen's seminar in Berlin in 1882, it was not only to equip himself for an academic career as a historian. He had been sent there on a '*mission*' by the French government, as a kind of industrial spy. As Fustel de Coulanges, Jullian's teacher in France, insisted: 'In order to defeat Germany, it is necessary to emulate her'.[7] However, as the American (and to some extent the British) experiences indicate, rivalry was not always the sole or the chief motive behind an intellectual transfer.

Waves of revolutionary activity from 1789 onward had forced the opening of hitherto highly secret archives. Improved communications made it possible to exploit the new openings. It was not least the introduction of the railway that was to be of vital importance in facilitating research trips. They need not even be planned. One German historian purportedly arrived at his local railway station not knowing which train he would catch or in which direction, and even when he had decided on one, at which station along the line he would alight to visit an archive. Archivists for many miles around are said to have lived in terror of his unannounced visits and peremptory demands for documents.[8] Doctoral students and their teachers alike took on the appearance of societies of explorers, venturing out into archives far and wide, discovering their content, and returning to report excitedly to their peers on their findings. The German historian ought, Ranke insisted, to be ready to 'traverse Germany in all directions in order to hunt down the remains of this world, which is half sunken and yet so close to us. We pursue unknown grasses into the deserts of Libya: how can the life of our forefathers, in our own country, not deserve the same zeal?'[9]

United Kingdom

If, as a result of its incorporation into university curricula, history within the United Kingdom, as was discussed in the previous chapter, became more socially exclusive, effectively the preserve of highly educated men, it also acquired a set of more explicit procedures and a renewed sense of purpose that would continue for more than a century to shape the ways in which a majority of professional historians in Britain practised their craft.

The new emphasis by historians on the interrogation of documents, for instance, presupposed the existence of accessible archives. The systematic collection and cataloguing of documents was already underway at the beginning of the nineteenth century, with governments and a civil service eager to put their own historic papers in order. The Record Commission began the task of publishing medieval sources in 1802, while the Parliamentary Commission, which had been set up two years earlier to investigate the condition of public records, recommended in 1838 the establishment of the Public Records Office as Britain's first official archive. In 1858, work began on a purpose-built repository and reading room in Chancery Lane to house public records, the first of its kind in the world. At the same time, thematic and regional interest groups emerged in many parts of Britain to initiate and broaden the study of history and to make collections of historical sources more widely available. 'This', Macaulay had written in 1823, 'is the age of societies',[10] describing, among others, the striking growth in England since the end of the eighteenth century of archaeological, antiquarian and genealogical societies. Many of these, in turn, became associations for the printing and dissemination of historical documents. These included the Surtees Society, focusing on England's northeast and Borders counties, established in 1834, the Camden Society of 1838 (which in 1897 was amalgamated with the Royal Historical Society), the Manchester-based Chetham Society in 1843, and the Haklyut Society and the Ecclesiastical History Society in 1846. Other material, such as the Sussex Archaeological Collections, began to be published by the Sussex Archaeological Society from 1848. The social composition of these societies was overwhelmingly professional, comprising such occupations as lawyers, journalists and a particularly high proportion of clergymen.[11] These developments in both government and the voluntary sector were continued during the second half of the nineteenth century. From 1857, for example, Lord Romilly, Master of the Rolls, began an ambitious sequence of archival publications, while new local historical societies continued to be formed, such as the Bradford Historical and Antiquarian Society in 1876, and the Birmingham Historical Society in 1881.

The fundamental importance of documents, the centrality of the seminar as an 'historical laboratory', which was regarded by Stubbs in 1867 as 'a grand republic of workers',[12] and a growing conviction that the study of history was, in Seeley's words, 'one of the most wholesome mental exercises',[13] or, in G. W. Prothero's later formulation, a 'good training for the mind',[14] ensured that history had acquired a legitimacy and a structure which it had never before possessed. By 1876, Stubbs could look back on his ten years as Regius Professor at Oxford and reflect on how the subject was 'becoming a professional, even a co-operative, discipline, with international networks of information and standards of performance'.[15] While in some respects the frontier between the professional and the popular remained porous – witness for example the huge popular success of Seeley's *The Expansion of England* (1883), which suggests intense, historically based public enthusiasm for Britain's late-nineteenth and early-twentieth century imperial project – the kind of history experienced by most people, in newspapers, music-hall acts, village pageants and tours of 'historic' buildings, had little contact with the paid historians who toiled away at the state papers of the realm. Where historians did have public lives, they tended to be in politics and high culture. Macaulay, Lecky and Acton served as M.P.s and in more senior political posts, whereas Burrows had begun his career as a naval officer, and Maitland as a barrister. Stubbs became a bishop (of Chester in 1884 and Oxford in 1888), while Froude and Prothero were editors of major literary and political journals, respectively *Fraser's Magazine* (1860–74) and the *Quarterly Review* (1899–1922).

This newly professionalised strata of historians increasingly insisted on the autonomy of their discipline, and were eager to create and nourish their own public sphere of societies, publishing projects and new educational initiatives. The early history of the Royal Historical Society provides a telling illustration of the way in which professional historians were drawn to, and then came to dominate, the historical world of the amateur and the antiquarian. The RHS was founded in November 1868 by a Presbyterian clergyman and journalist, Charles Rogers, who had migrated south to London having been declared bankrupt in his native Scotland, where, among his other campaigns, he had raised funds for the erection of the Wallace memorial in Stirling.[16] Once in London he established the 'the Royal Historical Society of Great Britain', which improperly used the style of 'royal' at its first meeting, which was subsequently, and wisely, abandoned. Having set himself up as the society's 'Historiographer' at a salary of £100 a year plus 10 per cent of all publication receipts, not a minor income for the time, he canvassed the support of prominent figures, and the subscriptions of fellows, who were, in the main, clergymen, physicians, lawyers, army officers, bank managers and journalists. Its first president, elected in 1870, was George Grote, Vice-chancellor of the University of London, while the first volume of its annual *Transactions* was issued in two parts in 1871–2. It was, by all accounts, a ramshackle affair, remote from the unfolding developments in university history taking place at Oxford, Cambridge, Manchester and elsewhere. Worse, it was assailed in the *Athenaeum* in 1879 for the mismanagement of its affairs. Following the reluctant resignation of Rogers in January 1881, however, the society began to assume the characteristics of a more professional association. The influx of new fellows, including Lord Acton, F. W. Maitland, Mandell Creighton, William Lecky and John Seeley, all elected between 1884 and 1886, marked the beginning of the end of the 'age of the dilettanti'.[17] In 1887, it organised a conference on the teaching of history in schools, and won its royal charter of incorporation in 1889 under the presidency of H. A. Bruce, Lord Aberdare, who, in typically Victorian interdisciplinary fashion, was also president of the Royal Geographical Society. The Camden Society was merged with the Royal Historical Society in 1897, and the first Alexander Prize was awarded the following year.[18] In 1899, A. W. Ward became the first president who was also a 'working historian', while in 1902, G. W. Prothero initiated the idea of an historical bibliography, on which work began in 1909. In less than twenty years, the society had been transformed from a loose body of interested amateurs into a group of research historians with strong university connections intent on building the first national structures of the new discipline.

At the same time, historians were engaged in a range of other activities which would extend the accessibility of historical documents and the reach of historical knowledge. In April 1869, the Historical Manuscripts Commission was established by royal warrant as Britain's central advisory body on archives and manuscripts, and in 1882 work began on the *Dictionary of National Biography* (*D.N.B.*), the first volume of which appeared in December 1884. Inspired by publisher George Smith, and funded from profits made from the sale of Apollinaris mineral water from a German spring, the *D.N.B.* was edited until 1891 by Leslie Stephen, then editor of the *Cornhill Magazine*, who was then succeeded by Sidney Lee. The final instalment, which ended with William Zuylestein, was completed in 1901. The first major periodical devoted to history also appeared in the vibrantly formative 1880s. Efforts to establish an *English Historical Review*, first conceived by James Bryce and J. R. Green in 1867, were initially thwarted both by the Macmillan publishing house's reluctance to take the financial risk involved in starting such a new venture, and by Green's illness. A similar approach to Cambridge University Press in 1883 also failed.[19] It was finally launched in 1886, under Mandell Creighton's editorship, as a journal that sought to communicate historical knowledge to both the specialist and the 'general reader'.[20] In its initial manifesto, it saw its role as being a means by which readers would be offered 'a full and critical record of what is being accomplished in the field of history, to bring Britain and its colonies into line with European states, and to support history in the universities'. Acton penned its first article, appropriately on the subject of 'German Schools of History', and, in addition to the main articles, it included a 'notes and documents' section and book reviews. It put historians across the country in touch with each other and with developments on the continent, and, in Acton's words, it enabled 'a Sacred Band of University workers' to begin to think of themselves as a historical community, and of history as a collective endeavour.[21] It made little money, paid derisorily low rates to contributors, and was never, in its early years, a serious competitor to the major literary Victorian periodicals. Although Gladstone once offered to write an article in order to broaden its appeal, in 1889 the *English Historical Review* acknowledged its specialist nature and cut its print run from 1,000 to 750 per issue. After 1900, however, its numbers gradually increased until it regained its initial circulation in the 1920s.[22] Above all, Creighton's intention of fostering through the journal a new generation of historians was being realised.[23] Partly in response to the place it had gained within the nascent profession of history in England, an *American Historical Review* was established in 1895, and a *Scottish Historical Review*, a new series of the *Scottish Antiquary* (also founded in 1886), was launched in 1904. These developments of the 1880s were augmented by the appearance of the first volumes of the English Victoria County History series in 1899, and the launch in 1901 of the *Cambridge Modern History* series.

United States

The relationship between history and the natural sciences, and the nature of historical objectivity, so prominent in the era of professionalisation in Germany, were seen differently in the USA in the 1880s and 1890s. There, the rhetoric of scientific investigation was pervasive: the research seminar was described as a 'historical laboratory' or 'workshop'; the footnote citations and bibliographical references that supported a historical monograph were known as the 'scholarly apparatus'; Herbert Baxter Adams referred to the documents presented to his students as 'specimens' to be examined and tested. Adams, like many of his contemporaries, believed that adoption of the new methods of critical scholarship would bring history close to the ideal of 'pure science'. What, then, were the components of the new 'scientific' method of historical investigation as perceived by American historians in the late nineteenth and early twentieth centuries?

Of paramount importance was the study of primary documents. The historian should return to the original sources, instead of relying on secondary accounts which had become encrusted with prejudice and error. Like the scientist with his microscope inspecting the material world at first hand, the historian must go into the archives to examine the documentary traces of the period that he was studying, applying the methods of textual criticism developed in Germany early in the nineteenth century. Only then would truth emerge from the mists of historical time; only then could historical 'facts' be discovered.

In the second place, the historian should devote himself, in the words of the Columbia historian William Archibald Dunning, to the 'absorbing and relentless pursuit of the objective fact – of the thing that actually happened [one of many such statements to paraphrase Ranke] in the form and manner of its happening'.[24] According to George Burton Adams, 'the conquest of the unknown' began with the accumulation of facts.

> To lay such foundations, to furnish such materials for later builders, may be a modest ambition, but it is my firm belief that in our field of history, for a long time to come, the man who devotes himself to such labor, who is content with this preliminary work, will make a more useful and a more permanent contribution to the final science ... of history, than will he who yields to the allurement of speculation and endeavors to discover in the present stage of our knowledge the forces that control society, or to formulate the laws of their action. ... The field of the historian is, and must long remain, the discovery and recording of what actually happened.[25]

In the eyes of John Franklin Jameson, what the discipline needed was 'a great deal of thoroughly good second-class work'.[26] Historians should be prepared to beaver away in the archives for the benefit of future generations, patiently fabricating the materials out of which the future historiographical edifice would be constructed (a common metaphor this), so that out of their endeavours a 'temple made of monographic bricks' would eventually arise.[27]

Implicit in their epistemological reflections was an inductivist model of science. Contemporaries believed that the natural sciences had attained their impressive understanding of the material world through a simple sequence of observation followed by generalisation. Scientific laws like those of evolution were immanent in the structure of the universe; they were not invented or imposed by the scientist but were simply there to be uncovered by his investigations. Rather than testing previously constructed hypotheses against the evidence, the scientist should examine the evidence, with his mind in effect a *tabula rasa*, so that the laws of nature could reveal themselves. So common was this inductivist view of science in the nineteenth century that even Darwin amended the story of his own 'discovery' of natural selection in order to make it appear like an epiphany vouchsafed to him by the finches of the Galapagos Islands. Historians, like Albert Bushnell Hart, addressing the AHA in 1910, regularly urged their colleagues to follow the Baconian model of scientific research:

> What we need is a genuinely scientific school of history which shall remorselessly examine the sources and separate the wheat from the chaff; which shall critically balance evidence; which shall dispassionately and moderately set forth results. For such a process we have the fortunate analogy of the physical sciences; did not Darwin spend twenty years in accumulating data, and in selecting typical phenomena before he so much as ventured a generalization? History, too, has its inductive method, its relentless concentration of the grain in its narrow spout, till by its own

weight it seeks the only outlet. In history, too, scattered and apparently unrelated data fall together in harmonious wholes; the mind is led to the discovery of laws. ... That is the way in which Darwin came upon his universally guiding principle of natural selection; is it not the way in which historians must work?[28]

However, like Ranke, whom they wrongly venerated as an incarnation of pure empiricism but who, in fact, held firm convictions about the kind of transcendent reality that would emerge from historical research, American historians of this period believed equally profoundly in the process of institutional evolution that would become manifest when the work of sifting and sorting had been completed.

Third, the historian must address his source objectively, that is, without prejudice or bias or any 'predetermined principles of classification and organization'.[29] That meant the exclusion of religious or political beliefs, but also the avoidance of any prior assumptions or hypotheses. After all, there was no need for prior interpretation since the 'facts when justly arranged interpret themselves'.[30]

That was the ideal of 'scientific history' as it was held in the United States around 1900. It was attractive to academic historians very largely because it validated their claim to professional authority. It was, says Peter Novick, the rock on which the enterprise of professional historiography was founded. It served to justify both the new social role of the historian and the narrowly specialised research in which most historians were engaged. It conferred an aura of modernity on their subject. The 'founding myth' of 'objectivity' suited the members of a new profession anxious to establish its claim to respect by aligning itself with the more prestigious field of natural science. By later standards the American historical profession was remarkably untroubled by serious discord over questions of epistemology and method. Ernst Breisach notes that there was no *Methodenstreit* in America – not at least until after the First World War.

Finally, the promulgation of a 'scientific' method was also advanced by the establishment of the *American Historical Review*, established by a ginger group of younger academic historians in 1895. Following the example of proximate disciplines, which had already established scholarly journals, as well as historians in Germany, France and Britain, they believed that a journal was necessary for more effective communication and the dissemination of appropriate methodologies. The publication of a separate journal was a clear indication of the extent to which academic historians had become a separate audience, clearly demarcated from the general lay readership for historical writing. Jameson, who served thirty years as the *Review*'s managing editor, laid down three criteria in evaluating articles for inclusion: 'that they shall be fresh and original in treatment; that they shall be the result of accurate scholarship; and that they shall have distinct literary merit'.[31] The *Review* contained book reviews which were intended both to keep readers informed of recent publications and, in theory at least, to weed out work that did not meet satisfactory standards of scholarship. Its function, said Jameson, was 'to regularize, to criticize, to restrain vagaries, to set a standard of workmanship and compel men to conform to it'.[32] Finally, it published news of documentary collections, conferences, appointments, scholarships and grants. In practice, most of the articles published in the early years, in Morey Rothberg's words, 'followed well-worn paths of institutional and political history' and exemplified diligent scholarship rather than literary excellence, while the reviews were mostly uncritical.[33] In consequence, the journal carried out its function of monitoring standards of professional competence less effectively than its function as an organ of communication for the nascent historical profession.

Notes

1 A. Grafton, *The Footnote. A Curious History*, Cambridge MA, Harvard University Press, 1997, p. 15.
2 L. von Ranke, 'Die großen Mächte', *Historisch-politische Zeitschrift*, 1833, vol. 2, pp. 1–51; here pp. 50–1.
3 Grafton, *The Footnote*, p. 36.
4 B. G. Smith, *The Gender of History: Men, Women, and Historical Practice*, Cambridge MA, Harvard University Press, 1998, p. 119.
5 H. Cymorek, *Georg von Below und die deutsche Geschichtswissenschaft um 1900*, Stuttgart, Franz Steiner, 1998, pp. 220–3; quotation p. 222.
6 G. von Below, 'Über historische Periodisierungen, mit besonderem Blick auf die Grenze zwischen Mittelalter und Neuzeit', *Archiv für Politik und Geschichte*, 1925, vol. 4, pp. 1–29; 170–214; quotation, p. 22.
7 K. F. Werner, 'Historisches Seminar – École des Annales. Zu den Grundlagen einer europäischen Geschichtsforschung', in J. Miethge (ed.) *Geschichte in Heidelberg*, Berlin, Springer, 1992, pp. 1–38; here pp. 3–8.
8 R. Chickering, *Karl Lamprecht. A German Academic Life, 1856–1915*, New Jersey, Humanities Press, 1993, p. 79.
9 Cit. after Grafton, *The Footnote*, p. 49.
10 Lord Macaulay, 'On the Royal Society of Literature', in *idem, Biographical, Critical and Miscellaneous Essays and Poetical Works*, 1892, p. 391.
11 Sixty-five per cent of the membership of the Buckinghamshire antiquarian society in 1854 were clergymen, P. Levine, *The Amateur and the Professional: Antiquarians, Historians and Archaeologists in Victorian England, 1838–1886*, Cambridge, Cambridge University Press, 1986, pp. 184–5.
12 B. Smith, 'Gender and the Practices of Scientific History: the Seminar and Archival Research in the Nineteenth Century', *American Historical Review*, 1995, vol. 100, pp. 1154–8, 1160.
13 J. R. Seeley, 'The Teaching of Politics: An Inaugural Lecture Delivered at Cambridge', in J. R. Seeley, *Lectures and Essays*, London, Macmillan, 1870, p. 295.
14 G. W. Prothero, *Why Should We Learn History? An Inaugural Lecture Delivered at Edinburgh, 16 October 1894*, Edinburgh, 1894.
15 J. W. Burrow, *A Liberal Descent. Victorian Historians and the English Past*, Cambridge, Cambridge University Press, 1981, p. 98.
16 R. A. Humphreys, *The Royal Historical Society 1868–1968*, London, Royal Historical Society, 1969, p. 1.

17 Humphreys, *The Royal Historical Society*, p. 20.
18 Humphreys, *The Royal Historical Society*, p. 26.
19 D. S. Goldstein, 'The Origins and Early Years of the *English Historical Review*', *English Historical Review*, 1987, vol. 101, pp. 6–9.
20 'Prefatory Note', *English Historical Review*, 1886, vol. 1, pp. 1–2.
21 Goldstein, 'The Origins and Early Years', p. 10.
22 *Ibid.*, pp. 12–14.
23 *Ibid.*, p. 18.
24 W. A. Dunning, 'Truth in History', *American Historical Review*, 1914, vol. 19, p. 219.
25 G. B. Adams, 'History and the Philosophy of History', *American Historical Review*, 1909, vol. 14, p. 236.
26 J. Higham, *History: Professional Scholarship in America*, New York, Harpers, 1965, p. 6.
27 L. R. Veysey, *The Emergence of the American University*, Chicago, University of Chicago Press, 1965, p. 146.
28 A. B. Hart, 'Imagination in History', *American Historical Review*, 1910, vol. 15, pp. 232–3.
29 E. P. Cheyney, quoted in P. Novick, *That Noble Dream: The 'Objectivity Question' and the American Historical Profession*, Cambridge, Cambridge University Press, 1988, p. 39.
30 A. J. Beveridge, quoted in W. Stull Holt, *Historical Scholarship in the United States*, Seattle, University of Washington Press, 1967, p. 23.
31 John Franklin Jameson, 'The *American Historical Review*, 1895–1920', *American Historical Review*, 1920, vol. 26, p. 8.
32 M. D. Rothberg, ' "To Set a Standard of Workmanship and Compel Men to Conform to It": John Franklin Jameson as Editor of the *American Historical Review*', *American Historical Review*, vol. 89, 1984, p. 965.
33 *Ibid.*, p. 961.

Chapter 3

The primacy of political history

Robert Harrison, Aled Jones and Peter Lambert

The founding generation of professional historians, in Germany, in America, and in Britain, had a narrow view of the subject-matter of history, concentrating their efforts on the study of political history. One reason for doing so was that the methods of 'scientific history' were more easily applied to political topics. The archives of state and federal governments and the collected papers of prominent political leaders provided the most easily accessible documentary material. Therefore states, rather than peoples, became their principal subjects.

Germany

In the case of Germany, in addition to the demands of scientific method, state sponsorship of the emergent discipline, and state patronage of historians, provided a second motive for the particular focus on political history, while the Lutheran propensity to defer to state authority furnished a third. Though they rejected almost every other aspect of his work, historians echoed Hegel in pronouncing the state to be the greatest achievement of human endeavour. Johann Gustav Droysen associated the state with the divine; Friedrich Dahlmann attributed more human attributes to it: those of a 'corporially and spiritually eligible personality'. Thus, a first step was taken toward reconciling a focus on the state *in general* with historians' conviction that their concern should be with the historically *particular*: the state was itself an individual! The second step was contrived when the historian's task was declared to be the propagation of his own *nation*-state. Where Ranke's earlier work had combined a defence of traditional authority with a measure of universalism, Prussian loyalism with an interest in the relations between states, and exhibited a sceptical attitude towards nationalism, his political allegiance and academic agenda subsequently shifted toward Germany. Even so, as early as 1833 Ranke had argued that only those states capable of 'awakening' the 'slumbering spirits of the nations' were also capable of surviving in post-French Revolutionary Europe. The hundred years before 1789 had witnessed the rise of the 'great states'; since then, the 'nationalities' had 'consciously entered into the state'. The 'national principle' had furnished the state with a 'moral force' and so given it a new lease of life. In Germany after 1809, the result was the defeat of Napoleonic France, a victory predicated on the fact that 'inherited strife was finally really forgotten, and unity seriously achieved'.[1] The next generation of German historians was thus rather misleading in its allegation that Ranke lacked patriotism, and that his 'objectivity' led to 'bloodlessness' and 'want of character'. But what this, the Prussian School of historians (including Droysen, Dahlmann and Heinrich von Sybel) *did* introduce was, first, a specific vision of a 'small German' nation-state (i.e. one excluding Austrian Germans) and, second, the notion that it was Prussia's 'mission' to unify Germany. Third, in contrast to Ranke, they wrote principally about German history. In the aftermath of the failure of the 1848 Revolution, Prussian School historians sought to mobilise bourgeois opinion behind Prussian statescraft and simultaneously, through advice, to encourage Prussia's politicians to undertake German unification. Thus Droysen's study of the role of York von Wartenberg in ensuring that the Prussian army deserted France and swung behind the Russians, thereby contributing to Prussia's and Germany's 'liberation', was consciously designed to jolt contemporary Prussian statesmen into undertaking similarly patriotic adventures. The hopes of the Prussian School, of course, were realised – in 1866, with the effective removal of Austria from German affairs and then, in 1870–1, with the defeat of France and the establishment of the German Empire. Historians were prominent contributors to the development of a cult of personality around Bismarck and to the celebration of the foundation of the empire not only in 1871 itself, but in speeches and articles commemorating its anniversaries thereafter. So complete did the convergence between the political and historiographical programme of the Prussian School on the one hand, and the political outcome on the other, appear to be, that historians were puzzled to find further causes in politics and inspiration for scholarship. The very fact of triumph brought its own dilemmas for Heinrich von Sybel: 'The object of all our desires and efforts for twenty years has now been fulfilled in so endlessly marvellous a fashion! Whence should we take new goals for further life in the remaining years of my life?'[2]

The next generation of historians solved this problem in a so-called 'Rankean Renaissance'. Max Lenz and Erich Marcks in particular contributed to this further shift of emphasis within historism. Their central concern was with the legitimation of the actually existing German state. Accordingly, the history they wrote lacked the stridency and urgency of the Prussian School. Sedate tones were more appropriate to defence of the *status quo*; Lenz argued that 'objectivity' had necessarily taken a back seat in the struggle for national unification. Now, 'passions had calmed' and, 'thanks to Bismarck even more than Ranke', a higher historical objectivity was possible: 'The Reich had to be founded before the sense for reality, the sure eye for reality in respect also of the past, could reawaken'.[3] In terms of lectures, research and publications, the outcome of this proclaimed feel for the past was a redoubled concentration on external relations, indeed, an insistence that there was a 'primacy of foreign policy' which should be reflected in the writing of history. If this reinforced a Rankean hierarchy of importance in kinds of history, it was marked also by a seepage of Darwinian, and sometimes racialist, ideas into the study of international relations, whose dynamics were henceforth reduced to a law of the jungle in which only the fittest would survive. Within this consensus, which was as much political as historiographical, there was still room for variations in emphasis. Dietrich Schäfer and Johannes Haller, for instance, outflanked governmental nationalism and were steadfastly and self-consciously reactionary. While there was broad support for the imperialist ambitions of Wilhelmine governments, statist historians like Friedrich Meinecke and Hans Delbrück ventured a number of particular criticisms of the domestic policies pursued in the Reich. Meinecke advocated a conciliatory policy toward the Social Democrats, implying that successive governments' treatment of them as 'vagrants without a fatherland' needlessly reinforced their Marxism and internationalism. Delbrück, though well connected with the imperial dynasty itself, was twice threatened by the authorities for venturing criticisms of government policy. On the second of these occasions, remarks objecting to anti-Danish policies in North Schleswig nearly cost him his post at Berlin and an effective demotion to a lesser university. Wilhelmine governments and historians found it difficult to distinguish in practice between legitimate disagreement about how the interests of state and nation could best be served on the one hand, and more fundamental, and therefore impermissible, critiques of the Wilhelmine state and society on the other. Were the first kind of dissent to be too narrowly defined, the claim to academic liberty would be jeopardised, and the historians' claim to be able to address the public in the national interest might be forfeited altogether.[4] In relation to the second species of dispute, however, historians frequently preempted the state by ruthlessly policing the statist and nationalist perimeters of the guild and of the history its members produced. In a sense, historism itself was more clearly and certainly more programmatically defined in response to a sequence of challenges to the dominance of political history.

These came from the spasmodic development of cultural, social and economic history. It was not that they necessarily appeared threatening in themselves. Ranke had never denied social history a place in principle; several of the chief exponents of Prussian School historiography had toyed with projects relating to the social history of their own class – though none had brought them to fruition.[5] However, the emergence of the disciplines of sociology and economics in German universities radically altered the context in which experimentation was received. Both these disciplines employed theoretical models, and thus diverged fundamentally from historians' understanding of knowledge itself. Each was also concerned with the past; both were proving attractive to students. History seemed in imminent danger of being knocked off its pedestal; historians' effective public monopoly on the interpretation of the past was equally at risk. In principle, historians could respond either by opening doors to the possibilities of interdisciplinarity, or by battening down the hatches and preserving the distinctive qualities and claims of the discipline.

In the early 1890s, one young but already established historian, Karl Lamprecht, brought the Trojan horse of interdisciplinarity into history in the first three volumes of his *German History*.[6] A hostile review by von Below objected in principle to its neglect of political history, but concentrated on cataloguing errors of detail in an attempt to destroy its author's professional credentials. Neither the review itself, nor even Lamprecht's litigious reaction to it, caused the real storm, however. Ironically, what sank Lamprecht – and with him, his methodological approach and its many disciples among his students – was a single positive review. Praise for his work as a 'major ... step forward in bourgeois historiography' came from a reviewer who read it as confirmation of a view 'that in every historical epoch the content of spiritual life must be derived, to a greater or lesser extent, from material and social preconditions'. Now, an explicitly political dimension was added to a scholarly debate which had degenerated into personal bickering. The reviewer in question, Franz Mehring, was not a professional historian but a Marxist writing in a Marxist theoretical journal and alleging that Lamprecht's ground, like the Marxists', was that of historical materialism. Conservative historians who had harboured the suspicion that social history might tend to imply socialist history saw their worst fears born out.

Young and ambitious historians lined up to establish their credentials in the guild – and perhaps also endear themselves to potential ministerial patrons – by attacking Lamprecht, restating the case for a primacy of political history and so rescuing history itself as they understood it. Lamprecht himself, who was very far from having any political sympathy with Marxism, neither defended the historical materialism he had seemed to champion, nor surrendered to his critics. Instead, he launched into a series of intellectually even more adventurous – but also far less persuasive – attempts at interdisciplinary history.[7]

The *Methodenstreit* surrounding Lamprecht's work had established to the satisfaction of the vast majority of historians that methodological innovation converged with left-wing politics – a witches' brew which could destroy careers and lead to the ostracisation of anyone foolhardy enough to toy with it. A handful of further cases reinforced the sharp lesson. Ludwig Quidde's *Caligula* was easily decoded by the authorities as a satire aimed at Wilhelm II; in a country in which *lèse majesté* remained a crime, the book ended Quidde's occupation of a full chair of history. The left-liberal Veit Valentin suffered a similar fate when the *venia legendi* (effectively the state's certification of an academic's right to teach at a university) was withdrawn from him.

Heterodox historiography was still practised by a few individuals on the peripheries of the guild, but its statist core had been confirmed. At the same time, social history *did* secure a foothold within the historical community. The process by which it did so can best be understood through the changing fortunes of a single periodical, the *Journal of Economic and Social History*

(*Zeitschrift für sozial- und Wirtschaftsgeschichte*) and its relaunch in 1903 as the *Social and Economic History Quarterly*. This was a journal which, in its first (1890s) incarnation, had been edited by two Austrian Marxist historians working wholly outside the profession. They had contrived to set an ambitious, theoretically informed agenda and to attract an impressively international array of contributors. The revived journal's *de facto* managing editor was Georg von Below, the arch-enemy of Lamprecht's work! 'A charming joke on world history' was von Below's own retrospective comment on his apparent transformation from gamekeeper to poacher. But precisely because he had been Lamprecht's first assailant, he was ideally placed to make social history respectable. He contrived the trick by transforming a hitherto intellectually radical journal into one whose pretensions were strikingly modest. Von Below's was a variant of social history which deliberately avoided theoretical abstractions, fought shy of links with adjacent disciplines, and – above all – took itself to be no more than a subservient adjunct to statist history. Once it had acquired a recognition at all, therefore, the lowly status of social history ensured that no more than a passing nod of acquaintance with it need be made by historians writing national history in the orthodox mould.[8] Dietrich Schäfer wrote for many when he declared in his *German History* that the 'quantitatively and qualitatively increased insight with which economic and social studies have furnished us … is to be greeted with joyful thanks. If, however, these studies claim to put historical understanding on a new basis, they must be decisively contradicted'. So it was a matter of course that economic and social questions should remain in the background of Schäfer's work. 'History is not a "fight for the fodder trough"', he announced in a remark perhaps more nearly reflecting his real estimation of the value of social and economic history, 'and the state is not a product of society. Social organisation has developed only on the basis of the state, and economic questions have certainly been able to influence, but rarely to govern, its development'. If anything, he had even less time for the history of material culture, since

> for the great questions through whose solution the making of our people and its place in humanity was determined, whether one fought with the spear or the automatic rifle, in chain-mail or an army service jacket, spoke in a robe or in tails, gained one's nourishment from bacon and beans or dined on the *cuisine* of a French chef is all irrelevant.[9]

The First World War, Germany's defeat, revolution, the inauguration of a parliamentary-democratic republic and the imposition of the Treaty of Versailles intensified the quality of historians' political engagement and the divide between the right and left wings of the guild already evident in the Wilhelmine period. During the war, history was employed to justify Germany's war aims. Historians disagreed merely on how expansionist those aims should be, and on whether a measure of democratisation would enhance or weaken national unity in the prosecution of the war itself. The fault line of that divide prefigured historians' divergent responses to the creation of the Weimar Republic and to the Treaty of Versailles. A significant minority within the guild argued that it was necessary, as Friedrich Meinecke put it, 'to throw overboard some conservative ballast' in order to preserve as much as possible of the old order, and in particular to fend off the threat of proletarian revolution. Meinecke coined a new set of political expressions to define this position: it was possible, while remaining a 'monarchist at heart', to become a 'Republican by virtue of reason', but not a 'Republican by dint of conviction'. The point was that the essence of the German state should survive the regime change. The majority of historians rejected the Weimar Republic out of hand. Similarly, a minority stressed the possibilities of a sober and gradual revision of the terms of the Versailles settlement, while a majority mined the past in order to propagate the values of militarism and power politics. They dreamed not of revising the Versailles settlement, but of smashing it. Nevertheless, the evidence of what continued to unite the guild is as impressive as that of discord within it.

So closely had historians been aligned with Imperial Germany and with the broad thrust of its foreign policy, that the collapse of the monarchy and the fact of military defeat were simultaneously also a defeat of German historism. Nevertheless, what ensued was not a paradigm shift, but the redoubled assertion of established historiographical norms. While social history – even in the self-deprecatory mode encouraged by von Below – all but vanished from the pages of the *Vierteljahrsschrift für sozial- und Wirtschaftsgeschichte*, traditional diplomatic history in particular was even re-invigorated in the aftermath of the war.

The so-called 'war guilt clause' of the Treaty of Versailles was interpreted as an attempt at indictment of the historical and moral record of the German Reich, and as disabling the development of a present and future German foreign policy. The statesmen of the old regime were keen to see themselves, the regime in general, or both, vindicated. They wrote memoirs, made themselves available for interview with historians, and sometimes approached historians to edit and publish their papers. Successive Weimar governments opened the Foreign Ministry archive to hand-picked historians, and oversaw not only the publication of a vast edition of its documents, but secured clandestine funding for an array of purportedly independent organisations seeking to popularise a campaign to establish Germany's innocence in the causes of the war. A flood of primary sources thus became available to historians. Medievalists like Johannes Haller (an expert on the medieval papacy) and early modernists like Richard Fester (who had previously worked on Machiavelli) transformed themselves into historians of the origins of the war. Whether inspired primarily by a desire to defend the reputation the Bismarckian and Wilhelmine Reich, or by a wish to serve the foreign policies of Weimar governments, German historians carried their 'world war of the documents' both to the German people and abroad.[10]

More generally, the concept of a German *Sonderweg*, of a peculiar German path which had departed historically from a presumed Western norm of development on the basis of natural rights and towards parliamentary democracy, was – as Bernd Faulenbach has argued – fully developed and celebrated only in the Weimar Republic. German historiography, it was asserted, had not only documented the *Sonderweg*, but made a vital contribution to it. From this perspective, parliamentary democracy could be denounced as an alien imposition on Germany, obedience to the state as an historic German virtue, and the pursuit of power as the just and necessary task of the state.[11]

It is tempting to suggest that, in 1918–19, professional German historiography had reached a turning point – and failed to turn. That it did *not* turn is certainly not testimony to any inherent virtues of the historist position, nor yet to the want of public interest in a more critical engagement with the past. Left-liberal amateur historiography had wide appeal in 1920s Germany. Emil Ludwig's iconoclastic biographies of Bismarck and Wilhelm II were best-sellers.[12] Rather, what the resilience of historism illustrates is the capacity of an organisation to immunise itself from the effects of political and social upheaval. Once severed by revolution and parliamentarisation from its moorings in the esteem of the ruling elites of Imperial Germany, the historians' guild could demonstrate to the full its collective capacity to continue to regulate the composition and scholarly code of conduct of its membership. The 'pull' factor of patronage and the 'push' factor of censorship still tended to keep young historians' work broadly in line with their elders', accentuating the consequences of the lack of change in the social composition of the new generational cohorts of history students. On the rare occasions when Weimar authorities sought to rid themselves of some of the most virulently anti-democratic professors, the democrats were accused of violating academic liberty. No thorough-going democratisation of the profession was even attempted.[13]

Convinced democrats, in contrast, met with unremitting hostility from the guild without receiving compensatory support from Republican governments. Where a young historian dared to combine left-wing politics with historiographical innovation, he scotched his own career in German academe. Eckart Kehr must have seemed socially highly acceptable to the guild. He was a member of a Prussian aristocratic family with a distinguished record of service to the state. However, when Kehr argued that a primacy of *domestic* policy had operated in Wilhelmine Germany, and that its navy-building had been undertaken not in response to an international threat, but in order to shore up the unity and power of Germany's political and economic elites, he hit raw patriotic and historist nerves. His own teachers denounced him as a 'Bolshevik'. Fully aware that he would never find a post at a German university, Kehr emigrated to the United States of America. Even there, the hostility of his former professors pursued him, as they sought – albeit unsuccessfully – to dissuade their American colleagues from employing him. Thus, it had not taken the advent of the Nazi dictatorship to deprive the German historical profession of one of its most promising talents. That promise was not to be fulfilled. Kehr died at the age of thirty-one in 1933, probably in consequence of syphilis 'inherited' from his father, a brutal Junker who had beaten his son throughout Eckart's childhood. Kehr's tragic death appears almost as a metaphor for the fate of politically and methodologically progressive German historiography between the wars.

Only where methodological innovation was clearly not linked to left-wing politics, and where it could appear to serve the interests of German nationalism, did it stand any chance of gaining ground within the profession. One version of history did meet these conditions: *Volksgeschichte* – 'folk' history. Tolerated, sometimes even encouraged, by statist historians, 'folk' history nevertheless made only a limited impact on guild historiography before 1933. Only in the aftermath of the Nazi 'seizure' of power, and with the direct aid of the Nazi party-state apparatus, did it really come to the fore. Its place in the history of German historiography will be discussed in Chapter 6 below. In other respects, the rise of Nazism failed to generate significant rethinking on the part of German historians.

United Kingdom

At the heart of the nineteenth-century endeavour to establish history as a discipline, which, in Britain, spanned university reform, the creation of professional societies and the issuing of new publications, was a belief that history could demonstrate and confirm the supremacy of the English political, religious and social institutions that dominated the British state and which helped define its 'national' culture. Like its research methodology, this too was adapted from the Rankean model which proposed that states, being the result of historical growth, constituted both 'moral energies' and the 'thoughts of God'. The primary task of historians was to reveal the 'existing order as God had willed it'.[14] This emphasis on constitutional history enabled history in the 1860s and 1870s, as we have seen, to become a more respectable academic subject. For the half century that followed the publication of Stubbs' three-volume *Constitutional History of England* (1873–8), professional history was focused almost exclusively on the history of law and administration.[15] Even Seeley's *Ecce Homo*, a study of the life of Christ published anonymously in 1865, was, according to Sheldon Rothblatt, 'really an attempt to define the social role of élites' which drew pointed parallels between the 'collapse of antiquity' and the 'collapse of aristocratic society' in Seeley's own time.[16] Its moralistic and philosophical reflections on the human condition appealed strongly to such Liberal politicians as W. E. Gladstone, who warmly sympathised with its historicist purpose.[17] Creighton, in the first issue of the *English Historical Review* in 1886, had defined history in much the same terms, as

> the record of human actions, and of thought only in its direct influence upon action. States and politics will be the chief part of its subject, because

the acts of nations and of individuals who have played a great part in the affairs of nations have usually been more important than the acts of private citizens.[18]

In similar vein, Acton, who had described Ranke as 'my own master',[19] and Mommsen and Treitschke as 'the two greatest of living writers',[20] could say with confidence in 1895 that 'knowledge of the past … [was] eminently practical, as an instrument of action and a power that goes to the making of the future'.[21] Not until Louis Namier began to explore the 'structure' of politics after the First World War did the influence of the mid- to late-Victorian constitutional historians on the practice of political history really begin to wane.[22]

The constitutional historians left a complex legacy. On the positive side, they developed distinctive (in their own terms, 'scientific') ways of reading, analysing, contextualising and comparing historical sources, had secured for history a place and a purpose as a mainstream university and, later, as a school subject, and had developed a body of published work which both laid the foundations of the discipline and, in some significant instances, crossed into the broader public domain. On the other hand, their preoccupation with demonstrating the 'Whiggish' continuities of English institutions, and their formative role in the making of the British state, inclined them, in Philippa Levine's words, 'towards the preservation of a disintegrating social and intellectual network', so that the 'paradoxes at work in Victorian society were mirrored in those of the newly emergent university history'.[23] This should come as no surprise, because these historians, too, were inescapably present in their own historically shaped worlds, and while they succeeded in avoiding the pressures nakedly to promote state interests in ways which many historians on the European continent did not, they nevertheless embodied many of the cultural and social assumptions of men of their position. Their emphasis on the Englishness of Britain's key institutions, for instance, effectively excluded non-English ethnic groups from the 'chief part', as Creighton had put it, of history's subject. Significantly, those left out of the picture in Ireland, Scotland and Wales, responded by writing, and inventing, their own 'national' histories,[24] while others formed separate historical associations – the Jewish Historical Society, for example, was founded in 1893. History's essentially conservative outlook, combined with its narrow social base, also helped ensure the general exclusion of women from both university posts in history, and from the 'seminar culture' of Rankean research activity.[25] Professionalisation in its early years may thus be seen to have reinforced certain kinds of 'identity history', while effectively excluding others.

But if women were marginalised by the male imperatives of university history, a hidden history of women historians may be found in the schools of early twentieth-century Britain, where they too were involved in an extension of the process of professionalisation. The Historical Association was founded in 1906 explicitly with the view, as T.F. Tout put it, to build up 'a corporate spirit among members of the profession of teachers of History' in schools, and to campaign for 'adequate recognition' for history as a school subject. With some 1,000 members in fourteen branches in England by 1911, when a separate Scottish section was established, the association was sufficiently confident in 1912 to launch its own periodical, *History*, aimed specifically at 'the student and the teacher'.[26] One of its early female contributors, Hilda Johnstone, wrote enthusiastically of the 'new glow of fervour' with which she sensed 'the recent awakening of interest in historical teaching, as well as in historical study' and the self-examination to which it had given rise.[27]

That process of self-reflection took many forms. G. P. Gooch's *History and Historians in the Nineteenth Century*, published in 1913, outlined 'the achievements of historical research and production' over the previous century, and analysed their effects on 'the life and thought of their time'.[28] Already by that time, however, historians were broadening their horizons. A. F. Pollard had noted in 1911 how the severity of the labour unrest of that year had fuelled the growth of economic history, which W. J. Ashley and the Oxford Economic Society had been fostering since 1886.[29] The first university lecturer in economic history had been appointed in 1904, the *Economic History Review* was established in 1927 and the first chairs in economic history were established in Manchester in 1910 and at the London School of Economics in 1921. Chairs in economic history followed at Cambridge in 1929 and in Oxford in 1931.[30] The years that followed the First World War were productive for history in other ways, too. In 1921, Pollard set up the Institute of Historical Research in London, which finally realised the long-held desire of the Royal Historical Society to establish a national school of historical research. Pollard, as Head of the History Department at University College London, also encouraged a more comprehensive approach to British history in his own institution by creating in 1924 a new lectureship in Scottish history, the first of its kind outside Scotland.[31] If English constitutional history had led the initial assault on the old universities in the 1860s and 1870s, the emergence of a postwar generation of university-educated historians began the long process of diversifying the practice of history, and thus of challenging the claims of the 'national' constitutional historians to an exclusive authority over the discipline.

United States

In the United States of America before the First World War, historians like Jameson saw insurmountable difficulties in the study of social history. As he told Frederick Jackson Turner,

> I have always thought it more difficult to document with any sense of security, the social and economic history of the United States than the political or constitutional. You do not have definitely limited bodies of material, handed down by authority, like statutes or other manageable series, but a

vast blot of miscellaneous material from which the historian picks out what he wants, and so the effort to document it must often be a process of selection, and if selection, always open to the suspicion of being a biased selection, or one made to sustain a set of views.[32]

In fact, Jameson was deeply interested in social history but, ever conscious of the problems of evidence, was reluctant to publish his work in the field.

The emphasis on political events followed also from professional historians' conception of their public function – a conception which sat oddly alongside their 'scientific' truth claims. University teachers were not civil servants, directly dependent for their living on the federal government or, except indirectly in some instances, on the states, while the administrators who hired and fired them were much more attuned to the desires of wealthy alumni and business donors than those of the agencies of government. Nonetheless, historians' conception of their political responsibility was not markedly different from that of their European equivalents. Their public role, they believed, included a responsibility to promote American nationalism by tracing the history of the United States and its institutions. The veneration of the past contributed to the validation of the present. The production of history gave content to an American nationhood which was not far beyond its infancy, which had just emerged from a threatening sectional conflict, and which now faced the challenges of growing ethnic diversity and widening class divisions. The task of the American historian, then, was to trace the development of American political institutions back through the history of the United States and beyond and hence to play his part in the ongoing process of nation-building.

What emerged was a story of progress, an American version of the 'Whig interpretation of history'. History was presented as a continuous process of development, the end-product of which was American democracy and the growth of the United States of America. It was very much a national, indeed a nationalist, vision, dismissive for the most part of local or sectional histories. Believing, in John Higham's words, that 'the national state ... constituted the highest form of organisation mankind had yet achieved', constitutional historians of the late nineteenth century 'recorded the slow upbuilding of national organisation'.[33] From the identification of the 'germs' of American liberty supposedly planted in the New World by the first English settlers, through the reinterpretation of the War of Independence as a disturbance in the British imperial system rather than as a social revolution, to the handling of the troubling subject of sectional conflict, the emphasis was on continuity rather than discontinuity, consensus rather than conflict, in the ongoing process of institutional development. A generation after the Civil War, the tendency among professional historians, as among most other white Americans, was to play down the bitter recriminations that had marked interpretation of the conflict in the immediate postbellum years. Instead, sectional differences were finessed by an agreement that the North had been right about the Civil War, that is about the need to restore the Union and abolish slavery, and that the South had been right about Reconstruction, that is about the need to maintain white supremacy after the war. Here, most obviously in Dunning's works on Reconstruction, which commanded the field for over a generation, an implicitly, sometimes explicitly, racist formulation was accepted. Insofar as they contemplated more recent political events, historians tended to reflect the views of the social group from which they came. They sought, in the manner of the genteel reformers of the Gilded Age, to steer American politics in a conservative direction at a time of social upheaval and political corruption. 'In the improvement of the existing order', said Herbert Baxter Adams, 'what the world needs is historical enlightenment and political and social progress along existing institutional lines. We must preserve the continuity of our past life in the State'.[34]

According to Edward Channing, the theme of his *History of the United States* was

> the victory of the forces of union over those of particularism. ... The guiding idea in the present work is to view the subject as the record of an evolution, and to trace ... the story of living forces, always struggling onward and upward toward that which is better and higher in human conception.[35]

This essentially Rankean vision was shared by many American historians of the period. They were confident that an account of institutional progress and national consolidation would emerge unbeckoned from the historical record, taking for granted that their evolutionist view of American history was politically neutral. 'Their confident evolutionism', observes Novick, 'gave an implicit moral meaning to history which made explicit moralising superfluous'.[36] Like Ranke, they saw no discrepancy between the ideals of disinterested scholarship and patriotic citizenship.

'What is striking about the literature of this era', noted Richard Hofstadter, 'is the narrow range of the historians' social sympathies'.[37] Historians during the years around 1900 exhibited a remarkable degree of ideological consensus, certainly in comparison with American society as a whole during an era of intense social conflict. Their narrow view of history reflected the narrow social base from which they spoke. Despite their claims to 'scientific' objectivity, it is clear that they articulated the views of the social class from which most historians were drawn: nationalism, racism, nativism, social conservatism and (for the most part) Republicanism. Unwilling, perhaps unable, to examine their own assumptions, they offered up their own version of the past as 'scientific history'.

During the first two decades of the twentieth century a number of younger historians, notably Charles A. Beard, Carl Becker, John Harvey Robinson and Frederick Jackson Turner, began to challenge established ways of doing history. The 'Progressive' historians, as they came to be known, called for a broadening of the scope of history to include social and economic trends, and they expressed a willingness to learn from the social sciences. History, they maintained, should be 'of practical value'. Its goal was the 'historical explanation of the present' rather than the contemplation of the past 'for its own sake'. Beard and Robinson set out to write history that would serve the needs of social and political reform. Progressive history grew out of the reformism of the Progressive Era. Most of its major proponents were associated to some degree with reform politics, and it was from that position that they challenged the (unstated) assumptions of conservative historiography.

They did this largely by exploring the 'social forces' that underlay the political struggles of the past. 'Beneath the constitutional forms and ideas, beneath political issues run the great ocean currents of economic and social life, shaping and reshaping political forms to the changes of this great sea, which changes continuously', declared Turner (in a metaphor that anticipates Braudel).[38] Turner emphasised the influence of the geographical environment in a series of essays on the significance of the frontier and the influence of sectionalism in American history. Beard, whose influence over the next generation of historians was considerable, imported into American historiography a simplified form of economic determinism which involved looking for the motivations of human motivation in class interests. Political principles, argued Beard, 'originate in the sentiments and views which the possession of various kinds of property creates in the minds of the possessors'.[39] He offered economic interpretations of the formation of the Constitution, Jeffersonian democracy and the origins of the Civil War. Beard believed that, since individuals do not usually admit to their motives, the historian could not rely upon the documentary record as evidence of the sources of their actions. It was necessary to look beneath the surface to reveal their underlying motives. The historian, like the 'muckraking' journalist of the Progressive Era, had to peer through the smoke-screen of official pronouncements and pious, self-serving rhetoric in order to discern the deeper realities of interest and power. Such an approach clearly challenged the orthodoxies of 'scientific history', with its faith in the evidential quality of written documents and its injunction against the introduction of prior theoretical suppositions. Economic determinism was not derived from the evidence but was an explanatory model to some extent imposed upon it. Hence Beard's *An Economic Interpretation of the Constitution of the United States* (1913) elicited a storm of criticism on account of its methodology as much as its challenge to the integrity of a sacred text.

The Progressive historians' challenge to conventional historiography was not just a reformist critique of history written from an implicitly conservative stance; it also pointed the way to a critique of the whole idea of 'scientific' history, of the very possibility of historical 'objectivity'. This, in part, reflected the intellectual currents of the early twentieth century, particularly of the interwar years. As Novick puts it, 'Interwar culture was overflowing with "relativistic", "pragmatic", and iconoclastic ideas'.[40] The effect of modernist impulses in various academic disciplines and various forms of cultural practice – relativity, the indeterminacy principle, pragmatism, Freudian psychology, the sociology of knowledge – was, in different ways, to replace fixed standards of judgment with multiple viewpoints. Neither the Newtonian universe nor the Baconian methodology which was believed to inform scientific discovery appeared credible in the intellectual climate of the new century.

It was American involvement in the First World War that did most to shake historians' claims to scholarly detachment. Many scholars, including Beard and the other Progressive historians, gleefully joined in the propaganda campaign which was designed to justify the American war effort and discredit Imperial Germany, much as historians in the other belligerent nations were doing. Their contributions included some shabby writing which was clearly designed for political effect. Some of its authors felt a certain shame, in some cases to the extent of going round the country buying up as many copies as possible of their wartime writings; others did not, convinced either that the story they told was a true one or, if it was not, that the circumstances warranted a certain amount of embroidering of the truth. It was difficult in either case to reconcile their efforts with the prewar ideal of professional detachment. After 1918 historians became embroiled in an impassioned debate over war guilt. It was disturbing to find that different historians could use the same evidence to reach diametrically opposite conclusions. As one of the participants observed,

> We used the same documents and read the same biographies and memoirs in preparing our respective books – and came up with quite different interpretations. ... Is there something wrong with our methods of historical study and training when two scholars drew such conflicting conclusions from the same evidence?[41]

Like the parallel controversy over the origins of the Civil War, in which economic determinists like Beard sparred with 'revisionists' who argued that the war was unnecessary, a consequence of political miscalculations rather than irreconcilable differences, such a dispute could clearly not be settled by an examination of the 'facts'. Contesting views were grounded in *a priori* assumptions about causality, human motivation and even the morality of war. In the face of this and other seemingly intractable historical controversies, the ideal of 'objective', incontestable historical truth was unrealised, and maybe unrealisable.

By the 1930s the American historical profession had become involved in a fully fledged debate on the question of historical 'relativism'. A series of essays by Becker and Beard set out the familiar arguments for relativism. They argued that the past could not be accessed directly, but only through the documentary traces that had been left behind. Historical 'facts', therefore, rather than being 'found', were constructed by the historian herself. History does not have an inner structure, an immanent pattern, other than that imposed by the historian.

Historical interpretation, therefore, must inevitably involve the application of 'transcendent' concepts and hypotheses that come from the mind of the historian rather than from the evidence. It was impossible to exclude human prejudices and presuppositions from the process of interpretation, since the subject-matter of history was inevitably charged with values. Much better, argued Beard, that those values should be progressive rather than reactionary ones.

So bald a statement of the relativist position was hotly contested by traditionalists like Theodore Clarke Smith, not just on epistemological grounds but because it appeared to call into question the whole enterprise of professional historiography. Their sense of the profession's standing and public role was so bound up with the ideal of 'objectivity', with their confidence in historians' capacity to arrive at positive 'knowledge', that they condemned the relativists in the manner of church leaders 'denouncing and excommunicating heretics'. Objectivity, claims Novick, 'can be seen as the founding myth of the historical profession; the pursuit of the objective truth its sacred mission and raison d'être'.[42] Smith's 1934 presidential address to the AHA indicates the intensity with which the old values were held:

> It may be that another fifty years will see the end of an era in historiography, the final extinction of a noble dream, and history, save as an instrument of entertainment, or of social control will not be permitted to exist. In that case, it will be time for the American Historical Association to disband, for the intellectual assumptions on which it is founded will have been taken away from beneath it. My hope is, none the less, that those of us who date from what may then seem an age of quaint beliefs and forgotten loyalties, may go down with our flags flying.[43]

Thus the ideal of 'scientific history' became highly compromised and hotly contested during the interwar years. So did the 'conservative evolutionist' version of political history that had prevailed before 1917, although the study of past politics still claimed the attention of most historians. To some extent, Progressive history offered itself as an alternative paradigm. 'Between the two world wars progressive influence became so great in American historiography that it seemed for a time virtually to overwhelm all other conceptual possibilities', claims Higham.[44] However, while Progressive history offered a new master narrative of the American past, in which the 'people' engaged in repeated struggles to overcome moneyed 'interests' that sought to exploit government power for selfish gain, the controversy over relativism left the profession in substantial disarray over questions of epistemology. The confident assurance with which the earlier generation had worked towards a 'scientific' understanding of human history could not easily be reproduced in the troubled interwar decades.

Notes

1 L. von Ranke, 'Die großen Mächte', *Historisch-politische Zeitschrift*, 1833, vol. 2, *passim*.
2 Heinrich von Sybel to Hermann Baumgarten, 27. 1. 1871, cit. after F. Jaeger and J. Rüsen, *Geschichte des Historismus*, Munich, C. H. Beck, 1992, p. 92.
3 M. Lenz, *Die großen Mächte. Ein Rückblick auf unser Jahrhundert*, Berlin, 1920, p. 26.
4 See A. Thompson, ' "Prussians in a good sense". German Historians as Critics of Prussian Conservatism, 1890–1920', in S. Berger, M. Donovan and K. Passmore (eds) *Writing National Histories: Western Europe since 1800*, London, Routledge, 1999, pp. 97–110.
5 U. Haltern, 'Geschichte und Bürgertum: Droysen – Sybel – Treitschke', *Historische Zeitschrift*, 1994, vol. 259, pp. 59–107.
6 K. Lamprecht, *Deutsche Geschichte*, 12 vols, Berlin and Freiburg, 1891–1909.
7 R. Chickering, *Karl Lamprecht. A German Academic Life, 1856–1915*, New Jersey, Humanities Press, 1993; quotations, p. 175.
8 Chickering, *Karl Lamprecht*, pp. 262 ff.
9 D. Schäfer, *Deutsche Geschichte*, vol. 1, Jena, 1910, 6th edn, 1918, pp. 10–11.
10 U. Heinemann, *Die Verdrängte Niederlage. Politische öffentlichkeit und Kriegsschuldfrage in der Weimarer Republik*, Göttingen, Vandenhoeck & Ruprecht, 1983; H. H. Herwig, 'Clio Deceived: Patriotic Self-Censorship in Germany After the Great War', in K. Wilson (ed.) *Forging the Collective Memory: Government and International Historians through Two World Wars*, Providence RI and Oxford, Berghahn, 1996, pp. 87–127.
11 B. Faulenbach, *Ideologie des deutschen Weges. Die deutsche Geschichte in der Historiographie zwischen Kaiserreich und Nationalsozialismus*, Munich, C. H. Beck, 1980.
12 See C. Gradmann, *Historische Belletristik. Populäre historische Biographien in der Weimarer Republik*, Frankfurt a.M., Campus, 1993.
13 P. Lambert, 'Generations of German Historians: Patronage, Censorship and the Containment of Generation Conflict, 1918–1945', in M. Roseman (ed.) *Generations in Conflict. Youth Revolt and Generation Formation in Germany 1770–1968*, Cambridge, Cambridge University Press, 1995, pp. 164–83.
14 G. G. Iggers, *Historiography in the Twentieth Century: From Scientific Objectivity to the Postmodern Challenge*, London, Wesleyan University Press, 1997, p. 26.
15 J. Tosh, *The Pursuit of History. Aims, Methods and New Directions in the Study of Modern History*, 2nd edn, London, Longman, 1991, p. 76.
16 S. Rothblatt, *The Revolution of the Dons. Cambridge and Society in Victorian England*, Cambridge, Cambridge University Press, 1981, p. 157.
17 W. E. Gladstone, *"Ecce Homo". A criticism of "Ecce Homo" by J. R. Seeley. Reprinted from "Good Word"*, 1868.
18 'Prefatory Note', *English Historical Review*, 1886, vol. 1, p. 2.
19 Lord Acton, 'Inaugural Lecture on the Study of History', in Lord Acton, *Lectures on Modern History*, London, Collins, 1960, p. 26 (delivered at Cambridge, June 1895).
20 Acton, 'Inaugural Lecture', p. 27. See also, for 'the German Inheritance', J. W. Burrow, *A Liberal Descent. Victorian Historians and the English Past*, Cambridge, Cambridge University Press, 1981, p. 97.
21 Acton, 'Inaugural Lecture', p. 17.
22 For the fullest discussion of this transition, see L. Colley, *Lewis Namier*, London, Weidenfeld and Nicolson, 1989, *passim*.

23 P. Levine, *The Amateur and the Professional: Antiquarians, Historians and Archaeologists in Victorian England, 1838–1886*, Cambridge, Cambridge University Press, 1986, pp. 162–3.

24 See, for example, H. Trevor-Roper, 'The Invention of Tradition: The Highland Tradition of Scotland', in E. Hobsbawm and T. Ranger (eds) *The Invention of Tradition*, Cambridge, Cambridge University Press, 1983, pp. 15–42.

25 B. Smith, 'Gender and the Practices of Scientific History: The Seminar and Archival Research in the Nineteenth Century', *American Historical Review*, 1995, vol. 100, *passim*; Iggers, *Historiography*, p. 30.

26 T. F. Tout, 'The Duties of an Historical Association', *History*, 1912, vol. 1, pp. 32–3.

27 H. Johnstone, 'The Seven Deadly Sins of Historical Teaching', *History*, 1912, vol. 1, p. 91.

28 G.P. Gooch, *History and Historians in the Nineteenth Century*, 1913, p. vi.

29 'History and the General Public. An interview with Professor A. F. Pollard, President of the Historical Association', *History*, 1912, vol. 1, pp. 244. See also Chapter 4 below, p. 67.

30 R. N. Soffer, *Discipline and Power: The University, History and the Making of an English Elite, 1870–1930*, Stanford, Stanford University Press, 1994, p. 58. See also Chapter 4 below, pp. 67–8.

31 Walter Seton of Abercorn, *Some Historians of Scotland. A Public Inaugural Lecture delivered at University College, London, in the presence of Her Majesty the Queen, on 21st February 1924*, Edinburgh, 1924, p. 6.

32 M. D. Rothberg, ' "To Set a Standard of Workmanship and Compel Men to Conform to It": John Franklin Jameson as Editor of the *American Historical Review*', *American Historical Review*, vol. 89, 1984, p. 967.

33 J. Higham, *History: Professional Scholarship in America*, New York, Harpers, 1965, pp. 159–60.

34 D. Ross, *The Origins of American Social Science*, Cambridge, Cambridge University Press, 1991, p. 72.

35 Higham, *History*, p. 169.

36 P. Novick, *That Noble Dream: The 'Objectivity Question' and the American Historical Profession*, Cambridge, Cambridge University Press, 1988, p. 85.

37 R. Hofstadter, *The Progressive Historians: Turner, Beard, Parrington*, New York, Alfred A. Knopf, 1968, p. 23.

38 R. Billington, *Frederick Jackson Turner: Historian, Scholar, Teacher*, New York, Oxford University Press, 1973, p. 101.

39 C. A. Beard, *An Economic Interpretation of the Constitution of the United States*, New York, Macmillan, 1913, pp. 13–14.

40 Novick, *That Noble Dream*, pp. 133–4.

41 Bernadotte Schmitt, quoted in Novick, *That Noble Dream*, pp. 223–4.

42 Novick, *That Noble Dream*, p. 268.

43 *Ibid.*, p. 269.

44 Higham, *History*, p. 190.

Conclusion to Part I

Impulses toward the professionalisation of history, and the adoption of an approach to history which showed a remarkable degree of uniformity irrespective of national borders, all had indigenous roots in the three societies we have addressed in these case-studies. However, as we have also suggested, the professionalisation of history can only be understood if we take into account the interrelatedness of these national experiences. It was a process with international dimensions and was marked by cultural transfers. Especially after 1945, the pattern was replicated beyond the 'Western' and European examples we have discussed. Today, history can claim to be a global discipline, albeit one beset by difficulties. Where, until 1945, the principal obstacles members of the profession had in communicating with one another had been wars between nations, for half a century after 1945 the Cold War presented similar barriers. In recent years, difficulties have surfaced in the conduct of a dialogue between historians in 'the West' and some of their colleagues in the Third World. Whether the habits of thought ingrained in 'Western' historiography, the categories 'Western' historians employ, even history itself might be an imposition on the Third World is a matter of current debate.[1]

The particular *historist* paradigm we have explored in Part I was limited spatially and in its longevity. After World War II, 'the historical traditionalists were', as Eric Hobsbawm has put it, 'fighting a rearguard engagement in a losing battle'. The 'garrison' of their 'central stronghold' – the German historical guild – had been 'put out of action by its association with National Socialism'.[2] In Part II we will explore some of the ways in which subsequent approaches to history diverged from the path laid out in the period of professionalisation. But we should also bear in mind the extent to which the new 'paradigms' or schools of history, the questions they asked and the tools they employed in addressing them were consciously 'revisionist'. The adoption of new methods and different perspectives did not mean forgetting, but engaging critically with the past of the discipline. Path-breaking innovations which transformed the practices of some historians also occurred within institutional settings which would still have been recognisable to a late nineteenth-century historian. And innovations themselves simultaneously betrayed continuities with historism – whether in their emphasis on research, in their veneration of documents, or in the very fact of their search for meaning in history. Besides, some of the core concerns of historism have in fact survived the fragmentation of the historist paradigm. There are still plenty of historians who work on 'high' politics, the relations between states or the development of the state itself, who research diplomatic documents, and whose only primary sources are documents. Nor is there any shortage of historians who see their vocation as a political calling and even, for that matter, as a contribution to nationalism.

But statist and political history has been knocked off its pedestal. It deserved to fall. Had its rise (to return to one of Kuhn's key concerns about scientific revolutions) really been associable with progress in the first place? Hobsbawm has replied to the question with a loud 'no'. 'The nineteenth century, that age of bourgeois civilization, has several major intellectual achievements to its credit, but the academic discipline of history which grew up in that period is not one of them'. It was regressive by comparison with Enlightenment historiography 'in all *except* the techniques of research' (our emphasis). Enlightenment historiography had sought 'to comprehend the transformation of human societies', but had done so on the basis of wild speculation. In the mid-late twentieth century, historians tried to eradicate the worst and build on the best elements of both these traditions. They applied the 'empirical criteria' established by Rankean scholarship to the ambitious projects first attempted in the era of industrialisation and the French Revolution.[3]

Notes

1   See J. Rüsen (ed.) *Western Historical Thinking. An Intercultural Debate*, New York and Oxford, Berghahn, 2002, and, for a general discussion of the uneven institutional and intellectual global expansion of academic history, P. Lambert, 'The Professionalization and Institutionalization of History' in S. Berger, H. Feldner and K. Passmore (eds) *Writing History: Theory and Practice*, Hodder and Stoughton, 2003, pp. 42–60.

2   E. Hobsbawm, *Interesting Times: A Twentieth-century Life*, London, Allen Lane, 2002, p. 290.

3   E. Hobsbawm, 'What Do Historians Owe to Karl Marx?', 1968, reprinted in *idem*, *On History*, London, Weidenfeld and Nicolson, 1997, pp. 141–56; p. 141.

Further reading

While there are many works on the professionalisation and institutionalisation of history limited to single national case-studies, there is as yet no full-scale attempt at a global overview of the process. Of the handful of brief surveys which are available, see: Chapter 1 of G. Iggers, *Historiography in the Twentieth Century: From Scientific Objectivity to the Postmodern Challenge*, London, Wesleyan University Press, 1997; Chapter 8 of M. Bentley, *Modern Historiography: An Introduction*, London, Routledge, 1999; P. Lambert, 'The Professionalization and Institutionalization of History', in S. Berger, H. Feldner and K. Passmore (eds) *Writing History: Theory and Practice*, London, Arnold, 2003, pp. 42–60 (with guidance to reading on national experiences beyond those considered in the present volume). K. Boyd (ed.), *Encyclopedia of Historians and Historical Writing*, 2 vols, London and Chicago, Fitzroy Dearborn, 1999, serves as a valuable general resource. B. Smith, *The Gender of History. Men, Women, and Historical Practice*, Cambridge MA and London, Harvard University Press, 1998, provides not only a fascinating account of the introduction of the seminar as the historian's training ground, but also of the parallel developments of professionalisation and of the exclusion of women. Other uncomfortable characteristics of the nascent profession, characteristics with whose legacy academic historians are still obliged to deal, include its nationalism and 'Western' cultural bias. The former problem is critically assessed in S. Berger, M. Donovan and K. Passmore (eds) *Writing National Histories: Western Europe since 1800*, London, Routledge, 1999; the latter is addressed in F. Cooper, 'Africa's Pasts and Africa's Historians', *Canadian Journal of African Studies*, 2000, vol. 34, pp. 298–336.

The classic account of historism, the statist political and intellectual agenda of German historians in the nineteenth century, is G. Iggers, *The German Conception of History*, 1968, 2nd edn 1983. Equally readable is S. Berger's more recent study: *The Search for Normality: National Identity and Historical Consciousness in Germany since 1800*, Oxford, Berghahn Books, 1997. S. Crane, *Collecting and Historical Consciousness in Early Nineteenth-Century Germany*, Ithaca NY and London, Cornell University Press, 2000, is an illuminating discussion of the relationship between antiquarian and professional routes to the past. An early challenge to the statist paradigm, and how and why the challenge was seen off, is the subject of R. Chickering, *Karl Lamprecht. A German Academic Life, 1856–1915*, New Jersey, Humanities Press, 1993. Germany's defeat in the First World War served only to harden the historist mindset. See W. J. Mommsen, 'German Historiography During the Weimar Republic and the Émigré Historians', in H. Lehmann and J. Sheehan (eds) *An Interrupted Past. German-Speaking Refugee Historians in the United States after 1933*, Washington DC, German Historical Institute and Cambridge, Cambridge University Press, 1991, pp. 32–66. How little the tenacity of the historist paradigm had to do with its intellectual merits, and how much with patronage and censorship, is underlined by W. Weber, 'The Long Reign and Final Fall of the German Conception of History: A Historical-Sociological View', *Central European History*, 1986, vol. 2, pp. 385–95. Nor was it only in Germany that the 1914–18 war and the Treaty of Versailles acted initially as a powerful stimulant to political and especially to diplomatic history. See K. Wilson (ed.) *Forging the Collective Memory: Government and International Historians through Two World Wars*, Providence RI and Oxford, Berghahn, 1996.

Once they had been established in one country, patterns of professionalisation and institutionalisation, and 'models' of how to practise history at large, were available to be emulated in others. But they were often imperfectly understood, and in any case subject to eclectic borrowings and modified to suit local traditions and needs in the 'importing' countries. Transnational historiographical relations are the subject of a rapidly growing body of work. See G. Iggers and L. Powell (eds) *Leopold von Ranke and the Shaping of the Historical Discipline*, Syracuse NY, Syracuse University Press, 1990; E. Fuchs and B. Stuchtey (eds) *Across Cultural Borders: Historiography in Global Perspective*, Lanham MD, 2002; Q. E. Wang and G. Iggers, *Turning-points in Historiography: A Cross-Cultural Perspective*, Woodbridge, Boydell and Brewer, 2002.

The way in which German models of historical scholarships were adapted to American conditions are explored in Dorothy G. Ross, 'On the Misunderstanding of Ranke and the Origins of the Historical Profession in America', in Iggers and Powell, *Leopold von Ranke and the Shaping of the Historical Discipline*. Two excellent histories of American historical writing are J. Higham, *History: Professional Scholarship in America*, revised edn, Baltimore, Johns Hopkins University Press, 1989; and Peter Novick, *That Noble Dream: The 'Objectivity Question' and the American Historical Profession*, Cambridge, Cambridge University Press, 1988. Novick's primary topic is historians' views on objectivity, but he approaches it through a richly detailed and contextualised account of American historical practice. He, like Higham, is successful in relating intellectual trends within the nascent historical profession to the process of institutional development. D. G. Ross, *The Origins of American Social Science*, Cambridge, Cambridge University Press, 1991, places history in the context of the wider development of the social sciences. Studies of the origins of some of the central institutions of the historical profession which also shed light on the broader processes that shaped the discipline are D. D. Van Tassel, 'From Learned Society to Professional Organization: The American Historical Association, 1884–1900', *American Historical Review*, 1984, vol. 89, pp. 929–56; M. D. Rothberg, ' "To Set a Standard of Workmanship and Compel Men to Conform to It": J. Franklin Jameson as Editor of the *American Historical Review*', *American Historical Review*, 1984, vol. 89, pp. 957–95. On the growth of the 'New History', see R. Hofstadter, *The Progressive Historians: Turner, Beard, Parrington*, New York, Knopf, 1968.

P. H. Slee, *Learning and a Liberal Education. The Study of Modern History in the Universities of Oxford, Cambridge and Manchester 1800–1914*, Manchester, Manchester University Press, 1986, is still the most comprehensive account of the growth of history as a discipline in British universities, while J. W. Burrow, *A Liberal Descent. Victorian Historians and the English Past*, Cambridge, Cambridge University Press, 1981, provides an excellent account of the intellectual environment in which nineteenth-century British historians were researching and writing. For a stimulating analysis of the changing social function of the university, and in particular of history's role in its evolution, see R. N. Soffer, *Discipline and Power: The University, History and the Making of an English Elite, 1870–1930*, Stanford, Stanford University Press, 1994; while P.

Levine, *The Amateur and the Professional. Antiquarians, Historians and Archaeologists in Victorian England, 1838–1880,* Cambridge, Cambridge University Press, 1986, broadens and complicates the picture by exploring the relationships between professional and non-professional history writing; whereas P. Mandler's *History and National Life*, London, Profile Books, 2002, is a sophisticated but highly accessible account, relating the development of professional history in modern Britain to its social value. On the construction of a range of institutions integral to the process of professionalisation, see D. Goldstein, 'The Organisational Development of the British Historical Profession, 1884–1921', *Bulletin of the Institute of Historical Research*, 1982, vol. 55, pp. 180–93. Accounts of the major historians of nineteenth-century Britain may be found in J. Kenyon, *The History Men*, London, Weidenfeld and Nicolson, 1983, and in individual biographical studies such as O. Dudley Edwards, *Macaulay*, London, Weidenfeld and Nicolson, 1988.

Part II

Challenges to the statist paradigm

In Part II, we identify the emergence of variants of a new, theory-friendly and 'critical' history in the USA and much of Western Europe in the mid-twentieth century. In the 1960s and 1970s its impact looked first potentially and then actually revolutionary. 'Critical' historiography was united in reacting to the methodological and political conservatism of professional historians, to their ingrained habit of identifying with powerful vested interests, and to their use of scholarship to legitimise nation-states. 'Critical' historians were emancipatory in their aspirations, identified with underdogs and were internationalist in outlook. They saw themselves 'as allies' belonging to a modernising international historiographical movement.[1] As the essays below will show, they also betrayed their respective points of national origin, and diverged from one another not only in the pace with which they developed and the scale of the influence they exerted, but also in form and content. By 1970, 'a common flag had been found for the far from homogeneous popular front of the innovators: "social history"'.[2]

Phillipp Schofield's chapter describes the early stirrings of economic and social history in Britain from the late Victorian period to the interwar years. At first, economic historians saw their work as expanding the established paradigm of political and constitutional history, whose confidence about the British past and present they shared. Around the turn of the century, however, the study of economic and social history in Britain became infected by a growing sense of unease. Britain was overtaken by Germany as Europe's leading industrial power; promoters of 'national efficiency' looked to Germany for inspiration; labour unrest and the gradual emergence of independent working-class political representation were too important to be ignored, yet could not be explained in the terms of the old paradigm. Some historians looked to social and economic history to provide lessons in social control of the unruly and indisciplined. Others came to economic and social history in order to inform a radical and socialist agenda. Increasingly, they became open to interdisciplinarity, borrowing variously from economics and from sociology. Schofield describes a lively and energetic community of scholars, but one which was to remain a small minority, aside from the mainstream of professional history. Its members were subject to influences too varied to allow of a single cohesive programme.

Perhaps their only unifying characteristic was their atypicality: the practitioners of economic and social history were largely 'outsiders', whether men disappointed by the failure of Oxford and Cambridge adequately to advance their careers, or women debarred by their sex from enjoying full membership of those universities. The very institutions in which they flourished were eccentric and experimental by the standards of early twentieth-century academia. Some of the potential for a paradigm shift was present in Britain by 1930, but it was not to be realised until after the Second World War.

The innovative roles of outsiders, and of historians whose life- or intellectual experiences were undergone literally at the peripheries of nation-states, feature repeatedly in the remaining chapters. Michael Roberts, writings on the French *Annales* school, draws attention to the close relationship between its founders' centrifugal choices of location for their education and training and their centrifugal attitudes to their own discipline. The slogan 'unlearning from Germany' might as well have been emblazoned on the frontispiece of their journal,[3] and 'unlearning' necessarily pertained also to French historiographical traditions which were themselves in hock to German historism. But then, as Roberts shows, the *Annales* historians exaggerated the revolutionary qualities of their intellectual movement for dramatic effect. They owed more than they acknowledged – in respect, for instance, to the kinds of sources they regarded as lying within the competence of the historian's craft – to an earlier generation and more particularly to *its* outsiders. However, while furnishing the *Annales* with a long genealogy, Roberts highlights moments of striking change – not least in the formative, interwar years when the journal *Annales* offered an alternative to 'normal science' as explicitly modern in style as in content. After 1945, *Annales* historiography was to attract more admirers and imitators internationally, and to spark off a greater array of tangential developments, than any school of history with paradigmatic pretensions had or has done since Ranke and his immediate disciples.

The *Annales*' was a highly specific species of social history. It comprised the exploration of mentalities and structures over the long term, aiming at no less an ambition than the construction of *total* history. *Annales* historians did not just exhibit sympathy with victims of oppression in past societies, but attached agential power to them. Thus far, the history they wrote was congruent with their emancipatory contemporary concerns: their anti-fascism and their use of history as a kind of education for active citizenship. Yet there was another side to the coin of *Annales* scholarship. It embraced a structural determinism which tended to contradict the possibility of human choice and agency and sat ill with an advocacy of active citizenship in the present.

A similar predicament, as Peter Lambert argues, bedevilled West German critical social history from the 1960s on. The so-called Bielefeld School adhered to the same democratic values as their colleagues across the Rhine, but its members were structural determinists with a vengeance. Where the tensions were contained within the *Annales* school, in Germany they erupted into outright conflict between the *Bielefelder* and a slightly younger generational cohort of historians whose concerns were not with grand structures but with the minutiae of everyday life. Allegations were hurled between them: of anti-quarianism and romanticism from one side; of dehumanising schematics from the other. Narrower and less flexible in their interpretative framework than the *Annales* historians, and less widely read abroad, the Bielefeld historians' impact at home and on the understanding of German history was certainly comparable to that of the *Annales* in and about France. That is because their political engagement was clearer and more direct. The experience of the Second World War, of Nazi occupation of one part of France, and of the collaborationist Vichy regime in the other, informed the sensibilities of *Annales* historians, but after 1945 it led them also to avert their gaze from the twentieth and even nine-teenth centuries. By contrast, the Bielefeld School tackled precisely that late modern period, and unambiguously confronted the problem of Nazism's place in German history.

The cultural and political turmoil of the 1960s left an indelible mark on the *Annales*, while the very emergence of critical social history in West Germany was directly related to the changes and struggles of that decade. In the USA, too, the 1960s inspired the production of a self-consciously 'new' social history. As Robert Harrison shows, this became the most numerous – and by no means the least vibrant – 'community' of practitioners of social history in the world. Notwithstanding a rough political consensus among them, the American 'new' social historians pursued radically divergent research agendas and employed an array of methodologies. Where the Bielefeld and *Annales* schools progressively lost the cohesiveness commensurate with paradigmatic qualities, 'new' social history in the USA had never possessed these in the first place. In a sense, US social history was precocious in being 'post-paradigmatic', generating a plurality of approaches to the past with which other 'national' historiographies have since caught up. Some historians fear that the outcome has proved to be fragmenta-tion. They worry that the 'grand conversation' of a community of professional historians has collapsed. Insular villages of historians assemble round the parish pumps of sub-disciplines and arcane specialisms to discuss problems that do not matter to the inhabitants of neighbouring villages, in a dialect they do not understand. Postmodernists, as we will see later in this volume, celebrate precisely this condition as a liberating one since, they allege, every attempt at constructing a 'grand narrative' necessarily involves strategies of exclusion and is inherently oppressive. One might object that, in pre-emptively delegitimising each and every attempt at over-arching synthesis, postmodernists are themselves oppressive – even anti-intellectual – in their programmatic hostility to ambi-tiously conceived explanation. And indeed there are still historians who try to reassemble syntheses in the spirit of 1960s and 1970s experimentation.[4]

Notes

1   E. Hobsbawm, *Interesting Times: A Twentieth-Century Life*, London, Allen Lane, 2002, p. 289.
2   *Ibid.*, p. 290. Cf., on the connections between the Popular Front and national histories, p. 184 (Chapter 12).
3   See P. Schöttler, ' "Désapprendre de l'Allemagne": Les *Annales* et l'histoire allemande dans les années trente', in H.-M. Bock, R. Meyer-Kalkus and M. Trebitsch (eds) *Entre Locarno et Vichy: Les relations culturelles franco-allemandes dans les années 1930*, Paris, CNRS-Editions, 1993, pp. 439–61.
4   Cf. the nuanced discussion in S. Berger, 'The Rise and Fall of "Critical" Historiography? Some Reflections on the Historiographical Agenda of the Left in Britain, France and Germany at the End of the Twentieth Century', *European Review of History*, 1996, vol. 3, pp. 213–30, which ultimately sides with postmodernists in warning against any revival of attempts at grand syntheses.

Chapter 4

The emergence of British economic history, c.1880–c.1930

Phillipp Schofield

In a lecture,'The economical interpretation of history', delivered in the late 1880s at Oxford, James E. Thorold Rogers, then professor of political economy at Oxford and of economic science and statistics at King's College, London, began by lamenting that

> in nearly all histories, and in nearly all political economy, the collection and interpretation of economical facts, by which I mean such records as illustrate social life and the distribution of wealth at different epochs of the history of mankind, have been habitually neglected.

This 'neglect', as he saw it, rendered 'history inaccurate or at least imperfect'.[1] Though Rogers continued in similar vein in this and in other lectures, his main point had already been made, namely that historical investigation which failed to embrace an economic or social element (in other words that 'type' of history which he and his contemporaries would refer to as 'economic history' but which later generations would come to call either 'economic and social history' or, as separate sub-disciplines, 'economic' and 'social' history[2]) was fundamentally flawed and that, by extension, the vast bulk of historical endeavour which he witnessed being undertaken within the universities suffered for that very reason. Rogers was quite prepared to acknowledge that 'the solid study of history has made considerable progress' so that the 'narrative is no longer merely one of war and peace, of royal genealogies, of unrelated dates'. However, he firmly believed both that a vast array of historical material was overlooked by academic historians and, most importantly, that in their historical preoccupations lurked prejudices and partisanships which the nature of their explorations and the quality of their sources encouraged.[3] For Rogers, there was a striking contrast between a present historical investigation which sought to infer motive from the actions of statesmen and of princes and a possible future engagement with sources of a more quantitative and thereby more robust nature, which, in turn, would cultivate 'the wise habit of developing inferences from evidence'.[4]

Roger's pointed observations, in which we may also be able to detect the badgering tone of the political activist and professional politician which he also was, were the expression of a man who had laboured for many years, often ploughing an entirely discrete furrow, to illustrate the value of the sources for economic history. His six-volume *History of Agriculture and Prices*, published between 1866 and 1887, was a work of Herculean proportions and remains a standard authority to the present. But it was presented more as a stimulus to research than as a response to it. This is not to say, of course, that Rogers laboured entirely alone. By the time of Rogers' lecture, there were already examinations in 'economic history' at Cambridge, even if there was little in the way of supporting material or academic personnel to supervise study there. Cunningham's *The Growth of English Industry and Commerce* (first edition 1882), it has been suggested, was a response to the limited teaching resources for this field of study. There were also other historians and social and political commentators keenly interested in topics that would, in more recent times, come to be associated with the sub-discipline of economic history. The intense, and politically informed, debate regarding the nature and development of the village community, for example, or the investigation by Seebohm and Gasquest into the impact of the Black Death upon Europe, find their places in the canon of late nineteenth-century British historiography. A striking feature of much of this work, however, is the lack of reference to secondary literature, indicative not so much of a nineteenth-century publishing convention, as of the dearth of studies with which the author could compare and in relation to which he could develop his own thesis. Gasquet's study of the Black Death in England cites Rogers, *Six Centuries of Agriculture and Prices*, on a number of occasions and makes passing reference to a half-dozen or so other works, but has little in the way of other reference to secondary literature; Maitland's pioneering discussion of the history of a Cambridgeshire manor in the late Middle Ages, a topic which would excite keen and varied interest in the twentieth century, confines itself largely to description and engages with no secondary material at all.[5]

Furthermore, much of this investigation, while raising issues normally beyond the interest of mainstream historians, was nevertheless still trapped within statist approaches to the material. In particular it exhibited a broadly qualitative and narrative-bound engagement with the period or topic discussed. Thus Gasquet's discussion of the impact of the Black Death both urged that historians acknowledge the potential of the plague to alter the course of human history, and employed a range of what were broadly socioeconomic and certainly under-used source types. Yet his analysis was still rooted in methodologies and issues, especially the over-reliance on chronicle evidence, that were the stuff of political narratives.[6] Of greatest importance is the evident perception in the earliest works of economic history, that the late nineteenth-century economy had achieved its apogee. This perception, a product of statist history relayed effortlessly into the study of economic history, is illustrated in the nineteenth-century historiographical preoccupation with *growth*.[7]

Institutionally, there was little or nothing in the way of infrastructure to support such initiatives. Within the academy, no posts in economic history had been established by the end of the nineteenth century in Britain; there were no seminars or postgraduates offering vitality to the sub-discipline, and little in the way of direct teaching of these topics within British universities.[8] Looking back almost fifty years, to the early 1880s, Sir William Ashley could write in 1927 of the failure of history teaching at Oxford to encourage students to engage directly with their sources, all of which were 'political'. If history as taught at Oxford in the late nineteenth century had a saving grace, it was, according to Ashley, to be found in the papers offered on political science and economic theory which served 'to check or modify a merely narrational frame of mind'.[9] Furthermore, the outlets for expression were also few, with no dedicated journal as yet available for the publication of articles on social or economic history. Famously, R. H. Tawney had, in 1913, been obliged to publish early research (effectively two articles on the assessment of wages in England by Justices of the Peace) in the German journal *Vierteljahrschrift für Sozial- und Wirtschaftsgeschichte*, since he was unable to find, in the England of the second decade of the century, a journal whose editors would contemplate carrying the 'damn thing'.[10]

Despite the impediments of an underdeveloped literature, a historical mindset rooted in a Whiggish conception of the past, and an academy ill equipped and/or ill disposed to the study of economic history, in the half-century between 1880 and 1930, the foundation which Rogers and others had laid was reinforced by their successors and, to a limited extent, some building above ground level was attempted. University posts were created, the numbers of publications and conferences grew, societies for the study of economic history were founded, and a dedicated journal, *Economic History Review*, established.

Along with Rogers, historians such as Cunningham, Toynbee and Ashley set about the promotion of economic history within the universities in the last decades of the nineteenth century. While Ashley had to move to North America to become the first Professor in Economic History in the English-speaking world (a chair inaugurated at Harvard in 1892), his and his colleagues' efforts began to bear fruit in Britain in the first years of the twentieth century in appointments to lectureships, and in a chair established at Manchester in 1910. 'By the early 1920s', as Harte records, 'economic history was well established in its original quadrilateral between Cambridge, Oxford, LSE and Manchester'.[11] Within these universities, economic history was taught and examined, with the first, precocious, instance now finding company in courses taught at those other institutions.

Burgeoning university courses encouraged publications. Reflecting upon the lectures of Ephraim Lipson,[12] Julia de Lacy Mann, Assistant Editor of the *Economic History Review* at its inception and, prior to that in the early 1920s, a student at Oxford, noted that

He [Lipson] said everything twice very slowly so that you could take it all down. I can't say it was inspiring; but ... it was very useful and of course his books – the later books – weren't published then so your lecture notes were what you relied on, and he was fully conscious of that, I think.[13]

Lipson's *Economic History of England* met, and was no doubt intended to meet, the expectations of students such as Miss Mann; in exactly the same way, and a generation earlier, Cunningham had, as already noted, produced a general text-book, *The Growth of English Industry and Commerce* (1882), which, in its subsequent expansion into fuller later editions, did much to promote and to facilitate the study of economic history in English universities.[14] It was in the same spirit that, in 1924, Tawney and Power published a collection of sources, *Tudor Economic Documents*, which was 'designed primarily for the use of under-graduate members of that University [London], who are taking the economic history of the Tudor period as their special subject'.[15]

The emergence of scholarly journals and societies, typically at the initiative of these same university academics, provided foundation to economic history. Lipson was a driving force in the establishment of the *Economic History Review* which, along with, and, it has been suggested, in some competition with, the newly launched economic history number of the *Economic Journal*, provided vital publishing opportunities for economic historians. Launched in the wake of a major economic history session of the second Anglo-American history confer-ence, which was held in London in 1926, the *Economic History Review*, in particular, became the beacon of economic history in Britain. Its editors, in its first quarter-century, Power, Tawney and Postan, set the pace and tone of the discipline.[16] Beyond the academy moves were afoot to encourage the teaching of economic history within schools, while adult education, and especially the Workers Educational Association (WEA), provided a natural home for themes which combined interest in the past with political engagement with the present, a point to which we shall return.

This work, both within and beyond the academy, provided a sound enough base from which the study of economic history in Britain could proceed. But before we measure the ultimate success of this development as a challenge to the dominant statist paradigm, we need to consider further the range of forces which shaped it.

The emergence of British economic history offers, in this respect, a useful case-study for the emergence of an historical tradition that stood in contrast to the established historical tradition operating in British universities at the close of the nineteenth century. In searching for the explanation(s) of that emergence we will need to look at, but also beyond, what may be considered an *intellectual* process of change and development. For, as well as the intellectual or strictly academic imperative for the emergence of non-statist history in Britain, of which economic history offers the best and earliest example, there were other important causes. It is a point which Rogers would, no doubt, have been keen to stress. The sub-discipline of economic history was not born only in the politicking of professors in senior common rooms, but was a product of a range of external forces, including the wider socio-economic developments of the late nineteenth and early twentieth centuries and the political turmoils of those decades. While, of course, none of the factors to be discussed was capable of existing in total isolation, it is with the overtly intellectual factors that we shall begin.

As the comments of Rogers have already indicated, there were, by the late nineteenth century, individual historians who were disinclined to accept that the chief subject matter of history should be high politics or, more importantly, that explanations of historical causation should be confined to the policy shifts of political leaders. While this was undoubtedly a reflection of discussion conducted within the core of academic history, it is also a reflection of the fact that different questions were being asked of the past from the last decades of the nineteenth century onward.

If history as a discipline could not, of itself, generate all such questions, other disciplines could. It was to these that the early economic historians looked for guiding principles. In the most obvious instance, economics, as a discipline, enjoyed a well established canon of work by the second half of the nineteenth century; the works of Adam Smith, David Ricardo and John Stuart Mill provided principles of study, but eschewed application.[17] As Cunningham's long discussion of method, set out in an introductory chapter to his *Growth of English Industry and Commerce*, illustrates, late nineteenth-century historians distanced themselves from 'hypothetical' study and engaged closely with 'circumstance'.[18] But, while economics departments did not prove natural homes for the study of the past, a fact that made history rather than economics the mother of economic history as a university subject, economics was obviously capable of generating key issues that helped mould the thought of historians.[19] During the 1920s at the London School of Economics (LSE), a progressivist institution with no formal separation, along departmental lines, of economists from historians, the opportunity for such intellectual exchange was especially abundant and, given the dynamism of economic historians working there during that period, especially fruitful.[20]

As with economics, so with sociology, some of whose earliest exponents shared agendas with and were stimulants to the work of the central figures of English economic history. Tawney's engagement with the work of Weber, for example, is an example of an intellectual response which, while in no way slavish in its adherence, benefited greatly from the Weberian perspective, a perspective born in history and honed in the social sciences.[21]

The contribution of Weber, a response to a distinctive German tradition which had separated methodologies in the natural sciences from those of the humanities, serves also to remind us that there was an international dimension to the advance of economic history in Britain. While, as Harte has noted,

'Economic history in England was largely – though not exclusively – home-grown', it is possible to identify certain points of contact with other national historical traditions which informed the development of the sub-discipline.[22] The work of German historians long before the close of the nineteenth century had already done much to provide models for economic history in other European countries. Unlike in England, German economists had been prepared to apply principles to the study of economic activity in the past. This had, as a direct consequence, generated an industrious economic history in Germany from at least the 1840s, the influence of which in England was far from immediate but could, on occasion, be held up as a model of the possible. Some of the leading economic historians within Britain, above all Ashley, enjoyed a degree of contact with leading German figures, such as Schmoller.[23] Seebohm, in his introduction to *The English Village Community* (1883) singles out the contribution of German historians in providing students with 'a working hypothesis by means of which the study of the economic problem [here, the relation between agrarian organisation and the emergence of village communities in past society] has been materially advanced'. In tones of exasperation, Seebohm notes that, while German historians have pointed the way, 'no English student has as yet followed it up by an adequate examination of the remarkably rich materials which lie at the disposal of English Economic History'.[24] A generation later, French and Belgian historians also provided new intellectual impetus to the work of English economic historians. Their contribution to the discipline was recognised and encouraged through their involvement, as 'foreign correspondents', with the *Economic History Review* from its inception in 1927. Finally, the study of British, and above all English, economic history in the late nineteenth and early twentieth centuries, was indebted to continental scholars not just for the methodological and theoretical advances which they brought but also for the empirical work which they carried out. German and Russian historians, in particular, encouraged by their own intellectual and political agendas, dived into English sources and carried out some of the earliest quantitative studies of English economic history.[25]

If academics recognised, from within the academy, the advantages which a more 'economical' study of the past brought to their discipline, they also responded to a wider, extra-academic, engagement which both transcended the narrowly political and narrative-bound and reflected desires to treat the past as an explanation and justification for the travails of the present. An impetus for the growth of economic history came from within the economic circumstances of the period. A deep commitment to economic history amongst a readership beyond the academy helped galvanise an early generation of economic historians who were, themselves, operating both within and beyond the university. In the first decade of the twentieth century, a time of 'social ferment' and 'popular agitation', when 'public education had just started on the second stage of its great career', when 'the world of Labour was heaving with the long groundswell', 'the prevalent demand [in WEA classes] was for Economic History and Theory'.[26] Much of the work of economic historians also, therefore, met the expectations of an increasingly politicised and literate population in the first decades of the twentieth century;[27] work which explored the past with close reference to the present proved highly popular and was widely sought after. While some of that engagement took place within the classroom, much else was informal. The work of historians and social commentators found a large readership. Volumes such as *Industrial Democracy* by Sidney and Beatrice Webb, which had sold 13,000 copies by 1914, or Townsend Warner's *Landmarks in English Industrial History*, which was published in 1899 and of which 27,000 copies had been printed by 1913, gave further significant impetus to the subdiscipline.

The economic history of Britain was, therefore, virgin territory at the end of the nineteenth century, open to colonisation by pioneers with discrete expectations of what they would find there.[28] By *c*.1900 the race into a past of landlords and tenants, of factory owners and workers, was under way, and those who travelled into that territory carried an assortment of maps and tools in their intellectual knapsacks. The origins of a significant dynamism for the discrete study of the past, which encompassed more than the affairs of state and the nature of the constitution, was always likely to emerge from within a working class. In that sense, economic history, while it enjoyed association with other political subgroups, was a response to the expectations of those who saw themselves separated from political processes. As John Elkin, a miner and WEA student, argued in the spring of 1912,

> This society [the WEA] is going to have a great deal to do with the education of the workers, especially in teaching economics and industrial history, and the workers ought to see that their point of view receives attention. We know how some of these people teach industrial history, that governments have always been moved by a kind consideration for the people, and that people are poor through their own fault. ... The truth is that through the ages the workers have been bottom dog, and we've got to see that the education given is of a kind to make them realize that.[29]

Those charged with that education responded with equal enthusiasm. Tawney, as a tutor appointed by the Oxford University Tutorial Classes Committee, a body established to implement the report of the 1908 Oxford conference on Working-Class Education, toured the northwest, taking four classes each week. In lieu of a fifth class, and with the encouragement of the Tutorial Classes Committee, Tawney wrote *The Agrarian Problem in the Sixteenth Century* (1912).[30] This book, a seminal work prompted by the needs of teaching for the Workers' Educational Association, was dedicated to its president and secretary. In such ways did classes in history for working men help prompt new departures in the discipline which, in turn, redirected academic study. 'The friendly smitings of weavers, potters, miners, and engineers, have taught me much about the problems of political and economic science which cannot easily be learned from books', wrote R. H. Tawney in April 1912 in his preface to *The Agrarian Problem*.[31]

Others, by inclination social engineers of a different hue, saw in the socio-economic study of the past a crude device to placate and to control, bringing very different prejudices to that study. Thus, a generation before the WEA classes aimed at a dialogue with industrial workers, improving lectures were offered to local audiences by their social superiors. In 1882 the Reverend Augustus Jessop delivered a lecture on 'Village Life in Norfolk Six Hundred Years Ago' in the public reading-room of the village of Tittershall, Norfolk. Subtitled 'The rude forefathers of the hamlet ... ', his talk, the Reverend Jessop noted, 'was listened to with apparent interest and great attention by an audience of farmers, village tradesmen, mechanics and labourers'.[32] In an extraordinary contrast to the agenda of the later WEA classes, but with that same zeal to find in the past a truth with which to improve the present and future, Jessop begins his lecture to the Norfolk villagers in a tone of strict paternalism: 'few things have stuck me more forcibly since I have cast in my lot among country people, than the strange ignorance which they exhibit of the *history of themselves*' (his italics). That this ignorance needs to be dispelled is vital, 'for we and ourselves are what we come to, partly by our sins and vices, but partly (and much more than some like to believe) by the sins, negligences, and ignorances of those whose blood is in our veins'.[33] If comprehending their lot by reviewing the weaknesses and failings of their forebears did not wholly appeal to Jessop's Norfolk villagers – and since Jessop left the reading-room by the door and not the window we cannot gauge other than by Jessop's own account how his talk was received – it did indicate one manner in which the economic history of the past could be employed and, as already noted, it does compare, but with a very different emphasis, with the enthusiasm with which the self-same 'mechanics and labourers' set about their exploration of the past in order to counter this type of construction of their own past.

But it was also the political interest of academics themselves that prompted such explorations. The early historiography of economic history in Britain was informed, and indeed generated, by agendas other than those that were strictly intellectual/historical. Thus, for instance, the historical study of the village community, a key focus of interest for socio-economic historians in the late nineteenth century, 'pullulated with contemporary relevance'.[34] According to Dewey, the nature of the village community in past society became contested property, and the right to impose an identity upon it, whether as the forerunner of a liberal utopia to which society should aspire or as the stultifying lag on economic development from which society was increasingly fortunate to distance itself, was fought over by radical and conservative respectively.[35]

Nowhere was this more obvious than in the association between socialism and economic history in the decades either side of 1900. While it was in the decades immediately after the Second World War that economic history and Marxism would enjoy a particularly fruitful union, it was the leading lights of British socialism that appeared as dominant figures in an earlier historiography. The Webbs wrote a history of trade unionism because they were passionately engaged in a commentary on the inequalities of their day and anxious to chronicle 'the contrast between the wage-earners who had enjoyed the advantages of collective regulation ... and those who had been abandoned to the rigours of unrestrained individual competition'.[36] Their direct involvement in the foundation of the LSE reflected their desire to reform society through collectivist endeavour, an approach which, unsurprisingly, gained support from academics, including historians, within the LSE.[37] Tawney also, whose analysis of acquisitive society drew him close to Leninism but whose insistence upon collective application of the correct moral choices repudiated pragmatism in favour of idealism, was driven to his history by the force of his beliefs. Hence his life-long commitment to the WEA, to education more generally, to the relief of poverty and the desire to implant a sense of collective endeavour into the life of the nation. The director of the LSE in the 1920s and 1930s, Sir William Beveridge combined work in the social sciences with large-scale historical projects, including the gathering of huge amounts of price data from the Middle Ages to the modern era.[38] Much of this work remains unpublished, a hidden monument to an inductivist approach married to a revised liberalism.

Within the discipline of history itself, the rise of economic history was marked by the contribution of historians who could be identified, in relation to the established ordering of that discipline, as outsiders. Some of its early and significant contributors, such as Lipson, the forceful promoter of the *Economic History Review* and its first editor, were alienated, or perceived themselves to be alienated, from the core of the discipline.[39] Most obviously, it is women who feature in the early emergence of economic history in Britain. While the first chairs went to men, many of the earliest lecturers, including Lillian Knowles and Eileen Power, both at the LSE, were women. In 1931, Power became Professor of Economic History at the LSE, an institution comfortable with the strengths of female academics and quite capable of promoting them. By the 1930s, it has been suggested, women historians at the LSE were integrated to the extent that they did not see themselves as distinctive, an impossible situation at Cambridge where women were yet to receive full degrees. In that sense, it was in the more radical institutions that there was room both for intellectual and for social departures; the attraction of economic history for women was, in a certain respect, that in its challenge to assumptions about role and relevance, it replicated their own contemporary experience.[40] Not just in posts, but also in publications, women, by the early twentieth century, were a driving force for economic history. To think of the contributors to medieval economic history, a substantial component of the corpus of the new sub-discipline, is to review a list which includes seminal contributions from women historians, including Eileen Power, Ada Levett and F. M. Page.

'History is a jade who periodically renews her vigour by marrying oncoming youths', wrote N. S. B. Gras in the first volume of the *Economic History Review*.[41] The reader of that first volume from 1927 is certainly confronted with a Clio flush with the excitement of a new encounter. Association with her beau had not, however, caused her to surrender her principles. There is much in the early work of economic historians to allow us to identify new approaches to, for instance, the gathering and dissemination of material, including the application of quantitative data. There is also, again in that first volume as in the article by Postan on 'Credit in Medieval Trade', an early rejection of a progressivist narrative in favour of something more processual. Postan explicitly distances his work from that of a first generation of economic historians, including Cunningham, who 'set out to describe … the story of how England's economic power steadily waxed from the early middle ages'.[42] However, as Postan was obliged to acknowledge at the time, these were early stirrings. For the greater part, the developments discussed in this chapter did not have widespread effect for another generation. It was the period after the Second World War that saw the major promotion of branches of economic history in the guise of 'new social history', the rise of Marxist history, and econometrics. As data published at various intervals by the Economic History Society show, per annum publications in economic history increased from about eighty in the mid-1920s to about 1,200 by the mid-1970s.[43] If such an increase in publication can be employed as a crude measure of real growth, then clearly economic history grew in the half-century after its founding generation. But, as Harte, the compiler of these statistics, notes, the identification of articles as 'economic' rather than, say, 'political' or 'constitutional' poses problems to an extent that would not have been possible in 1925. 'Much of straight historical writing has been fundamentally changed by the rise of economic and social history', wrote Harte in 1975, so that, by an absorption of approach, of interest, of topic, the study of the past had undergone a shift of its own. Much of this chapter has been about the ways in which that shift was occasioned. The development of economic history reflected a demand that history be about more than the machinations of the state and its politics; the demandants, including the historians, in pursuing that other kind of history also brought new methodologies to their work, and admitted novelties into the discipline which would ultimately come to challenge more than content.

Notes

1   J. E. T. Rogers, 'The economical interpretation of history', in *idem*, *The Economic Interpretation of History (Lectures delivered in Worcester College Hall, Oxford, 1887–8)*, London, T. Fisher Unwin, 1888, p. 2.

2 Throughout this chapter, we will employ 'economic history', in its contemporary sense, as a term of use for 'economic and/or social history'. For a recent brief discussion of the development of terminology in this respect, see E. Royle, 'Economic (*and Social?*) History', in P. Hudson (ed.) *Living Economic and Social History*, Glasgow, Economic History Society, 2001, p. 315.

3 *Ibid.*, p. 5.

4 *Ibid.*, p. 8.

5 F. Seebohm, 'The Black Death and Its Place in English History', *The Fortnightly Review*, 1865; F. A. Gasquet, *The Great Pestilence*, London, 1893; F. W. Maitland, 'The History of a Cambridgeshire Manor', *English Historical Review*, 1894, vol. 35. See also the useful discussion of the work of Seebohm and responses to it, in N. Hybel, *Crisis or Change*, Aarhus, Aarhus University Press, 1988, p. 1ff.

6 Gasquet, *Great Pestilence*.

7 See, for instance, W. Cunningham, *The Growth of English Industry and Commerce*, 5th edn, Cambridge, Cambridge University Press, 1910, pp. 13–15; also F. Seebohm, *The English Village Community*, London, Longmans, Green and Co., 1883, pp. 439, 441.

8 For some few notable exceptions, see, for example, the brief discussion by N. Harte, 'The Economic History Society, 1926–2001', in Hudson (ed.) *Living Economic and Social History*, p. 1.

9 Sir W. Ashley, 'The Place of Economic History in University Studies', *Economic History Review*, 1927, vol. 1, p. 7.

10 Interview with M. M. Postan cited in T. C. Barker, 'The Beginnings of the Economic History Society', *Economic History Review*, 1977, vol. 30, p. 6.

11 Harte, 'Economic History Society', p. 2. For further narrative acounts of these developments, see also D. C. Coleman, *History and the Economic Past. An Account of the Rise and Decline of Economic History in Britain*, Oxford, Clarendon, 1987, pp. 38–9. Harte's discussion, cited above, draws upon his earlier and fuller piece: 'Introduction: the Making of Economic History', in N. B. Harte (ed.) *The Study of Economic History. Collected Inaugural Lectures, 1893–1970*, London, Frank Cass, 1971, pp. xxiii ff.

12 Reader in Economic History at Oxford in the 1920s and the motive force for the establishment of the *Economic History Review* in 1927, see also above, p. 73.

13 Barker, 'Beginnings of the Economic History Society', p. 10.

14 See the comments of L. L. Price on Cunningham and Ashley, who, he wrote, 'have created Economic History for English students', quoted in Harte, 'Introduction', p. xxvi.

15 R. H. Tawney and E. Power (eds) *Tudor Economic Documents*, 3 vols, London, Longmans, 1924, p. v.

16 Barker, 'Beginnings of the Economic History Society', pp. 12–13.

17 Harte, 'Introduction', pp. xii–xiii.

18 Cunningham, *Growth of English Industry and Commerce*, pp. 21–2.

19 *Ibid.*, p. xix.

20 M. Berg, *A Woman in History. Eileen Power, 1889–1940*, Cambridge, Cambridge University Press, 1996, p. 144.

21 A. Wright, *R. H. Tawney*, Manchester, Manchester University Press, 1987, p. 127. See also below, pp. 139–40 (Chapter 9).

22 Harte, 'Introduction', p. xiv.

23 W. J. Ashley, 'On the Study of Economic History (Harvard, 1893)', in Harte (ed.) *Study of Economic History*, pp. 6–7.

24 Seebohm, *The English Village Community*, pp. x, xi.

25 See also below, pp. 181–2 (Chapter 12).

26 R. H. Tawney, 'The Workers' Educational Association and Adult Education', in *idem, The Radical Tradition*, Harmondsworth, Penguin, 1964, pp. 88–90; see also Barker, 'Beginnings of the Economic History Society', p. 4.
27 See also below, pp. 78–9.
28 See also above, p. 47.
29 *R. H. Tawney's Commonplace Book*, eds J. M. Winter and D. M. Joslin, Cambridge, Cambridge University Press, 1972, p. 3. Tawney records that he has noted the substance of Elkin's comment, though not the exact words.
30 R. H. Tawney, *The Agrarian Problem in the Sixteenth Century*, London, Longman, 1912, Preface; see also A. Wright, *R. H. Tawney*, Manchester, Manchester University Press, 1987, pp. 5–6; R. Terrill, *R. H. Tawney and His Times. Socialism as Fellowship*, London, Andre Deutsch, 1973, pp. 39ff.
31 Tawney, *Agrarian Problem*, Preface.
32 Rev. A. Jessop, 'Village Life in Norfolk Six Hundred Years Ago. "The rude forefathers of the hamlet ... " ', in *idem, The Coming of the Friars and Other Historic Essays*, London, T. Fisher Unwin, 1889, p. 55.
33 *Ibid.*, pp. 56, 58.
34 C. Dewey, 'Images of the Village Community: A Study in Anglo-Indian Ideology', *Modern Asian Studies*, 1972, vol. 6, p. 292.
35 *Ibid.*, p. 292; also R. M. Smith, ' "Modernization" and the Corporate Medieval Village Community in England. Some Sceptical Reflections', in A. R. H. Baker and D. Gregory (eds) *Explorations in Historical Geography*, Cambridge, Cambridge University Press, 1984, p. 151.
36 B. Webb, *My Apprenticeship*, 2 vols, Harmondsworth, Pelican, 1938, ii, p. 395.
37 Berg, *Woman in History*, pp. 68, 148.
38 Berg, *Woman in History*, p. 146.
39 Barker, 'Beginnings of the Economic History Society', pp. 9–10.
40 Berg, *Woman in History*, pp. 142–3.
41 N. S. B. Gras, 'The Rise and Development of Economic History', *Economic History Review*, 1927, vol. 1, p. 12.
42 M. M. Postan, 'Credit in Medieval Trade', *Economic History Review*, 1927, vol. 1, p. 235.
43 N. B. Harte, 'Trends in Publications on the Economic History of Great Britain and Ireland, 1925–1974', *Economic History Review*, 1975, vol. 50, p. 24.

Further reading

There have been important and thorough attempts to chart the rise of economic history in Britain. The introduction by N. B. Harte to an edited collection of inaugural lectures by economic historians offers the most substantial assessment: 'Introduction: the Making of Economic History', in N. B. Harte (ed.) *The Study of Economic History. Collected Inaugural Lectures, 1893–1970*, London, Frank Cass, 1971. For another valuable account, see also D. C. Coleman, *History and the Economic Past. An Account of the Rise and Decline of Economic History in Britain*, Oxford, Clarendon, 1987; A. Kadish, *Historians, Economists and Economic History*, London, Routledge, 1989. Just after this chapter was completed, a further piece on economic history in Britain also appeared, P. Hudson, 'Economic History', in S. Berger, H. Feldner and K. Passmore (eds) *Writing History. Theory and Practice*, Arnold, 2003, pp. 223–42. Taking a different approach, in particular in its assessment of the long-term challenges to economic history, Hudson surveys the progress of economic history throughout the twentieth century.

Important players in the establishment of economic history have themselves commented upon the process. See, for instance, Sir W. Ashley, 'The Place of Economic History in University Studies', *Economic History Review*, 1927, vol. 1, pp. 1–11; N. S. B. Gras, 'The Rise and Development of Economic History', *Economic History Review*, 1927, vol. 1, pp. 12–34. There are also the various contemporary reflections on the emergence of the discipline articulated through inaugural lectures: Harte (ed.) *Study of Economic History*; also *R. H. Tawney's Commonplace Book*, eds J. M. Winter and D. M. Joslin, Cambridge, Cambridge University Press, 1972. Reflection on the state of the sub-discipline continues to the present; see the collection of short musings in P. Hudson (ed.) *Living Economic and Social History*, Glasgow, Economic History Society, 2001. Leading figures in the early years of the economic history have also been the subject of biographers who, in turn, have discussed the history and development of the discipline: A. Wright, *R. H. Tawney*, Manchester, Manchester University Press, 1987; R. Terrill, *R. H. Tawney and His Times. Socialism as Fellowship*, London, Andre Deutsch, 1973; of particular note in this respect is the insightful study of Eileen Power, M. Berg, *A Woman in History. Eileen Power, 1889–1940*, Cambridge, Cambridge University Press, 1996. Here see also the useful list of relevant obituaries, *ibid.*, pp. 282–3. On the role of women in the sub-discipline, see M. Berg, 'The first women economic historians', *Economic History Review*, 1992, vol. 45, pp. 308–29. As well as studies of individuals, histories of institutions also shed light on the emergence of economic history; see S. Caine, *The History of the Foundation of the LSE*, London, G. Bell and Sons, 1963.

On the origins and subsequent growth of the Economic History Society, see N. Harte, 'The Economic History Society, 1926–2001', in Hudson (ed.) *Living Economic and Social History*, pp. 1–12; T. C. Barker, 'The Beginnings of the Economic History Society', *Economic History Review*, 1977, vol. 30, pp. 1–19; N. B. Harte, 'Trends in Publications on the Economic History of Great Britain and Ireland, 1925–1974', *Economic History Review*, 1975, vol. 50, pp. 20–41. Most recent is a piece published for the 75th anniversary of the society: E. A. Wrigley, 'The Review During the Last 50 years', http://www.ehs.org.uk/othercontent/wrigley50yearsEssay.pdf.

Chapter 5

The *Annales* school and historical writing

Michael Roberts

The historians associated with the French journal *Annales* have exerted probably the single most marked influence on the character of historical writing
since the Second World War. This is largely because in the twenty years after its
foundation in 1929 the journal's editors developed an effective paradigm within
which research findings from an ever-widening range of historical subjects and
approaches could be assimilated and given coherence. Their ambitions to
compose an integrated, 'total history', attentive both to the breadth of geography and the subtleties of the human outlook or 'mentality' (usually expressed
in the plural as *mentalités*), were combined with a fascination with the experience of time resolutely appropriate to the twentieth century. This became the
framework for much cutting-edge work in France, and increasingly elsewhere
from the 1960s onwards. The voluminous publications of the journal's editors,
even more than articles in the journal itself, are now widely regarded as classics,
and have become staple fare in courses on historical methodology. The achievement is all the more remarkable for having extended a programme shaped by
French preoccupations during the 1870–1914 period into a genuinely trans-
national pattern for research. Its application has made the historiographical
world at large a kind of France, and France less straightforwardly a 'nation' than
a microcosm for the world, a test-bed for questions about the relation between
physical surroundings, social arrangements and the mental habits of communities in the past.

The impetus which lay behind the *Annales* owed much to the energy and
vision of its founding editors, Lucien Febvre and Marc Bloch. By self-
consciously dramatising their differences with an earlier, first generation of
professional historians in France, they helped attract to the journal sufficient
contributors and readers to make the new venture viable in an economically
very unpropitious climate. Their success in the 1930s parallels that of French
cinema, which evolved a distinctive method of 'artisanal low-budget produc-
tions' that enabled it to thrive when the delayed impact of the Depression was
felt after 1931. As attendances at theatres, music halls, concerts and cabarets
fell, cinema audiences more than doubled.[1] The *Annales* did not match this feat
but their annual output was more than twice the bulk of the Economic History

Society's UK equivalent.[2] This was due in part to their determination to address contemporary economic problems in a deliberate dialogue between the present and the past: several early articles dealt with the contemporary financial situation, with collectivisation of Soviet agriculture, and with the Great Depression in the USA.[3] But it also owed much to the lingering need in France to realign the national past with the facts of a succession of defeats.

French scholarship after the Franco-Prussian War has been described as 'the continuation of war by other means'[4] but the efforts to modernise historical studies through seminar teaching, journals, book reviewing and the establishment of university chairs had achieved only modest success by the early 1900s, when *professional* historians, teachers and archivists were still very much a minority of those producing historical publications, and most historians were still concentrating on political history. This limited progress tended to enhance the self-image of the prestigious École Normale Supèrieure in Paris as a model of interdisciplinary work, and a source of innovation (the school also prided itself on its wide regional recruitment). Febvre studied there during 1898–1902, and Bloch in 1904–8. In so centralised a culture, both establishment and innovators had somehow to coexist within the same metropolitan frame of reference, hence the importance of the concepts of the avant-garde, the outsider, and the marginal in French culture. These informed the way in which the *Annales* historians combined the geographical and the temporal realms, and their determination to succeed in establishing, in a new Sixth Section of the École Pratique des Hautes Études after the Second World War, what was in effect a counter-faculty.

Christophe Charle has recently suggested that this aspect of French academic life corresponds to Kuhn's model of scientific change, whereby 'normal science' is pursued and directed at the centre by patrons manipulating power in traditional fashion, whilst innovation comes from 'les outsiders'. It was not the two professors of history at the Sorbonne, Ernest Lavisse and Alfred Rambaud who set up the *Revue historique* in 1876 to help shape history as a 'positive science', but Gabriel Monod, who was employed at the entirely new Fourth Section of the École Pratique, and Gustave Fagniez, an archivist.[5] Their aim was to develop a more powerful, because more complex, form of historical understanding. But the very nature of that consciousness was also coming into question in this very period.[6] The main problem lay with the definition of a sufficiently rigorous scientific method by which human experience over time could be understood. The adoption of scrupulous techniques of source criticism promised to minimise the distortions introduced by biased evidence, and the construction of a historical profession offered the security of mutual criticism and regular public exposure for work in progress. But the plausibility with which a 'scientific' method could be elaborated also depended on a relatively circumscribed view of the historian's proper field of enquiry. Pressure for its expansion came from several directions during the last quarter of the nineteenth century. Interest in the effects of collective human behaviour had been growing since the first French Revolution of 1789, and was now finding systematised form in the emerging disciplines of economics and sociology. But there was also pressure for the deepening of historical analysis through attention to human psychology. As a student, Lucien Febvre had been impressed by the lectures of the philosopher Henri Bergson, with their suggestion that intuition was a better way of understanding human experience than scientific reason. Bergson also had interesting ideas about the layering of time, and the incommunicability of our innermost self and memories. Time at that level, he thought, moved very differently than at the public level of minutes and hours. If politics and history were categorically distinct for the scientific historian, for Bergson our personal past and present were inseparable. These questions were being explored in contemporary literature, too, by writers like Proust, Joyce and Woolf, whilst the sociologist Durkheim had explored the relationships between private and social experience in *The Elementary Forms of Religious Life* (1912).[7] The importance, and the mystery, of the individual experience of time was meanwhile being thrown into high relief by ever more uniform and precise notions of public time. In 1912 Paris hosted the first International Conference on Time in order to determine the basis for accuracy on a global scale, and in July 1913 it was from the Eiffel Tower that the first time signal transmitted around the world was beamed electronically. Mastery over this high-tech time was becoming a matter of national pride, as France and other countries resisted English kitemarking of the common mean. The task given the Russian anarchist in Joseph Conrad's *The Secret Agent* (1907) was to blow up Greenwich Observatory.[8]

These circumstances made the modernisation of historical practice an urgent but problematic task. Charles V. Langlois and Charles Seignobos had laid out a model for archivally based historical method in their *Introduction aux études historiques* (1897). This actually very thorough and reflective volume sought to establish the distinctiveness of the 'scientific' method in its application to history, and thus both its rigour and the fact that 'the rational methods of obtaining historical knowledge differ so widely from the methods of all other sciences'.[9] But its very scrupulousness also demonstrated just how much subject matter its authors and their generation were not investigating. It was against this confinement that the creators of the *Annales* found themselves in revolt. Febvre, born in Nancy in 1878 and the elder by eight years, was the son of a teacher; Bloch, the son of an eminent professor of ancient history. Both were equipped with the confidence and breadth of vision inculcated at the École Normale, and thus predisposed against too much deference towards their elders. They were also attracted by the sociologist Émile Durkheim's study of collective behaviour, and the philosopher Henri Berr's quest for a synthesis of the human sciences. 'We were a group of young historians at the École Normale who were beginning to find our studies banal, and were just about to quit', recalled Febvre, when Berr's *Revue de synthèse historique* appeared in 1900.[10] In 1903 the *Revue* conducted a questionnaire survey of history at

French universities which revealed, aside from a great deal of unresponsive complacency, pockets of enthusiasm for something new. 'The time for a new "integral history" [*l'histoire intégral*] has come', responded one professor from Caen.[11]

Febvre contributed to the *Revue de synthèse* from 1905 onwards, and Bloch's first contribution in 1912 was an article exploring the subject of his doctoral thesis. In their early work both historians were indebted to the strong geographical interests of former historian Paul Vidal de la Blache (1843–1918), who had turned towards geography after 1870 in an effort to understand France's defeat. His emphasis on observation and description, on the long stabilities of rural landscape, sustained a series of regional monographs, which gave a direct example to historians bored with events and origins. We see this in Febvre's *Philippe II et la Franche-Comté* (1911); and his *La terre et l'évolution humaine* (1922; translated as *A Geographical Introduction to History*, 1925); and Bloch's *L'Ile de France* (1913; translated into English 1971). The careers of both men were interrupted by military service during the First World War, an experience which reinforced their patriotism and sense of purpose. Their sense of civic duty was shared by many veterans, and helps to explain the militant, even combative, tone of the early *Annales*.[12] For Bloch at least, the war also brought a lasting admiration for the qualities of the ordinary people of France, and a willingness to view the past of a peasant society literally from the grass roots up. After the war this was combined with a pronounced interest in ideas and perceptions, which seems to have had a Bergsonian stimulus: Bloch's *Les rois thaumaturges* (1922; translated as *The Royal Touch*, 1973) also drew on his fascination with the force of rumour and 'false news' experienced in the trenches. Meanwhile Febvre deepened his interest in the sixteenth century by considering the way in which its history had been framed by the assumptions of later investigations. In 1929 he contributed a long article to the mainstream *Revue historique* on the origins of the French Reformation, presenting the search for origins as a 'badly put question' and concluding violently that 'Specificity, dating and nationality are words which need to be struck off the historian's vocabulary list. They are problems of no substance – stuffy old controversial subjects, old cast-offs which still lie around in our books of learning'. It was far more important to recognise that what later generations came to call the Protestant Reformation was for contemporaries a much more complex and confused crisis of faith in general, affecting all facets of Christian belief and spilling across national boundaries.[13] Though starting as the historians of particular provinces, Bloch and Febvre thus evolved an unusually open, comparative understanding of European history through their willingness to study subjects outside the strait-jacket of national political histories.

With strong family and affective ties to northeastern France, both historians found themselves after the war working in the hot-house atmosphere of the re-founded university of Strasbourg, where the innovations introduced during the German occupation were now being consolidated by a crack team of academics hired to turn the university into an equally impressive shop window for French scholarship and values. The location encouraged an approach to the past which could put national sentiment in its place, and explore those large-scale, extra-national experiences which had shaped Europe and its civilisation, such as the ebb and flow of Roman imperial power, the development of feudalism, or the fracture of Christendom at the Reformation. The promise, or threat, of the Soviet Revolution after 1917, and the economic difficulties of the 1920s and 1930s likewise required explanations beyond national boundaries. A scientific history defined through the scrupulous criticism of largely political source materials did not seem well equipped to take these questions further. Accordingly, when *Annales* eventually appeared in 1929 it was launched as 'a national review with an international spirit'. Its editorial committee of ten included only two Sorbonne professors (Demangeon, a historical geographer, and the economic historian Hauser), alongside several non-historians to ensure interdisciplinary credibility. Its name, *Annales d'histoire économique et sociale*, presaged a contemporary approach, not unlike that announced shortly before by the British *Economic History Review*.[14]

From the beginning, the journal formed only part of the apparatus by which 'the almost virgin soil of social history' was to be tilled.[15] Bloch's lectures on the character of French rural life delivered in Oslo in 1929 showed a similarly experimental attitude, offering a synthesis in advance of 'a host of analytical studies' since 'there are times when for once the formulation of problems is more urgent than their solution'. To 'the immutability of agrarian custom' Bloch counterposed a dynamic reading of the landscape:

> in more than one place the pattern of the fields is older by far than even the most venerable stones. But, and this is the point, these survivals have never been 'ruins'; they are better compared to a composite building of archaic structure, never deserted but constantly remodelled by each fresh generation of occupiers.[16]

This was a lively past which survived as 'the last reel of a film which we must try to unroll, resigned to the gaps we shall certainly discover, resolved to pay due regard to its sensitivity as a register of change'.[17] Bloch saw the contemporary exodus of the rural proletariat as the outcome of 'an age-old antagonism between *manouvriers* and *laboureurs*, the end of a story whose earlier chapters are written in medieval parchments which set manual and ploughing services in opposition to one another'.[18] In dignifying contemporary struggles with this long pedigree, Bloch also called for an unsentimental approach to rural history: 'what discipline is more imperious in forcing its practitioners to come to grips with history as it really is?' Rural history for Bloch did not entail an avoidance of the political, so much as a more realistically conceived idea of politics itself.[19]

During the war, the Nazi Occupation made the future of *Annales* itself a political issue. To continue production at all required that Bloch, as a Jew, remove his name as editor and contribute pseudonymously. The Swiss historian Philippe Burrin has recently shown how extensive were the accommodations reached with the occupying power, and how these tacitly acknowledged that France might have a plausible future in a Nazi Europe, even if this was tantamount 'to accepting the prospect of a future with no more Jews'.[20] Yet to historians shaped by the struggle for justice in the Dreyfus affair, and for whom the renewal and enriching of historical method was a matter of deep pride in the cultivation and openness of French society, the journal's closure would also amount to a defeat. Several historians were in direct danger. When in August 1942 Febvre decided to circumvent regulations by issuing an irregular *Mélanges d'histoire sociale* in place of the *Annales* itself, its first number reported the Germans' incarceration of Pierre Vilar, Fernand Braudel and Henri Brunschwig as prisoners of war. He wrote with desperate optimism how Braudel had drafted out what would be an epoch-making thesis on 'the Mediterranean in the period of Phillip II'. As for Bloch, before his arrest and murder by the Gestapo as a Resistance leader in 1944, he contributed indefatigably to the underground press.[21] For his part, Febvre published during the war a number of articles giving expression to the continuing fruitfulness of a 'French' perspective on a pointedly chosen set of problems: intellectual freedom, cultural regression, death and remembrance.[22]

War thus consecrated the broader conception of political commitment, which was already embodied by the *Annales*. The journal was relaunched in 1946 under a new declamatory title: *Annales: économies-sociétés-civilisations*. As in Strasbourg after 1918, the impetus towards postwar reconstruction, and political rivalry with an enemy (this time the Soviet Union), encouraged new initiatives, drawing on funding from the Rockefeller Foundation, thanks to the connections of Charles Morazé, then secretary for the International Committee of Historical Sciences.[23] A new centre for interdisciplinary research (the Sixième Section of the École Pratique des Hautes Études) was established in 1948 under Febvre's direction, with Braudel in charge of the historical wing. Later grants and government funding over the next twelve years allowed the number of posts in the section to grow to eighty.[24] Historians were thus playing the leading role within an increasingly confident social science community.

For Febvre, who served as French delegate to UNESCO during 1945–50, the postwar *Annales* promised to become the vehicle of vast collaborative research projects upon subjects of obvious public interest.[25] One of the most direct ways in which historians could contribute to national revival after the war was through the exploration of the very conditions of life, and in particular the study of the demography of France. Public preoccupation with a declining population had led to the introduction of family allowances in 1932, and thereafter the birth rate began to recover, spurred in response to political defeat by what the demographer Alfred Sauvy called the 'collective conscience'. Demographic studies demand, above all, reliable data over long periods of time, and it was to the study of parochial records of baptisms, marriages and burials that much time was now devoted. This allowed specialists in the sixteenth and seventeenth centuries, in which such registration had been first widely applied, to make a genuinely original contribution to contemporary understanding, whilst preserving the continuity of chronological emphasis within the *Annales*.

The period between 1950 and 1970 has been dubbed 'le temps des thèses ardues', after the sequence of large regional studies which issued from the Sixth Section, written by historians who had scarcely been born when *Annales* itself was founded.[26] These decisively shifted the emphasis of French historiography. By 1961 more than 40 per cent of all modern history theses in progress in France were on economic and social history.[27] After Febvre's death in 1956 the journal was effectively under Fernand Braudel's control, and was given its now familiar chic appearance in a white cover with red lettering. Its contents had doubled in size by 1960. Braudel contributed little to the journal itself after an initial discussion of his ideas about history over the long term, preferring to work on such an enormous canvas that his own massive multi-volume books served as a kind of parallel exemplar to the journal itself. Braudel offered a magnificent personal example of the energy and vision required. The son of a mathematics teacher, his historical awareness was enlivened by the traditional household of his maternal grandmother, whose ancestors he claimed had built the local seigneurial mill.[28] This kindled his life-long interest in peasants and their markets. His commitment to a wider world began whilst working as one of a number of young French scholars who helped establish the university of Sao Paolo in Brazil in the mid-1930s. To this he brought a taste for innovation, pioneering the microfilming of primary source materials with the use of a second-hand film camera. Thus equipped, he embarked on a study of the entire Mediterranean world during the time of Phillip II of Spain. The accumulated mass of evidence might have defeated even Braudel, but for the accident of his incarceration in a German prisoner of war camp. The resulting work carried the logic of total history to its conclusion through its multi-faceted detail, whilst its organisation threw into sharp relief the opposition between the history of the geographical, economic and social Mediterranean on the one hand, and the historian's traditional focal point, political events, on the other. Phillip, and the Battle of Lepanto, were relegated to a very late appearance towards the end of the book.

By 1963, when a second edition was issued, Braudel had predictably accumulated more material, but he had also re-thought his priorities as to what should be included, and how the material should be organised. It was at this point that he also made explicit his interest in the interplay between continuity and change, through the introduction of the terms 'structure' and 'conjuncture' from the field of economics. The elaboration of a three-level theory of time, 'l'histoire de la longue durée ... des conjonctures ... de la durée courte' (history over the long term; conjunctural history; short-term history), allowed Braudel to retain for historians the claim to scientific leadership which was now threatened by the impact of structuralism in the study of anthropology, linguistics, and what we would today call cultural theory. Introducing the new edition, he contrasted the familiar 'conspicuous history' with 'that other, submerged, history, almost silent and always discreet, virtually unsuspected either by its observers or its participants, which is little touched by the obstinate erosion of time'.[29]

Braudel's equation of the barely moving long term with geography was evocative, but marked a move away from Febvre's geographical 'possibilism'[30] towards a determinism which even began to shape the history of *mentalités*. Braudel considered that 'mental frameworks' could 'form prisons of the *longue durée*'.[31] As this phrase illustrates, however, part of the achievement of Braudel and his younger colleagues such as Emmanuel Le Roy Ladurie, lay in their rhetorical packaging of work that was often arduous and arcane.[32] Ladurie glamorised the results of patient long-term quantification as 'history that stands still' (*l'histoire immobile*'). By thus combining quantitative studies with a continuing interest in mental frameworks, and an imaginative, question-posing attitude to exposition, the *Annales* historians were able to absorb the full impact of the fashion for 'hard' social science in the 1960s and to emerge with new ideas when the fashion faltered. There was an impressive variation in the scale and character of the books emerging from individual authors: Bloch and Febvre had worked like this already, and the pattern has been continued most impressively by Le Roy Ladurie (in this respect at least a more representative figure than Braudel) and Alain Corbin. The use of numbers itself became one more illustrative device, an invitation to look again rather than not to look at all. Despite much of the rhetoric, the underlying appeal of this work was made less at the level of 'science' than through the histories' imaginative breadth.

This proved to be an important legacy when the history of 'events' returned with a vengeance to the France of the late 1960s. Between 1960 and 1975 the number of professional historians in France grew from 450 to 1,448. The associated expansion of the student market and of paperback publishing saw print runs increase, and even weighty regional studies by Pierre Goubert or Le Roy Ladurie became available in cheap, abbreviated editions. History, and historians, emerged as successful media figures, beginning with the interview in *Le Nouvel Observateur* with Emmanuel Le Roy Ladurie in 1966 about his thesis on the peasants of Languedoc.[33] Ladurie's integration of long-term price and rent movements with conjunctural shifts and immediate crises lent his work a majestic drama. Peasant prosperity repeatedly came up against 'stumbling blocks in the way of expansion'. But these 'were not all of a material nature. I sensed the presence of a formidable obstacle in mental attitudes ... I learned to identify these spiritual stumbling blocks in the chronicle of hopeless popular revolts and in the bloody history of peasant religions'.[34]

Much of Ladurie's later work has elaborated in imaginative ways on that thwarted world, perhaps most memorably (though also controversially) in his study of the medieval community of *Montaillou*, which to the author and publisher's surprise had sold 150,000 copies by 1987.[35] Historians were having a similar impact in other media. In 1977 French TV viewers voted historical programmes more popular than variety or sport.[36] On this basis, the former radical Régis Debray identified a pattern of shifts in the location of intellectual power, moving from the church to the universities (1880–1930) to the big publishers like Gallimard (1930–68) then to the media.[37] Media success brought a change of emphasis. The *médiatique* media-friendly personality seemed to need different qualities to those tried and tested for an academic career by the ten-year production of a regional *thèse*.[38] It also encouraged the adoption of a simpler style, less encumbered with footnotes. Georges Duby, whose *Le Dimanche de Bouvines* had helped usher in the return to events in 1973, not only reflected perceptively on the problems of turning such a work into film, but contributed to the development of the new medium itself through support for a production consortium.[39] The popularity of history in film and TV saw a return to national and political history, Braudel's former student Marc Ferro playing a key TV role. The agenda has also been shifted by the high-quality popular history magazines, which have often concentrated on political history, contemporary history, and commemoration. Even Braudel's last work, *The Identity of France*, can be seen as an extensive commentary on contemporary debates about regionalism and economic development, fulfilling the early promise of the *Annales* towards transnational cooperation.[40]

By the time of his death, Braudel had also played a large part in the export of the *Annales* approach outside France, particularly to the Americas, which had been taking place since the mid-1960s.[41] The resources and energy of the Sixth Section had ensured that the social and economic history of Europe, particularly during the centuries of early capitalist development, was dominated by work from France during the 1960s, and Braudel's later work extended its reach to cover the whole world.[42] Not long after the 'events' of May 1968 the journal began to include English-language summaries of its articles. Interest in the United States was considerable, and reciprocated: a centre for research into long-term change was set up in Braudel's name at the State University of New York at Binghamton in 1976, and the following year Georges Huppert was observing enthusiastically that half the world's historians were American.[43] Braudel's international ascendancy in the 1980s, when sales of *The Mediterranean* took off suddenly, was also associated with waning interest in Marxian interpretative schemes, for which his emphasis on three levels of time, and on the workings of the world economy offered a kind of substitute. The journal itself benefited from this global reach. By 1994 subscriptions came from 2,179 French institutions, and 1,813 outside France, with a further 1,577 copies sold, making a total of 4,023 for the year.

Meanwhile, in France itself, the impending bicentennial of the 1789 Revolution crystallised personal, professional and ideological differences between historians who might otherwise be thought of as members of a single *Annales* school. The need to commemorate the Revolution (or to find some alternative to commemoration) forced historians to re-examine their understanding of the political realm, and of its relation to 'the social'. Indeed, the historian's own social role, as puncturer of national myths or renewer of national solidarity, seemed to need re-examination. Responses were very varied. Whilst Francois Furet emphasised the autonomy of political experience, representing political history as 'a narrative of human freedom',[44] Roger Chartier sought to reinvent a kind of social analysis without relying on Marxism, by focussing on what he calls the autonomy of cultural practices. At the same moment, historians were invited to adopt a more autobiographical, confessional mode.[45] The editors of *Annales* recognised the impending crisis in 1988–9 by describing the historical scene as resembling a canvas increasingly illegible through the variety of its contents.[46] The effect in Georges Duby's view was also one of suffocation and lack of direction, whilst for the young scholar François Dosse the *Annales* had left history in pieces.[47] The school's very success in stimulating innovative work elsewhere now meant that the coherence and integrity of the project, and the use of the microcosm of France as a laboratory for the whole world, were being eroded by the adoption of other models: Italian micro history, British social history, German *Alltagsgeschichte*, and the American linguistic turn.[48] This made the particularity of the pre-1980s *Annales* more visible.[49]

One of its blind-spots, the history of women, was recognised by Georges Duby, who in the early 1970s began a long research project dealing with women and the medieval family, and lectured to packed audiences at the Collège de France on the subject in the 1980s, eclipsing even his colleagues Barthes and Foucault in his popularity.[50] Another, surprisingly, was the way in which histories were written (as opposed to how they were researched and organised). This meant that critics like Roland Barthes and Julia Kristeva were misled into thinking of historical writing as one-dimensional,[51] whilst an entirely separate conceptualisation of work with the past was developed by the non-historian Michel Foucault.

It may be, however, that the bold interdisciplinarity of the *Annales* project could only have been sustained on the basis of a relatively unreflective attitude towards writing and epistemology. As reflectiveness has increased, the pressure on the individual historian grows, though this need not end in disaster, as we can see from the transformation of the history of mentalities at the hands of Alain Corbin (1936–), whose early work on archaism and modernity in the nineteenth-century Limousin was influenced by Febvre and Duby. The approach he adopts also owes much to the pioneering work of Robert Mandrou, the first to show the primacy of hearing and touch and the other senses of 'déquipement sensoriel' in his majestic but deceptively titled work *Introduction à la France moderne 1500–1640* (1961). Mandrou continued Febvre's fascination with the history of emotions, and Corbin has transferred this approach to the relatively under-explored nineteenth century. This offers the historian an anthropological 'marqueterie' (mosaic), and Corbin's readers have become familiar with the ideas of a *paysage sonore* or a *paysage olfactif*. But

Corbin has been insistent on the need to avoid geographical, social or literary reductionism; his approach strives to recover a total history by being prepared to

> map the boundaries of what the mind can imagine, identify the mechanisms driving new emotions, trace the origins of desires, and the way in which suffering or pleasure was experienced at a given time, describe habitus, and reconstitute the logic behind the systems of vision and evaluation.[52]

This ambition is strikingly true to the spirit of 1929 in its completeness, whilst turning away from postwar rigidities: 'It is time for historians to call into question the idea of long-term prison and the out-of-step rhythms of Braudelian temporality'. Indeed, there needs to be a return to that other, passionate Braudel: 'Specialists of cultural history now know how to examine institutions, objects and practices. They will not, however, *let themselves* tackle emotionally charged systems' (emphasis added).[53] Corbin's interest in the methodological problems of practising 'cultural history' of this kind have led him most recently to reverse the bias by which all preceding history has been written, by selecting at random an entirely forgotten individual as the protagonist of his reconstituted history.[54] By experimenting, Corbin has recreated another Montaillou, a veritable Mediterranean of sensations nestling beneath the forests of the Perche. The creative capacity of the historian, working with scrupulously tended armouries of innumerable, inconsequential fact, is the *Annales'* still living legacy.

Notes

1   C. Crisp, *The Classic French Cinema 1930–1960*, Bloomington IN, Indiana University Press, 1997, pp. 3–7.
2   J. H. Hexter, 'Fernand Braudel and the *Monde Braudellien'*, *Journal of Modern History*, 1972, vol. 44; reprinted in *idem*, *On Historians: Reappraisals of Some of the Makers of Modern History*, London, Collins, 1979, p. 68.
3   F. Dosse, *New History in France: The Triumph of the Annales*, Urbana, University of Illinois, 1994, pp. 42–50 (first published as *L'histoire en miettes: Dès 'Annales' à la 'nouvelle histoire'*, Paris, La Découverte (Armillaire), 1987.
4   P. den Boer, *History as a Profession: The Study of History in France, 1818–1914*, Princeton NJ, Princeton University Press, 1998, p. 102; originally published as *Geschiedenis als Beroep: De professionalisering van de geschiedbeoefening in Frankrijk (1818–1914)*, Nijmegen, 1987.
5   C. Charle, 'Produire et diffuser les idées', in J-C. Ruano-Borbalan (ed.) *L'histoire aujourd'hui*, Paris, Éditions Sciences Humaines, 1999, p. 24.
6   H. Stuart Hughes, *Consciousness and Society: The Reorientation of European Social Thought 1890–1930*, New York, Knopf, 1959.
7   S. Kern, *The Culture of Time and Space 1880–1918*, Cambridge MA, Harvard University Press, 1983, ch. 1.
8   *Ibid.*, p. 16.
9   C. V. Langlois and C. Seignobos, *Introduction to the Study of History*, trans. G. G. Berry, 1898, PAris, Hachette et Cie, p. 8.

10 M. Siegel, 'Henri Berr's *Revue de synthèse historique*', *History and Theory*, 1970, vol. ix, 328.

11 F. Simiand, 'Méthode historique et science sociale', *Revue de synthèse historique*, 1903. The article was reprinted by *Annales* in 1960, vol. 15.1, pp. 83–119, as an example to a younger generation.

12 M. Bloch, *Memoirs of War, 1914–15*, trans. C. Fink, Cambridge, Cambridge University Press, 1988; A. Prost, *In the Wake of War: 'Les Anciens Combattants' and French Society*, Oxford, Berg Publishers, 1992; R. A. Nye, *Masculinity and Male Codes of Honor in Modern France*, Oxford, Oxford University Press, 1993, p. 228. In the articles reprinted in *Combats pour l'histoire*, Paris, Libraire Armand Colin, 1953, Febvre lambasted colleagues for faint-heartedness.

13 L. Febvre, 'The Origins of the French Reformation: A Badly-put Question?', in Peter Burke (ed.) *A New Kind of History from the Writings of Lucien Febvre*, London, Routledge and Kegan Paul, 1973, p. 88, originally published in the *Revue historique*, 1929, vol. 161.

14 For which see also above, p. 68.

15 Peter Burke, *The French Historical Revolution: The Annales School 1929–89*, Cambridge, Polity, 1990, p. 22.

16 *Ibid.*, pp. xxix–xxx.

17 M. Bloch, *French Rural History: An Essay on Its Basic Characteristics*, trans. Janet Sondheimer, London, Routledge and Kegan Paul, 1966, p. xxx.

18 *Ibid.*, pp. 246–7.

19 In 1940 Bloch was to see the defeat of France as in large part the defeat of its rural charm: R. O. Paxton, *French Peasant Fascism: Henry Dorgères's Greenshirts and the Crises of French Agriculture, 1929–1939*, Oxford, Oxford University Press, 1997, p. 177.

20 P. Burrin, *La France à l'heure allemande, 1940–1944*, Paris, Editions du Seuil, 1995, translated as *Living with Defeat. France under the German Occupation 1940–1944*, London, Edward Arnold, 1996.

21 These clandestine writings have been republished in M. Bloch, *Etrange défaite*, Paris, 1993; cf. C. Fink, *Marc Bloch: A Life in History*, Cambridge, Cambridge University Press, 1989, p. 280.

22 Burke (ed.) *New Kind of History*, chs 2, 5 and 8.

23 The Director of the foundation's social sciences division wrote in 1946 that 'In France, the outcome of the conflict and the choice between communism and democracy appears in its most acute form. It is a field of battle or a laboratory': Dosse, *New History in France*, p. 99 (using 'accused' for acute). In Britain the equivalent initiative came with the foundation of *Past and Present* in 1952 by a largely Marxist group of historians, for which see also below, p. 182.

24 Dosse, *New History in France*, pp. 99–103.

25 Cf. C. Lévi-Strauss, *Tristes Tropiques*, trans. J. and D. Weightman, London, Cape, 1973, p. 101 for a parallel statement by Lévi-Strauss in 1955.

26 The concept of region varied elastically across this range of works: R. Baehrel, *Une croissance: la basse Provence rurale*, Paris, SEVPEN, 1961; P. & H. Chaunu, *Séville et l'Atlantique, 1504–1650*, Paris, SEVPEN, 1955–9.

27 H. Stuart Hughes, *The Obstructed Path: French Social Thought in the Years of Desperation 1930–1960*, New York and London, Harper and Row, 1969, p. 63.

28 P. Braudel, 'Les origines intellectuelles de Fernand Braudel: un témoignage', *Annales E.S.C.*, 1992, vol. 47.

29 Cf. G. Duby, *History Continues*, Chicago, University of Chicago Press, 1994, p. 66, for the impact of structuralism on the *Annales* agenda.

30 Febvre's *A Geographical Introduction to History*, London, Kegan Paul, 1924, developed a 'possibilism' whereby geography could be modified by human action, and set

outer limits rather then determining outcomes. Febvre published his article on the term 'frontier' in Berr's *Revue de synthèse* in 1928.

31 *On History*, Chicago, University of Chicago Press, 1980, p. 32, first published 1969.

32 Ernest Labrousse's supervision of theses in this field was also critical, together with the adaptation of the techniques of 'serial history' to the study of religious and political behaviour in the work of Michel Vovelle and François Furet.

33 R. Rieffel, 'Les historiens, l'édition et les médias', in F. Bédarida (ed.) *L'Histoire et le métier d'historien en France 1945–1995*, Paris, Editions de la MSH, 1995, p. 65.

34 E. Le Roy Ladurie, *The Peasants of Languedoc*, Urbana, University of Illinois Press, 1974, p. 8.

35 Rieffel, 'Les historiens', p. 67.

36 *Ibid.*, p. 66.

37 R. Debray, *Le Pouvoir Intellectuel en France*, Paris, Ramsay, 1979.

38 Duby, *History Continues*, p. 50, for the decline of the doctorate as a vehicle of professional advancement by 1968.

39 *Ibid.*, pp. 108–14.

40 J. Ardagh, *France in the New Century: Portrait of a Changing Society*, London, Penguin, 2000, p. 356: on Lyons and the scope for trans-national regional cooperation.

41 The years 1965–75 were those in which the new history made its first marked impact on the English-speaking world, with articles by R. R. Davies (*History*, 1967) and W. H. Sewell (*History and Theory*, 1967) on each side of the Atlantic. Treatments in book form appeared from Stuart Hughes, *Obstructed Path*; G. Iggers, *New Directions in European Historiography*, Middletown CT, Wesleyan University Press, 1975; and an *Annales* 'paradigm' was identified by T. Stoianovich in *French Historical Method*, Ithaca NY, Cornell University Press, 1976. Individual articles from *Annales* were also gathered together in English translation from the early 1970s onwards in collections edited by Peter Earle; Peter Burke; Marc Ferro; and a sequence of volumes edited by Robert Forster and Orest Ranum.

42 P. Earle (ed.) *Essays in European Economic History, 1500–1800*, Oxford, Clarendon Press, 1974, Preface.

43 A similar centre devoted to public policy research on inflation was founded in Sao Paolo in 1987.

44 For which he received Gertrude Himmelfarb's approval in an otherwise stringent critique of the *Annales*; *The New History and the Old*, Cambridge MA, Belknap, 1987, citing Furet's Introduction to *In the Workshop of History* (French, 1981; English, 1984).

45 P. Nora (ed.) *Essais d'égo-histoire*, Paris, Gallimard, 1987.

46 J. Revel and L. Hunt (eds) *Histories: French Constructions of the Past*, New York; New Press, 1995.

47 Dosse, *New History in France*. The French title has history in 'crumbs': *L'histoire en miettes. Des Annales à la Nouvelle Histoires*, Paris, la Découverte, 1987.

48 Though the continuing relevance of Marc Bloch's commitment to comparative studies has recently been emphasised: M. Kammen, 'The Problem of American Exceptionalism: A Reconsideration', in his *In The Past Lane: Historical Perspectives on American Culture*, Oxford, Oxford University Press, 1997, p. 186.

49 G. Huppert, 'The *Annales* Experiment', in M. Bentley (ed.) *Companion to Historiography*, London, Routledge, 1997. The sense of an overcomplicated development is suggested by Peter Burke's wryly titled book *The French Historical Revolution: The Annales School, 1929–89*, Cambridge, Polity, 1990, which contains a 'Glossary' of 'The Language of *Annales*', including a number of the terms which came into use during the 1960s and later.

50 Duby, *History Continues*, p. vii; a translation of *L'histoire continue*, Paris, Odile Jacob, 1991.

51 P. Carrard, *Poetics of the New History: French Historical Discourse from Braudel to Chartier*, Baltimore, 1992, pp. 24–7.
52 A. Corbin, *The Lure of the Sea*, Harmondsworth, Penguin, 1995, originally published in French by Flammarion, Paris, p. vii.
53 Corbin, *Lure*, pp. 283, vii.
54 *Le monde retrouvé de Louis-François Pinagot, sur les traces d'un inconnu, 1798–1876*, 1998 now translated as *The Life of an Unknown: The Rediscovered World of a Clog Maker in Nineteenth-century France*, New York, Columbia University Press, 2001.

Further reading

Since one of the main aims of the *Annales* has been to raise historians' methodological self-consciousness, it is not surprising that key articles from the journal provided staging posts in the process by which a French journal came to re-shape historical practice outside France itself after the Second World War. Representative collections in translation include M. Ferro (ed.) *Social Historians in Contemporary France: Essays from 'Annales'*, New York, Harper and Row, 1972; P. Burke (ed.) *A New Kind of History From the Writings of Lucien Febvre*, London, Routledge and Kegan Paul, 1973; P. Earle (ed.) *Essays in European Economic History, 1500–1800*, Oxford, Clarendon Press, 1974. The scholarly world against which the *Annales* originally reacted has been thoroughly anatomised in P. den Boer, *History as a Profession: The Study of History in France, 1818–1914*, Princeton NJ, Princeton University Press (originally published in Dutch at Nijmegen, 1987), whilst the contemporary intellectual landscape is brilliantly covered by H. Stuart Hughes, *Consciousness and Society: The Reorientation of European Social Thought 1890–1930*, New York, Knopf, 1958. An important transitional journal is examined in M. Siegel, 'Henri Berr's *Revue de synthèse historique*', *History and Theory*, 1970, vol. ix, pp. 322–34. The establishment of the *Annales* as the hegemonic institutional influence in France itself is sardonically chronicled in F. Dosse, *New History in France: The Triumph of the Annales*, Urbana, University of Illinois, 1994 (first French edition, Paris, 1987). H. Stuart Hughes, *The Obstructed Path: French Social Thought in the Years of Desperation 1930–1960*, New York and London, Harper and Row, 1969, deals with the parallel course of intellectual history. T. Stoianovich, *French Historical Method*, Ithaca NY, Cornell University Press, 1976, identified a distinctive *Annales* 'paradigm'. J. H. Hexter affectionately parodied its geographical structuralism in 'Fernand Braudel and the Monde Braudellien', *Journal of Modern History*, 1972, vol. 44, pp. 480–539, reprinted in *On Historians: Reappraisals of some of the Makers of Modern History*, London, Collins, 1979, pp. 61–145. A similarly amused admiration is evident in the valuable synthesis by P. Burke, *The French Historical Revolution: The Annales School 1929–89*, Cambridge, Polity, 1990, written whilst the commemoration of the original French Revolution was seriously dividing opinion amongst historians in France itself. Biographies and memoirs exemplify a genre which has come to hold a more central place in latter-day French historical discussion. These include C. Fink, *Marc Bloch: A Life in History*, Cambridge, Cambridge University Press, 1989; G. Duby,

History Continues, Chicago, University of Chicago Press, 1994; F. Braudel, *On History*, Chicago, University of Chicago Press, 1980 (first French edition Paris, 1969). A wonderful compendium of extracts documents the shifting emphases of the *Annales* with a similar attention to the role of individuals: J. Revel and L. Hunt (eds) *Histories: French Constructions of the Past*, New York, New Press, 1995. Attention to the way in which *Annaliste* history was *written* has also recently intensified: P. Carrard, *Poetics of the New History: French Historical Discourse from Braudel to Chartier*, Baltimore, Johns Hopkins University Press, 1992.

Chapter 6

Social history in Germany

Peter Lambert

For a brief period in the mid-1970s, the triumphal progress of a new, social-scientific approach to writing history in the Federal Republic of Germany was widely heralded. At the head of the march, two young historians – Hans-Ulrich Wehler and Jürgen Kocka – based at the new university of Bielefeld were making confident strides into territories so far unexplored by German historians. Reference to them, to their close colleagues, and to their students as the 'Bielefeld school' was quickly adopted as a convenient short-hand for a rapidly growing body of work informed by shared convictions and aspirations. Here, at last, was a progressive and theoretically informed historiography which was simultaneously firmly anchored within the West German university system – a new paradigm which had supplanted the decaying but hitherto ubiquitous intellectual vegetation of statist and nationalist political history. Apologias for the German past had now given way to a stringent critique. Purportedly stagnant and isolated until the 1960s, German historiography now seemed both to be lively and to have 'returned to the West'. Where German historiography had been hostile to theory, the *Bielefelder* readily embraced it. Where historical agency had been accorded to individuals, it was now attached to impersonal forces and structures. Nostalgic, pessimistic anti-modernism gave way to a confident identification of modernity with progress. And this historiography seemed faithfully to have reflected abrupt departures in German politics, society and culture.

A quarter of a century on, the story can no longer be told so simply. It is tempting to suggest that the *observation* of trends in (West) German historiography has itself undergone a paradigm shift. What had appeared to be a new orthodoxy, thoroughly to be welcomed, now seems to have enjoyed only a fleeting moment's dominance, and to have deserved its downfall. There are three reasons for this. First, the arrival of the *Bielefelder* did not mark the disappearance of the older traditions of German historical scholarship. Purveyors of a nationalist historiography of high politics and of the state merely ducked their heads under the parapets of ivory towers in old universities, waiting for better times.[1] Indeed, from the 1980s onward, changes in the domestic political climate and international position of the Federal Republic of Germany (FRG) were to encourage a revival of their confidence and public presence.[2] Second, the *Bielefelder* rapidly found themselves outflanked, as it were, on their left. Third, some of their critics from both right and left – but in a sense even some of the *Bielefelder* and their students themselves – have begun to argue that the 'new' social history in fact had 'brown roots'.

'Brown', in this connection, means Nazi! Attention has, in other words, shifted from the immediate context within which critical social history emerged in the 1960s and 1970s. A longer and disconcerting perspective on its development has been suggested. But how can the emphatically left-leaning, liberal and social-democratic, anti-nationalist and anti-Nazi historians associated with the Bielefeld school simultaneously have carried over methodologies and practices developed by Nazis and their collaborators? On the face of it, the question seems perplexing, even pernicious. The answer leads through the *Bielefelder*'s teachers, and their teachers' teachers, to developments within German historiography after the First World War.

The argument runs like this. Social history was firmly established in West Germany in the course of the 1950s and 1960s by a network of already established scholars who then smoothed the *Bielefelder*'s path into academic careers. These older historians, including Hermann Aubin, Otto Brunner, Theodor Schieder and – above all – Werner Conze, were the real innovators in the construction of structuralist social history, and had made it acceptable to the wider community of German historians. However, they had forged their careers before 1945, as practitioners of *Volksgeschichte* ('folk-' or 'race-history'). Much or all of their work before 1945 had been contaminated by an ultra-nationalist, racialist vocabulary. But the ease with which they cleansed their own texts of the offending language after 1945 highlights the essentially scholarly quality of the content and still more of the methodology of their research and writing. *Volksgeschichte* had constituted a coherent and cohesive challenge to the dominant statist paradigm. In particular, it had encapsulated an openness to interdisciplinarity unprecedented in German historiography, and had programmatically advanced an attempt at understanding societies in their 'totality' and over the long term. Historians must comprehend the 'inner' workings of the societies they studied. This agenda, in turn, dictated a massively expanded definition of the historian's sources. Altogether, the questions *Volksgeschichte* posed, its techniques and its raw materials, gave it at the very least an innovative potential. Though its lasting value is half-concealed by the words in which its concepts were couched, *Volksgeschichte* is thus an integral part of the history of modern social historiography in Germany, not only in terms of overlap in personnel, but also intellectually. *Volks*-history, indeed, began the onslaught on the staid and state-centred orthodoxies of German historism which the critical social historians of the last third of the twentieth century merely continued. As Otto Brunner had put it in 1938, 'the concept of the people [*Volkstum*]' as defined by folklore and tradition moved to centre-stage; 'not the state' but 'the people becomes the prime directive'. Historians whose work was informed by it were alert to 'the smallest of everyday occurrences'.³ Thus, not just the state itself, but relations between states, the study of diplomatic papers, wars, great events themselves, were all knocked off their shared pedestal. All these characteristics parallel those of the early *Annales*.⁴ Only in the politics of their practitioners did the two intellectual movements part company.

What had caused the advent of this 'history from the perspective of the *Volk*', and what had propelled it into prominence? Hermann Aubin, in a retrospective account, had located its birth in a moment of 'dreadful awakening' at the disastrous end of the First World War. At that point, 'Reich-Germans had been torn out of the security of the nation-state which they thought had been realised in the foundation of the Reich in 1871'. As the familiar 'system of states' had collapsed, the consciousness of community in the *Volkstum* had 'gained new force'. Its 'essence' lay in 'heredity, language and historical experience', and not in the artificial borders which were a legacy of dynastic power-politics.⁵ The rise of new states in eastern Europe, dictated by the victorious powers and legitimated partly by the principle of national self-determination, partly with reference to ethnicity, gave this conceptual shift an added urgency. *Volk* was now to be mobilised in the contestation of the Versailles settlement. The object was not a return to the borders of 1914, but an altogether more ambitious re-ordering of Europe based on the premise that *all* Germans belonged in a single, expanded Reich. From the 1920s onward, the Austrian historian Heinrich Ritter von Srbik propounded a *gesamtdeutsch* (whole-German) view of history as a means of transcending old historiographical-cum-political battle-lines. By refusing the divisive legacy of nineteenth-century state-formation, Srbik made a crucial if indirect contribution to the advance of *Volksgeschichte*. But historians' hyper-nationalist ambitions did not end with the incorporation into the Reich of territories inhabited predominantly by Germans and whose population was, like that of the 'Sudetenland' and of Austria, denied the right to national self-determination after the First World War. Evidence of specific patterns of settlement and of the cultivation of the land were taken to be evidence of an originally German conquest from nature of still wider lands. To these also, irrespective of the ethnicity of their present inhabitants, *Volkshistoriker* laid claim on Germany's behalf. Thus *Raum* (space) ranked alongside *Volk* as a key concept, giving *Volks*-history an over-arching identity. Most sought it in the east, and *Ostforschung* functioned as an historiographical spearhead of the *Drang nach Osten*.⁶ A smaller group of historians turned their research to the west (*Westforschung*), articulating similar designs on Belgian and French territories and using the same research techniques and ideological constructs.⁷

Encouraged by a handful of grandees among already established professional historians, notably the Berlin historian and archive-director Albert Brackmann, a young generation of German nationalist historians began to employ *Volk* as an organising concept. Strikingly, many of them were born around or beyond the borders of the Reich. Innovative impulses, as the case of the *Annales* suggests, do tend to come not from the geographical cores, but from the peripheries of national cultures. *Volks*-historians' sensibilities, however, were more particularly informed by their experiences of border struggles in ethnically mixed areas: in the Baltic territories, in territories disputed with Poland, in the Sudetenland and in Alsace-Lorraine, for instance. Their work typically entailed the study of demography and human geography, and accorded unprecedented significance to the peasantry. The new interests demanded research techniques which were beyond the repertoire of German professional historiography. Historians therefore forged links with geographers and cartographers, demographers and sociologists, ethnologists and folklorists. The emergence of *Volks*-history betrays a marked resemblance – in terms both of ideological affinities and of its causes – to the wider transformation of the German right which culminated in Nazism.[8] Like *Volks*-history, and in contrast to the traditional German right, Nazism entertained no particular veneration of the state, lauded rural life, was associable with a generational shift and possessed a leadership within which men born in border regions or outside the Reich were disproportionately strongly represented. The growth in *Volks*-history accelerated from around 1930 (the year of the Nazis' national electoral breakthrough), and again under the auspices of the Nazi regime itself. While the job market for historians in the universities stagnated in the Third Reich, new and generously funded research institutes mushroomed. Young historians working within them became valued members of the Nazis' functional elite.[9] In mapping out demographic patterns of east-central Europe, they contributed to planning Nazi population policy.

Volks-history had at least some of the hallmarks of a new 'disciplinary matrix', but it did not destroy the statist paradigm. Where it gained ground, it rarely did so at the direct expense of the older emphasis on political history. It flourished in a handful of border universities – at Königsberg and at the (re-)Germanised University of Straßburg, for instance – while it had little impact at Berlin. It dominated the contents of journals like *Jomsburg*, newly founded in the Third Reich, and of the history teachers' journal *Vergangenheit und Gegenwart* (Past and Present), but was accorded little space in the pages of the *Historische Zeitschrift*, which remained the principal organ of professional German historians.[10] Some strident programmatic expositions of the supremacy of *Volksgeschichte* as against archaic, inadequate statist history notwithstanding, the two approaches coexisted comfortably more often than they clashed. There was no real debate as to the respective merits of their perspectives and methodologies. In part, this was because advocates of both positions were determined that there should not be one. They may have been nationalists of rather different kinds, but German nationalism was nevertheless common to both.

So, too, was widespread collaboration with the Nazi regime. Walter Frank, Director of the Nazi 'Reich Institute for the History of the New Germany', though an advocate of ideologically committed scholarship and initiator of purges from positions of influence within the discipline of some eminent older historians, fell far short of his ambition of transforming German historiography. Among his victims were his former teacher Hermann Oncken and Friedrich

Meinecke, who had hired Frank as an editorial assistant on the *Historische Zeitschrift*. Significantly, neither was purged primarily because of the history he wrote. The point was that both had supported the Weimar Republic. Frank found room for statist history *and* for *Volksgeschichte* in his academic empire. Where he could not mediate between unusually truculent adherents to the two camps, he buried their differences.[11] In any case, he was himself incapable of arriving at an intellectual judgment between them. Other young historians, whether because they were less vindictive than Frank, or simply because their teachers had been traditionalist right-wing opponents of Weimar democracy, avoided inter-generational disputes which would have entailed an appearance of disloyalty to their sometime patrons. Finally, practitioners of *Volksgeschichte* like Werner Conze also wrote in the idiom and on the classic subjects of political history. Implicitly, Conze was suggesting that the old history and the new were mutually complementary.

Rooted in the experiences of war and defeat, infected by the cultural pessimism of neo-conservative circles in Weimar Germany, and tending increasingly towards a racial interpretation of history, *Volksgeschichte* was profoundly anti-democratic. Its techniques may have been 'modern'; its content was not. Those least touched by modernity – isolated rural communities of 'Germans' in east-central Europe – were both its subjects and its heroes. The innovations with which it has been credited were too patchy and narrow to amount to a new methodology. Under its auspices, interdisciplinarity was more often regressive than progressive, since its alliances were broadly with racist deformations of other disciplines.[12] The keywords it employed – *Volk*, *Raum* and *Boden* – were conceptually too hazy to function as cornerstones of a coherent intellectual edifice. Comparison with the early *Annales* overlooks Mark Bloch's dissection of historiographical trends across the Rhine, and in any case yields only superficial resemblances.[13] Much of *Volksgeschichte* does not warrant description as *social* history at all. Very few of its exemplars are worth reading today for their inherent value to scholarship; most ended in an intellectual as well as a political cul-de-sac. Their chief interest lies rather in their contributions to the planning of the Nazi regime's murderous demographic policies;[14] their 'total history' is better described as *totalitarian* history. In its original form, it was to survive the end of the regime only in nooks and crannies of West German academe.

Practitioners of *Volks*-history regrouped under the banner of 'structural history'. Their subjects and methods were often as clearly characterised by seamless continuity as their language was by an abrupt shift. The purposes underpinning their research, however, had undergone some real alterations. *Westforschung* was a dead letter. However, the onset of the Cold War furnished a context in which anti-Slav prejudice, now subsumed under anti-communism and so acceptable to the West, could survive among old hands of *Ostforschung*. But sometimes the Cold War mentalities and revisionist ambitions of the West German political establishment, rather than those of historians, presented a problem.

Thus, in 1951, Theodor Schieder accepted a contract from the FRG's Ministry for Expellees and Refugees to oversee the creation and publication of a collection of documents on Germans removed from east-central Europe in and after 1945. The ministry secured a very wide distribution of the resultant publications, in particular of a translation into English, hoping to delegitimise the postwar European settlement. Schieder and his team wanted to round off their series with a concluding volume locating the expulsion of Germans in a broader context of forced demographic changes in European history, and in particular to relate it to Nazi population policies. The ministry saw that the editors' proposal threatened to undermine the political impact of the earlier volumes, and the conclusion never appeared. Schieder and his team had not buckled under the authorities' pressure, but their endeavours to complete the project independently of the ministry fell foul of a complication. Since they had themselves been implicated in the authorship of Nazi population plans, they found themselves uncovering their own traces in the historical record of criminality.[15] While they were prepared in principle to subordinate a contemporary political agenda to the dictates of historical truth, and to engage critically with Nazi crimes, they were not prepared to encounter their own past. And it is perhaps the besetting sin of the founders of social history in the FRG that they did not themselves systematically reflect on the relationship between their past and their present practices as historians.

Schieder himself promoted social history – but never wrote any. It was his colleague Werner Conze who was the prime mover both as an 'academic entrepreneur', in the institutionalisation of social history in the FRG, and in shaping it intellectually. In 1957 he was appointed to an established chair at Heidelberg where (with Erich Maschke, another former *Volks*-historian) he created an Institute for Economic and Social History. In the same year, he played a pivotal part in establishing a Working Group for Modern Social History.[16] He gave social history – which he argued was conceptually 'too narrow' – a peculiar profile as 'structural history', embedded sociology within it, and conflated it with 'constitutional history'.[17] Conze and his collaborators were concerned to do nothing that might ruffle the feathers of conventional political historians. Dalliance with social history of any kind still stirred up uncomfortable memories of the 'Lamprecht dispute'.[18] Yet avoidance of controversy was rendered possible by dint of the fact that Gerhard Ritter, chief representative of the historiographical old guard in the early years of the FRG, had formally declared the discipline open to extension through the absorption of sociological influences – so long as generalisations were not ventured at the expense of concern with the particular and individual.[19] Conze's version of structural history met Ritter's criteria to perfection. He advertised it as an expansion of the horizons of political history, not as an alternative. Structures, for him, delineated the room for manoeuvre available to the individual historical actor, but never determined any particular course of action. It followed that structural history was no more a challenge to the importance of a history of events than it was to historist views of individual agency: structures simply furnished the context within which these should be understood. Nor was Ritter likely to suspect reds lurking under structural history's bed. Conze's structural history was emphatically anti-socialist, played the virtues of domestic order off against the vices of revolution, and constituted a search for ways in which conservative values could be preserved under conditions of modernity.[20]

Conze himself inspired new work on the family, on agrarian history, on industrialisation, on political parties and even on the labour movement. Thus a remarkable diversification of research topics, pursued in the name of uncovering the structural transformations of society since the eighteenth century, took place in the absence of attacks on political historians and without a major controversy about methodology. But prospects of a conflict-free evolution of the discipline rapidly proved to be illusory. No sooner had Conze's version of social history as 'structural history' gained its 'victory', Thomas Etzemüller points out, than its 'downfall' began.[21] Its success was attributable to the congenial context afforded by the conservatism of the political culture of the FRG in the 1950s; it did not survive the leftward shift of the 1960s. Society was changing. The newly established form of social history failed to keep up with the changes. Conze and his colleagues may have opened the gates of German historical scholarship to social history. But where they had imagined an influx of new craftsmen whose work would build on the old edifice, what ensued was a hostile invasion, intent on destroying much of the old, and rebuilding with new materials and different purposes. An explicitly *critical* social-scientific interpretation emerged to challenge and supplant the entire nationalist tradition of German historiography.

If the promotion of 1950s social history had *facilitated* a more radical and profound change (unintentionally, by dint of 'softening up' and expanding the national disciplinary definition of what constituted 'normal science'), that change was actively *encouraged* by influences of a very different order. Historians exiled by the Nazi regime had begun to visit the FRG. Their lecture tours introduced history students to a social-scientific US historiography which drew on the modernisation theories of Talcott Parsons, for instance, but also on Max Weber's sociology. Weber's ideas were thus 'returned' to Germany after their virtual exile by the Third Reich. What drew students to the émigrés? First, student numbers were undergoing unprecedented expansion. With expansion, the social composition of the student body became more varied. The usefulness of history became a pressing concern for the new intake. More than ever, the agenda of statist historism seemed archaic; social history promised to furnish students with skills pertinent to a society itself undergoing modernisation. But the indigenous version of social history pursued by Conze and Schieder was too static, and still too troubled by modernity to appeal. In particular, it had failed seriously to address Nazism and its relationship with the authoritarian traditions of the German state. Students arriving at university in the 1960s constituted the first generation to have been socialised wholly in postwar Germany, and they evinced a willingness to ask questions about the Third Reich which their predecessors had fought shy of raising. As the Cold War gave way to détente, anti-communism ceased to function as an effective obstacle to completing the process of de-Nazification. When Willi Brandt, who in 1969 became the first Social Democrat to lead a German government since 1930, announced his intention to give real content to a parliamentary-democratic constitution by democratising German *society*, he struck a chord. Finally, US student and protest movements served to spur on radicalisation in Germany. Younger, educated Germans could now 'return to the West' without turning into Cold Warriors.

Fritz Fischer, though he worked on orthodox diplomatic and literary sources and on foreign policy, did much to clear a way forward. Fischer's work broke a West German taboo by arguing that Germany's war aims in 1914–18 had been so ambitious as to bear comparison with those of the Nazis, and that the outbreak of the First World War had been desired, even planned, by the German elites. For them, foreign policy adventurism provided a means of escape from impending domestic crisis. Where Gerhard Ritter, the last great exponent of the historist paradigm, notoriously proclaimed Nazism to have been 'an accident in the works' of German history, Fischer was locating the Third Reich at the logical end of a line of continuity.

Fischer himself, and the school which rapidly gathered around him, were at first hounded by the nationalist historical establishment. But the attempt to censor or silence them failed. Their case rested on a mass of evidence, painstakingly referenced, so that pinning charges of unscholarly conduct on them was always going to be difficult for their opponents. The latter were obliged to take them on in public debate. Where student audiences in the interwar years had howled left-wing historians down, their 1960s counterparts took the Fischerites' side. Fischer's own work increasingly incorporated observations on the links between the domestic and foreign policies of Imperial Germany, and so helped to promote the interest in social history on which the mature *Sonderweg* thesis was to rely.

The fundamental, unifying tenet of the new critical approach to history was the identification of a German *Sonderweg*, a peculiar and aberrant German path to modernity. In rendering it visible, and showing that it had culminated in the calamities of Nazism, historians made their own contribution to a 'return to the West'. British, French and US national histories were held up as models against which Germany's was measured and found wanting. These three had (allegedly) undergone 'bourgeois revolutions' which had secured the primacy in politics of representative parliamentary institutions and removed the arbitrariness of monarchs. As a result, they had created the necessary conditions for industrialisation, capitalism and democratisation to go hand-in-hand. In Germany, by contrast, 'bourgeois revolution' had failed – spectacularly so in 1848. Defeated and demoralised, the bourgeoisie had retreated from politics. The aristocracy, still possessing semi-feudal power on the lands, held on to its positions of dominance in Imperial Germany's governments, civil service and army officer corps.

It did so right through the period of Germany's industrialisation. Adult men might vote for political parties in *Reichstag* elections, but the Kaiser could and did ignore them, and appoint unelected aristocrats to the principal ministries of state.

Thus, from around 1900 (when Germany's economy overtook Britain's), the leading industrial power in Europe was led by a class whose power *should* have been broken. Assailed by democratising forces, it had sustained itself artificially – by forging an 'alliance of the elites', buying the loyalty of the bourgeoisie through offering unswerving support against the emerging labour movement, protection and guaranteed markets for the products of German industry, and especially by seeking to create the dumping grounds called 'Empire' for its excess products. To this end, the elites whipped up aggressive, expansionist nationalism. Simultaneously, they sought to deflect grievances of the lower middle class and peasantry on to purported 'enemies of the Fatherland' within Germany – internationalist, Marxist Social Democrats; ultramontane Roman Catholics; Jews. Thus an exclusivist national unity was maintained through 'social imperialism' and a strategy of 'negative integration', binding some social groups to itself by constructing others as alien threats. Mass participation in politics could not altogether be prevented, but it could be channelled in directions favourable to the elites. Thus the elites sponsored pressure-group politics, whose ultimate purpose was to persuade citizens that their interests would be served better by direct appeal to the throne than through party politics. This amounted to a highly complex strategy of elite domination, which was simultaneously also increasingly unstable.

As the early engagement with modernisation theorists, but also with Marxism, suggests, Wehler, Kocka and many of their contemporaries liked to think of their work as being *driven* by theory. And, far from displaying any wariness of interdisciplinarity, they came to term their work 'history as critical social science'. Thus, Jürgen Kocka's exploration of the impact of the 1914–18 war on the German state and society began with a Marxist model of class society, proposing a movement from the inherent opposition of the objective interests of the bourgeoisie and proletariat in a class society, through the emergence of tensions which grew as these classes became conscious of the discrepancies in their interests, to fundamental conflict between them. But he used the model in a way that was 'removed from the context of a Marxian philosophy of history, and complemented by new findings in conflict research'. Still more specifically, it was a 'Weberian' employment of Marxism, not exactly in order to test hypotheses against historical evidence, but to construct 'a model which then served as an instrument for historical understanding by permitting the description and explanation of the variable "distance" between model and reality' to be measured against a yardstick of 'historical reality'.[22]

Wehler's path-breaking study of Imperial Germany – first published in Germany in 1973, the year in which Kocka's book had first appeared – was, he later claimed, intended to 'advance hypotheses' in order to 'stimulate further critical reflection'; his determination 'not to evade critical questions' encouraged him to essay hypotheses irrespective of whether or not they were 'meticulously substantiated'.[23] But in fact his history of an authoritarian society was laid out as a sequence of scientific laws, each followed by its own proofs. Wehler laid himself open to the objection that his authorial voice was so authoritative as to be stentorian. In depicting a ring-fenced elite system of elite rule, he had created a totalising and hermetically sealed explanatory framework. It did not, perhaps, bode well for his receptivity to the subsequent development of alternative approaches.

The *Bielefelder* had begun with a combination of programmatic statements of an intent to supplant individualising and event-fixated, conservative and nationalist historism on the one hand, and historical studies functioning not least as exemplars of how the programme could be put into practice on the other. Kocka's book on the impact of 'total war' had, he emphasised, been designed explicitly 'to demonstrate ... the superiority of theory-orientated history over plain narrative'.[24] The challengers were highly self-conscious about their own aspirations to destroy the remnants of the old 'normal science' and themselves to establish the new. They therefore called on Kuhn's name and conceptual categories almost as if they were magic words. Thus, in 1979, Wehler characterised the previous two decades as having been distinguished by 'open competition between rival interpretations' which had been 'symptoms of a paradigm shift'. By the time of writing, however, Wehler appeared to suggest that the paradigm had indeed shifted. 'Social and economic history are firmly established. The noise of battle-cries shouted in programmatic statements has therefore abated. In its stead, research has got underway'. Wehler fortuitously overlooked Kuhn's refusal to identify a paradigm shift with an improvement. He and his colleagues were brim full of faith in the progressive forward march of historiography and of history itself. Wehler drew on Kuhn rhetorically, in order to propagate the potential of his own version of history, to maximise its distinctiveness and, at least implicitly, to help establish it as the new normal science.[25] Yet he did *not* pretend that 'history as social science' was or should become the sole variant of the discipline within West Germany. On the contrary, he welcomed a variety of approaches – at least in principle, and so long as they were mutually tolerant. His recognition both of the fact and of the desirability of a plurality of scholarly communities, methodologies and agendas seems incompatible with his simultaneous proclamation of a paradigm shift. However, Wehler asserted that it was the very act of prising open the illiberal, intolerant, anti-socialist and anti-theoretical, closed system of German historiography that constituted a paradigm shift. Accepting that one could think about history in many ways, not one, entailed a more fundamental redefinition of the discipline than a mere substitution of one sub-species of history by another.

The Bielefeld school enhanced its claims through a detailed engagement with past positions of German historiography.[26] In the act of apprehending the old paradigm (as well as recovering mavericks who lay outside its fold), they reinforced their case for being regarded as a new, cohesive and viable force in advancing historical study. The ever-cautious proponents of the earlier 'structural history' had ostentatiously garbed themselves in the robes of Rankean source-criticism in order to make their appearance the more acceptable in the eyes of conventional political historians. The *Bielefelder*, by contrast, challenged even these fundamental assumptions about the uncontestable status of hermeneutics as the key to 'understanding' the past. Individual historical actors in past societies were incapable of grasping the wider structures to which they were subordinate. How could they do so? Structuralism had not yet been invented! The documents they left behind were therefore essentially naive, and historians whose sole dependency was upon them were trapped by their limitations, doomed to replicate their naivety. Theory alone allowed the historian to comprehend the real course of history. How abstract, 'vague, impoverished in its content and formal' had the character of merely 'structural history' been in this regard! For – again in stark contrast to structur*al* historians, the structural*ist* critical historians believed that structures *determined* individuals' decisions and actions. Narrations of individuals, the 'choices' they made (or rather seemed to make) and the resultant events, were all well and good. But to begin with them would be 'absurd'. Historians who did so condemned themselves to treating only superficialities, since the structures they neglected were what really mattered, and could alone account for long-term stability and processes of change alike.[27]

The critical social history, then, did have some roots in structural history. That was inevitable. Where else was a budding social historian in West Germany to find willing and competent supervision? But, while there certainly were significant continuities between *Volks*-history and structural history, there were none between *Volks*-history and critical historical social science. Structural history had, for instance, maintained the close connection with geography forged by *Volks*-historians, and gone on using *Raum* (if not the more specific idea, inextricably linked to Nazism, of *Lebensraum* – living space) as an organising principle. The Bielefeld school used no such categories, and the link with geography was broken. It had not grown from 'brown roots'. As Thomas Welskopp has argued, 'on the level of central concepts ... no continuous genealogical line may be drawn' from *Volks*-history to critical social history.

Critical social historians took issue both with orthodox political historians and with structural historians intellectually. It is to the intellectual rather than the moral criticisms made of them that we should now turn. First, it has been noted that the *Bielefelder* were not as rigorous in their structural determinism as they liked to imagine. A gap opened between their programmatic statements and the histories they wrote. Wehler's account of the German Empire in fact told two parallel stories: one of structures, the other of Bismarck's manipulative politics. Thus Wehler had found no practical solution to the puzzle of what role to accord the individual in history.[28] Second, the *Sonderweg* thesis was really just an inversion of older historiographical adages about the superiority of a

'German path' over the path followed in the West.[29] Third, and as a result, German history remained the basic focal point of research. Comparisons with the West were made in order to seek out differences.

From an early point, Wehler and Kocka had identified comparative history and work on the German bourgeoisie as research desiderata. These gaps began rapidly to be filled. But the manner in which the new work was produced, and the results it yielded, did not conform to the 'mopping-up' operations typical of the expansion of 'normal science'. Paradoxically, the most powerful and direct assault on critical social history so far to have been mounted came from two British neo-Marxist historians. Working within a comparativist framework and on the bourgeoisie in particular, declaring themselves on 'fundamental issues' to be in the 'camp' of West German critical social historians, David Blackbourn and Geoff Eley tore into the *Sonderweg* model.[30] It was, they argued, presaged on assumptions about 'bourgeois revolution' which were unwarrantable and a Western normality which was a chimera. Thus they highlighted, for instance, survivals of aristocratic influence and pre-democratic politics in Britain into the twentieth century. A 'bourgeois revolution' of the kind supposed by proponents of the *Sonderweg* thesis to have characterised the West was nowhere to be found, while pre-1914 Germany had in fact undergone a 'silent bourgeois revolution' in its economy, society and culture. Blackbourn's and Eley's views had been shaped by radical challenges to the Whig interpretation of British history, whose basic tenets had been unthinkingly adopted by the *Bielefelder*. One national variant of left-wing social history thus exposed the complacencies of another.[31] And, in general, as studies on the German bourgeoisie undertaken within and beyond the circles of the *Bielefelder* proliferated, so they became harder to contain within the Bielefeld paradigm.[32]

The reaction to complacent historiographical 'Whiggishness' and smug belief in the progressive unfolding of British history was accompanied by a broader scepticism about the optimism of modernisation theory. Another West German historian, Detlev Peukert, argued that modernity was an ambiguous condition which had a 'dark side' and was associable not only with progress but also with 'pathologies'. He argued that the collapse of the Weimar Republic and the Nazi seizure of power could be explained in relation to the *weakness* of the old elites, not to the strength the *Bielefelder* had imputed to them; Weimar Germany had suffered not from backwardness, but from a 'crisis of classical modernity'. Like Kocka, Peukert had drawn heavily on Max Weber, but where Kocka had used Weber's writings as allies in his own advocacy of modernisation, Peukert detected a critque of modernity in them.[33] Here, changes in historiography were once more reflecting changes in West German politics and society. By the mid-1970s, the ruling Social Democratic-Liberal coalition government, with which the *Bielefelder* were identifiable, was running out of steam. At the same time, mushrooming of citizens' initiatives, and women's and green groups were signalling a transformation of the German Left. It acquired historiographical counterparts: histories of everyday life (*Alltagsgeschichte*) and a new cultural history. In the more pluralist historical profession they had hoped for, the *Bielefelder* have frequently been on the back foot, obliged to respond to other people's agendas. Nevertheless, they have managed to modify the *Sonderweg* thesis, and in its modified form, it continues to appeal internationally and to some of the most influential historians – Ian Kershaw among them – of modern Germany.[34]

Commentators have latterly lined up to diminish or at least to relativise all sorts of the critical social historians' achievements and breaks with the past practices of their discipline. For Thomas Etzemüller, 'In fact, there was no paradigm shift from traditional to critical historiography, though "Bielefeld" tried to stylise history that way'. The 1960s critical history of society was rooted in 1950s structural history; the transition from the latter to the former was 'smooth'. But his conclusion is too confusing to get us very far. The shift was like that experienced in 'most revolutions': 'only small – though decisive – parts were changed'. If the change was indeed 'revolutionary', then why does the advent of 'Bielefeld' fail to pass the tests of a paradigm shift? And even if the changes really were 'small', is it not enough that they were simultaneously also 'decisive'? Thomas Welskopp, on record as regarding the critical history of society as possessing the hallmarks of a 'disciplinary matrix' to an especially marked degree, also denies its emergence the status its own exponents had laid claim to: the arrival of the critical history of society emphatically did not constitute a paradigm shift at all.[35] Perhaps they have set the standards for qualification as a paradigm shift too high. If the breakthrough of the Bielefeld school failed to meet them, few scholarly communities – if any – have succeeded. But, if the sights are set lower, and if it may be admitted that *any* revolution will be less than comprehensive, entail elements of contradiction, leave lines of continuity unbroken in some directions and yet break them in others, we have not reduced all revolutions to evolutions. Measured by these less exacting criteria, the change wrought by critical social history in West Germany still seems dramatic and enduring.

Notes

1   Wolfgang Weber, 'The Long Reign and Final Fall of the German Conception of History: A Historical-Sociological View', *Central European History*, 1986, vol. 2, pp. 385–95.
2   See R. J. Evans, *In Hitler's Shadow: West German Historians and the Attempt to Escape from the Nazi Past*, London, I. B. Tauris, 1989; S. Berger, 'Historians and Nation-building in Germany after Reunification', *Past and Present*, 1995, vol. 148, pp. 187–222.
3   O. Brunner, 'Österreichs Weg zum Großdeutschen Reich', *Deutsches Archiv für Landes- und Volksforschung*, 1938, vol. 2, pp. 519–28; here, p. 526.
4   Cf. above, p. 80ff.
5   Hermann Aubin, cit. after Willi Oberkrome, *Volksgeschichte. Methodische Innovation und völkische Ideologisierung in der deutschen Geschichtswissenschaft 1918–1945*, Göttingen, Vandenhoeck & Ruprecht, 1993, p. 22.

6 M. Burleigh, *Germany Turns Eastwards. A Study of Ostforschung in the Third Reich*, Cambridge, Cambridge University Press, 1988.

7 P. Schöttler, 'Die historische "Westforschung" zwischen "Abwehrkamp" und territorialer Offensive', in *idem* (ed.) *Geschichtsschreibung als Legitimationswissenschaft 1918–1945*, Frankfurt a.M., Suhrkamp, 1999, pp. 204–62.

8 Cf. P. Fritzsche, *Germans into Nazis*, Cambridge MA and London, Harvard University Press, 1988.

9 M. Fahlbusch, *Wissenschaft im Dienst der nationalsozialistischen Politik? Die 'Volksdeutschen Forschungsgemeinschaften' von 1931–1945*, Baden-Baden, Nomos, 1999.

10 On the foundation and early role of the *HZ*, see above, p. 27.

11 H. Heiber, *Walter Frank und sein Reichsinstitut für die Geschichte des Neuen Deutschland*, Stuttgart 1966.

12 For sociology, see J. Z. Müller, *The Other God that Failed: Hans Freyer and the Deradicalization of German Conservatism*, Princeton, Princeton University Press, 1987; for folklore, J. R. Dow and H. Lixfeld (eds) *The Nazification of an Academic Discipline. Folklore in the Third Reich*, Bloomington, Indiana University Press, 1994; for geography and cartography, G. H. Herb, *Under the Map of Germany. Nationalism and Propaganda 1918–1945*, London, Routledge, 1997.

13 For correctives to superficial comparisons, see P. Schöttler, 'Marc Bloch as a Critic of Historiographical Nationalism in the Interwar Years', in S. Berger, M. Donovan and K. Passmore (eds) *Writing National Histories: Western Europe since 1800*, London, Routledge, 1999, pp. 125–36; *idem*, 'Die intellektuelle Rheingrenze. Wie lassen sich die französischen *Annales* und die NS-*Volksgeschichte* vergleichen?', in C. Conrad and S. Conrad (eds) *Die Nation Schreiben: Geschichtswissenschaft im internationalen Vergleich*, Göttingen, Vandenhoeck & Ruprecht, 2002, pp. 271–95.

14 See G. Aly, *Macht – Geist – Wahn. Kontinuitäten deutschen Denkens*, Berlin, Argon, 1997, esp. pp. 153ff.

15 T. Etzemüller, *Sozialgeschichte als politische Geschichte. Werner Conze und die Neuorientierung der westdeutschen Geschichtswissenschaft nach 1945*, Munich, R. Oldenbourg, 2001, pp. 319–22.

16 W. Schulze, *Deutsche Geschichtswissenschaft nach 1945*, 1989, 2nd edn, Munich, Deutscher Taschenbuchverlag, 1993, pp. 254ff.

17 Etzemüller, *Sozialgeschichte*, pp. 130, 161.

18 Cf. pp. 41–2 above (Chapter 3).

19 G. Ritter, 'Gegenwärtige Lage und Zukunftsaufgaben deutscher Geschichtswissenschaft', *Historische Zeitschrift*, 1950, vol. 170, pp. 1–22.

20 Etzemüller, *Sozialgeschichte*, pp. 232–6 and 278ff.

21 Etzemüller, *Sozialgeschichte*, pp. 310 and (in an English-language abstract) 359.

22 J. Kocka, *Facing Total War. German Society 1914–1918*, Leamington Spa, Berg, 1984, pp. 8, 1, 168.

23 Translated as H.-U. Wehler, *The German Empire 1871–1918*, Leamington Spa, Berg, 1985.

24 Kocka, *Total War*, p. 2.

25 Wehler, 'Zur Lage der Geschichtswissenschaft in der Bundesrepublik 1949–1979', first published 1979 and reprinted in *idem*, *Historische Wissenschaften und Geschichtsschreibung. Studien zu Aufgaben und Traditionen deutscher Geschichtswissenschaft*, Göttingen, Vandenhoeck & Ruprecht, 1980, pp. 13–41. Here, p. 22 for the initial discussion of Kuhn; quotations p. 33. I have preferred my own translation, though the essay is available in English as 'Historiography in Germany Today' in J. Habermas (ed.) *Observations on the 'Spiritual Situation of the Age': Contemporary German Perspectives*, translated and with an introduction by Andrew Buchwalter, London and Cambridge MA, MIT Press, 1984, pp. 221–59.

26 H.-U. Wehler (ed.) *Deutsche Historiker*, 9 vols, Göttingen, Vandenhoeck & Ruprecht, 1971–82.

27 J. Kocka, *Sozialgeschichte*, Göttingen, Vandenhoeck & Ruprecht, 1977, 2nd edn 1986, pp. 76, 79, 82; and the discussion in T. Welskopp, 'Grenzüberschreitungen. Deutsche Sozialgeschichte zwischen den dreißiger und den siebziger Jahren des 20. Jahrhunderts', in C. Conrad and S. Conrad (eds) *Die Nation Schreiben*, Göttingen, Vandenhoeck and Ruprecht, pp. 296–332, esp. pp. 310–12.

28 O. Pflanze, 'Bismarcks Herrschaftstechnik als Problem der gegenwärtigen Historiographie', *Historische Zeitschrift*, 1982, vol. 234, pp. 561–99.

29 See above, pp. 100–1.

30 D. Blackbourn and G. Eley, *The Peculiarities of German History. Bourgeois Society and Politics in Nineteenth-Century Germany*, Oxford, Oxford University Press, 1984. Quotations p. 32.

31 See A. Bauerkämper, 'Geschichtsschreibung als Projektion. Die Revision der "Whig Interpretation of History" und die Kritik am Paradigma vom "deutschen Sonderweg" seit den 1970er Jahren', in S. Berger, P. Lambert and P. Schumann (eds) *Historikerdialoge. Geschichte, Mythos und Gedächtnis im deutsch-britischen kulturellen Austausch 1750–2000*, Göttingen, Vandenhoeck & Ruprecht, 2003, pp. 383–438.

32 See the contributions to D. Blackbourn and R. J. Evans (eds) *The German Bourgeoisie. Essays on the Social History of the German Middle Class from the Late Eighteenth to the Early Twentieth Century*, London, Routledge, 1991.

33 See D. Crew, 'The Pathologies of Modernity: Detlev Peukert on Germany's Twentieth Century', *Social History*, 1992, vol. 17, pp. 319–28.

34 J. Kocka, 'German History before Hitler: The Debate about the German *Sonderweg*', *Journal of Contemporary History*, 1988, vol. 23, pp. 3–16; I. Kershaw, ' "Working towards the Führer": Reflections on the Nature of the Hitler Dictatorship', in *idem* and M. Lewin (eds) *Stalinism and Nazism: Dictatorships in Comparison*, Cambridge, Cambridge University Press, 1997, pp. 88–106; p. 89.

35 Etzemüller, *Sozialgeschichte*, p. 359; Welskopp, 'Westbindung auf dem "Sonderweg". Die deutsche Sozialgeschichte vom Appendix der Wirtschaftsgeschichte zur Historischen Sozialwissenschaft', in W. Küttler, J. Rüsen and E. Schulin (eds) *Geschichtsdiskurs* vol. 5: *Globale Konflikte, Erinnerungsarbeit und Neuorientierungen seit 1945*, Frankfurt a.M., Fischer, 1999, pp. 191–237; *idem*, 'Grenzüberschrietungen', p. 299.

Further reading

The rise of German *Volksgeschichte* between the two World Wars went largely unnoticed by contemporary British historians. In the USA, however, O. Hammen published an insightful account, which is still worth reading: 'German Historians and the Advent of the National Socialist State', *Journal of Modern History*, 1941, vol. 13, pp. 161–88. Several of the essays in H. Lehmann and J. Van Horn Melton (eds) *Paths of Continuity: Central European Historiography from the 1930s to the 1950s*, Cambridge, Cambridge University Press, 1994, are relevant, though a number of the contributors exaggerate *Volks*-historians' innovatory achievements while downplaying their politically culpable associations. These are given due prominence, in: M. Burleigh, 'Scholarship, State and Nation, 1918–1945', in J. Breuilly (ed.) *The State of Germany*, London and New York, Longman, 1992, pp. 128–41; *idem*, *Germany Turns Eastwards. A*

Study of Ostforschung *in the Third Reich*, Cambridge, Cambridge University Press (1988); K. Schönwälder, 'The Fascination of Power: Historical Scholarship in Nazi Germany', *History Workshop Journal*, 1997, vol. 43, pp. 133–54; H. Schleier, 'German Historiography under National Socialism: Dreams of a Powerful Nation-state and German *Volkstum* Come True', in S. Berger, M. Donovan and K. Passmore (eds) *Writing National Histories: Western Europe since 1800*, London, Routledge, 1999, pp. 176–88.

The decisive break with historiographical nationalism and challenge to the dominance of political history, came in the second half of the twentieth century. Readers wishing to get a flavour of the new approaches will find G. Iggers (ed.) *The Social History of Politics: Critical Perspectives in West German Historical Writing since 1945*, Leamington Spa, Berg, 1985, a good starting point. Fritz Fischer helped clear the path for a new social history in West Germany, and incorporated social historical perspectives increasingly into his examination of foreign policy. For a brief statement of his thesis, see F. Fischer, *From Kaiserreich to Third Reich: Elements of Continuity in German History, 1871–1945*, London, Allen and Unwin, 1986, translated and with an introduction by R. Fletcher. The most important of Fischer's earlier works are also widely available in English translation. They, their context in 1960s and 1970s German society and academic culture, and continuing relevance to subsequent debate, are at the core of A. Mombauer, *The Origins of the First World War: Controversies and Consensus*, London, Longman, 2002. Two of Germany's most eminent social historians have furnished accounts of the changes they helped bring to their country's historiography: H.-U. Wehler, 'Historiography in Germany Today', in J. Habermas (ed.) *Observations on the 'Spiritual Situation of the Age': Contemporary German Perspectives*, London and Cambridge MA, MIT Press, 1984, pp. 221–59; G. A. Ritter, *The New Social History in the Federal Republic of Germany*, London, German Historical Institute, 1991. The broad sweep of the latter makes it an especially useful starting-point, not least because it puts German social history in an international perspective. So too does S. Berger, 'The Rise and Fall of "Critical" Historiography? Some Reflections on the Historiographical Agenda of the Left at the End of the Twentieth Century', *European Review of History*, 1996, vol. 3, pp. 213–32.

Chapter 7

The 'new social history' in America

Robert Harrison

'Without much question', noted Peter Stearns in 1988, 'the rise of social history has been the most dramatic development in American historical research over the past two decades'.[1] As in Britain, social history was a feeble presence in the academy up to about the 1950s. During the following decades, however, the volume of publications rose dramatically, as newcomers poured into the field and whole new areas were opened up for scholarly investigation. The rapid growth of the 'new social history' marked a dramatic shift in the centre of gravity of historical writing in the United States. 'In the historical profession as a whole', observed Gertrude Himmelfarb in 1987, 'the new history is the new orthodoxy'. In turn, traditionally minded political and intellectual historians like Himmelfarb felt marginalised and deprived of recognition: 'What was once at the center of the profession is now at the periphery'.[2] Before we identify the rise of social history as a classical paradigm shift, we must recognise that the new subdiscipline was itself a broad church. Its devotees approached it from many different directions, bringing with them different agendas and ideological presuppositions and favouring very different methodologies with which to uncover the lived experience of the American past. Moreover, its period of hegemony was decidedly short-lived. We must consider therefore whether the 'new social history' was either coherent enough or enduring enough to constitute a major historical paradigm.

American historiography in the immediate postwar era was dominated by the theme of consensus. Although this label, conventionally applied to the political and intellectual life of the late 1940s and 1950s, places too confining a straitjacket on so diverse and idiosyncratic an array of individuals as academic historians, it nevertheless conveys a few essential truths about historical writing during those troubled decades. Richard Hofstadter, perhaps the most influential, and the most intellectually complex, of the so-called consensus historians, called for a reinterpretation of the American political tradition which gave due weight to the values shared by most Americans:

> The existence of such a climate of opinion has been much obscured by the tendency to place political conflict in the foreground of history. ... The

fierceness of the political struggles has often been misleading; for the range of vision embraced by the primary contestants in the major parties has always been bounded by the horizons of property and enterprise. ... The sanctity of private property, the right of the individual to dispose of and invest it, the value of opportunity, and the natural evolution of self-interest and self-assertion, within broad legal limits, into a beneficent social order have been staple tenets of the central faith in American political ideologies.[3]

While playing down the importance of class conflict, or any other kind of conflict, in the American past, and while playing down discontinuities in fundamental beliefs and values, historians of the postwar era stressed instead those qualities that differentiated Americans from other people. Key texts like Hofstadter's *The American Political Tradition* (1948), Daniel Boorstin's *The Genius of American Politics* (1953) and Louis Hartz's *The Liberal Tradition in America* (1955) pointed to a belief in possessive individualism, in free enterprise and political liberty as characteristic of Americans, but also (paradoxically perhaps) praised their empirical, pragmatic, non-ideological cast of mind.

It is important to recognise the political context in which historians operated in the early years of the Cold War. The global confrontation with international communism, like that with fascism that preceded it, presented itself to American historians as a defence of Western civilisation, of freedom in contradistinction to 'totalitarianism'. The critical difference between East and West, they believed, was the commitment to freedom of speech and, more specifically, the tolerance of academic freedom. On certain fundamental principles the USA was emphatically right and the USSR was emphatically wrong. Many historians concluded that there could be no place for communists in a scholarly community whose core values they could not possibly share. Communists, and perhaps historians of the left more generally, were accused of putting scholarship to political purposes, serving the interest of the Party rather than historical truth. They were believed to be incapable of 'objective' scholarship. Scores of communists were dismissed or barred from university posts; loyalty oaths were required of academics as well as other public servants. Where they did not wholeheartedly endorse such proceedings, other scholars felt at best ambivalent, at worst cowed. Under such circumstances dissenting voices were muted. In a 1955 survey of social scientists, including 681 historians, about one half acknowledged that they had become more cautious in expressing their views for fear of being labelled subversive. Little in any case was written, or at least submitted for publication, that might possibly be termed subversive.

Although historical writing of this period tended to be sensitive to a wider range of social forces than its predecessors, more complex in its interpretations, more sophisticated in its methodology and more open to influences from the social sciences, its subject-matter was still predominantly political. Historians were mostly preoccupied with the standard questions of American political development. The leading subjects of historical writing and debate were the

American Revolution and the making of the Constitution, Jacksonian politics, the origins of the Civil War, Reconstruction, Populism, Progressivism and the New Deal. A narrative of political development remained the central spine of American history.

Social history had, of course, been written in the United States before the 1960s. Commonly dismissed as 'pots and pans history', it encompassed an often colourful but unsystematic and theoretically unsophisticated account of otherwise neglected topics like fashion, folklore and foodways. From about 1960, however, the field underwent a dramatic expansion. The proportion of dissertations devoted to social history topics quadrupled between 1958 and 1978, by which date it had overtaken the proportion written on political history, while similar trends were observable in the history catalogues of the major university presses and on the contents pages of mainstream historical journals. In 1967 the *Journal of Social History* was founded, to be followed a few years later by *Social Science History* and the *Journal of Interdisciplinary History*, along with more specialised journals like *Labor History*, the *Journal of Urban History* and *Family History*. Several subfields were opened up for investigation, like the history of immigration, family history, urban history, the 'new labor history' and the history of work and leisure, while subjects like the history of education and religion began to be tackled by social historians rather than exclusively by practitioners working within each profession's own intellectual frame of reference. It was, comments John Higham, as if an earthquake had 'split the dam and released a flood of waters across the entire terrain of scholarship'.[4]

The reasons for the growth of social history are actually quite various. It can be attributed in part to the dynamics of disciplinary expansion. The historical profession roughly quintupled in size between 1940 and 1970. By the early 1970s the American Historical Association had a membership in excess of 18,000, while Ph.D.s in history were pouring off the production-line at a rate of over 1,200 a year. Although, as it turned out, the profession had attained its peak in numerical terms in that decade, the number of practising historians remained large, and their published output showed few signs of slackening off during the closing decades of the century. Moreover, the GI Bill of Rights and the postwar expansion of the universities gave educational opportunities to a great many young men and women from blue-collar households and of recent immigrant stock, many of whom went on to do graduate work and later to take up teaching posts in history. In particular, the postwar decades witnessed the entry into the profession of a large number of Jewish historians.

As the profession grew, larger numbers of scholars and research students were looking for their own piece of historical terrain to stake out. The development of social history gave access to a whole new territory for historical research, equivalent to the opening up of a new tract of land in the American West – a kind of historiographical equivalent of the Oklahoma Land Rush. Second, this was a period in which the social sciences enjoyed considerable prestige. Disciplines like sociology and social anthropology appeared to offer a compelling example of methodological sophistication in analysing social relations. They, Keith Thomas suggested, provided the 'tools' with which the social historian could work. Third, and perhaps most importantly, research in social history was driven by a desire to incorporate the viewpoints of social groups which had been largely excluded from the mainstream version of American history, like African-Americans, industrial workers, women and children, and the urban poor. Inevitably, the incorporation of alternative viewpoints meant recognising the diversity of those viewpoints and, inevitably also, the prevalence of social conflict in the American past, as was so evident in the American present. In this respect social history was very much a child of the 1960s.

Whereas postwar America appeared to be blessed with a pervasive social and political consensus, during the course of the 1960s the nation was torn by a series of serious and disturbing conflicts. As the decade wore on, issues of civil rights which had seemed soluble within the terms of the liberal consensus, in the face of urban riots, the rise of 'Black Power' and the 'white backlash', came to seem increasingly divisive and intractable. Rather than an anachronistic and atavistic Southern folkway, racial prejudice appeared to be deeply embedded in American culture and institutions. From 1965 the war in Vietnam provoked further divisions. Many opponents of the war, disgusted both at what America was doing to Vietnam and at what Vietnam was revealing about America, graduated from a critique of US foreign policy to a critique of American society, which they condemned as indelibly imperialist, racist and dominated by the so-called 'military-industrial complex'. Some of the elements of this critique had already been aired by spokespersons of the New Left. Radical students associated with Students for a Democratic Society had graduated from criticism of the practices of their universities to a broader denunciation of American imperialism and American corporate society. Student radicals tended to be moved by sympathy for oppressed peoples, such as Southern sharecroppers, ghetto blacks, Chicano fruit-pickers and the beleaguered inhabitants of Cuba and Vietnam, rather than by a commitment to abstract ideas. Their intellectual influences, such as they were, were highly eclectic, ranging from Henry David Thoreau to Frantz Fanon and Herbert Marcuse, but increasingly they turned to Marxism for their ideas (particularly as modified by twentieth-century Western Marxists like Antonio Gramsci). The 1960s and 1970s saw the emergence, almost for the first time, of a substantial body of Marxist writing in America.

The New Left was well represented among American historians. Its influence, particularly at institutions like the universities of Michigan and Wisconsin, led to the development of a sizeable and vigorous oppositional tendency within the profession. Radical historians rejected the core assumptions of consensus historiography and the core values of postwar American culture. They insisted, like the New Historians of the 1910s but more stridently, that history should be used as a tool for changing the world, that it should be made 'relevant' to contemporary concerns. Some, like Eugene Genovese and Christopher Lasch, operated within the academy; others, like Staughton Lynd and Jesse Lemisch, rejected it as elitist in character, repressive in behaviour and conformist in its influence. Some laid claim to ideals of historical detachment and 'scientific' objectivity; others wrote avowedly committed history to serve the interests of the socially oppressed. In the long run, not surprisingly, many of the former managed to find a place within the profession, perhaps to the extent of becoming acculturated to its norms and values, while many of the latter operated outside it and, correspondingly, had less influence on the way in which the writing of academic history in the United States developed over the next generation.

Social historians wrote from every point on the political compass, but it is fair to say that a majority were more or less radical in their politics. Much of the intellectual momentum behind social history came from the politics of the New Left. Many leading practitioners emerged from the student radicalism of the 1960s; some were closely associated with the New Left; nearly all were strongly influenced by the social and political movements of the decade. Although most were probably not explicitly Marxist in their politics, to a much greater degree than any previous generation of American historians they were familiar with the categories of Marxist analysis. The historical questions that they sought to answer grew out of that background of social turmoil and radical politics. As Jonathan Wiener explains,

> In general radical historians have focused on issues of exploitation, domination, and oppression; they have argued that existing patterns of domination are not natural or inevitable, but rather have historical origins; thus they can be abolished. In seeking those historical origins, they have focused on ordinary people rather than political elites, on groups rather than individuals, and on human agency rather than abstract or general processes of change.[5]

Thus their political imperatives impelled a large number of historians influenced by the radical movements of the 1960s towards the study of social history.

Social history meant a lot of different things, but to the generation that emerged from graduate school in the 1960s and 1970s it had two compelling purposes. The first was to recapture the experience of social groups which had been previously hidden from history. According to Peter Stearns, editor of the *Journal of Social History*,

> The clearest general definition of social history in the United States focuses on its concern with the general membership of a society, and not just individuals among the elite. ... not only the mass of people but also the framework of their daily lives – their families, artifacts, community life, their births and deaths.[6]

With its focus on political events, diplomatic negotiations and military engagements, past historical writing had concerned itself almost exclusively with the activities of elites, narrowly defined in terms of class, gender and ethnicity. Social history involved, in effect, turning the image of society upside down and, in the phrase current at the time, writing history 'from the bottom up' – from the point of view, not of political elites, but of ordinary people in all their variety. A second challenge of social history was to restore a sense of agency to social groups which had been regarded as passive receptors of social change, such as peasants, women, non-unionised workers and even slaves, in order to demonstrate that they had 'lives of their own' that they partially shaped through their own actions. A powerful influence, and a model of how this kind of history might be written, came from the work of E. P. Thompson, especially *The Making of the English Working Class*, which was probably cited more often by American social historians than any historical work published on their own side of the Atlantic.

Beyond this general impetus to uncover ordinary lives, social history was extraordinarily eclectic both in subject-matter and method. There was no dominant school or journal, no characteristic methodology accepted by all or even most practitioners. It was not 'a coherent subdiscipline', notes James Henretta, so much as 'a congeries of groups' which 'begin from contradictory epistemological premises' and 'accept divergent standards of proof'.[7] At least two very different tendencies can be distinguished.

The first was what was known as 'social science history'. This was history which drew heavily for its methods and, to a lesser extent, its theoretical models, on the social sciences. Above all, 'social science history' was marked out by its dependence on quantitative methods. Quantification became the 'rallying cry' of the 'new history'. It offered a means of exploring the experience of sections of the population which left few written records by analysing the traces that they did leave behind, in the form of manuscript census returns, tax-lists, city directories, military enlistments and company records. The timely arrival of the computer, and the extraordinary advances in processing-power that followed, permitted large-scale statistical analysis of social trends and distributions and the relationship between variables which sometimes confirmed or rejected prior hypotheses about social processes, sometimes suggested wholly new ones. Prominent examples of quantitative social history include Stephan Thernstrom's and Thomas Kessner's studies of social mobility, using census records and city directories; studies of the distribution of wealth by Edward Pessen and Michael B. Katz; the investigation of demographic trends by Robert Wells, Tamara Hareven and Maris Vinovskis; studies of the residential and occupational distribution of immigrants by John Bodnar and Josef Barton; the analysis of segregation and ethnic-group separation by Olivier Zunz and Theodore Hershberg; the study of industrial workers on the basis of company records by Thomas Dublin and Tamara Hareven; and studies of crime and violence on the basis of court records, for example by Roger Lane and Michael

Hindus. Much hope was vested in large-scale investigations, such as the Philadelphia History Project, which translated into machine-readable form 2.5 million individual census entries relating to the population of Philadelphia between 1850 and 1880, in the hope that their analysis would turn up definite knowledge about the social structure of a nineteenth-century industrial city. It did so in only the most trivial respects, proving, for example, that most workers resided within a mile of their workplace, something which had been long suspected on the basis of documentary evidence, not to mention common sense. As Lawrence Stone suggests, such gargantuan projects 'may turn out to be rather like the project to put a man on the moon, more remarkable for the evidence they provide of man's vaunting ambition, vast financial resources, and technical virtuosity in the 1960s than for their scientific results in the advancement of knowledge'.[8] It soon became evident that quantification could capture only some aspects of social history. It turned out to be more useful in identifying problems for analysis than in solving them, more useful in clearing away the undergrowth of unfounded hypotheses than in providing convincing historical explanations.

A second variety of social history consisted of attempts to recover the experience of ordinary people, not through statistical analysis but through a more sensitive reading of the surviving documentary (and also pictorial) evidence. This embraces much of the so-called 'new labor history', as well as studies of immigrant communities and much early work in women's history. Thus working-class culture has been investigated through a careful reading of scattered documents, occasional autobiographies and, where possible, oral testimony. From such evidence, in the work of for example Sean Wilentz, has emerged a compelling account of working-class life in the early years of industrialisation; similarly Lizabeth Cohen has produced an impressive reconstruction of working-class communities in Chicago in the interwar years. Even more impressively, a number of historians, including most conspicuously Eugene Genovese, Herbert Gutman and Lawrence Levine, have constructed out of the documentary record of slavery, supplemented by oral narratives collected by the federal Works Progress Administration in the 1930s, a vivid picture of the culture and community relationships of antebellum slaves. Like historians of the working class, historians of slavery have tried to demonstrate how communities resisted oppression through culture. In doing so, and in reaffirming the agency of ordinary people, they set out to show 'how even ordinary people construct their own lives'.[9]

The approach of such historians, as Alice Kessler-Harris points out, was essentially phenomenological: 'the "self-experiences" of historical actors served as the filters through which historians viewed and interpreted an issue or problem'.[10] From cultural anthropologists like Clifford Geertz and Victor Turner social historians learned how to interpret symbolic acts and 'read' social rituals, almost as if they were texts. Thus historians of working-class culture engaged in a detailed analysis of events like street parades, riots and protest actions, prize-fights and the culture of saloons and minstrel shows. By the 1980s a substantial portion of social history was shading into cultural history. Historians were becoming interested in questions of meaning rather than material existence, investigating symbols, ritual and discourse rather than social structure or social behaviour. Cultural representations began to be regarded not as mere reflections of the social world but as objects of study in themselves. Thus cultural historians moved beyond group behaviour to examine the cultural conventions that informed it – conventions relating to work, time, family, class, race and, above all, gender. In the words of Anthony Molho and Gordon Wood,

> they came to believe that the societies they were studying were culturally constructed, mere assemblages of meanings. ... Borrowing heavily from anthropology and literary theory, cultural historians tended to break up the past into discrete ethnographic moments, imagining that cultures could be studied as if they were texts, with no more than a tenuous relationship to anything outside themselves.[11]

Under the influence of poststructuralist theory, they came to question whether cultural 'texts' could be regarded as evidence of any underlying social reality, and indeed whether 'society' or the 'social' had any validity as objects of investigation. Although most practising social historians proceeded relatively untroubled by the 'linguistic turn', the intellectual foundations of the subdiscipline were seriously shaken.

By 1980 historians had generated an exceptional body of work and produced fascinating insights into a kaleidoscopic variety of topics in social history. What they had not produced was a 'history of American society'. Their output consisted typically of microstudies of particular groups in particular localities. 'The most innovative work done in the last fifteen years', noted Thomas Bender,

> has explored the culture of groups in American society ... the private or *gemeinschaftlich* [communal] worlds of trades, occupations, and professions; locality; sisterhood; race and ethnicity; and family. What we have gotten are the parts, all richly described. But since they are assumed to be autonomous, we get no image of the whole.[12]

Kessler-Harris concurs: 'The subject matter carried with it waves of exciting new knowledge, but coherence, purpose, and direction all floundered in the churning water'.[13] During the 1980s many prominent figures worried publicly about the problem of integration in American history.

There were some, like Eric Monkkonen for example, who argued that the task of synthesis was impossible. It was futile to attempt to generalise about the whole American experience or to explain how it changed over time, since that would entail the reduction to a few simple statements of a complex social reality. All the historian could do was to seek to describe it, or a portion of it, in the fullness of detail. Instead of 'the working class', she should study individual working-class communities, differentiated by locality, ethnicity and the particularity of their experience. Instead of trying to fabricate comprehensive models of social change or to construct global explanations, she should seek to uncover the meaning of change for particular individuals and groups. In a way, notes Kessler-Harris, 'fragmentation is implicit in the conception of a history that insists on the importance of the unique event and reifies the diversity of ordinary people'.[14] Indeed, proposals for synthesis, such as Bender's suggested focus on the making of 'public culture', were criticised for being insensitive to the experience of minority groups and for favouring the 'core' over the 'peripheries'. Any master narrative, it was contended, was inherently ideological, giving priority to one hegemonic interpretation of reality over a multitude of competing voices. Such criticisms were most trenchantly voiced by historians of gender.

The neglect of politics was another source of criticism, both from historians on the right, like Gertrude Himmelfarb, and on the left, like Elizabeth Fox-Genovese and Eugene Genovese. The Genoveses, for example, admitted that the study of oppressed groups to recapture experiences hidden from history, of which Eugene Genovese's own study of slavery was a strikingly successful example, was a worthy aim, but they warned against a tendency to romanticise those experiences:

> To speak bluntly, as admirable as much of the recent social history has been and as valuable as much of the description of the life of the lower classes may eventually prove, the subject as a whole is steadily sinking into a neo-antiquarian swamp presided over by liberal ideologues, the burden of whose political argument, notwithstanding the usual pretense of not having a political argument, rests on an evasion of class confrontation.[15]

If social historians ignore the structures of power that constrain people's lives, they ignore the most crucial determinants of their world: they would depict slavery without the slaveholder, as certain 1970s studies of slave culture seemed close to doing, or working-class life without corporate power. 'A romantic view of the slaves or workers that denies a reciprocal influence with the oppressors in effect denies the history they actually lived'.[16] Instead, historians were urged to integrate social history with studies of political power and the growth of the state.

The 'new social history', for all its influence, was never dominant enough, nor was it coherent enough, to be classed as a ruling paradigm. As a perusal of the contents pages of most of the mainstream historical journals in recent years would confirm, though very much alive and kicking, social history is no longer as dominant as it once was. Although a great deal of important and informative work is still being done in almost all of its principal subfields, it cannot be denied that social history has lost its place at the cutting-edge of scholarship and lost its claim to represent the heart of the historical enterprise in the United States. The challenge of cultural history, the 'linguistic turn' in historical studies, the resurgence in various forms of political history and the impact of postmodernism have all in different ways undermined the central premises of the 'new social history' while, at the same time, offering an unimaginable range of subject-matters and an almost infinite variety of ways of 'doing history'.

Neither American social historians, nor indeed American historians in general, shared a sufficient measure of agreement over their research agenda, their methodology or their epistemology. As Bender noted in 1986, the historical kingdom was fragmented into a large number of separate provinces, each 'studied in its own terms, each with its own scholarly network and discourse'.[17] What had emerged was a profusion of subfields, each with its own central concerns, its own controversies, its own methodology, often its own association and its own journal. Seventy-five specialist historical associations were affiliated with the AHA. Bernard Bailyn described research as 'ramifying in a hundred directions at once [with] no coordination among them', and he was only one of a number of leading figures to regret 'The absence of effective organizing principles in modern historiography – its shapelessness, its lack of general coherence'.[18] Kuhn describes early scientific inquiry as 'pre-paradigmatic', lacking the intellectual coherence and institutional coordination of mature science. Modern historiography, on the other hand, could be perhaps described as 'post-paradigmatic'. Whereas it may be possible to talk of a dominant paradigm in American historiography in the late nineteenth or early twentieth century, maybe even in the 1950s, contemporary historical studies have become far too eclectic in subject-matter, in methodology and in standards of proof for that to be the case.

Notes

1 P. N. Stearns, 'Introduction: Social History and Its Evolution', in *idem* (ed.) *Expanding the Past: A Reader in Social History*, New York, New York University Press, 1988, p. 3.
2 G. Himmelfarb, *The New History and the Old: Critical Essays and Reappraisals*, Cambridge MA, Belknap, 1987, p. 4.
3 R. Hofstadter, *The American Political Tradition*, New York, Knopf, 1948, pp. xxxvi–xxxvii.
4 A. Kessler-Harris, 'Social History', in Eric Foner (ed.) *The New American History*, Philadelphia, Temple University Press, 1990, p. 163.
5 J. Wiener, 'Radical Historians and the Crisis in American History, 1959–1980', *Journal of American History*, 1989, vol. 76, p. 399.
6 P. N. Stearns, 'Towards a Wider Vision: Trends in Social History', in M. Kammen (ed.) *The Past before Us: Contemporary Historical Writing in the United States*, Ithaca NY, Cornell University Press, 1980, p. 212.

7 J. Henretta, 'Social History as Lived and Written', *American Historical Review*, 1979, vol. 84, p. 1295.
8 L. Stone, *The Past and the Present Revisited*, London, Routledge and Kegan Paul, 1987, p. 38.
9 D. G. Ross, 'The New and Newer Histories: Social Theory and Historiography in an American Key', in Anthony Molho and Gordon S. Wood (eds) *Imagined Histories: American Historians Interpret Their Past*, Princeton, Princeton University Press, 1998, p. 96.
10 Kessler-Harris, 'Social History', p. 168.
11 'Introduction', in Molho and Wood (eds) *Imagined histories*, p. 12.
12 T. Bender, 'Wholes and Parts: The Need for Synthesis in American History', *Journal of American History*, 1986, vol. 73, p. 127.
13 Kessler-Harris, 'Social History', p. 164.
14 *Ibid.*, p. 178.
15 E. Fox-Genovese and E. Genovese, 'The Political Crisis of Social History', in Fox-Genovese and Genovese, *The Fruits of Merchant Capital: Slavery and Bourgeois Property in the Rise and Expansion of Capitalism*, Oxford, Oxford University Press, 1983, p. 201.
16 *Ibid.*, p. 198.
17 Bender, 'Wholes and Parts', p. 128.
18 P. Novick, *That Noble Dream : The 'Objectivity Question' and the American Historical Profession*, Cambridge, Cambridge University Press, 1988, p. 579.

Further reading

Two excellent histories of American historical writing are J. Higham, *History: Professional Scholarship in America*, revised edn, Baltimore, Johns Hopkins University Press, 1983; and P. Novick, *That Noble Dream: The 'Objectivity Question' and the American Historical Profession*, Cambridge, Cambridge University Press, 1988. Although Higham's account ends in the early 1960s, it examines the character and context of 'consensus' historiography, which, indeed, Higham (in an article published in *Commentary* in 1959) was among the first to identify. Novick's primary topic is historians' views on objectivity, but he approaches it through a richly detailed and contextualised account of American historical practice. An illuminating discussion of the relationship between the 'new social history' and radical politics in the 1960s is J. Wiener, 'Radical Historians and the Crisis in American History, 1959–1980', *Journal of American History*, 1989, vol. 76, pp. 399–434. That social history is still associated in the popular mind with the left is demonstrated by the political attacks to which it has recently been subjected. See 'Special Issue: Social History and the American Political Climate – Problems and Strategies', *Journal of Social History*, 1995, vol. 29, supp.

There are several reviews of the development of social history in the United States since the 1960s, including P.N. Stearns, 'Trends in Social History', in M. Kammen (ed.) *The Past before Us: Contemporary Historical Writing in the United States*, Ithaca NY, Cornell University Press, 1980; O. Zunz, 'American Social History', in *idem* (ed.) *Reliving the Past: The Worlds of Social History*, Chapel Hill, University of North Carolina Press, 1985; and A. Kessler-Harris,

'Social History', in E. Foner (ed.) *The New American History*, Philadelphia, Temple University Press, 1990. The changing priorities and prospects of social history can be traced through a sequence of review essays by Peter Stearns in his role as editor of the *Journal of Social History*: 'Social History Today ... and Tomorrow', *Journal of Social History*, 1976, vol. 10, pp. 129–55; 'Social History and History: A Progress Report', *ibid.*, 1986, vol. 19, pp. 319–34; and, most recently, 'Social History, Present and Future', *ibid.*, 2003, vol. 37, pp. 9–20.

Criticism of the 'new social history' for its alleged inattention to politics comes from Elizabeth Fox-Genovese and Eugene Genovese, 'The Political Crisis of Social History', in *eaedem*, *The Fruits of Merchant Capital*, New York, Oxford University Press, 1983 (from the left); and G. Himmelfarb, *The New History and the Old: Critical Essays and Reappraisals*, Cambridge MA, Harvard University Press, 1987 (from the right). On the development of cultural history, see L. Hunt (ed.) *The New Cultural History*, Berkeley, University of California Press, 1989. For one among many comments on the supposed fragmentation of American historiography, see T. Bender, 'Wholes and Parts: The Need for Synthesis in American History', *Journal of American History*, 1986, vol. 73, pp. 120–36; and the responses in 'A Round Table: Synthesis in American History', *ibid.*, 1987, vol. 74, pp. 107–30.

On recent trends in American historical writing, see '*AHR* Forum: The Old History and the New', *American Historical Review*, 1989, vol. 94, pp. 654–98; 'The Practice of American History: Special Issue', *Journal of American History*, 1994, vol. 81, pp. 933–1174; A. Molho and G. S. Wood (eds) *Imagined Histories: American Historians Interpret their Past*, Princeton, Princeton University Press, 1998.

Part III

Interdisciplinarity

As we have seen, history, as practised in the twentieth century and especially as its practitioners began to challenge or to develop the approaches of their nineteenth-century forebears, employed concepts and methodological approaches borrowed from other disciplines. While certain disciplines predated the appearance of academic history and were present, often to significant effect, at the birth – political economy, for instance, or law – others began to flourish as the infant history also grew. Nurture, including the influence of peers as well as elders and those who may have presumed themselves betters, has been important, though whether as important as nature remains a vital question.

In fact, there are a number of other significant questions that inform the contributions to this part of the volume. To what extent have the 'outside' influences of neighbouring disciplines modified historians' perspectives and practices? How are disciplinary boundaries drawn (and redrawn)? When and why have disciplines acted as barriers? When and why have they been treated rather as lines over which ideas are exchanged? What are the implications of different, discipline-specific discourses to the prospects and potentials of interdisciplinarity? As in other parts of the volume, the chapters here offer case-studies which address some or all of these issues from within the particulars of history's relationship with another discipline. In three of the instances here the contributors are historians who have worked closely with practitioners and/or the work of practitioners from a cognate discipline; in one instance, the chapter by Tim Woods, the author is himself a practitioner from one such neighbouring discipline, literature.

Not all disciplines are, of course, constructed in the same ways and not all approaches to interdisciplinarity accord in their particulars of focus. While we can recognise sociology or anthropology as disciplines in a conventional sense, including their strong institutional presence within the academy, other 'disciplines' do not display the same characteristics but are more easily identifiable as movements adjacent to or located within disciplines. Siân Nicholas, in her study of 'psychohistory', moves between psychoanalysis and psychohistory as the disciplinary foundations of her chapter, just as the earliest practitioners, of whom the first was of course Freud, did also. It was Freud whose publication on Leonardo da Vinci 'launched "psychohistory" as a discipline': the original psychoanalyst was also the original psychohistorian. Freud's studies were aped to limited effect by contemporaries and near contemporaries, but their conclusions and approach did not gain the wholesale support of historians any more than psychoanalysis appealed universally to psychologists. As Nicholas points out, what historians found unpalatable, in reviewing these early studies, was that psychoanalysis and its product, psychohistory, appeared as 'pseudo-sciences', disreputable poor relations of the science of psychology. And, of course, in that psychoanalytic history contradicted, or seemed to contradict, some of the fundamentals of rules of evidence to which historians, fully paid-up members of the guild, had to subscribe.

Neither sociology nor anthropology have posed the same fundamental questions of approach. Historians have found in each discipline not challenges to their ideas about how historical argument should be constructed but encouragements to explore the past in ways that are distinctive. Sociology, as Robert Harrison's chapter describes, shares a series of agendas as well as its intellectual origins with history; while sociologists may be more overt in their application of theory, their study of 'human social life' hardly forces an obvious distinction with the work of the historian. While historical sociologists investigate past society, it is the present-centredness of sociology that most evidently distinguishes its disciplinary identity from that of history. In its search for general patterns of behaviour, sociology's employment of research techniques, including the statistical analysis of large sets of data, also reveals elements of difference from traditional historical practice. As Harrison notes, however, history has taken a great deal from sociology, both in terms of the broad theories of development and concepts of societal function and also in terms of research method and approach. In return, history has stimulated in sociology a desire to investigate past society. As a result, sociology, in effect, employs historians as field researchers in the archive. By helping establish, for instance, research agendas in social structure or demography, sociologists have encouraged the opening up of sources and the development of historical techniques which historians and they themselves can exploit.

The same is true of anthropology. As John Davidson describes in his chapter, the shared agendas of anthropology and history, essentially the explication of the actions of one people to another people, but rooted either in different space (anthropology) or different time (history), have encouraged a good deal of common effort by practitioners from each discipline. Just as in the case of sociology, anthropology has brought an intellectual agenda and aspects of methodology which have greatly influenced the work of some historians to immediate effect and that of a greater number by more subtle means, even unconscious adoption. Striking in the case of both anthropology and sociology is the particular direction these disciplines have given to the work of social historians in the last half-century. Part of that drive came from within history; as the number of practitioners of social and economic history as well as cultural history expanded, they sought out comparative material and analytical approaches. Inevitably, some of that absorption within the discipline was at second or third remove. Le Roy Ladurie's famous microstudy of early four-teenth-century Montaillou, which drew upon cultural anthropology, encouraged similar endeavour within the discipline. It is, therefore, possible to conceive of a second or third historiographical generation (that is, post-*Montaillou* in this instance) who came to their anthropology via their history.

In recent decades anthropology, especially the cultural anthropology of Geertz, has engaged in its own interdisciplinary exchanges with disciplines other than history. The rise (or resurrection) of cultural studies, of narrative, of literary studies, has seen energetic cross-fertilisation between literary theorists and cultural anthropologists. Tim Woods notes the contribution of Geertz and *Annales* to the work of the 'new historicists' of literary studies. He also acknowledges the apparent contradiction that, while micro-narratives such as *Montaillou* may have been 'fostered by postmodernist theories of history', such ventures are still subject to the theoretical challenge of literary theory.

Certain other elements of the relationship between the developing discipline of history and its academic neighbours emerge forcefully in each of the four chapters. The chronology of 'take-up' is noteworthy. In emerging disciplines, such as anthropology or sociology, a process of internal development, with a first wave of pioneers giving way to revisionists just as the discipline hardens its institutional base, shares common elements with other disciplines, including history. Quite when history catches up with the emergent cognate discipline and begins to share with and learn from it, is revealing. In some cases, it is clear that history, as any discipline, is capable of learning late, perhaps too late, from sister disciplines. Davidson, for instance, makes the point that a symbolic inter-pretive anthropology was in a process of decline within anthropology, just as outside disciplines, including history, embraced it. In that sense, interdisci-plinarity is a case-study of history repeating itself. In acknowledging Marx's commentary on that two-stage process, we would not expect to find tragedy in the first stage of interdisciplinarity but, as Nicholas' discussion of the potential historiography of the psychoanalysis of psychoanalytical historians neatly illus-trates, we may anticipate moments of farce in the second stage.

There is also a reverse chronology of unlearning as much as learning from other disciplines. Disciplines can become caricatured, offered as exemplars of the wrong against which an earnest new discipline or sub-discipline may look to set the world to right. The 'New Historicism' of literary studies set itself against an 'old' historicism; Tim Woods quotes Louis Montrose on the textuality of history. Montrose argues that 'we can have no access to a full and authentic past'; but, of course, it is hard to conceive that any 'old' historicist would disagree. The evolution of disciplines often means that their own practitioners have a closer and more immediate sense of what goes on within them, the potential for a heightened self-reflection, compared with those, from 'outside', who observe and learn from them. This is not to say, of course, that 'outsiders' are incapable of nuanced and novel observation, that they cannot point to flaws in what they observe. But it can mean that, if they do not look closely or if they stop looking too soon, they describe a veneer and call it a core.

Even so, the reckless characterisations and poorly conceived analyses of commentators from beyond, as within, disciplines can stimulate responses. From these the discipline can prosper. It has been one of a number of the achievements of a postmodernist approach to history to encourage historians to reflect closely upon the nature of what they do and especially also to attempt, or rather to revisit, a more literary style of analysis.[1]

Note

1   R. J. Evans, *In Defence of History*, London, Granta, 1997, pp. 248–9.

Chapter 8

History and psychoanalysis

Siân Nicholas

Freud's theories of the human mind, derived from his experiences as a neurologist and paediatrician in turn-of-the-century Vienna, shaped the intellectual climate of the twentieth century, transforming the way we saw ourselves and our society, bringing a new vocabulary ('ego', 'repression', 'projection' and, of course, 'psychoanalysis') into everyday language, and influencing fields as diverse as medicine, art and literature, education, the social sciences – and history. Over the past hundred years the 'psychoanalytic' approach pioneered by Freud, the search for the hidden, unconscious forces that have shaped human history, has become one of the most controversial of all historical methodologies, because it seems to call into question some of our most basic assumptions about historical method, the use of sources, even human nature itself. This chapter seeks to describe the essence of the psychoanalytic approach to history, and to explain why it was so revolutionary, what made it so controversial – and why it remains so contentious to this day, both exalted by its proponents as the greatest of interpretive approaches to history and vilified by its detractors as a pseudo-science more akin to a cult belief than a philosophy of history.

What is the psychoanalytic approach?

'Psychological' approaches to history did not, of course, originate with Freud. The ancient historians wrote character sketches of their principal actors, and used human nature as an explanatory tool. The notion of a 'collective psyche' influencing the character and development of societies was current in the eighteenth century in the work of Vico, Herder and others. In the nineteenth century 'national character' was widely (if vaguely) discussed. During the late nineteenth and early twentieth century historians and sociologists pondered the psychological dynamics of history, most famously in Gustave le Bon's *The Psychology of Crowds* (1895) and Max Weber's *The Protestant Ethic and the Spirit of Capitalism* (1904). Johan Huizinga's *The Waning of the Middle Ages* (1924) was a path-breaking attempt to address the psychology of medieval society. Meanwhile the *Annales* historians followed Lucien Febvre's call for an 'historical psychology', to investigate the concept of collective mentalities (*mentalités*), for instance in Georges Lefebvre's *La Grande Peur de 1789* (1932). Such approaches inevitably relied heavily on the historian's imaginative sympathy. Freud, however, proposed a more rigorous, psycho*analytic*, approach to historical research, based on his observations as a clinician, which claimed to offer a new theory of human character and motivation based on the revelation of the unconscious mind.

Freud's theory of human personality famously rests on concepts of infantile sexuality and the dynamic unconscious. He posited that the human personality has three elements, the id (the unrestrained human personality, impelled by libido, or sexual drive), the superego (the personality restrained by social, cultural and familial forces) and the ego (the unique self, produced through the taming of the id by the superego, and comprising both the visible, socialised mind, and the subconscious, repressed mind). Childhood experience is key to the development of the adult personality; thus infants progress through three developmental stages (oral, anal and genital) in which their biological desire for pleasure is first realised (through breastfeeding, defecation, masturbation) then socially restrained (by weaning, toilet-training, sexual taboos), followed by a formative experience of intergenerational conflict (Freud's notorious 'Oedipus complex') by which they learn to accommodate their intuitive resentment of their parent of the same sex as a rival for the affections of their parent of the opposite sex (hence the crude aphorism that boys unconsciously wish to kill their father and have sex with their mother). In addition girl infants suffer low self-esteem related to their lack of male genitalia. The effects of these experiences – particularly when resolved unsuccessfully or traumatically – are repressed in the individual's subconscious, or unconscious mind, but reveal themselves in dreams, word association, neurotic symptoms and/or pathological behaviour. Psychoanalysis was the means by which these unconscious impulses could be identified, explained and perhaps resolved.

If historism classically concerned itself with recorded fact and rational explanation, psychoanalytical theory immediately offered the way into something quite different: the unconscious motivations that shape human action: 'the aggression, sexuality, passions, fantasy and emotional states of the inner world of its subject'.[1] This 'inner world' is key, for it alone fully explains the outer actions. Psychoanalysis, by uncovering the formative experiences of key historical personalities, could reveal the true character and motivation for their actions. More than this, Freud believed, by applying the psychoanalytic method to groups or societies in the past, one might explain not simply outbreaks of collective psychosis but the very origins of cultural attitudes, prejudices, mythology, religion, indeed human civilisation itself. And by embracing psychoanalytic theory, the historian's own relationship to his or her discipline would be transformed. One of the most passionate defenders of psychoanalytic history, the historian of ideas Peter Gay, has stated that his training in psychoanalytic theory opened up for him a new dimension of historical analysis: a sharpened sensitivity to sources, a more perceptive reading of texts (for instance, what they repress as much as what they admit), an enhanced recognition of the unconscious shared fantasies underpinning cultural attitudes, or of the sexual and aggressive drives that precipitate individual or collective actions. 'Many historians have heard the music of the past but have transcribed it for penny whistle' – to Gay, historians without psychoanalytic insight, however accomplished, remain merely 'craftsmen' and only the psychoanalytic historian can write the score for full orchestra.[2]

Psychohistory as a discipline: its origins and development

Freud effectively launched 'psychohistory' as a discipline with his *Leonardo da Vinci and a Memory of his Childhood* (1910), in which he sought to investigate Leonardo's artistic inspiration by analysing the few facts known about his life (namely, his illegitimacy, his parental background – servant mother, and gentleman father with whom he went to live as a child – and the absence of any known love affairs in adulthood), plus the record of his life's work, and a childhood memory mentioned in his notebooks, that a bird – a vulture – had flown down to his cradle and put its tail in his mouth. Freud concluded that Leonardo was obviously homosexual, that this could be attributed to the repression, when he went to live with his father, of his peculiarly intense relationship with his natural mother, but that the fixation on his mother remained in his subconscious. This was revealed for posterity in his artistic preoccupations with idealised female (and especially maternal) figures, most clearly in his 'double-mother' portrait of the Christ child, the Virgin and her mother St Anne – and also in his dream-memoir, since the vulture of Leonardo's childhood recollection (for which read, subconscious fantasy) was also the ancient Egyptian symbol of motherhood. In the second edition of his book (1919), Freud added a 'remarkable' footnote: his contemporary, Oskar Pfister, had discovered in the portrait of Christ, the Virgin and St Anne, the outline of a vulture, unconsciously delineated in the folds of Mary's clothing and with its tail close to the mouth of the infant Christ.[3]

These intriguing conclusions sparked a minor flood of speculative, purportedly psychoanalytic biographies in the 1920s, which probably did more harm than good to the academic profile of psychoanalytic history. But Freudian psychoanalysis was becoming increasingly fashionable in academic and artistic circles in interwar Britain, continental Europe and the USA. Simultaneously the work of the *Annales* historians, and such historical studies as George Dangerfield's *Strange Death of Liberal England* (1935), which described British society undergoing in effect a collective nervous breakdown in the years immediately preceding the First World War, strengthened interest in psychological approaches. The Second World War, though, proved a turning point in the development of psychoanalytic history. First, during the war itself, psychoanalysis gained a new popular currency, as a succession of practitioners in Britain and the USA, including European exiles from Nazism, sought to explain the 'psychopathology' of both Hitler himself and the German people who had supported his rise to power.[4] The most celebrated of these, Walter Langer's psychoanalytic study of Hitler, carried out for the US government in 1943, examined Hitler's relations with his young and adored mother and elderly and despised father, his suspected illegitimacy, his mother's death (while being treated, it was noted, by a Jewish doctor), his youthful rejection as an artist and traumatic military service during the First World War, to conclude (to no-one's surprise) that Hitler was a paranoid hysteric.[5] Second, the war undermined the confidence of some historians in their discipline: the conventional explanations of historical developments seemed inadequate, and the simple label 'evil' too problematic, to explain the rise of totalitarianism and the atrocities of the death camps. Psychoanalytic theory offered a new intellectual direction, a *science* of human behaviour that might provide answers to these otherwise unanswerable questions.

In 1957 William Langer (brother of Walter), President of the American Historical Association, appealed to the association to consider what the psycho-analytic approach might contribute to the historical discipline. The publication of his address in the following year, together with the appearance of Erik Erikson's psychoanalytic study, *Young Man Luther*, marked the creation of a new interdisciplinary academic field. Both men developed and broadened Freud's approach. Langer argued that psychoanalysis offered the means to discover the irrational and repressed motivations not just of historical individuals but groups, for instance modern totalitarian movements, French revolutionary mobs or European society after the Black Death. Erikson's analysis of Luther's 'search for identity' introduced a greater degree of historical context than Freud had essayed, and modified the primacy of infant experience with a theory of 'ego psychology' that placed the individual's development in the context of familial and societal forces and adult as well as childhood influences. But his championing of the psychoanalytical approach went further than Langer's: history was too important to be left to 'non-clinical observers' or to professional historians 'immersed' in the 'very disguises, rationalizations and idealizations of the historical process from which it should be their business to separate themselves'.[6] This new approach struck a chord, particularly among the postwar cohort of young American historians such as Peter Loewenberg, drawn to investigate the 'two generations molded by two world wars, the Russian Revolution, fascism and nazism ... that saw the power of psychotic fantasy to turn words into nightmares lived'.[7] In the next two decades, psychohistory established itself as an historical sub-discipline its own right. Seminars in history and psychoanalysis were launched by Erikson at Harvard and Bruce Mazlish at the Massachusetts Institute of Technology. Mazlish addressed the Royal Historical Society on 'What is Psycho-history?' in 1970. The *American Historical Review* was the first mainstream historical journal to publish scholarship in psychoanalytic history. The *Psychohistory Review: Studies of Motivation in*

History and Culture was launched in 1972, and the former *History of Childhood Quarterly* relaunched in 1976 as *The Journal of Psychohistory*. From the 1980s history journals such as *History and Theory* have regularly featured psychohistorical research; in more recent years *History Workshop Journal*, for instance, has published two special issues on psychohistory.[8]

Psychohistorical literature falls into two principal elements: studies of individuals ('psychobiography'), and of groups or societies. Psychobiographies have tended to focus on authoritarian leaders such as Napoleon, Stalin and Hitler, monarchs or statesmen who appear to have failed great political tests (for instance Wilhelm II or Woodrow Wilson), or politicians whose careers have proved particularly controversial (e.g. Richard Nixon, Ronald Reagan or Margaret Thatcher). Interesting attempts have also been made to integrate psychoanalytic biography with the history of ideas, for instance Mazlish's celebrated study of John Stuart Mill's anguished relationship with his father, *James and John Stuart Mill: Father and Son in the Nineteenth Century* (1975).

The shift in focus among psychohistorians from individuals to societies had been presaged in the work of Erich Fromm, and the 'Frankfurt School' of European Marxist exiles in the USA, who sought to fuse Freudian and Marxist thought into a new strand of historical sociology.[9] However, the psychohistorians went further by focusing on specific historical events or social phenomena such as racism, political ideology or family relationships.[10] One of the most controversial studies of the past twenty years, John Demos' *Entertaining Satan: Witchcraft and the Culture of Early New England* (1982), used a variety of psychoanalytic approaches to analyse the Salem witch-craze, identifying a radical misogyny directed at the accused and attributing it to the effects of child-rearing practices and familial, namely sibling, rivalries. Following Loewenberg among others, Klaus Theweleit's *Male Fantasies* (two volumes, 1987/1989) highlighted, first, the paternal brutality and withdrawn maternal affection characteristic of male childhood and adolescent socialisation in Imperial Germany, and second, the literal association in the 1920s and 1930s of 'Reds' with threatening femininity, that drove young Germans towards the masculine warrior-ethos of fascism.

The backlash against psychohistory

Almost from the start, psychohistory came under attack from the mainstream of the historical profession; indeed, few methodologies have polarised historiographical opinion so thoroughly.[11] Psychohistories have constituted a closed alternative historiography, rarely if ever cited by the mainstream. As early as 1919 the youthful Karl Popper dismissed the psychoanalytic approach as 'pseudo-science'. Reviewing Bullitt and Freud's *Thomas Woodrow Wilson, A Psychological Study* (1967), A. J. P. Taylor asked, 'how did anyone ever manage to take Freud seriously?' Lawrence Stone criticised Freud's theories of child development as unhistorical. To Geoffrey Barraclough, psychohistory was simply 'bunk'. Of leading postwar British historians only Lewis Namier was prepared to admit a fascination with Freudian theory.[12]

Part of the problem has been the quality of the psychohistories themselves. Even such a staunch advocate of the psychoanalytic approach as Peter Gay has admitted that too many psychohistories have been characterised by 'irrelevance, irresponsibility and vulgarity'.[13] Certainly the two most celebrated early examples, Freud's psychobiography of Leonardo and Erikson's of Luther, have aged badly. Freud's descriptions of Leonardo's eroticised infant relationship with his mother are based not on material evidence but on Freud's own supposition that Leonardo was homosexual, and deploy a theory of the origins of homosexuality that few would accept today; his critique of Leonardo's paintings ignores some of the basic conventions of fifteenth century art, and his analysis of Leonardo's bird-story is based on an unfortunate mistranslation (Leonardo described a kite, not a vulture!). Erikson's account of Luther is likewise based on unreliable evidence, fails in its description of Luther's allegedly traumatic home life to take into account the norms of a late-medieval upbringing, and, by leading the reader to the inescapable conclusion that Luther's bowel problems were instrumental in the origins of the Protestant Reformation, rather undermines the high seriousness of his analysis.[14] Though both works have been defended as explorations in psychohistory rather than serious historical expositions, they exemplify a fault-line in the psychohistorical literature: too many psychohistories have been written either by amateur historians or by amateur psychoanalysts.

Moreover, the way that psychohistories (psychobiographies in particular) have seemed to reduce major historical episodes to the emotional crises of a handful of prominent individuals, can be troubling. This odd updating of the old 'great men' thesis of history, by which one can trace the flaws in American policy in the early twentieth century to Woodrow Wilson's ego problems, German totalitarianism to Hitler's childhood traumas or the ignominy of Watergate to Nixon's childhood maternal obsession, causes unease among historians trained to see historical development as a more complex phenomenon.[15] The use of psychoanalysis to investigate past societies is also fraught with difficulties, notably when historically specific twentieth-century theories of childcare, maternal attitudes, etc., are transposed to past societies to explain phenomena such as infanticide.[16]

But do failures in the practice of psychohistory invalidate the theory itself? Are the failures of particular psychohistories (namely, that their conclusions are unsubstantiated by the evidence; that they are reductionist; and that they are anachronistic) implicit in their methodology or just the growing pains of a relatively new academic discipline? Freud and his successors considered psychoanalytic theory to be a scientific tool, providing models against which individuals or groups could be (psycho)analysed. But is psychoanalysis as scientific an approach as its adherents claim?

As has often been pointed out, one cannot psychoanalyse the dead. Childhood records are often scarce or non-existent. Any surviving personal records – letters, diaries, etc – are presumably the product of the subject's conscious mind. So what evidence do we have – *can* we have – for the inner lives, the secret and unacknowledged motives, of historical subjects? For, by definition, the existence of the unconscious mind cannot be proven, its condition in any single case only inferred by external signs and clues that the psychoanalyst/historian interprets according to his or her theoretical perspective. While all historical research is inductive rather than deductive (i.e. working backwards to seek reasons for known outcomes), and historians are perpetually warned against identifying only the evidence that supports their hypothesis, in psychohistory the danger appears endemic, with hypotheses about childhood development inferred from and then in effect used to explain adult behaviour. Moreover, with no two psychoanalytical interpretations ever guaranteed to be alike, the scientific credentials of the approach are questionable at best. To outsiders, psychohistory, far from being a 'science of history', appears to bear approximately the same relation to history as astrology does to astronomy: a highly theorised yet seemingly infinitely malleable doctrine, whose layers of explanation allow practitioners to 'prove' almost anything they wish, and whose adherents too often display a cult-like reverence for, rather than a critical distance from, Freud and his theories. More recent attempts by practitioners (especially in the USA) to introduce a greater theoretical rigour into the discipline, for instance by requiring formal training in both history and psychoanalytic theory, have not been wholly successful, too often presenting the casual reader not with greater clarity or plausibility but with a mystifying technical vocabulary and intuitively implausible inductive leaps.

A theory-driven argument is not necessarily a circular argument. But it is not susceptible to proof in the usual sense. A telling example used in Peter Gay's defence of psychoanalytic history is Gladstone's notorious proclivity for rescuing 'fallen women'. Rather than attributing his motivation to sexual prurience and leaving it at that, Gay properly points out that such campaigns were a common philanthropic interest in late-Victorian Britain, and suggests that they derived much of their impetus from an unconscious desire to rehabilitate strangers. He then goes further, arguing that this 'rescue fantasy' is itself a disguise for the 'far more potent wish to restore the purity of the mother who, though officially an angel, does mysterious and terrible things with father behind closed bedroom doors'.[17] Many historians will happily take on board the former proposition; most would probably baulk at the latter. Whether we accept it or not depends on whether we accept the Freudian theory in the first place.

Reductionism is another problem. Leo Abse's psychobiography of Margaret Thatcher, *Margaret, Daughter of Beatrice* (1990), may be an unforgettable read (her hard-line social policy traced to her allegedly abrupt weaning by her distant mother; her monetarist philosophy attributed to her presumably harsh potty training), but it barely begins to explain what it was about the political, economic or electoral condition of Britain in the 1980s that permitted an unprecedented three successive Conservative election victories.[18] More seriously, the explanation of such phenomena as the rise of Nazism in terms of the developmental traumas of either the individual (i.e. Hitler) or the collective (German society) can appear appallingly glib. The fact that psychohistories are almost invariably psychopathologies, labouring to tell us much about dysfunctional individuals, societies and times, but little about 'normal' life, remains a problem. If the psychoanalytic approach is indeed universal in application, it should surely be just as important in explaining rational behaviour?[19]

As for getting the facts wrong about the attitudes or lifestyles of past eras, this may be a feature of bad psychohistorical practice rather than theory. But to some, the very historicity of psychoanalytic history is rooted in paradox. On the one hand it offers a theory premised on the immutability of human nature and character development across societies, cultures and historical epochs, thus arguably ahistorical to its core. On the other, critics have argued that Freud's notion of childhood development is essentially predicated on the late nineteenth-century middle class opinions and child-rearing practices of Freud, his patients and his social milieu, and so is hardly representative of late nineteenth-century Viennese, let alone European or pre-nineteenth century, society as a whole. Although theorists after Freud have sought to accommodate a wider perspective, psychohistory is clearly open to the accusation of cultural parochialism in extreme form.[20]

Freudian theory is of course no simple creed. The standard edition of his psychological works runs to twenty-four volumes. Most psychoanalytic historians tend to be convinced Freudians, but Freud's own attitudes modified considerably over the course of his life; many of Freud's followers substantially modified parts of his theory (e.g. Adler's work on the inferiority complex, Klein's views on child development); and many rivals posited alternative schemata (e.g. Jung's theory of the collective unconscious). The technical problems of applying a historically located, highly theoretical *and* internally contested discipline to historical study are considerable.

This prompts the question: far from offering universal insights into the human condition, will Freudian theory prove to be no more than an historical phenomenon itself? Certainly, many of Freud's key psychoanalytic insights (e.g. penis envy, or the roots of homosexuality) are largely discredited. As scientific knowledge has increased, psychoanalytical explanations of historical phenomena have been joined by medical ones (were the witch-crazes of medieval Europe or seventeenth-century Salem, Massachusetts, sparked by ergot poisoning, for instance, or Wilhelm II's irrationality by hereditary porphyria?[21]) It may well be that in the twenty-first century advances in genetics, biochemistry or the behavioural sciences will supersede the Freudian explanations of human action so characteristic of the twentieth. The relative enthusiasm of American historians in the last third of the twentieth century – compared to the scepticism of most European historians – for the psychoanalytic approach could perhaps itself be viewed simply as another instructive historical as well as historiographical phenomenon.

An accommodation? Thoughts and conclusions

Yet it is too easy simply to dismiss psychohistory as bunk. As one recent commentator pointed out, 'As a dogmatic structure, Freudianism is largely unconvincing: yet in diffuse form, Freudian ideas have become an indispensable part of our common-sense understanding of humanity'.[22] We all have a vague notion of Freudian theories, the language of psychoanalysis is now part of common parlance, and historians have for decades blithely used words such as 'repression', 'inferiority complex', 'transference', 'death wish', etc., even when their conceptual grasp of these terms has been impressionistic to say the least.[23] And historians are still left with the conundrum: how does one begin to explain the irrational, the non-rational, the frankly baffling, in human history? Even if psychohistory has proved to be something of a theoretical strait-jacket, perhaps the generalised psychoanalytic approach could be said to offer at the very least a broad working thesis. After all, psychology has always been part of mainstream historical explanation. The field of social psychology, i.e. the study of cultures, belief systems, gender identities, etc., is an area in which the boundaries between the psychological and the psychoanalytic often seem to blur.

In recent years psychoanalytic historians themselves have mounted a considerable defence of their field. They have argued that true psychoanalytic history (*not* mere 'psychohistory') is a multi-layered and sensitive approach, combining 'straight' historical analysis with 'social science models, humanistic sensibility and psychodynamic theory and clinical insights, to create a fuller, more rounded view of life in the past'.[24] They point out that psychoanalysis should be one tool among many at the disposal of the historian, and that psychoanalytic history should be used to complement, not replace, traditional historiographical genres and methods. They argue that the psychoanalytic historian should be trained as both historian and psychoanalyst, and pay just as much attention to historical method as to psychoanalytic theory. Some propose a much-modified Freudianism, in which the basic precepts are filtered through a historical perspective – though others argue that this reduces the theoretical element to little more than the 'common-sense' psychological approach that Freud sought to theoretise in the first place. More rewarding, perhaps, are recent studies that consider the historical role of psychoanalysts themselves in a critical historical and psychoanalytic context, such as recent work on the role of wartime psychoanalysts and the impact of the Blitz on London children.[25]

However, new directions in psychoanalytic history only partly redress the problem. For instance, a recent trend towards 'psychoanalysing the psychohistorian' has seen Freud's own major works reinterpreted to a significant degree as exercises in disguised or symbolic self-analysis.[26] Psychohistorians such as Erikson and Langer have been subject to psychoanalytic studies to discover their own inner lives and motivations. As Loewenberg warns, 'No phenomenon has an inherent meaning. The historian's personality accounts not only for the historical material and themes selected but also for the conscious and unconscious conceptual schemata imposed upon it'.[27] This rather terrifying modification of the old historian's injunction to beware personal bias cuts to a further paradox at the heart of the modern psychoanalytic endeavour: it is a purportedly scientific approach, but it increasingly recognises its practitioners *not* as scientific observers but as subjective consciousnesses in the whole enterprise. Far from historians maintaining an intellectual distance, in some accounts the psychohistorians' own personalities threaten to take on as much significance as the events they purport to address. One fears the *reductio ad absurdum* of a historiography comprising an unending spiral of psychohistorians analysing other psychohistorians.

Psychoanalytic history remains a sub-discipline whose conclusions, to sceptics, too often appear either irredeemably banal or else impenetrably abstruse. In arguing that true psychoanalytic historians must be trained as both psychoanalysts and historians, the sub-discipline has gained in analytical rigour, but in so doing has arguably both reinforced its intellectual exclusivity and continued effectively to alienate non-believers. To some, psychoanalysis will continue to be the key to historical understanding. To others it will no doubt continue to be bunk. Yet if Freud failed to supply convincing answers, he certainly raised questions about human motivation and the influence of irrationality and emotion in historical endeavour, that no historian can reasonably ignore.

Notes

1 P. Loewenberg, 'Psychohistory', in M. Kammen (ed.) *The Past Before Us: Contemporary Historical Writing in the United States*, New York, Cornell University Press, 1980, p. 409.
2 P. Gay, *Freud for Historians*, New York, Oxford University Press, 1985, pp. xiv, 77, and *passim*.
3 Sigmund Freud, *Leonardo da Vinci and a Memory of His Childhood*, New York, Norton, 1964, pp. 65 n. and *passim*.
4 For instance, W. Brown, 'The Psychology of Modern Germany', *British Journal of Psychology*, 1944, vol. 34, pp. 43–59, characterises Germany as a sick nation, whose perennial attacks of manic depression and persecution complex mirror Hitler's own hysterical and paranoid tendencies.
5 W. Langer, *The Mind of Adolf Hitler*, London, Secker and Warburg, 1973.
6 W. L. Langer, 'The Next Assignment', *American Historical Review*, 1958, vol. 63, pp. 283–304; E.H. Erikson, *Young Man Luther: A Study in Psychoanalysis and History*, New York, Norton, 1958, p. 20 and *passim*.
7 P. Loewenberg, *Decoding the Past: The Psychohistorical Approach*, Berkeley, University of California Press, 1984, p. 7 and preface. Loewenberg was born in 1933 to German parents but spent his earliest years in Shanghai, from where he was evacuated on a French gunboat; he spent the war years as a child in the USA; his father was a psychiatrist.
8 B. Mazlish, 'What is Psycho-History?' *Royal Historical Society Transactions*, 1971, vol. 21, pp. 79–100; *History Workshop Journal*, 1988, vol. 26, and 1998, vol. 45.
9 See for instance T. Adorno, *The Authoritarian Personality*, New York, Harper, 1950; E. Fromm, *The Sane Society*, London, Routledge and Kegan Paul, 1956.
10 See, for instance, W. D. Jordan, *White Over Black: American Attitudes Toward the Negro 1550–1812*, Chapel Hill, University of North Carolina Press, 1968; R.

Hofstadter, *The Paranoid Style in American Politics, and Other Essays*, New York, Vintage Books, 1967; D. Hunt, *Parents and Children in History: The Psychology of Family Life in Early Modern France*, New York, Basic Books, 1970.

11 Perhaps only postmodernism comes close.

12 See Gay, *Freud for Historians*, pp. 62–3; A. J. P. Taylor, *New Statesman and Nation*, 12 May 1967, pp. 653–4; L. Stone, *The Family, Sex and Marriage in England 1500–1800*, London, Weidenfeld and Nicolson, 1977, pp. 15, 161; G. Barraclough, 'Psycho-history Is Bunk', *The Guardian*, 3 March 1973; L. Namier, 'Human Nature in Politics', in his *Personalities and Powers*, London, Hamish Hamilton, 1955.

13 Gay, *Freud for Historians*, p. 4.

14 For a detailed critique of Freud on Leonardo, see D. Stannard, *Shrinking History: On Freud and the Failure of Psychohistory*, New York, Oxford University Press, 1980; for Erickson see R. A. Bainton in R. A. Johnson (ed.) *Psychohistory and Religion: the Case of Young Man Luther*, Philadelphia, Fortress Press, 1977.

15 Or, since in Freudian analysis the mother is the central external figure in child development and in most of the cases cited the individuals' mothers play a key role, perhaps one should posit a new 'Bad Mothers of Great Men' thesis?

16 See, for instance, B. A. Kellum, 'Infanticide in England in the Later Middle Ages', *History of Childhood Quarterly*, 1974, vol. 1, pp. 367–88.

17 Gay, *Freud for Historians*, pp. 188–9.

18 L. Abse, *Margaret, Daughter of Beatrice*, London, Jonathan Cape, 1989. Cf. his *The Man Behind the Smile: Tony Blair and the Politics of Perversion*, London, Robson Books, 1996.

19 For the problem of rationality and psychohistory, see G. Izenberg, 'Psychohistory and Intellectual History', *History and Theory*, 1975, vol. 14, pp. 139–55.

20 Stannard, *Shrinking History*, p. 30. Meanwhile, as pedants point out, Freud's Oedipus complex may or may not be a valid theory of child development, but has little to do with the Oedipus of Greek mythology, who *did not know* either that the man he killed was his natural father or that the widow he subsequently married was his natural mother until it was too late. The 'Electra complex', the female equivalent, has barely more classical validity: Electra, daughter of Agamemnon, does incite her brother Orestes to kill her guilty mother after her father's murder, but out of revenge not desire. Psychohistorians might of course argue that Sophocles' *Oedipus Rex* and Aeschylus' *Oresteia* were sublimated rather than explicit expositions of the collective Oedipal subconscious.

21 L. Caporeal, 'Ergotism: the Satan loosed in Salem?', *Science*, 2 April 1976, vol. 192; M. K. Matossian, *Poisons of the Past: Molds, Epidemics and History*, New Haven, Yale University Press, 1989; J. C. G. Rohl (historian), M. Warren (biochemist) and D. Hunt (geneticist), *Purple Secret: Genes, 'Madness' and the Royal Houses of Europe*, London, Bantam, 1998, p. 311.

22 Ritchie Robertson, *Times Literary Supplement*, 27 October 2000, p. 11.

23 Ironically, Lawrence Stone attributes the twentieth-century sexual revolution in part to popular Freudianism itself, the articulation of Freudian sexual theory fuelling an increase in sexual expectations.

24 Loewenberg, *Decoding the Past*, p. 14.

25 A. Phillips, 'Bombs Away', *Historical Workshop Journal*, 1998, vol. 45, pp. 183–98.

26 For a recent study, see, for instance, L. Breger, *Freud: Darkness in the Midst of Vision*, Chichester and New York, John Wiley, 2000.

27 Loewenberg, *Decoding the Past*, p. 12. Loewenberg suggests that all research students would benefit from psychoanalysis; indeed he goes further, 'We need to introduce psychoanalytic education in our graduate curriculum in the social sciences' (p. 78).

Further reading

Discussions of psychoanalytic history among historians have rarely been disinterested, tending to be either defences of or attacks on the notion that the psychoanalytic approach might contribute anything to historical understanding. The most important early statement by a leading historian of support for psychoanalytic history is William L. Langer's Presidential Address to the American Historical Association in 1957, reprinted as 'The Next Assignment', *American Historical Review*, 1958, vol. 63, pp. 283–304; see too Bruce Mazlish's address to the Royal Historical Society in 1970, reprinted as 'What is Psycho-History?' *Royal Historical Society Transactions*, 1971, vol. 21, pp. 79–100. Further defences of the psychoanalytic approach can be found in P. Loewenberg, *Decoding the Past: the Psychohistorical Approach*, New York, Alfred A. Knopf, 1983; in Loewenberg, 'Psychohistory', in M. Kammen (ed.) *The Past Before Us: Contemporary Historical Writing in the United States*, New York, Cornell University Press, 1980; and in Peter Gay's admirably lucid *Freud For Historians*, New York, Oxford University Press, 1985.

A leading critical account of 'psychohistory' (that includes a searing critique of Freud on Leonardo da Vinci) is D. E. Stannard, *Shrinking History: On Freud and the Failure of Psychohistory*, New York, Oxford University Press, 1980; for a similarly detailed critique of Erik Erikson's work, see for instance R. A. Johnson (ed.) *Psychohistory and Religion: The Case of* Young Man Luther, Philadelphia, 1977.

Other overviews include Geoffrey Cocks and Travis L. Crosby (eds) *Psycho/History: Readings in the Method of Psychology, Psychoanalysis and History*, New Haven and London, Yale University Press, 1987; G. Izenberg, 'Pyschohistory and Intellectual History', *History and Theory*, 1975, vol. 14, pp. 139–55; F. Weinstein, 'Psychohistory and the Crisis of the Social Sciences', *History and Theory*, 1995, vol. 34, pp. 299–319; T. G. Ashplant, 'Psychoanalysis in Historical Writing', *History Workshop Journal*, 1988, vol. 26, pp. 102–19. For feminist and gender perspectives, see S. Alexander, 'Feminist History and Psychoanalysis', *History Workshop Journal*, 1991, vol. 32, pp. 128–33; and R. Minsky (ed.) *Psychoanalysis and Gender: An Introductory Reader*, London and New York, 1996.

For Freud and Freudian theory, see S. Frosh, *The Politics of Psychoanalysis: An Introduction to Freudian and Post-Freudian Theory*, Basingstoke and London, Macmillan, 1999. A brief but useful exploration of post-Freudian developments in psychoanalytic historical approaches (with specific reference to Anna Freud, Melanie Klein, Lacan and Kristeva), can be found in G. Walker, 'Psychoanalysis and History', in S. Berger, H. Feldner and K. Passmore (eds) *Writing History: Theory and Practice*, London, Arnold, 2003, pp. 141–60.

Of 'psychohistories' themselves, as Walker (*op.cit.*, p. 141) points out, psychoanalytic theory has 'made a particular contribution to the fields of historical biography, early modern witchcraft and Holocaust studies'. A list of some of the most important full-length studies in psychoanalytic history would thus include B. Mazlish, *James and John Stuart Mill: Father and Son in the Nineteenth Century*, New York, Basic Books, 1975; J. Demos, *Entertaining Satan: Witchcraft and the Culture of Early New England*, New York, Oxford University Press, 1982; L. Roper, *Oedipus and the Devil: Witchcraft, Sexuality and Religion in Early Modern Europe*, London and New York, Routledge, 1994; K. Theweleit, *Male Fantasies*, Oxford, Polity, 1987/89; Dominick LaCapra, *History and Memory After Auschwitz*, Ithaca NY and London, Cornell University Press, 1998. See too the *Journal of Psychohistory*, produced by the Institute for Psychohistory (www.psychohistory.com) in New York.

And, for its sheer brio of execution this author would put in a word for Leo Abse's extraordinary psychobiography of Margaret Thatcher, *Margaret, Daughter of Beatrice*, London, Jonathan Cape, 1990.

Chapter 9

History and sociology

Robert Harrison

Of history's cognate disciplines, sociology has always seemed the closest, but at the same time the most intrusive, the most hectoring, the most contemptuous of historical practice. This chapter examines the origins and development of sociology. It looks at some of the ways in which sociologists have set about the investigation of society, at how their work has influenced the writing of history in recent decades, and finally at the growing penetration of various kinds of historical thinking within sociology itself.

According to Anthony Giddens, 'Sociology is the study of human social life, groups and societies'. It has 'as its subject-matter our own behaviour as social beings'.[1] How, though, does this differ from the subject-matter of history, which the nineteenth-century French historian Fustel de Coulanges identified as 'the science of human societies'?[2] The most obvious difference is that history deals with the past, while sociology deals with the present. Although such a generalisation would accurately describe the research activities of most historians and most sociologists, there is a sense in which the sociologist's construction of the 'ethnographic present' and the historian's claims to exclude the demands of the present from her investigation of the past are equally fictitious. More importantly, there is a flourishing school of historical sociology which includes in its ranks such influential figures as Barrington Moore and Immanuel Wallerstein, who study historical events in order both to test sociological theories and to construct models of social change. They are doing no more than many of the founding fathers of sociology, including Marx and Weber, both of whom mixed studies of history and sociology. Indeed, classical sociology originated as a reaction to social change, as a way of coming to terms with the social and political revolutions of the nineteenth century.

A second, equally obvious, distinction is that historians concern themselves with the interpretation of particular events, whereas sociologists seek to establish general patterns. This also is substantially true, although historians are commonly praised for work whose 'significance' transcends its immediate subject-matter, a 'significance' which, argues Gareth Stedman Jones, is ultimately 'dependent on some explicit or implicit theory of social causation'.[3] 'In works of history', notes Richard Johnson, 'the organising ideas and presuppositions may lie very deep. They none the less exist'.[4] However, sociologists are usually more explicit in creating their theoretical models of reality. Sociology has always claimed a position among the social sciences, a status which most historians have been decidedly reluctant to assume. Sociology aspires to the status of a 'science' in its attempt to devise a precise and value-free language, in its approach to data-gathering and analysis, and in the elaborate and sophisticated nature of its theory. Many historians might feel sceptical about such pretensions. They might question the usefulness of sociological 'jargon', the capacity of social scientists to collect unimpeachable 'scientific' evidence about human societies, and the value of sociological theories which they find either mundane or incomprehensible. They might question the status of sociology as a 'science'. If so, they would be doing no more than echo the criticisms of many sociologists, not all of whom subscribe to the positivist approach to their subject that prevailed, at least in Anglo-American sociology, for much of the last century. It is important to recognise that there is more than one way of doing sociology. Indeed, sociology departments probably harbour a greater diversity of contesting schools, diverging widely in both methodology and thematic focus, than do history departments. Thus any attempt to examine the relationship between history and sociology must constantly bear in mind variations in practice within both disciplines.

The reason for posing what might appear to be an elementary question about the differences between history and sociology is that the two disciplines have not always been separate. They share common origins in Enlightenment philosophy. Writers like Charles de Montesquieu, Adam Ferguson and John Millar wrote comparative analytical works on what Millar called 'the philosophy of society' but also regarded themselves as 'philosophical historians'. They shared an analytical approach to history and sought to comprehend the laws governing society by historical studies.

The social theorists of the nineteenth century continued their interest in historical development, that is in the evolution of social institutions. Auguste Comte, the French scholar who invented the word 'sociology', regarded the study of social history as indispensable to the articulation of social theory. His work, which could essentially be described as an exercise in the speculative philosophy of history, consisted of an account of the successive stages through which humankind has passed. Karl Marx produced what was as much a theory of history as a theory of society. Indeed, he maintained that the structure of society could only be understood historically, in terms of a sequence of modes of production and social organisation. Herbert Spencer, the English theorist who made the most systematic efforts to apply Darwinian notions of natural selection to human society, made considerable use of historical materials to illustrate the process of social evolution. Emile Durkheim drew on historical materials in his sociological studies and also wrote on the history of education in France. The German sociologist Max Weber penned numerous historical works, up to and including *The Protestant Ethic and the Spirit of Capitalism*, and his studies of social and economic organisation drew heavily on historical case-studies.

Weber and the other founders of the discipline were essentially historical sociologists. They were preoccupied with what was fundamentally an historical problem, that of coming to terms with the new society that had arisen in the wake of what Alexis de Tocqueville called 'the continuing revolution' of the nineteenth century. Old institutions, old values had largely lost their meaning. The result was a profound feeling of social confusion and 'intellectual anarchy'. 'These times are times of chaos', observed Jules Lamartine during the last years of the July Monarchy in France; 'opinions are a scramble; parties are a jumble; the language of new ideas has not been created ... It is the problem of the time to classify things and men. The world has jumbled its catalogue'.[5] The aim of social theorists was to create a 'language of new ideas', to find new ways 'to classify things and men', and, in so doing, to unjumble the world's catalogue. They attempted to understand the new society by comparing it with the old. Marx saw the key in the structure of capitalism and class formation, Weber in rationalisation and the growth of bureaucracy, Durkheim in the social implications of the division of labour, but they shared a common preoccupation with the interpretation of the new industrial society.

If they were interested in history, they were not terribly interested in the work of historians. During the late nineteenth century historians were moving away from the broad sweep of the 'philosophical historians'. The new modes of 'scientific history' required the close study of official documents. Taking as their central subject the evolution of the nation-state, members of the newly established historical profession confined themselves almost exclusively to political topics, narrowly defined in terms of time and place. The paradigm of statist history that was established along with the professionalisation of the discipline during the late nineteenth century defined the practice of the majority of academic historians for a generation or more.

Just as history became less sociological, sociology became less historical. Indeed, under the influence of the functionalist theories which largely held sway during the early twentieth century, it became decidedly anti-historical. What were seen as genuinely 'sociological' explanations displaced historical explanations. This tendency was reinforced by the institutionalisation of sociology as an academic discipline, especially in the United States, which provided the principal home of sociological research after the First World War. Sociologists, like historians, established their own departments, their own learned societies, their own journals in which they refined their own concepts, theories and research procedures, their own professional standards and modes of socialisation. In other words, they created a form of 'normal sociology'. Thus the institutionalisation of academic life during the late nineteenth and early twentieth centuries tended to separate scholars in cognate disciplines, each eager to establish its claim to intellectual and institutional autonomy.

There were, of course, many different ways of doing sociology, but two approaches prevailed during the early and mid-twentieth century. One was structural-functionalism, which was so dominant during the years between 1920 and 1960 as virtually to constitute *the* sociological method; the other was positivism. Though analytically distinct, structural-functionalism and positivism tended to cohabit the same intellectual space. Functionalist theories seek to explain social institutions and social behaviour in terms of their present functions rather than their historical development. Society is conceived of as an integrated whole whose various parts fit together. Its normal condition is one of equilibrium. Social institutions should be investigated in terms of their functions, that is the manner in which they contribute to the maintenance of societal equilibrium. Such functions could be either manifest, that is explicit and intentional, or latent, that is unintended and indirect. Structural-functionalism in sociology owed much to the anthropological theories of A. R. Radcliffe-Brown, which, in turn, drew heavily on the writings of the late nineteenth-century French sociologist Emile Durkheim. It was carried to its furthest conclusion, some might say to the point of *reductio ad absurdum*, in the elaborate theoretical systems of Talcott Parsons.

Positivism means, first of all, a belief that the logic of explanation in the social sciences should be modelled on that employed in the natural sciences. Under the influence of philosophers of science like Carl Hempel and Ernest Nagel, social scientists were persuaded that the only valid form of explanation was one which called upon general laws, equivalent to the laws of science, and that their duty was, as far as possible, to create a body of theoretical knowledge of society. Second, social scientists should find methods of hypothesis-testing which were equivalent to those that had proved so successful in the hands of natural scientists. In other words, they had to find some kind of analogue to the experimental method.

Durkheim argued in his *Rules of Sociological Method* that 'social facts are to be treated as things': 'I consider extremely fruitful [the] idea that social life should be explained, not by the notions of those who participate in it, but by more profound causes which are unperceived by consciousness'.[6] Instead of using his and his subjects' ideas and preconceptions about society, the investigator should set out to uncover the underlying patterns by observing social behaviour. Since he was interested in 'social facts' he could not rely on individual understandings to access them. To Durkheim, as to later sociologists of a positivist cast of mind, the way to discover patterns and regularities in human behaviour was through the application of quantitative methods. A well known example is Durkheim's analysis of suicide. On comparing the incidence of suicides in various European countries with measures of other social variables, he discovered that suicide rates were higher in Protestant than in Catholic countries. The two variables, as he put it, 'go together'. This, he argued, was because Protestant communities were more individualistic, less well integrated than Catholic communities: 'suicide varies inversely with the degree of integration of religious society'.[7] This 'variable analysis' was equivalent to a scientific experiment. The social researcher obviously cannot experiment with human beings (especially when studying suicide), but he can use quantitative measures of social variables to identify correlations which indicate at least the possibility of a causal relationship. Although Durkheim's methodology was crude and his explanation seriously flawed, his study offered an early and influential example of the form which much sociological investigation was to take.

The next century saw a great elaboration of the methods of quantitative sociological research. Sociologists, indulging a growing fascination, even obsession, with measurement, devoted themselves to increasingly narrow empirical studies. Techniques for gathering data through questionnaires and social surveys were improved, while the statistical methods applied to the analysis of data became ever more complex. Much sociological research in the middle decades of the century was heavily dependent on quantitative analysis, with tables, charts and equations featuring heavily in the published output, not just as illustrative matter but as central terms in the argument. Between the twin poles of 'abstracted empiricism' and 'grand theory' identified by C. Wright Mills in 1959, there was little room within sociology for the contemplation of history.

Such was the conception of sociology that prevailed during the period when historians in Britain and North America, in search of new ideas and approaches, began to look jealously at the activities of the social scientists across the corridor. Although advocates of the 'new history' like James Harvey Robinson had urged their colleagues to dismantle the barriers between history and the social sciences, and although the *Annales* historians in France had made notable progress in that direction, little practical work drawing on sociological methods or theories was carried out in Britain and America before the 1950s. Why did historians at this point in time, in contrast to the indifference, if not repugnance, which most members of their tribe had shown in the past, begin to show an interest in what they could learn from sociology?

In part, historians acted out of a sense of deference towards the authority which the social sciences commanded in the postwar era. In the belief that sociologists could find definite answers to many of the besetting social problems of the time, governments and private foundations showered resources upon them which scholars in the humanities could only dream of. A number of historians suffered from something of an inferiority complex when faced with the self-confident assertiveness with which colleagues in the social sciences claimed to have attained positive understandings about the workings of society. In contrast, historians lamented the 'flaccidity', the 'intellectually invertebrate' nature, the tired traditionalism of most work in their own subject. Geoffrey Barraclough, reviewing the state of the discipline in 1955, felt that 'historical science was struck in a deep rut churned by the ponderous cart wheels of nineteenth-century historiography'.[8] Historians of the younger generation in particular, products of what might be called the 'baby boom' in higher education called to university teaching by the dramatic expansion of the postwar decades, were attracted to interdisciplinary approaches in their quest for subjects to research and write on. In the political ferment of the 1960s, sociology appealed to young Turks eager to challenge the historical establishment. In Britain at least, sociology had something of a radical image. Whereas in the United States sociology was a well established university subject and, in the absence of a strong indigenous Marxist tradition, a largely conservative one, at British universities little sociology had been taught before the 1960s. Sociology emerged, especially at the newer universities, in association with the social and political changes of the 1960s. For historians a willingness to learn from sociology took on a kind of symbolic significance: it was something which distinguished the innovative ambitions of young progressive historians from the fusty pedantry of the old brigade.

Above all, historians took an interest in sociology when the scope of their own research became broader. Most important was the rise of social history.[9] Once historians took for their subject-matter questions of social relationship and social structure, once they began to investigate family patterns, religion, social class and status, crime and deviance, urbanisation and acculturation, once they switched their attention from the individual to the group, it seemed foolish not to consider what social scientists had to say about the same topics. Many of the questions to which historians were now turning had long been investigated by sociologists. In each case a body of theory, a range of concepts and an arsenal of methods was already available. It was tempting for social historians, struggling with parallel research problems, to take sociological concepts, methods and explanatory theories, as it were, off the peg, without always recognising the extent to which, in nearly every case, those methods, concepts and theories were contested within their mother discipline.

When historians turned to the study of ordinary people, and sometimes more particularly to 'history from below', they found the traditional historical sources and methods decidedly unhelpful. Therefore they turned to different methods, many of them drawn from the social science. Most prominent for a while was quantification. Ordinary people do not commonly speak through the documentary record, but they are enumerated in parish records, census returns, muster rolls and tax lists. Sometimes the only way of learning about them is through the analysis of such sources. That is why social historians turned to statistical methods in order to process large sets of data extracted from these records, rather than poring over manuscripts and newspapers. The methods of quantitative analysis developed in the social sciences appeared to point the way forward. The growing interest in quantitative methods among historians in recent decades followed from the increasing prominence of social history.

The more enthusiastic calls for interdisciplinarity took on something of a messianic tone. For example, in one of a group of essays on 'New Ways in History' published in the *Times Literary Supplement* in 1966, Keith Thomas expressed his contempt for 'the old empirical tradition', whose practitioners, with their woolly concepts, impressionistic language and obscurantist method-ology, had condemned history to the status of 'a craft, not a cumulative science'. Instead, he urged historians to borrow from 'the new sciences of society': to refine their terms with greater precision and clarity, to utilise tried and tested sociological and anthropological theories, and to apply more rigorous techniques of verification, particularly through quantitative methods, which, he insisted, had already provided 'definitive answers' to longstanding historical controversies, particularly in the field of economic history. 'A more self-conscious statistical approach will enable historians to be objective where the facts are available, and refrain from unverifiable pronouncements when they are not'. 'The tools of reconstruction are at hand', he proclaimed; it remained to be seen whether historians had 'the will to use them'.[10] Although most historians who turned to the social sciences, probably including Thomas himself, did so in search of fresh insights to deepen their historical under-standing, there were some who hoped to revive an older dream of a 'scientific' history by replacing the 'impressionistic' methods of traditional historiography with the more rigorous procedures of positivist social science.

Sociological concepts and methods greatly influenced the writing of history during the 1960s and 1970s. The 'new history', as it was called in America, was characterised by an interest in the behaviour of masses rather than elites; an analytical, rather than a narrative, structure; a willingness to ask explicit ques-tions of the evidence and to frame explicit hypotheses articulated with reference to social science theory; greater precision in the use of language; and a readiness to adopt new methods in collecting and analysing data, including oral inter-views, content analysis, collective biography and quantification, and to be much more explicit in setting out its research methodology. The numerous examples include the studies of historical demography by E. A. Wrigley and D. V. Glass, of family history by Lawrence Stone and Edward Shorter, of social mobility by Stephan Thernstrom, of collective violence by Charles and Louise Tilly, of New England witchcraft by Paul Boyer and Stephen Nissenbaum. The influence of sociology was evident also in writing on urban history, the study of institutions of 'social control' like prisons and asylums, the study of social movements and many other fields.[11]

Several difficulties attended the application of sociological techniques and methods to historical data, and these were pointed out trenchantly by 'straight-line professionals' (to use Arthur Marwick's phrase) like Geoffrey Elton and Jack Hexter. Some of their criticisms were merely obscurantist in character, but others carried more force. History, argued E. P. Thompson, is a 'discipline of context'.[12] It involves placing events and texts in their proper historical context. In seeking to apply comparative frameworks and general theories of human behaviour, historians are likely to lose sight of the particularity of events. History is concerned with change over time. Since most social science theory is ahistorical in character, it cannot, by its very nature, provide an explanation of change. 'Attitudes towards sociological theory among sociologically inclined historians have often verged on the credulous', complained Gareth Stedman Jones, 'they have looked uncritically to sociology as a theoretical storehouse from which they could simply select concepts most serviceable for their individual needs'. Historians, rather than borrowing inappropriate theories from sociologists, should develop their own; 'theoretical work in history is too important to be sub-contracted to others'.[13]

By 1979 Lawrence Stone, in a widely reported article in *Past and Present*, noted that some of the more enthusiastic borrowers from the social sciences were becoming disillusioned with large-scale numerical analysis and deterministic models of human behaviour. Their various large-scale projects had failed to overturn the 'central propositions' of historical interpretation. Their attempts to offer 'coherent scientific explanations of change in the past' and their hopes that social science methodology would revolutionise the study of history were unrealised. Instead, he observed, historians like Emmanuel Le Roy Ladurie, in order to do justice to the complexity of human experience, were turning to more narrowly focused studies of individual communities and events (like Le Roy Ladurie's study of *Montaillou*). Instead of analysing mass behaviour, they were taking an interest in culture and *mentalité*. Instead of applying sociological theories and quantitative methods, they were looking for their inspiration to cultural anthropology and literary theory. And, instead of setting out their findings in an analytical format, they were returning to narrative modes of presentation.[14] As a number of commentators pointed out, Stone greatly overstated the degree of disillusionment of social science historians and read too much significance into two or three prominent microstudies, but his article on 'The Revival of Narrative', while by no means marking the end of historians' fascination with the social sciences, did perhaps denote a more sophisticated appreciation of the possibilities of interdisciplinary history and a more realistic understanding of its limitations than had been evident a decade or two earlier. He also correctly identified the 'cultural turn' in history which meant that, from the 1980s, sociology became much less influential than the neighbouring discipline of cultural anthropology, as well as literary theory and cultural studies.

Another problem that historians faced was that the social sciences themselves were in turmoil, sociology not least among them. The positivist tradition competed with various forms of 'interpretive sociology', including symbolic interactionism, phenomenology and ethnomethodology, each of which, in different ways, started from the position that human actions were meaningful. Meanwhile, in the social and political ferment of the 1960s and 1970s, unprecedented attention was given to various forms of Marxist sociology. But, in the eyes of most practitioners, Marxist theory was no more successful than the formerly dominant functionalist paradigm in making sense of an increasingly fragmented social reality. Sociology, was subject, no less than history, to the repercussions of the 'linguistic turn' in the human sciences and, in time, to the intellectually erosive impact of poststructuralism. By the 1980s the discipline, in the English-speaking world at least, had lost much of the cohesiveness it had once possessed, and with it the intellectual self-confidence and social authority of the postwar decades. It was a sign of the times when prestigious universities on both sides of the Atlantic decided to close their sociology departments.

One response to the crisis within sociology was a return to history. The last thirty years have seen a resurgence of historical sociology. The work of Barrington Moore, Perry Anderson, Immanuel Wallerstein, Theda Skocpol and Charles Tilly has revived an ancient and honourable tradition that goes back to Marx and Weber. It had been suppressed during the early and middle decades of the twentieth century, when sociologists either ignored history or perceived it in terms of a simple and invariant evolutionary process described as 'modernization', but developments since the 1960s encouraged a revival. The frustrations experienced by social scientists seeking to understand and facilitate the process of economic development in the Third World demonstrated that there was no one road to modernity. Ahistorical theories proved incapable of explaining the ways in which different societies developed. Nor did they offer clear-cut answers to the social problems of Western nations like the United States in an era of student protest, racial turmoil and generational conflict. As Abrams pointed out, 'many of the most serious problems faced by sociologists need to be solved historically'.[15] Social theorists found themselves in a situation similar to that which the sociologists of the previous century had experienced, one in which the world had 'jumbled its catalogue' and in which the old verities had lost their force. Neither orthodox Marxist nor Western evolutionary models were wholly adequate to explain the complexity of the late twentieth-century world. Thus historical sociology is built largely around a series of dialogues with the grand theories of the past – Anderson and Wallerstein with the Marxist tradition, S. N. Eisenstadt and Reinhard Bendix with structural-functionalism – in order to refine and modify them to meet changing historical circumstances.

The number of sociologists interested in historical development has grown considerably. The number of articles with historical content in the pages of the *British Journal of Sociology*, the *American Journal of Sociology* and the *American Sociological Review* has increased from virtually none at all in 1970 to nearly a quarter by 1980. In recognition of the trend, in 1982 the American Sociological Association established a section devoted to Comparative and Historical Sociology. At the same time, a growing number of sociologists interested in specialised topics like crime, demography, family structure, migration studies and urbanisation attend meetings of the Social Science History Association, where they now outnumber the historians.

One might ask how the endeavours of historical sociologists differ from those of social historians. As Skocpol explains, historical sociologists 'ask questions about social structures or processes understood to be concretely situated in time and space'; 'they address processes over time'; they 'attend to the interplay of meaningful actions and structural contexts'; and they 'highlight the *particular* and *varying* features of special kinds of social structures and patterns of change'.[16] So do historians. Historical sociologists sometimes carry out highly detailed historical research and engage in dialogues with historians interested in the same substantive issues. There is no definition of historical sociology that clearly demarcates it from history. Many would agree with Anthony Giddens that 'there are simply no logical or even methodological distinctions between the social sciences and history – appropriately conceived'.[17] Yet, if the disciplinary boundaries have become blurred, they are still clearly discernible. The work of historical sociologists tends to be more explicitly theoretical than that of historians. They engage in comparative analysis more frequently, more systematically and with a clearly theoretical intent. Historical analysis is used as a way to test and develop social theory, rather than to explore specific historical events. Moreover, most historical sociologists make it clear in their reaction to criticism from their fellow professionals that they see their intellectual and institutional home as located firmly within the boundaries of their home discipline.

Stuart Hughes, writing in 1964, predicted that 'the study of history today is entering a period of rapid change and advance such as characterized the science of physics in the first three decades of the twentieth century'.[18] When the dust had settled after the burst of innovation in the 1960s and 1970s it was clear that the paradigm shift implied by Hughes had not occurred. Certainly, the defenders of traditionalism were well entrenched. In 1978 Barraclough estimated that 90 per cent of historians were traditionalists, variously deterred from adopting the new methods by an innate conservatism, a desire for empathy with the past, a love of story-telling and the entrenched individualism of historical research. Conversely, Charles Tilly estimated that only about 1,000 out of over 15,000 professional historians in the United States regarded themselves as practitioners of social science history. Hexter found the writing of history almost unaltered by the efforts to transform it; it seemed to absorb the pressures placed upon it and resume its original shape like a foam cushion. From the vantage-point of the new millennium such dismissive claims seem unfounded. Outside the diminishing ranks of the old-style political historians, the writing of history has become more sensitive to problems of conceptualisation and methodology, more attuned to work in adjacent disciplines, more eclectic in the choice of sources and methods. Historians explore relevant work in related disciplines almost as a matter of course. However, they tend to do so in a pragmatic, *ad hoc* fashion. As Dorothy Ross observes, 'That loose and eclectic mode of operation often reflects historians' superficial engagement with social theory, but it also follows from their preference for empirical richness and complexity'.[19] Their very eclecticism, their very diversity of subject-matter and method, means that the relationship between history and sociology, still more between history and the social sciences in general, is a complex and a changing one. The outcome, as Tilly explains, is 'not one grand Synthesis, but several different syntheses of sociological and historical practice', as historians interested in diverse bodies of subject-matter develop working relationships with those segments of the social sciences that appear most applicable to their needs.[20] Those syntheses have changed continuously as the assumptions and agendas of historians have changed, and as the social sciences themselves have evolved in dramatic, sometimes unexpected ways; and they will continue to do so.

Notes

1 A. Giddens, *Sociology*, Cambridge, Cambridge University Press, 1989, p. 7.
2 M. Bloch, *The Historian's Craft*, Manchester, Manchester University Press, 1954, p. 25, n.
3 G. Stedman Jones, 'From Historical Sociology to Theoretical History', *British Journal of Sociology*, 1976, vol. 27, p. 296.
4 P. Abrams, *Historical Sociology*, Shepton Mallet, Open Books, 1982, p. xvi.
5 Quoted in P. Abrams, 'The Sense of the Past and the Origins of Sociology', *Past and Present*, 1972, vol. 55, p. 22.
6 Emile Durkheim, *The Rules of Sociological Method*, New York, Free Press, 1964, p. xliii. Numerous editions, originally published 1895.
7 E. C. Huff and G. C. E. Payne, *Perspectives in Sociology*, 2nd edn, London, George Allen and Unwin, 1984, p. 197.
8 G. R. Barraclough, *Main Trends in History*, New York, Holmes and Meier, 1979, p. 206.
9 See also above, p. 69.
10 K. V. Thomas, 'The Tools and the Job', *Times Literary Supplement*, 7 April 1966, pp. 275–6.
11 See also above, pp. 114–16.
12 E. P. Thompson, 'Anthropology and the Discipline of Historical Context', *Midland History*, spring 1972, vol. 1:3, p. 45.
13 Jones, 'From Historical Sociology to Theoretical History', p. 300.
14 Lawrence Stone, 'The Revival of Narrative', *Past and Present*, 1979, vol. 85, pp. 3–24. See also below, pp. 154–7.
15 Abrams, *Historical Sociology*, p. ix.
16 T. Skocpol, 'Sociology's Historical Imagination', in *idem* (ed.) *Vision and Method in Historical Sociology*, Cambridge, Cambridge University Press, 1984, p. 1.
17 A. Giddens, *Central Problems in Social Theory*, London, Macmillan, 1979, p. 230.
18 Barraclough, *Main Trends in History*, p. 44.
19 D. G. Ross, 'The New and Newer Histories: Social Theory and Historiography in an American Key', in A. Molho and G. S. Wood (eds) *Imagined Histories: American Historians Interpret Their Past*, Princeton, Princeton University Press, 1998, p. 96.
20 C. Tilly, *As Sociology Meets History*, New York, Academic Press, 1981, p. 4.

Further reading

For a general discussion of the relationship between history and sociology, see P. Burke, *History and Social Theory*, Cambridge, Polity Press, 1992 (an earlier version of which was published as *History and Sociology*); P. Abrams, *Historical Sociology*, Shepton Mallet, Open Books, 1982. A helpful explanation of the differences between the two disciplines can be found in K. Erikson, 'Sociology and the Historical Perspective', in M. Drake (ed.) *Applied Social Studies: An Introductory Reader*, London, Methuen, 1971. On the history and early development of sociology in Britain and America, see P. Abrams, 'The Sense of the Past and the Origins of Sociology', *Past and Present*, 1972, no. 55, pp. 18–32; D. G. Ross, *The Origins of American Social Science*, Cambridge, Cambridge University Press, 1991.

The growing willingness of historians to 'borrow' from sociology and the other social sciences can be traced in S. Martin Lipset and R. Hofstadter (eds) *Sociology and History: Methods*, New York, Basic Books, 1968; G. Barraclough, *Main Trends in History*, New York, Holmes and Meier, 1979, pp. 45–93; J. Morgan Kousser, 'Quantitative Social-Scientific History', in M. Kammen (ed.) *The Past Before Us: Contemporary Historical Writing in the United States*, Ithaca NY, Cornell University Press, 1980; L. Stone, 'History and the Social Sciences', in *idem, The Past and the Present Revisited*, London, Routledge, 1987; C. Tilly, *As Sociology Meets History*, New York, Academic Press, 1981. An especially enthusiastic expression of the optimism associated with the early stages of the process is K. V. Thomas, 'The Tools and the Job', *Times Literary Supplement*, 7 April 1966, pp. 275–6. A growing disillusionment with some of the more grandiose versions of social science history was identified by Lawrence Stone in a 1979 *Past and Present* article, reprinted in *The Past and the Present Revisited*. For a retrospective look at the relationship between the disciplines, see A. Abbott, 'History and Sociology: The Lost Synthesis', in E. H. Monkkonen (ed.) *Engaging the Past: The Uses of History across the Social Sciences*, Durham NC, Duke University Press, 1994; D. G. Ross, 'The New and Newer Histories: Social Theory and Historiography in an American Key', in A. Molho and G. S. Wood (eds) *Imagined Histories: American Historians Interpret their Past*, Princeton, Princeton University Press, 1998.

The rise, or rather revival, of historical sociology can be traced in Abrams, *Historical Sociology*, T. Skocpol (ed.) *Vision and Method in Historical Sociology*, Cambridge, Cambridge University Press, 1984; D. Smith, *The Rise of Historical Sociology*, Cambridge: Cambridge University Press, 1991.

Chapter 10

History and anthropology

John Davidson

According to Bernard S. Cohn, an American South Asianist who has straddled the disciplines more effectively than most,

> Historians and anthropologists have a common subject matter, 'otherness'; one field constructs and studies 'otherness' in space, the other in time. Both fields have a concern with text and context. Both aim, whatever else they do, at explicating the meaning of actions of people rooted in one time and place, to persons in another.[1]

Most historians have practised their craft uninfluenced by, and in many cases ignorant of, developments in anthropology. But from the earliest days of professional academic history some historians have shown an interest in anthropology and even envisaged a blurring of the disciplinary divide. Anthropologists, particularly British social anthropologists, were more sceptical. But in the 1960s and later, as some anthropologists moved away from natural science models, E. E. Evans-Pritchard and Clifford Geertz argued that social and cultural anthropology ought to align itself with history and the humanities rather than with positivist social science. In the period after 1945 historians began to interest themselves in the histories of societies in Africa and Asia hitherto thought of as the exclusive preserve of anthropologists. In the postcolonial intellectual and political context of the late 1960s and 1970s anthropologists began to research complex societies with well documented histories. In the early 1980s some social and intellectual historians took a marked 'cultural turn'. By the end of the twentieth century a substantial 'blurring of the genres', in Geertz's phrase, had indeed taken place.

Like history, anthropology emerged in its modern form in the thought of the French and the Scottish Enlightenments. Common to all its definitions is the notion that anthropology deals primarily with small-scale, technologically simple societies commonly characterised in the nineteenth century, and later, as 'primitive', 'savage' or 'tribal'. Such societies were encountered mainly in the world beyond Europe and particularly in Oceania, Africa and the Americas. The process of accumulating the necessary data by residence and observation, and the subsequent description of such societies was referred to as ethnography. In the nineteenth century the increase in the scale and density of information about the diversity of human societies stimulated writers, notably J. H. Maine, E. B. Tylor and L. H. Morgan, with intellectual backgrounds either in classics or in law to produce syntheses, which formed the basis of a new academic discipline. Unified professional associations were established; the British Anthropological Institute in 1871 and the United States Bureau of Ethnology in 1879. The 'Classical Evolutionists' differed substantially in emphasis and argument, but all sought to build a unilinear developmental framework that led from barbarism to civilisation, from status to contract, from promiscuity to monogamy. Contemporary savage societies were regarded as living ancestors preserved almost like fossils, stuck on a lower rung of the evolutionary ladder – perhaps for environmental, but more probably for biological reasons.

In the early twentieth century in both the United States and Great Britain, major changes took place in the practice and theoretical underpinnings of anthropology. They comprised a strong reaction against classical evolutionism and German geographical diffusionism. In both cases intellectual changes went together with further academic professionalisation. In both cases dominant founding fathers pioneered intellectual changes and trained the next generation of practitioners.

Franz Boas was born in 1858 in a liberal German Jewish family. He was educated in Germany, moved to the United States and was appointed to a chair at Columbia in 1899. His major contribution was to argue that culture and biology were radically separate. He attacked racist thinking, still alive and well among physical anthropologists as well as in public discourse in the USA, and argued that human culture was learned, not inherited. The cultures exhibited by particular peoples – Boas worked mainly on Native Americans – had to be understood in the context of their particular historical development.

Bronislaw Malinowski's major innovation was to establish extensive fieldwork as the defining method of professional anthropology. In the Trobriands, in 1915–16 and again in 1917–18, he became fluent in the vernacular and lived among the islanders as a genuine participant observer. His first major monograph, *Argonauts of the Western Pacific* presented an account of an exotic 'savage' society unparalleled in richness of detail and sympathetic understanding. Malinowski believed that Trobriand society made sense in its own terms. The key to understanding was to observe local society closely over long periods, to elucidate the function of the separate elements of social structure and show how each element fitted together to make an integrated whole. The central importance accorded to fluency in local languages and to long residence in the field, and the aspiration to provide a complete holistic account of the society studied, restricted the range of societies studied. The anthropologist's 'people' had to be small-scale and clearly bounded – it is no accident that so many early fieldworkers worked on islands. The account provided was inevitably synchronic, static and timeless. Both history and any consideration of processes of change contemporaneous with the fieldwork were largely excluded. The ahistorical emphasis was strongly reinforced by the influence of the other founding father of British social anthropology, A. R. Radcliffe-Brown. He drew heavily on Durkheim and emphasised the central importance of social structure as the object of analysis and the search for development of sound, law-type generalisations as the aim of a truly scientific anthropology.[2] That aspiration dominated British social anthropology until the 1960s.

In very different ways, Boasian cultural anthropology and British structural-functionalist social anthropology made available to students of human society a mode of analysis that disjoined culture and society from biology, and provided a possible framework of systematic comparison. But in the period between the two world wars contacts between historians and anthropologists were marginal. Before 1945 the most significant connections between historians and some of the theoretical concerns of anthropology were forged in France. There, concern for an understanding of 'primitive' society was less sharply distinguished from sociology as a whole than was the case in Anglo-Saxon academe. Emile Durkheim and his nephew Marcel Mauss wrote significant works of anthropology. Mauss' important book on *Le Don* (1923) drew on Malinowski's Trobriand and Boas' Kwakiutl ethnography. Lucien Levy-Bruhl wrote on religion and on 'primitive mentality'. All were important for the first generation of *Annales* historians, as teachers and intellectual influences. Marc Bloch's *Les rois thaumaturges* (1924) and Lucien Febvre's *Le problème de l'incroyance au 16e siècle: la religion de Rabelais* (1942) show most obviously the influence of anthropologists' concerns with ritual and systems of belief, and in Bloch's case with comparative history. But Braudel too used Mauss in his discussion of cultural exchange, while the aspiration to *histoire totale* owes something to the anthropological impetus to describe societies as integrated wholes.[3] Some historians outside France read Mauss or Levy-Bruhl, as for example did the Dutch historian Huizinga, an early pioneer of a broader cultural history.[4] But before 1939 cross-disciplinary contact outside France was partial and fragmented.

Political, social and economic change in the period 1939–c.1975 transformed the shape of the academy and of many of the disciplines that made it up. Particularly after the onset of the Cold War, an enhanced academic understanding of what came to be known as the Third World assumed a far greater importance. The number of anthropologists and historians interested in Asia, Africa, Oceania and Latin America expanded as a proportion of the total, and fieldwork attracted funding on an unprecedented scale.

The benefits to the relationship between history and anthropology were not immediate. The major African monographs produced by the British school between 1935 and 1965 are the classic instances of work written in the 'anthropological present', a timeless tense in which the anthropologist describes the social structure of the people in question. To the degree that these 'societies' were placed in time, that time was a notional 'just before the Europeans arrived', though in most cases the fieldwork had been conducted much later.

Few went so far as to claim that African societies were changeless. But the timeless monographs fixing Nuer and Tallensi forever in the anthropological canon along with Trobrianders were esteemed as making a greater contribution to theory than studies of urban life ever could.[5] In the United States, too, the claims of a positivist social science were pushed strongly in the period after the war, particularly at the Institute of Social Sciences at Harvard. Here many of the next generation of anthropologists were trained under the influence of Talcott Parsons.

Historians made the first moves that led to the blurring of the genres in the study of the world beyond Europe and North America. One of the consequences of political change in Asia and then in Africa was that new nations needed a history emancipated from the colonial framework. The impact this had on historiography can be illustrated with reference to Africa. The first generation of academic historians of Africa had of necessity to turn to other disciplines, and in particular anthropology. The debt to anthropology involved borrowing modes of analysis, methods and in particular the practice of fieldwork. The major statement of the theoretical implications of the new practice came from the work of Jan Vansina, a Belgian historian, trained as a medievalist, who went on to study anthropology at University College London and pioneered fieldwork techniques in the then Belgian Congo, Rwanda and Burundi.[6] In 1960, Vansina took up a post at the University of Wisconsin. There he directed the work of successive generations of American scholars who worked in the field in new ways.[7] The initial impetus of much of the work of the pioneers was to refute the then common calumny that Africa had no history. Great efforts were made to collect the oral traditions of major African states and to put together what was in a sense a statist metanarrative of the history of the continent. Subsequently doubts developed, among Vansina's students as well as elsewhere, about the reliability of oral tradition and the limitations of exclusive concentration on political history.

But, once forged, the bonds between history and anthropology could not be broken. Whatever status might be accorded formal court traditions, fieldwork and the gathering of all manner of oral texts remained central to research on recent as well as on pre-colonial history, and for social, cultural and economic as well as for political history. The alliance between history and anthropology was further assisted by a widespread rediscovery of history on the part of anthropologists concerned with Africa. As early as the 1950s and 1960s some Africanist anthropologists were writing what was in essential respects history, dealing with long time spans and with processes of change and using a full range of sources written as well as oral. By the mid-1970s, when African studies was well established particularly in the USA, the significant intellectual divides ran not between the disciplines but across history and anthropology. From the 1980s onwards the theoretical developments loosely characterised as 'postmodernism' have had an impact on African studies. The range of topics studied has, as elsewhere, been considerably extended from its earlier concentration on states and trade to include the history of disease, of religion, of women, of ethnicity, clothing, and alcohol use.[8] Great states continue to be studied, but with very different theoretical underpinnings.[9] But whatever the topic, whatever the theoretical purpose, anthropologists and historians of Africa are engaged in a shared enterprise. The classic ethnographies have now become part of the resource available to modern historians and to anthropologists revisiting the sites of earlier work. Thus Douglas Johnston and Sharon Hutchinson, by diligent archival study and heroic fieldwork, have restored Evans-Pritchard's Nuer to history.[10]

The development of a richer historiography of the world beyond Europe and North America necessarily involved historians in an encounter with anthropology and anthropologists in a closer consideration of the past. That was true for studies of Asia, Latin America and Oceania, as well as for Africa. Contact and cross-fertilisation between anthropologists and the larger body of historians concerned with the histories of Europe, North America and Australasia was much more episodic. Only in the last quarter of the twentieth century, when much significant work in French became available in translation and international academic exchange intensified, did a single, if fractured, conversation establish itself across the social sciences and humanities.

In Britain historians borrowed insights from particular pieces of anthropological theory or particular monographs. In 1963, Keith Thomas stressed that history might learn general lessons from anthropology.[11] Historians might learn to be self-conscious about the possibilities of broad comparisons. In particular, comparison across radically different societies could yield new insights, both by offering clues to the understanding of puzzling aspects of the 'Western' past and by pointing up that elements of Western society, family structure for example, taken for granted as normal, are actually highly unusual.

A major case for Keith Thomas was witchcraft beliefs and the pattern of witchcraft accusations. The key monograph was E. E. Evans-Pritchard's *Witchcraft Oracles and Magic among the Azande* (1937). Evans-Pritchard argued that Zande beliefs about magic – essentially that human misfortunes from death to crop failure have to be understood by reference to supernatural factors, which may nonetheless be manipulated by resort to oracles and to the use of good magic – make up a pattern of thought that makes sense to the Azande and can be explained to others. By concentrating on Zande thinking and paying close attention to problems of translation, Evans-Pritchard anticipated much later theoretical developments in the aftermath of the 'linguistic turn'. At the time, when Radcliffe-Brown's structural-functionalism remained the dominant theory in British social anthropology, the Zande ethnography encouraged African fieldwork that located witch-hunts in particular social settings. That ethnography stimulated historians to believe that medieval and early modern witchcraft was worth taking seriously and might be explained by analogy with accounts rooted in the social-structural analysis of the African monographs. In the early 1970s, two major books, *Religion and the Decline of Magic* by Keith Thomas and

Witchcraft in Tudor and Stuart England: A Regional and Comparative Study by Alan Macfarlane, drew on anthropology. In *Salem Possessed: The Social Origins of Witchcraft*, Boyer and Nissenbaum extended the style of analysis to the most famous New England case. The conjuncture between the disciplines, and the place of witchcraft studies within that context was, however, fairly brief. The style of anthropological analysis from which the historians, particularly Macfarlane, had drawn was passing out of fashion among anthropologists. Historians continued to be interested in witchcraft, but increasingly concentrated on questions of belief systems, consonant with the increasingly fashionable concerns of cultural and intellectual history, rather than continuing to emphasise the social context of witchcraft accusations.[12]

Other historians, working within the English Marxist tradition, most notably Eric Hobsbawm, especially in *Primitive Rebels* (1959) and Edward Thompson, in *The Making of the English Working Class* (1963) developed an interest in the notion of culture as something that might usefully broaden and complicate existing modes of analysis. Both were aware of the anthropologists' use of the notion of culture, as well as of its more English literary usage in the work of Raymond Williams. Hobsbawm gave drafts of *Primitive Rebels* as papers to Max Gluckman's seminar in Manchester, the centre of the group of British anthropologists most interested in processes of social change.[13] This body of work was read and appreciated by anthropologists, particularly by American anthropologists seeking to inject a clearer sense of the past into their accounts of culture. Renato Rosaldo recounts how Thompson's work assisted him in writing up his work in the essentially historical framework he gave *Ilongot Headhunters*.[14] General surveys of anthropological theory, particularly from the mid-1980s onwards, refer to Thompson as a significant influence on anthropologists and as an exemplar of one way of analysing past societies in a style that gives proper place to an anthropological understanding of culture.

In postwar France, as Michael Roberts' contribution to this volume shows, the *Annales* historians established themselves in key positions within the history profession.[15] Claude Lévi-Strauss's structuralism exercised a dominant influence extending well beyond anthropology. Other schools of anthropology, such as the structural Marxism developed by Maurice Godelier and others, flourished in the 1970s. Paul Bourdieu, a later proponent of the theory of 'practice', began his career as a North African anthropologist. For history written in France, the increased importance of anthropology sustained the emphasis on intellectual and cultural themes that re-emerged so strongly in the 1970s and 1980s, in the third generation of *Annales*, as confidence in the power of quantitative methods declined. In 1975 Le Roy Ladurie, hitherto committed to the use of quantitative data, published the best known French work of historical anthropology, *Montaillou*, an account of a Cathar village in the Pyrenees, based on the register of an early fourteenth-century inquisitorial interrogation, treated as an ethnographer's notebook and presented in the manner of an anthropological monograph.[16] From the early 1970s onwards scholars in North America and

Britain became aware of the range of French historical practice and the importance of the French post-structuralist theorists, Derrida, Barthes, Foucault and
Bourdieu. Hitherto distinct national traditions began, if not to elide, then at
least to fray at the edges.

Despite the impact of French theorists, for historians, particularly in North
America, late twentieth-century relationships with anthropology centred round
one American anthropologist, Clifford Geertz, whose intellectual roots were in
Boas and Weber. But Geertz sought to separate off anthropology from
Parsonian social science and to define culture as essentially a 'semiotic concept',
whose analysis is 'not an experimental science in search of law but an interpretive one in search of meaning'.[17] In 1970 Geertz moved from Chicago to the
Institute of Advanced Studies at Princeton. From that splendid ivy tower Geertz
exercised influence, and patronage, for the remainder of the century. His major
impact came not from a piece of brilliant ethnography in the manner of
Malinowski or Evans-Pritchard, but through two volumes of elegantly written,
allusive essays, *The Interpretation of Cultures* (1973) and *Local Knowledge:
Further Essays in Interpretative Anthropology* (1983). As read by some historians, Geertz's argument seemed fresh and suggestive, providing support from
within the citadel of social science for an anti-positivist account of the study of
human society and culture. In his mature work, Geertz argues that human
cultures are made up of a system of symbols expressed in language and in rituals
and other public, observable performances such as the famous Balinese cock-
fight. The task of the anthropologist is to read and interpret aspects of cultures
both exotic and familiar much as literary scholars might read and deconstruct a
text. Apparently minor, even trivial episodes can yield rich insights if closely read
and 'thickly' described.

A number of medieval and early modern historians, familiar with cultural
themes from *Annales*, were sympathetic to Geertz's arguments. A key figure
was Robert Darnton, who ran a joint seminar with Geertz at Princeton. In
1984 Darnton published *The Great Cat Massacre and Other Episodes in French
Cultural History*, in which the debt to Geertz is very clear and the claim made
that Geertz provides the rigorous theory of culture that earlier work had lacked.
Natalie Davis also acknowledges Geertz's influence. Elsewhere, as for example
in Italian *microstoria*, developments followed very similar but independent lines:
Carlo Ginzburg's *The Cheese and the Worms* provides a kind of 'thick description'. Geertz's impact extended to other historians. Students of the Colonial
period of the United States, notably Rhys Isaac, produced anthropological
history. The most significant impact on modernists was on US historians of
Europe, for example Lucy Hunt and William Sewell. But historians in Europe
also took note, for example Hans Medick, a key figure in the German concern
for the history of everyday life. Some, particularly those affected not only by
Geertz but also by French literary and social theory, sought to establish cultural
history as a distinct enterprise emancipated from the positivist overtones of
social and economic history. The range of publication of 'new cultural history'

hugely expanded in the last decades of the century, much of it consisting of 'cultural histories' of particular elements of culture ranging from science and technology, to disease, sugar and the pencil.[18]

Styles of anthropology other than the symbolic interpretive continued to be pursued, and challenges to Geertz from within anthropology grew even as his standing outside the discipline reached its peak. A younger generation of US anthropologists influenced by literary theory, who first made a major mark with the publication of *Writing Culture* in 1986, pushed Geertz's interpretivism further down the postmodernist road towards self-conscious reflexive concern for the process by which ethnography is produced. But even in the United States other traditions survived. The neo-evolutionist tradition continued, with a particular stress on ecological constraints, in the work of Eric Wolf and Sidney Minz. That tradition entailed a concern for history particularly in the *longue durée*, as exemplified by Eric Wolf's *Europe and the Peoples without History*. In the USA and in Europe some anthropologists maintained concern with social and political structures, with modes of production and with economic life generally. And everywhere anthropologists showed increasing interest in dealing with the past and in taking history seriously as a mode of understanding society and culture.

Tentative moves had been made as early as the 1960s to promote cooperation between historians and anthropologists. The journal *Comparative Studies in Society and History*, founded in 1958, drew its editorial board from American anthropologists and historians. In the last quarter of the century the greater ease of maintaining informal networks and the more widespread 'historical turn' enhanced cooperation and widened opportunities for publication. New journals and monograph series in Europe as well as in Britain and the USA gave increased attention to historical anthropology.

Much of that material dealt with the world outside Europe and North America and was often of interest mainly to regional specialists. Marshall Sahlins' analysis of the death of Captain Cook in Hawaii attracted attention as providing an example of someone in the American culturalist tradition engaged directly with questions of history. Bernard Cohn's work, for long known mainly to South Asian specialists, was reprinted in book form in 1987. Jean and John Comaroff's two-volume study of Tswana history, *Of Revelation and Revolution* (1991/1997) and their volume of essays on *Ethnography and the Historical Imagination* (1992) found readers outside African studies.[19] In Britain, anthropologists such as Jack Goody, Ernest Gellner and Alan Macfarlane published on large historical themes. The impact of historical anthropology written by anthropologists was enhanced by the increased tendency for anthropologists to work on European societies. Ruth Behar's *The Presence of the Past in a Spanish Village: Santa Maria del Monte*, and Marianne Heiberg's *The Making of the Basque Nation*, for example, use a combination of fieldwork and archival study to illuminate questions of interest both to anthropologists and historians.

Increasingly anthropologists and historians inhabit the same intellectual world, dealing in different ways with similar challenges from theory and from external pressures. The disciplines, however, remain separate. Anthropologists are more committed to theory than most historians. All anthropologists teach in the context of theory. Many historians do not. Historians, though acknowledging the gains in breadth and in self-awareness that contact with anthropology has brought, remain properly conscious of the dangers of too ready unconsidered borrowing. Fieldwork methods, even when supplemented by archival study, push analysis towards synchrony. Much anthropological analysis remains, in Nicholas Thomas' phrase, 'out of time'. That is as true of Geertz as of Radcliffe-Brown. *Negara*, Geertz's account of the nineteenth century Balinese 'theatre state' is set in the past. It is not history, but rather presents an essentially synchronic analysis of an 'ideal type'. Historians do write synchronic accounts of a system – Namier's *Structure of Politics in the Age of George III* for example. But history as a discipline deals with change over time and seeks to present the particular aspect of the past that is under close consideration in a broader context, and to provide an account of the process of change.

Anthropologists might respond that historians' concern to explain change implies a commitment, not often fulfilled, to theorize the process of change. Theory does matter and theoretical argument will continue to complicate the conversation between the disciplines and cast doubt on the status of historical anthropology or anthropological history. But the tradition of both disciplines provides escape from the anomie that exclusive concern with theory can bring, and draws their practitioners back to the archive and to the field and sometimes to both. Acknowledging the impact of recent work, they go there even more conscious of the problematic nature of archives, of texts, of field experience and of the status of the observer, ethnographer or historian. But most historians and many anthropologists still aspire to add to the useful record of what human beings have said and done and to produce work that can stand beside the classic ethnography and the most enduring historiography, to be read in the context of the theoretical debates to which it was addressed, but making a lasting contribution to the understanding of past societies.

Notes

1   B. S. Cohn, 'History and Anthropology: the State of Play', *Comparative Studies in Society and History*, 1980, vol. 22, reprinted in Bernard S. Cohn, *An Anthropologist among the Historians and Other Essays*, Delhi, Oxford University Press, 1987.

2   See also above, pp. 141–2.

3   P. Burke, *The French Historical Revolution: The Annales School, 1929–89*, Oxford, Polity Press, 1990, pp. 12–30, 38, 42.

4   P. Burke, *Varieties of Cultural History*, Ithaca NY, Cornell University Press, 1997, pp. 184ff.

5   S. Falk Moore, *Anthropology and Africa: Changing Perspectives on a Changing Scene*, Charlottesville and London, University Press of Virginia, 1994, p. 40.

6 J. Vansina, *De la tradition orale: essai de méthode historique*, Tervuren, musée royal de *l'Afrique Centrale*, 1961, translated as *Oral Tradition*, London, Routledge and Kegan Paul, 1965; J. Vansina, *Oral Tradition as History*, London, James Currey, 1985, is such a substantially revised version as to be in effect a new and different book.

7 J. Vansina, *Living with Africa*, Madison, University of Wisconsin Press, 1994; C. Keyes Adenaike and J. Vansina (eds) *In Pursuit of History: Fieldwork in Africa*, Portsmouth NH and Oxford, Heinemann and James Currey, 1996.

8 For recent reviews of the state of African history see J. C. Miller, 'History and Africa: Africa and History', *American Historical Review*, 1999, vol. 104. S. Feierman, 'Colonizers, Scholars and the Creation of Invisible Histories', in V. E. Bonnell and L. Hunt (eds) *Beyond the Cultural Turn: New Directions in the Study of Culture and Society*, Berkeley, University of California Press, 1999.

9 J. D. Y. Peel, *Ijeshas and Nigerians: The Incorporation of a Yoruba Kingdom 1890s–1970s*, Cambridge, Cambridge University Press, 1983; T. C. McCaskie, *State and Society in pre-colonial Asante*, Cambridge, Cambridge University Press, 1995. In both cases introductory chapters set out the historiographical context.

10 D. H. Johnson, *Nuer Prophets: A History of Prophecy from the Upper Nile in the Nineteenth and Twentieth Centuries*, Oxford, Clarendon Press, 1994; S. E. Hutchinson, *Nuer Dilemmas: Coping with Money, War and the State*, Berkeley, University of California Press, 1996.

11 K. Thomas, 'History and Anthropology', *Past and Present*, 1963, vol. 24.

12 S. Clarke, *Thinking with Demons*, Oxford, Clarendon Press, 1999; and I. Bostridge, *Witchcraft and its Transformations*, Oxford, Oxford University Press, 1997, provide two very different versions of an intellectualist approach. Recent developments in Africa have revived anthropologists' and historians' interest in the topic. See, for example, P. Geschiere, *The Modernity of Witchcraft: Politics and the Occult in Postcolonial Africa*, Charlottesville and London, University of Virginia Press, 1997.

13 E. Hobsbawm, *Interesting Times: A Twentieth Century Life*, London, Allen Lane, 2002, p. 347.

14 R. Rosaldo, 'Celebrating Thompson's Heroes: Social Analysis in History and Anthropology', in H. J. Kaye and K. McClelland (eds) *E. P. Thompson: Critical Perspectives*, Oxford, Polity Press, 1990.

15 See above, pp. 83–6.

16 E. Le Roy Ladurie, *Montaillou: Cathars and Catholics in a French Village, 1294–1324*, London, Scolar Press, 1978; for an anthropologist's response see R. Rosaldo, 'From the Door of his Tent: The Fieldworker and the Inquisitor', in J. Clifford and G. E. Marcus (eds) *Writing Culture: The Poetics and Politics of Ethnography*, Berkeley, University of California Press, 1986. See also above, p. 145 (Chapter 9).

17 C. Geertz, 'Thick Description: Towards an Interpretive Theory of Culture' in *The Interpretation of Cultures*, New York, Basic Books, 1973, p. 5.

18 J. Goodman, 'History and Anthropology', in M. Bentley, *Companion to Historiography*, London, Routledge, 1997, pp. 792–4, provides a substantial list and commentary.

19 See also S. E. Merny, 'Hegemony and Culture in Historical Anthropology', *American Historical Review*, 2003, vol. 108.

Further reading

No single volume deals with the whole story of the relationship between history and anthropology. The story has to be followed in the accounts of the development of the two disciplines and in the work of those who have sought to build bridges between them. Anthropology is well provided with general accounts of the nature and history of the discipline. T. H. Eriksen, *Small Places and Large Issues: An Introduction to Social and Cultural Anthropology*, 2nd edn, London, Pluto Press, 2002, provides a wide ranging overview. A. Bernard and J. Spencer (eds) *Encyclopedia of Social and Cultural Anthropology*, London, Routledge, 1996, is a useful reference work. T. H. Eriksen and F. S. Nielsen, *A History of Anthropology*, London, Pluto Press, 2001, is comprehensive. A. Kuper, *Anthropologists and Anthropology: The Modern British School*, 3rd edn, London, Routledge, 1996, and T. C. Patterson, *A Social History of Anthropology in the United States*, Oxford, Berg, 2001, for developments in the British Commonwealth and in the United States. M. Augé, *The Anthropological Circle: Symbol, Function, History*, Cambridge, Cambridge University Press, 1982, for France. A major historian of anthropology gives a brief overview in Kuhnian mode in G. W. Stocking Jnr, 'Paradigmatic Traditions in the History of Anthropology', in *idem, The Ethnographer's Magic and Other Essays in the History of Anthropology*, Madison, University of Wisconsin Press, 1992, pp. 342–61. A. Kuper, *Culture: The Anthropologists' Account*, Cambridge MA, Harvard University Press, 1999, discusses the development of a key anthropological concept, particularly in the work of modern American anthropologists.

For the development of the conversation between history and anthropology: E. E. Evans-Pritchard, 'Anthropology and History', in *idem, Essays in Social Anthropology*, London, Faber, 1962, pp. 46–65. K. Thomas, 'History and Anthropology', *Past and Present*, 1964, vol. 24, pp. 3–24. I. M. Lewis (ed.) *History and Social Anthropology*, London, Tavistock, 1968, in the Monograph series of the Association of Social Anthropologists of the Commonwealth dealt mainly with anthropologists' exploration of the African past. A later volume in the same series, E. Tonkin, M. McDonald and M. Chapman (eds) *History and Ethnicity*, London, Routledge, 1989, indicates the shift in interest in the intervening years. T. K. Raab and R. I. Rotberg (eds) *The New History: the 1980s and Beyond; Studies in Interdisciplinary History*, Princeton, Princeton University Press, 1982, contains a number of important articles by, for example, B. S. Cohn and N. Z. Davies.

Developments in cultural history are surveyed in L. Hunt (ed.) *The New Cultural History*, Berkeley, University of California Press, 1989, and in S. B. Ortner (ed.) *The Fate of 'Culture': Geertz and Beyond*, Berkeley, University of California Press, 1999. J. Goodman, 'History and Anthropology', in M. Bentley (ed.) *Companion to Historiography*, London, Routledge, 1997, pp. 783–804, gives a richly referenced survey of the relationship between the disciplines from a cultural historian's point of view.

Some participants have provided some account of their careers, notably J. Vansina, *Living with Africa*, Madison, University of Wisconsin Press, 1994, who gives an entertaining if idiosyncratic account of the development of the historiography of Africa, and C. Geertz, *After the Fact: Two Countries, Four*

Decades, One Anthropologist, Cambridge MA, Harvard University Press, 1995. E. R. Wolf, 'Introduction: An Intellectual Autobiography', in *idem*, *Pathways of Power: Building an Anthropology of the Modern World*, Berkeley, University of California Press, 2001, pp. 1–10, gives a personal introduction to a collection of his papers.

Chapter 11

History and literature

Tim Woods

The new shibboleth in recent literary studies has been the (re)turn to history. This has been partly governed by a range of institutional pressures: for example, the frantic necessity of securing research grants; the new ideological utilitarianism pervading literary studies in response to quality audits and research rankings; and the need to be *seen to be producing* research of an 'innovative' nature, which inexorably pushes scholars and research funding to (often 'untouched') historical archives. Yet the debate about 'historical' research versus 'literary' research has see-sawed in literary studies for at least the past twenty-five years now. There have been fierce arguments within literary studies about the ways in which theory neglects history, especially between poststructuralists and Marxists: how insofar as one attaches importance to theory, one excludes 'textuality' and 'the real'.[1] Faced with the imperative to 'return to history', many have been left in a quandary about where that history is to be located. It is clear that the very category of history that was once invoked so confidently is in fact deeply problematical. Within this crisis of the referential which has become so vexed with the refigurations of the relationship between the verbal and the social, this chapter will briefly consider the ways in which new hermeneutic practices in literary studies may offer useful perspectives to students of history. For example, what can historians see in literary studies (if anything) that they may not be doing themselves? In what ways can the writing of history learn from the critical practices of literary studies? How is historiography altered by the concerns of literary studies? In what ways may an interdisciplinarity be envisaged between history and literary studies? And finally, to try and turn this around, in what ways does literary study learn from the practices of historians?

'Always historicize!'. So exhorts Fredric Jameson's mammoth *Political Unconscious* as the principal law organising all Marxist and materialist critical study undertaken in the past thirty years. Jameson's historical imperative has been the characteristic of materialist literary criticism which sought to distinguish itself from 'traditional' literary criticism and its aestheticising affirmation of eternal literary values and from formalist, psychoanalytical or poststructuralist approaches. Indeed, the writing of history – historio-*graphy* – has been a perennial concern of literary studies, yet it is principally in the past twenty years that thinking of history as a specifically *textual* concern has entered the historical consciousness of literary studies. As has been widely documented,[2] historicism in some form or other has dominated the early development of literary studies, until New Criticism turned literary study towards textual analysis in the 1940s. Early forms of historicism either studied the explicit and hidden links between literature and topical events, or they described the way a literary work embodied the 'world picture' (the dominant values and understandings) of its age, where literary texts were typically understood to *reflect* history in an inert and passive manner.[3] Under the influence of such humanist approaches from influential literary critics like F. R. Leavis and I. A. Richards in Britain and the New Critics in the USA, literary studies had laboured under the assumptions that texts had some universal significance and essential ahistorical truths to impart, and that history was something from which literary analysis had to be protected.

In the late 1970s and early 1980s, Marxists and feminists in particular led a 'return to history', but their focus lay more on the politics of form rather than the earlier concern with the determining factors of economic and social history. Raymond Williams defined history as 'an account of real *past* events' and 'the organised knowledge of the *past*'. Yet this sits somewhat awkwardly with more contemporary understandings of 'history':

> It is necessary to distinguish an important sense of history which is more than, although it includes, organized knowledge of the past. ... One way of expressing this new sense is to say that past events are seen not as specific histories but as continuous and connected process. Various systematisations and interpretations of this continuous and connected process then become history in a new general and eventually abstract sense. Moreover ... history in many of these uses loses its exclusive association with the past and becomes connected not only to the present but also to the future.[4]

Yet the conservative ideological forces at work in the belief in the 'continuous process' of history had already been broached by Walter Benjamin in his 'Theses on the Philosophy of History'; and it was further questioned by Michel Foucault's analyses of power, which shifted interest away from the macronarratives of politics and economics towards the micrological discursive practices and knowledge/power regimes that construct different forms of domination. Foucault's work insists upon the necessity of shifting out of disciplinary divisions into that of discourse. Instead of studying the individual talents of writers, we are now urged to examine anonymous forces of dissipation, contradictions rather than totalities, while the rhetoric of discontinuities, gaps and ruptures is favoured over continuity, development and evolution. Citing the influence of Nietzsche's *The Use and Abuse of History*, Foucault's concern is with the irregularities that define discourse and the many possible interconnections of discourse in culture. Marxists and feminists have joined with Foucault in insisting upon the pressure exerted by historical contexts that have usually been ignored in formalistic literary studies. Yet discourse is not merely a lapse into a textual generality, a world of text and nothing but text, but an assertion of the particular and specific. It is an assault upon the centralising forces of continuity and unity in theory and practice and all forms of totalising thought that do not acknowledge their role in the very constitution of their objects of study. Postmodern narratives have been sceptical of accounts of 'continuous history', which have been described by Mark Poster as 'a means of controlling and domesticating the past in the form of knowing it', and the problem is that the historian (and the historical realist novelist) achieves control over the past 'without placing himself in question'.[5] Foucault's chief advantage in stressing *discontinuity* in the historical process is the challenge it presents to the position of the historian. For Poster, Foucault 'attempts to show how the past was different, strange, threatening. He labors to distance the past from the present, to disrupt the easy, cozy intimacy historians have traditionally enjoyed in the relationship of the past to the present'.[6] This formed part of the major attack on historians' tendencies to fetishise facts and to be hostile to theory.

By the early 1980s, the time was ripe for a riposte to the dominant textualism with a 'return to history'. Largely as a result of their theories, at least in the minds of the poststructuralists, history was no longer what it used to be – a background of ideas or a field of empirical facts. Heavily influenced by Foucault, the New Historicists argued instead for a view of history that emphasised the role of representation and discourse in social life. Underlying their position was the belief that neither history nor literature offers a firm ground from which the other can be securely surveyed. New Historicism has been an important force in the reassessment of history and literature in the past twenty years. Not so 'new' now, it took as its principal impetus the failure of the New Left in the 1960s to instigate social and political change.[7] The term 'New Historicism' can refer to all those historicist theories of both history and literature which are informed by textualist and poststructuralist ideas and which break with more traditional historicisms; but it can also more specifically refer to those (largely American) writers such as Stephen Greenblatt, Louis Montrose, Catherine Gallagher and Joel Fineman who are thus distinguished from those (mainly British) cultural materialists such as Jonathan Dollimore, Alan Sinfield, and Catherine Belsey, whose own New Historicism owes much more to a tradition of Marxist analysis, towards which their American colleagues have been antipathetic or hostile. One British critic distinguishes between 'old historicism' and 'New Historicism' in the following manner:

> Where the old historicism relied on a basically empiricist form of historical research, confident in its capacity to excavate and define the events of the past, New Historicism drew on post-structuralist theory, and accepted 'history' only as a contemporary activity of narrating or representing the past.[8]

A further definition in a recent collection of essays concerned with New Historicism reinforces this:

> For the most part new historicism can be distinguished from 'old' histori-
> cism by its lack of faith in 'objectivity' and 'permanence' and its stress not
> upon the direct recreation of the past, but rather the processes by which
> the past is constructed or invented. Unsettling, transgressive, at times
> contradictory, new historicism tends to regard texts in materialist terms, as
> objects and events in the world, as a part of human life, society, the histor-
> ical realities of power, authority, and resistance; yet at the same time, it
> rejects the idea of 'History' as a directly accessible, unitary past, and substi-
> tutes for it the conception of 'histories', an ongoing series of human
> constructions, each representing the past at particular present moments for
> particular purposes.[9]

Drawing on Foucault, the *Annales* school of social history, the cultural anthropology of Clifford Geertz, and deconstruction, New Historicist theorists like Greenblatt abandoned certain notions of the aesthetically autonomous work, the formally complete literary icon, the artistic genius at the origin, and the notion of a complete or whole reading. Instead, they suggested an approach in which criticism concern itself with collective beliefs, social practices, and cultural discourses that shape a particular work. These leave 'textual traces' in a work of literature (intruding rudely upon the 'purity' of the work) and connect it to the extra-literary representational systems of the culture in which it is embedded.

Although New Historicism's development of anti-foundationalist and non-transcendental positions has tended to emerge from studies of the Renaissance and Romanticism, postmodern fiction has also demonstrated similar stances. Narratives like those of E. L. Doctorow, John Barth, Thomas Pynchon, Salman Rushdie and Angela Carter, also forced a rethinking of the writing of history. As Paul Ricoeur's magisterial studies of narrative have shown, it is actually the writing of history itself that is '*constitutive* of the historical mode of under-standing'.[10] What we consider to be historical facts are established by historiography's explanatory and narrative structures of past events. This is the context in which 'postmodern' historical consciousness invests itself: eschewing the Enlightenment notions of progress and development, the Hegelian idealist world-historical process, or any essentialist Marxist notions of history. What has been termed 'historiographic metafiction' by Linda Hutcheon,

> puts into question, at the same time as it exploits, the grounding of histor-
> ical knowledge in the past real. ... It can often enact the problematic nature
> of the relation of writing history to narrativization and, thus, to fictional-
> ization, thereby raising the same questions about the cognitive status of
> historical knowledge with which current philosophers of history are also

grappling. What is the ontological nature of historical documents? Are they the stand-in for the past? What is meant – in ideological terms – by our 'natural' understanding of historical explanation?[11]

As Hutcheon argues, historiographic metafiction openly speculates about the way representation displaces the past and the ideological consequences of this displacement, about the ways one writes about the 'past real', about what constitute 'the known facts' of any given event.

This textual anxiety about history manifests itself as one in which interpreters have to be self-conscious about their complicit stance with the object of their enquiry. Clearly influenced by the work of Hayden White, who argued for a textual and narrativist understanding of history as early as 1973 in *Metahistory*, one of the leading New Historicists, Louis Montrose, makes an important distinction between the '*historicity of texts*' and the '*textuality of history*':

> By *the historicity of texts*, I mean to suggest the cultural specificity, the social embedment, of all modes of writing … not only the texts that critics study but also the texts in which we study them. By *the textuality of history* I mean to suggest, firstly, that we can have no access to a full and authentic past, a lived material existence, unmediated by the surviving textual traces of the society in question … traces whose survival we cannot assume to be merely contingent but must rather presume to be at least partially consequent upon complex and subtle social processes of preservation and effacement; and secondly, that those textual traces are themselves subject to subsequent textual mediations when they are construed as the 'documents' upon which historians ground their own texts, called 'histories'.[12]

Seeking a renegotiation of the relationships between texts and other signifying practices, going so far as to dissolve 'literature' into the historical context that academic literary studies has traditionally held in abeyance, New Historicists have clouded the conventional waters of literary studies. Central to the challenge mounted by 'New Historicism' was that it gave scholars new opportunities to traverse the boundaries separating history, anthropology, art, politics, literature and economics. As one commentator has described New Historicism:

> It attacked the doctrine of noninterference that forbade humanists to intrude on questions of politics, power, indeed on all matters that deeply affect people's practical lives – matters best left, prevailing wisdom went, to experts who could be trusted to preserve order and stability in 'our' global and intellectual domains.[13]

In this respect, New Historicism is suspicious of earlier literary historiographers' tendencies to use totalising or atomising methods:

By discarding what they view as monologic or myopic historiography, by demonstrating that social and cultural events commingle messily, by rigorously exposing the innumerable trade-offs, the competing bids and exchanges of culture, New Historicists can make a valid claim to have established new ways of studying history and a new awareness of how history and culture define each other.[14]

Despite the practitioners' heterogeneity of approach, H. Aram Veeser has summarised the following issues as the dominant characteristics of New Historicism:

- that every expressive act is embedded in a network of material practices;
- that every act of unmasking, critique, and opposition uses the tools it condemns and risks falling prey to the practice it exposes;
- that literary and non-literary 'texts' circulate inseparably;
- that no discourse, imaginative or archival, gives access to unchanging truths nor expresses inalterable human nature;
- finally, that critical method and a language adequate to describe culture under capitalism participate in the economy they describe.[15]

Although these definitions run the risk of homogenising the practices of different critics, nevertheless they do show the extent to which there is a dehierarchisation of the specifically *literary* text in favour of a more relativist perspective about cultural documents. It also shows the high degree to which New Historicists recognise their critical complicity with their interpretative object.

This dazzling rhetoric of New Historicism is part of a broader cultural articulation of a growing recognition that the past is much more complex, different and discontinuous, than had previously been recognised by more positivist or empiricist theories of history. These various changes to our notions of writing and conceiving history, have, on the one hand, encouraged the rise of very personalised accounts of the past – ethnic histories and gendered histories, where there is a heavy reliance on authenticity and firsthand experience. This appears to have been partially a consequence of the elevation of the micro-narrative or 'petite histoire' fostered by postmodernist theories of history. Yet, paradoxically, these same theories are also distinctly opposed to any stance of authentic discourse, to any claim for *authoritative personal experience*, based on what is perceived to be a questionable foundationalism vested in the narrating subject, as is evident in any testimonial literature. This is one of the contradictions of these theories of history, which makes way theoretically for micro-narratives, yet then removes their validity by undermining them on the very basis upon which they were accredited with a voice in the first place. Consequently, the burgeoning literature of 'postcolonial consciousness' across the world, from writers like Ngugi wa Thiong'o, Chinua Achebe, Maxine Hong

Kingston, Mudrooroo Narogin, Sandra Cisneros, Leslie Marmon Silko, M. Scott Momaday, Salman Rushdie and Toni Morrison (to name but a few), is caught in a complex political and ethical adjustment which involves inscribing a personal counter-history as a way of investing historical facts with racial and gender variations. Part of the reason for this perception of history's increased complexity in literary studies over the past two decades, is the increasing preoccupation with the role of memory in relation to history. This not only helps clarify the investments at work in postwar historical literature, especially the investigation of 'its own historically relative construction of history', but it also offers the opportunity to locate the growing commitment to historicism in literary studies within the wider culture.[16] Historicism, 'new' and 'old', postcolonial and feminist, is widely felt to be the 'the latest way forward for literary theory'[17] despite the apparent contradictions between historical relativism and the abstract atemporality of some theory. In cases where the dominant collective sense of the past is manifestly deficient in its recognition of other social groups, this is already acknowledged. Certain literary texts by black, feminist and working-class writers, for example, have offered such lucid and compelling narratives of hitherto suppressed pasts that they have helped create whole areas of literary study. This literature manifestly adds to historical knowledge, and directs attention to other cognate literary texts whose situation in history may have been less accessible.

Meanwhile a synchronous development within contemporary historical studies has been the concern with the troubling persistence of modes of thought that have traditionally been the preserve of the arts and literary study: narrative, imagination and memory. 'Is it not possible', asks Hayden White in the final sentence of an essay on narrative in history, 'that the question of narrative in any discussion of historical theory is always finally about the function of imagination in the production of a specifically human truth?'[18] Imagination and narrative are troubling for literary and cultural studies too, not least because of their long genealogy and the vestigial meanings attached to them, and so, despite their potential for rapprochement, memory is the field in which there is currently the greatest convergence between the two disciplines. The rapidly growing interest amongst historians in how trauma, 'notably including the deferred recognition of the significance of traumatic series of events', and sites of memory, have played a key role in the collective construction of pasts and their management by professional custodians, has a counterpart in the interest amongst literary and cultural theorists in memory as an important link between theory (particularly in psychoanalysis and theories of identity) and history.[19]

There has been a widespread conviction amongst contemporary literary and cultural critics, and historians, that the past has been killed, destroyed, or lost, or at best thinned out so much that it no longer seems relevant. Eras and epistèmes have disappeared and been replaced by new uncharted textualities. Consequently, they argue, people urgently need to do new 'memory work', 'to cast lifelines to the past and counteract our culture's undisputed tendency toward amnesia under the sign of immediate profit and short-term politics'.[20] Literary contemporaries also ask questions about the past, but usually suggest more complex images of the displaced or traumatic relation to the past. Some literary texts claim that the past is not where we expected to find it because of changes in the common experience of space and time, and such insights could help us better understand the consequences of science and technology for our current theories of postmodernity. Others show that what looks like historical amnesia may be misrecognition of new technologies of memory which seem like white noise to those expecting memory to play by traditional scales. In our recent book entitled *Literatures of Memory*, Peter Middleton and I have argued that new genres of writing about the past have developed phenomenologies of 'spacetime' that are not yet fully recognised and legitimised by either theory or the institutions of public history.[21] Narrative, memory, performance, and the production and circulation of texts, are all implicated in the new 'spacetimes', and history therefore takes many forms in contemporary literature, some of them far from obvious. Middleton and I argue that some of the most original investigations of historicity are taking place in literary practices that are especially aware of the changing conditions of life in space and time, and yet do not advertise themselves as historical literatures. That new historical literature of recent decades is part of the historical turn in literary studies and the turn to memory in historical studies. *Literatures of Memory* shows that historical literature articulates several issues that can contribute to current debate about the links between history and literature: the necessity for approaching representation of the past as a complex ethical problem; the need to recognise that memory is practised according to hegemonic paradigms which are deeply imbued with aesthetic and temporal features, notably the 'delayed coding' of the past; the complexity of the temporal and spatial locatability of the past; and the still unmapped cultural variety of the narrativity of the past. Neither a purely materialist, nor a wholly discursive approach is sufficient, because both entail too many presuppositions about memory, time and space to adequately recognise their diverse participation in social and cultural production.

The historian Jacques Le Goff calls for contemporary 'specialists in memory ... to make of the struggle for the democratization of social memory one of the primary imperatives of their scientific objectivity'.[22] Democratisation could mean no more than responsible popularisation, but it might also point us towards an ethical relation to the past, and from there towards a political activity of remembering, reconstructing, and textualising, the past. Yet Le Goff speaks only of objectivity. A democratisation might just as well open up the emotional working through of memory, as well as the aesthetic processes of self-reflexive, subjective fantasy. For fictional narrative frequently has the ability to transform and reconfigure the past, a process of reconfiguration which is not simply a judicial sifting of the documentary record, but a change of relation to the past. The new focus in literary studies upon social memory and textual memory aims to free us from the hold of linear time and the fixity of the past, both of which obstruct the development of new routes into the future. Fictional narration is not aimed at caging the beast of the past, but at transforming it.

One reason for this reconfiguration has been the attention increasingly given to the cultural studies of 'everyday life' and the anecdotal. It is possible to pinpoint here an instance where debates in history have offered literary studies useful methodological and conceptual equipment to conceive of new literary practices. For the recent attention to 'the practices of everyday life' derive in part from the anecdotal practice of the New Historicists, in part from theorists like Michel de Certeau and Henri Lefebvre, and also from Raphael Samuel's historical work in Britain and the *Alltagsgeschicte* movement in German historiography.[23] As I noted earlier, increasing interest has occurred in the witness narratives, autobiographical genres and personal histories which straddle orthodox literary and historical writing, as forms which are seeking to write a form of history which escapes or goes beyond practices hitherto understood as literary or historiographical. Like Foucault, de Certeau is against the hermeneutic tradition which seeks to establish a general meaning behind texts. In *The Writing of History*, de Certeau argues that modern historiography is a process of isolating a body of knowledge causing a rift between past and present which constructs the past as an 'other' in order to establish the present.[24] As Claire Colebrook argues, de Certeau regards the ritual of history writing as

> an act of both silence and retrieval; the specificity of the past is made quiet while a form and order are given to the events of the past. Historiography becomes a performative act of exorcism in which the loss of the past (its silence and mystery) are made present and reified in historical discourse.[25]

In order to counter conceptual ordering, strategic forms of representation, and conquering textual histories which *theorise* the (other) past, de Certeau argues that we need to pay more attention to memory, folk-tale and anecdote, practices and acts which resist historiographical authority by occurring in the interstices and margins of the historical text. Thus, de Certeau tries to think the other of theory, to resist institutionalised knowledge discourses which organise, objectify and 'tame' the contingencies and singularities of everyday life.

This argument that the way in which people experience identity (both individually and collectively) is deeply bound up with what they imagine history to be, points in quite another direction than heroic exceptionalism, however; it directs us towards the everyday understanding of what it means to be a historian. Countering the apparently widespread sense of ethical failure of historical awareness at the turn of the century, it is this ethical imperative in the uses and abuses of history which is currently the subject of wide discussion and debate within literary studies.[26] Literary studies has been preoccupied with finding a way to read the past from the present without appropriating it *for* the present. It has been searching for a method and practice which can genuinely respect the specificity of and radical difference of the social and cultural past while disclosing its polemics, forms, structures and struggles. For the 'good of history', it is ethically crucial that a reader maintains an open interrogatory stance towards his or her historical subject if the past is not to be subsumed or appropriated into the prevailing preoccupations of the present.

Notes

1 For a good study of these debates, see J. Hawthorn, *Cunning Passages, New Historicism, Cultural Materialism and Marxism in the Contemporary Literary Debate*, London, Edward Arnold, 1996.
2 See for example, L. Gossman, *Between History and Literature*, Cambridge MA, Harvard University Press, 1990; P. Hamilton, *Historicism*, London, Routledge, 1996.
3 A classic of its kind, this kind of historical approach is best exemplified in E. M. W. Tillyard, *The Elizabethan World Picture*, London, Chatto and Windus, 1943.
4 R. Williams, *Keywords*, London, Fontana, 1976, p. 146.
5 M. Poster, *Foucault, Marxism and Power*, Cambridge, Cambridge University Press, 1984, p. 75.
6 *Ibid.*, p. 74.
7 Although see C. Gallagher, 'Marxism and the New Historicism', in H. Aram Veeser (ed.) *The New Historicism*, London, Routledge, 1989, pp. 37–48, where she argues that New Historicism does owe a particular debt to the radical campaigns of the New Left in the 1960s and early 1970s.
8 G. Holderness, *Shakespeare Recycled: The Making of Historical Drama*, Hemel Hempstead, Harvester, 1992, p. 32.
9 J. N. Cox and L. J. Reynolds (eds) *New Historical Literary Study, Essays on Reproducing Texts, Representing History*, Princeton, Princeton University Press, 1993, p. 1.
10 P. Ricoeur, *Time and Narrative, Volume I*, trans. K. McLaughlin and D. Pellauer, Chicago and London, University of Chicago Press, 1984, p. 162.
11 L. Hutcheon, *A Poetics of Postmodernism*, London, Routledge, 1988, pp. 92–3.
12 L. Montrose, 'Professing the Renaissance: The Poetics and Politics of Culture', in H. Aram Veeser (ed.) *The New Historicism*, London, Routledge, 1989, p. 20.
13 H. Aram Veeser, 'Introduction', *The New Historicism*, p. ix.
14 *Ibid.*, p. xiii.
15 *Ibid.*, p. xi.
16 S. Connor, *The English Novel in History 1950–1995*, London, Routledge, 1996, p. 143.
17 P. Hamilton, *Historicism*, London, Routledge, 1996, p. 2.
18 H. White, *The Content of the Form, Narrative Discourse and Historical Representation*, Baltimore, Johns Hopkins University Press, 1987, p. 57.
19 See D. LaCapra, *History and Memory after Auschwitz*, Ithaca NY and London, Cornell University Press, 1998, p. 8. See also T. Woods, 'Mending the Skin of Memory: Ethics and History in Contemporary Narratives', *Rethinking History*, 1998, vol. 2:3, pp. 339–48.
20 A. Huyssen, *Twilight Memories: Marking Time in a Culture of Amnesia*, New York, Routledge, 1995, p. 254.
21 P. Middleton and T. Woods, *Literatures of Memory, Time, Space and History in Postwar Writing*, Manchester, Manchester University Press, 2000, presents a wide-ranging discussion of the concept of 'textual memory', the absence of the past, the

reconfiguration of time with space, and the relationship between history and literature.
22 J. Le Goff, *History and Memory*, trans. S. Rendall and E. Claman, New York,
Columbia University Press, 1992, p. 99.
23 See S. Berger, 'The Rise and Fall of "Critical" Historiography?', *European Review of
History*, vol. 3:2, 1996, pp. 213–32; R. Samuel, *Theatres of Memory*, vol. I, London,
Verso, 1994.
24 M. de Certeau, *The Writing of History*, trans. T. Conley, New York, Columbia
University Press, 1988, p. 3.
25 C. Colebrook, *New Literary Histories: New Historicism and Contemporary Criticism*,
Manchester, Manchester University Press, 1997, p. 132.
26 See *Rethinking History*, vol. 2:3, Autumn 1998, special issue 'The Good of History',
which addresses these points.

Further reading

The relationship of literature to history has been widely discussed in a number
of ways. Historicist approaches to literature have been evident right from the
outset of literary criticism in reflectionist approaches to history in literature in
such influential texts as E. M. W. Tillyard, *The Elizabethan World Picture*,
London, Chatto and Windus, 1943; B. Willey, *The Seventeenth-Century
Background*, London, Chatto and Windus, 1934; and idem, *The Eighteenth-
Century Background*, London, Chatto and Windus, 1940. The shift from the
very assertive use of the singular in these old reflectionist models to approaches
informed specifically by Marxist notions of history where there is a more tenta-
tive use of the plural, occur in the works of such British cultural materialist
critics as A. Sinfield, *Faultlines: Cultural Materialism and the Politics of
Dissident Reading*, Oxford, Oxford University Press, 1992; J. Dollimore and A.
Sinfield (eds) *Political Shakespeare: New Essays in Cultural Materialism: Theory
and Practice*, Manchester, Manchester University Press, 1985; and J.
Dollimore, *Radical Tragedy: Religion, Ideology and Power in the Drama of
Shakespeare and His Contemporaries*, Brighton, Harvester, 1984. Useful investi-
gations and discussions of cultural materialism occur in S. Wilson, *Cultural
Materialism*, London, Routledge, 1995; and J. Higgins, *Raymond Williams:
Literature, Marxism and Cultural Materialism*, London, Routledge, 1999.
    After poststructuralism, a 'linguistic turn' to history has been developed by
the work of scholars now grouped as the 'New Historicists'. Seminal texts
include S. J. Greenblatt, *Renaissance Self-Fashioning: From More to Shakespeare*,
Chicago, University of Chicago Press, 1980; idem, *Shakespearian Negotiation*,
Berkeley, University of California Press, 1988; T. Healy, *New Latitudes: Theory
and English Renaissance Literature*, London, Arnold, 1990; D. LaCapra,
Rethinking Intellectual History: Texts, Contexts, Language, Ithaca NY, Cornell
University Press, 1983; J. J. McGann, *Social Value and Poetic Acts*, Cambridge
MA, Harvard University Press, 1988; L. Montrose, 'Renaissance Literary
Studies and the Subject of History', *English Literary Renaissance*, 1986, vol.
16, pp. 5–12; C. Gallagher, *The Making of the Modern Body: Sexuality and*

Society in the Nineteenth Century, Berkeley, University of California Press, 1987. Many of these writers are anthologised in exemplary manner in H. A. Veeser (ed.) *The New Historicism*, London, Routledge, 1989 and *idem* (ed.) *The New Historicism Reader*, London, Routledge, 1994. See also J. Cox and L. J. Reynolds, *New Historical Literary Study: Essays on Reproducing Texts, Representing History*, Princeton NJ, Princeton University Press, 1993; and R. D. Hume, *Reconstructing Contexts: The Aims and Principles of Archaeo-Historicism*, Oxford, Oxford University Press, 1999.

Good explanations of the critical approach of the cultural materialists as distinct from that of the New Historicists occur in P. Barry, *Beginning Theory*, 2nd edn, Manchester, Manchester University Press, 2002, ch. 9; J. Hawthorn, *Cunning Passages: New Historicism, Cultural Materialism and Marxism in the Contemporary Literary Debate*, London, Edward Arnold, 1996; C. Colebrook, *New Literary Histories: New Historicism and Contemporary Criticism*, Manchester, Manchester University Press, 1997. Further useful texts are K. Ryan, *New Historicism and Cultural Materialism: A Reader*, London, Hodder, 1996; J. Brannigan, *New Historicism and Cultural Materialism*, Basingstoke, Palgrave Macmillan, 1998; with a good general discussion of the relationship between history and literature also to be found in P. Hamilton, *Historicism*, London, Routledge, 1996.

Part IV

Social movements and theory into history

> Theoreticians of all kinds circle round the peaceful herds of historians as they graze on the rich pastures of their primary sources or chew the cud of each other's publications. Sometimes even the least combative feel impelled to face their attackers.[1]

Eric Hobsbawm was perhaps not being altogether serious in imputing bovine characteristics to historians and the attributes of the hunter (or even the vulture) to theoreticians. But there was nevertheless a serious point to his allegations. For Hobsbawm was in deadly earnest when he argued that 'The nineteenth century, that age of bourgeois civilization, has several major intellectual achievements to its credit, but the academic discipline of history which grew up in that period is not one of them'.[2] Too readily, historians' insistence on empirical evidence had turned into dogmatic empiricism. An anti-theoretical bent has continued to be a hallmark of many an historian ever since. But the discipline as a whole has not continued to ignore theory or at most, when provoked beyond endurance, bullishly to confront it. In fact, there have been plenty of historians prepared to open gates to theorists, and even to trample down some fencing. Eric Hobsbawm himself has done much to encourage us to see the borders of what constitutes history not as obstacles, but as sites of intellectual trade. Similarly, the borders are themselves not set in nature or for all time, but are negotiable. The very act of imagining them in this way has helped historians to be responsive not only to theories as such, but also to some of the vehicles which serve to carry theories. In Part II, and more particularly in Part III, we have already encountered the ways in which other academic disciplines have served to convey theory into history, and noted also instances of social and political movements doing so. In the chapters which follow, we consider the latter more systematically.

Labour movements, socialist world views and, specifically, Marxist theory have been so influential that the general shape of twentieth-century historical scholarship cannot be understood without them. Marxism affords the classic example of an intellectual movement whose development was not immanent to the discipline of history. Marxists came into the historical profession already equipped with tools of analysis made by Marx and his followers, and having learned how to use them in left-wing political parties. Phillipp Schofield's chapter shows how the historical materialist perspective they brought to bear helped transform the questions asked about the past as well as how they were answered.

Schofield concentrates especially on British Marxist historiography. In the 1960s and 1970s, when their rise paralleled that of the *Annales* and Bielefeld schools, Marxist historians in British universities exerted a measure of influence on the profession at home and internationally that was out of all proportion to their relatively small numbers. Their strength within academe, according to one German commentator, is testimony to 'English tolerance and a pragmatic ability to learn'.[3] And in fact they *were* pragmatic and undogmatic in their application of Marxist theory – which is precisely why their versions of Marxism could appeal where those of Soviet-bloc historiography, which had declined into a subservient science of communist regime-legitimation, could not.

An examination of the relationship between the general attractiveness of Marxism in a particular society and its particular attractiveness to that society's historians yields surprising results. Curiously, in Britain the Communist Party was small, and the influence of Marxism on the Labour Party, the principal party of the labour movement, was negligible where the influence of Marxists, and especially of communists, on historiography was pronounced. By contrast, France had a strong Communist Party, and Marxism had always been a powerful current within French socialism, yet Marxist historians did not extend their institutional presence much beyond the Sorbonne, or their intellectual presence much beyond work on the French Revolution. Besides, as Schofield shows, the onward march of the British Marxist historians may have begun under the auspices of the Communist Party, but it accelerated as the Party haemorrhaged. Those of its historians who left did so because they could not stomach remaining in an international organisation whose leading force – the Soviet Union – was so evidently behaving as an oppressor of much of east-central Europe and institutionalising not even a dictatorship of the proletariat, but a dictatorship *over* it.

With the consequent collapse of faith in the 'leading role' of communist parties as forces for genuinely revolutionary change, and of the belief that they were necessary or for that matter conceivable instruments of liberation, came the possibility of attaching *agency* directly to the working class. In turn, this facilitated the development of a 'history from below' perspective, to which E. P. Thompson's work contributed decisively. It became a hallmark of the History Workshop movement and journal in Britain, which purveyed an otherwise generally ill-defined 'socialist history'. Initially uniting professional and amateur historians, and signalling a generation shift within the British left, its characteristic products provide a stark contrast to the majestic historical overviews in which Hobsbawm, among other older Marxists, excelled. History Workshop sought out lost stories of oppressed groups in history's nooks and crannies.

Where Thompson had still conceptualised 'below' and 'above' only in terms of class, History Workshop activists did not. The Workshop provided one of the milieux from which women's history emerged. As Michael Roberts' chapter shows, numerous women's historians began from precisely the same materialist propositions as Marxists. Women's history, no less than Marxism, was injected into academic history by the needle-sharp theories of a social movement: feminism. To some older male historians, it still feels like a foreign body within the profession. Hobsbawm alleges that – like the History Workshop movement – feminists 'were people for whom history was not so much a way of interpreting the world, but a means of collective self-discovery, or at best, of winning collective recognition'. This, he alleges, 'undermines the universality ... that is the essence of all history as a scholarly and intellectual discipline'.[4] But feminist historians, as Roberts again makes clear, themselves problematised their position between the postulates of passionate political motives and sound academic practices. As they did so, their work mutated. An undifferentiated notion of 'patriarchy' and a dependency on biology as a determinant of the subject of historical inquiry were thrown overboard when socially constructed gender roles, the relations between genders, and histories of men as well as women took off. Gender history is more widely accepted by male historians than feminist history had been in the 1970s.[5] We should ask whether this is because it has traded-in passion for academic respectability and so become a safe current within the 'mainstream' of a *still* predominantly male profession.

A burgeoning historiography of ethnicity is no less striking an example of emphatically political impulses driving academics' interests. John Davidson discusses the 'interaction of context and theory' characteristic of this body of work especially from the 1970s onward. His chapter is an account of the ways in which historians have responded both to the measurable impact of patterns of migration and to unquantifiable changes these have brought to political culture and national identity. Even inclusive definitions have, as Davidson argues in relation to the USA, proved to rest on comfortable illusions about the USA's capacity to function as a 'salad bowl' society. Those who held it to have demonstrated an infinite capacity rapidly to integrate new immigrant groups found themselves colliding not only with indigenous racism, but also with an assertive politics of identity articulated by underprivileged groups defining themselves in terms of ethnicity and ancestry – and so also of history. Historians' work has not only reflected these problems and how they have been aired, but debated the nature of ethnicity. This is a theme Davidson pursues further in the context of Africa, whose historians successively assumed 'tribal' identities as a given, then treated them as inventions and constructs, and finally tended to conclude that, while 'tribes' might have the qualities of 'imagined communities', their existence was not imagined out of thin air.

The first generations of African professional historians had been trained in the techniques and been encouraged to adopt the habits of mind of European historiography. The process of decolonisation brought into high relief the question of what categories and units were appropriate to understanding Africa. As well as historians researching 'tribes', there were pan-Africanists and nationalists seeking historically to legitimate their various post-colonial states. They vied with one another to produce viable and persuasive accounts of the past. Loss of empire, meanwhile, has been one factor in persuading British historians – and historians of Britain – to rethink the ways in which they have conceptualised their subject.

Paul O'Leary's contribution dissects a 'new British history' which has employed not ethnicity but national identity as its organising principle. It renders them vulnerable to two charges at the outset. First – and this is a weakness they share with many historians of ethnicity – that 'identity' is itself too blunt an instrument to serve the purposes of historical analysis;[6] second, that British historians are unwittingly exemplifying their insularity.[7] While certainly influenced by legacies of empire – as witness the signal contributions described by O'Leary of a New Zealand historian to redefining 'Britishness' – advocates of 'new British history' have responded more directly to reconfigurations of the British polity as proposed in campaigns for devolution and realised in the creation of a Scottish Parliament and a Welsh Assembly. They have succeeded in exposing the old trick of saying 'British' but meaning only 'English' – writ large – and simultaneously struggled to transcend ring-fenced Irish, Scottish, Welsh and English national historiographical traditions. In other respects, however, 'new British history' describes a continuing debate, not a paradigm. No consensus has emerged on whether Britain should be seen in an Atlantic or in a European context, or on whether Britain has functioned as a preservative for four inter-relating national identities, or has forged a new identity, dissolving the four in its melting-pot to make one mixture. In any case, observers of the disputes have offered trenchant criticisms of the terms in which they are conducted. They connect more readily, O'Leary points out, to the concerns of nineteenth-century political and constitutional history than to those of late twentieth-century social history, and tend to share the 'top-down' perspective, the teleological approach, even the conviction that Britain is the proper unit of historical analysis characteristic of the former. It is questionable whether 'new British history' will be of much interest beyond Britain and a few patches of her former empire, or has really broken through the banks of the long, sluggish stream of 'the conventional, completely English-centred ... political history, to be found in the *English Historical Review* for instance, the absolutely reliable sleeping pill available in every decent family medicine cabinet'.[8] One might add that 'new British history' lacks the theoretical sophistication we encounter in the subjects of all the other chapters in this part of the volume. Empiricism seems very much alive among the contributors to this debate. But then empiricism has arguably remained a besetting sin more commonly to be found in British than in other national cultures of historiography.

In his second contribution to this part of the volume, Michael Roberts returns to theory with a vengeance, and to an intellectual movement and community of scholars which is decidedly international: postmodernism. Paradoxically, postmodernism has also divided historians: between those who have carried on with their work oblivious or wilfully blind to its challenge and those who have responded to it. Among the latter, it has attracted some, repelled others, and enticed many who would not subscribe to all its propositions to draw eclectically from within their range. On both a geographical and an intellectual level, postmodernism's progress among historians illustrates the truism that integration and fragmentation, centripetal and centrifugal forces, are two sides of the same coin. For postmodernism is also associable with the recent vogue for articulating – indeed, celebrating – multiple identities, and insisting that no hierarchies of value should pertain to them. Its origins lie in aesthetics, but it is bound up also with the history of the academic left internationally in the late twentieth century, as it reflected on the defeats the left had suffered, on a long line of its pyrrhic victories, and on its fragmentation.

Notes

1   E. Hobsbawm, 'Preface', *On History*, London, Weidenfeld and Nicolson, 1997, p. vii.
2   *Ibid.*, p. 141 (from 'What Do Historians Owe to Karl Marx?', first presented as a paper in 1968, and reprinted here, pp. 141–56).
3   H.-U. Wehler, *Historisches Denken am Ende des 20. Jahrhunderts*, Göttingen, Wallstein Verlag, 2001, p. 32.
4   E. J. Hobsbawm, *Interesting Times. A Twentieth-Century Life*, London, Allen Lane, 2002, p. 296. Hobsbawm, it should be remembered, had problems of his own in squaring his political and academic commitments, *ibid.*, p. 291.
5   See e.g. Wehler, *Historisches Denken*, p. 24.
6   Cf. L. Niethammer, *Kollektive Identität. Heimliche Quellen einer unheimlichen Konjunktur*, Reinbeck, 2000.
7   K. Robbins, *Insular Outsider? 'British History' and European Integration*, Reading, Reading University, 1990.
8   Wehler, *Historisches Denken*, p. 29.

Chapter 12

History and Marxism

Phillipp Schofield

A basic model of economic determinism, manufactured from the writings of Marx, has presented historians with a compelling explanatory tool and one that could be used particularly effectively in the new subject areas which have emerged since the close of the nineteenth century. Social and economic historians found a use for or need of Marx where their statist forebears had not. A 'vulgar Marxism' encouraged historians to consider the claims for an economic-determinist interpretation of history. In turn, both engagement and conflict with a determinist Marxism also prompted historians to insist upon the importance of class struggle as historical agency, and to develop a perspective upon the past which admitted some, at least, of those who had not always seemed ripe for study. Developments such as these signalled the creation of a distinction between orthodox Marxism, focussed upon modes of production, and a 'cultural' Marxism, or socialist humanism, which we will revisit below. For historians in the late nineteenth-century, the impact of the key tenets of 'vulgar Marxism' have been described as 'concentrated charges of intellectual explosive', while for historians of later generations, awareness of Marxist historical materialism could have a 'liberating effect'.[1] The intellectual possibilities which Marxism offered historians, both as a model to be applied and as a theory of development to be tested, have inspired at least three generations of historians, as imitators and developers but also as respondents and critics. In this discussion, particular emphasis will be placed upon the way in which Marxist historians in the West, and notably, but not exclusively, Britain, offered signal impetus to the discipline from the middle years of the twentieth century. There was a very different application of a Marxist historiography in Eastern Europe during the same period, a point to which we also briefly return.

While a 'professionalised' Marxist historiography is not strongly evident in the West before the middle years of the twentieth century, the first historical application of Marxist thinking was, unsurprisingly, undertaken by Marx himself. Explorations of, for example, the rise of capitalism led to broad surveys of long-term developments, as in the case of his examination of the changing length of the working day, which charts labour legislation within the context of socio-economic change from the fourteenth to the nineteenth centuries

(*Capital*, Pt. 3, s.5). While these historical perspectives were subsumed within broader, economic discussion, Marx also wrote history in a narrower sense. *The Eighteenth Brumaire of Louis Bonaparte* was, as Engels noted in his preface to the third edition, an 'eminent understanding of the living history of the day'. Engels, more so in fact than did Marx, and later commentators and students of Marx also brought historical perspective to their analysis.[2] A Marxist orthodoxy, applied to historical change and based upon productive force determinism, was also strongly evident in a next generation of writers, including, of course, such key political figues as Lenin and Trotsky.[3]

In the late nineteenth century and the early twentieth century, where an orthodox Marxist dialectic (a model of historical development predicated upon the succession of a series of economic 'modes', their development explained in terms of mechanisms of transition, notably class struggle) was employed, it tended to be applied by Russian authors and in the particular historical context of Russian history.[4] Thus the work of Plekhanov, and subsequently of Lenin (in his *The Development of Capitalism in Russia* [1907]) was intended to explore, within a Marxist conception of history, the changing condition of the rural population of Russia. That, as we shall see below, the demands of the Soviet state came to dictate, in the most aggressive of ways, an historical agenda in Russia, is foreshadowed by the early and clear association of the work of Marxist historians with the establishment of that state and its claims for its own identity and legitimacy. In Russia, during the 1920s, surviving links with a relatively neutral or 'bourgeois' historism were eventually severed in favour of an energetic and ideological agenda.

At the end of the nineteenth century in the West, by contrast, a Marxist conception of historical development was virtually absent from professionalised historiography. Instead, it developed beyond the academy, in, for instance, Workers' Educational Association (WEA) classes. Where, beyond Eastern Europe and Russia by the early twentieth century, a Marxist dialectic did find root in mainstream historiography, it was not infrequently imported by Russian historians, offering comparative and theoretically engaged perspectives on different historical experiences. Kosminsky's examination of the economy and society of rural England in the Middle Ages, undertaken in the 1920s and 1930s, offers a fine example of this early application of Marxist-Leninist historical theory to a particular, non-Russian, past society.[5] Kosminsky investigates the feudal mode of production in thirteenth-century England and examines the extent to which feudalism displays traits of pre-feudal relations and, most importantly for him, the 'germs of new relationships, signs of the developing changes within feudalism towards a new mode of production – the capitalist'.[6] For Kosminsky, therefore, evolution in the form of rent, as a 'relation of production', was reflective of a changing 'mode of production'. Kosminsky, in the preface to the English translation of *Studies in the Agrarian History of England*, closely defines his object of study and his methodology since, although work done by English Marxists had 'to some extent familiarized the

English reader with this terminology ... I feel I must say more about the meaning of certain fundamental terms'.[7]

By the middle decades of the twentieth century, a generation of historians in the West, operating within the academy and employing the methods of research, instruction and dissemination shared with the practitioners of 'bourgeois' historiography, had certainly begun to advance the claims of Marxist theory within the historical mainstream. While the early stirrings of economic and social history in Greece, for example, attracted a good deal of Marxist commentary from professional historians, and this by the 1920s, the process was particularly evident in Britain in the years immediately after the Second World War.[8] There, a roughly contemporaneous generation of historians, Hill, Hobsbawm, Hilton, Thomas, Thompson, nurtured research agendas which, if they did not come to dominate British historiography by the 1960s, certainly grew into striking features of the historiographical landscape.[9]

In terms of what was perceived as important and energetic in mid-twentieth century British historiography, it would certainly be true to say that offshoots of the work of Marxist historians were central. Beginning with explorations of large-scale processes of change in the past, Marxist historians, over two or three decades from the end of the Second World War until the early 1970s, allowed their interest to focus increasingly upon those lives which moulded and were moulded by these developments or transitions. This change of emphasis, to what some practitioners described as 'history from below', furnished historians with broad analytical frameworks but also close, new research agendas. In terms of publications, the journal *Past and Present*, founded in 1952 by Marxists (but not a Marxist journal), rapidly achieved parity with the *English Historical Review* and the *Economic History Review*, and is still widely recognised as one of the three most important British history journals. At the same time, the first generation of Marxist historians had taken the ivory towers by storm. Writing in 1968, on the eve of student revolutions, Hobsbawm could reflect that 'the Marxists who reached the point of publishing widely read books and occupying senior positions in academic life in the 1950s were often only the radicalised students of the 1930s or 1940s, reaching the normal peak of their careers'.[10] There were, by then, Marxist professors at leading history departments, including those of the Universities of Oxford (Thomas), London (Hobsbawm), Cambridge (Hill), Birmingham (Hilton), and Warwick (Thompson).

In no other country in the West did the critical mass of Marxist historiography generated in the immediate postwar period match that to be found in Britain. Historians, as individuals and as groups, found themselves places within the historical profession from where they were able to engage with issues of Marxist dialectics and, in some instances, to generate debate of international proportions. Discussion, for instance, of the transition from feudalism to capitalism, initiated by the publication by Maurice Dobb in 1946 of *Studies in the Development of Capitalism*, employed Marxist orthodoxies to explore the process of development between historical periods. These periods were defined by their respective dominant modes of production. In responding to Dobb's assertion that the collapse of feudalism is explicable in terms of its own economic contradictions, Italian, French, British and American historians, Marxists and non-Marxists, participated in a theoretically charged engagement.

A couple of decades later, a further salvo from an American Marxist, Robert Brenner, which also directed attention to explanations of long-term change in late medieval and early modern Europe, produced a similarly powerful and provocative debate and one that, again, excited the interest of an international body of Marxist and non-Marxist historians.[11] But by the time of the Brenner debate, Marxism had effected another change in Western historiography, and one that in its emphasis upon experience in shaping class, Brenner's work exemplifies, namely 'history from below'. The socialist-humanist approach, most closely associated at its point of origin with E. P. Thompson, came to influence a raft of studies from the the the mid-to-late 1960s.[12]

This energy of a Marxist historiography has not been sustained into the twenty-first century for a plethora of reasons, as we shall see. From the 1980s the baton of a radicalised historical agenda has passed to a new generation of social, feminist and gender historians, as well as historians of culture. It would not be appropriate to suggest, however, that these developments ran counter to the work of early Marxist historians. While it is undoubtedly the case that, in certain instances, a generation of historians writing after the first wave of Marxist historiography in the West has seen in that work something to react against and to correct – as in the work of Scott and Clark, who have highlighted the limited awareness of gender in Marxist work, including that of the purveyors of 'history from below'[13] – it is also evident that a significant debt was owed to those who established an agenda which demanded exploration of the condition of labouring men and women.

If we are to explain the process of a fashioning of a Marxist historiography in the last century or so, it is clear that no single or prime mover can be identified, not least because identification of a single 'Marxist' historiography is, to all intents and purposes, an impossibility. It is quite evident however that, at the very least, a distinction needs to be made between the development of a Marxist historiography in the capitalist West and in the Eastern European communist bloc; we might also want to make distinctions between historians who promoted a Marxist orthodoxy, centred upon modes of production, and those socialist-humanist historians, who distanced themselves in their work from close engagement with the grand themes of Marxism and focussed instead on the particular detail of class struggle.

Raphael Samuel's discussion of the emergence of a British Marxist tradition highlights an array of both complementary and conflicting factors which helped generate it. These included the intellectual roots of an historical dialectic, an engagement with non-Marxists and earlier historians who, while not Marxists, identified historical questions or research areas which Marxists were later able to exploit, a Protestant non-conformist tradition, a tradition of political activism, of radical atheism. Above all, the political vicissitudes of the twentieth century have obviously played no smaller part in the development of a Marxist histori-ography than they have in that of other branches of the discipline. 'Where', pondered Eric Hobsbawm in reviewing the early appearance of a Marxist histor-ical endeavour in Britain, 'would we, as intellectuals, have been, what would have become of us, but for the experiences of war, revolution and depression, fascism and anti-fascism, which surrounded us in our youth?'.[14] The decades either side of the Second World War have, of course, seen significant shifts in perceptions of communism and the role of the communist state. Associated with these developments, there has been a shift in political fashion which has seen a rise and subsequent decline, if not demise, of Marxist historiography.

For Marxist historians operating in the West, early encounters with politics came through family – a radical liberal tradition, not infrequently developed out of nonconformity, being a near constant feature of the background of British Marxists born in the early decades of the twentieth century – and also through university, especially Oxford in the 1930s. There, a politicised student body witnessed both the Depression and the rise of fascism. They also, as a product of the shift in communist politics, experienced Popular Frontism which, as more than one commentator has noted, effected its own development in the histori-ography: notably an identification of the history of the common man and woman with 'an unremitting endeavour towards liberation'.[15] Historians in the West who espoused Marx and Marxism were also likely to be active members of the Communist Party. Their political association led to a containing of the historical engagement, as under Popular Frontism when communist parties across Europe, in a bid to secure alliances with non-Marxist socialists and to bolster nationalism in parliamentary democratic countries, sought out national democratic traditions and set their historians to write the sort of history that complemented their approach. Christopher Hill's lifelong engagement with the 'English Revolution', and its persistence through strands of radicalism, is trace-able to the climate created by Popular Frontism, and similar inspiration is evident in the work of other CP historians who learned their trade in and around the Second World War.[16]

If the Party was a cause of containment, it also provided an impetus and dynamic to the work of British Marxist historians, especially through the collec-tive endeavour of the Historians' Group of the Communist Party in the years 1946 to 1956, the period of the group's inception and seminal contribution. A response to the work of early British Marxists and non-Marxists, historians within the Party were, through the influence of a first generation including Maurice Dobb and Donna Torr, mobilised to investigate a Marxist dialectic in the context of historical sub-periods. Rodney Hilton (1916–2002), to quote one obvious example of a historian subject to this combination of influences, came from a politically active socialist background, was educated at Manchester

Grammar School and Oxford University, the latter from 1935 to 1939, where he read history, specialising in medieval topics. During his time at Oxford he also joined the Communist Party, as a member of which he was an active participant in its Historians' Group.

Beyond the calls of family, education and Party membership, the experience of war and of Cold War politics had often dramatic influences upon the development of Marxist historians in the East and in the West. The Second World War offered, for many Marxist historians, a first-hand confrontation with fascism. E. P. Thompson (1924–93), author of the *The Making of the English Working Class*, born into a liberal background, a Cambridge graduate and member of the Communist Party from the late 1930s, saw active service in Italy and France, after which he spent some time in Yugoslavia and Bulgaria as a volunteer state-builder. The experience of war, it has also been suggested, may have further generated, in its shared frustrations, successes and horrors, a sense of equality which informed later endeavours to give voice to the voiceless.[17] After the war, a combination of a failing communist experiment in the East, the workers' uprising in Hungary in 1956 and the Soviet invasion of Czechoslovakia in 1968, introduced doubts. A number of Marxists, including Hilton and Thompson, quit the Communist Party of Great Britain, and so also the Historians' Group of the Communist Party, and reconsidered their employment of an orthodox Marxist-Leninist schema. In the USA, by comparison, a political process, experienced elsewhere in the West but not with the same intensity, also impinged significantly upon the establishment of a Marxist historiography. As Eric Foner records, an active communist-led investigation of, for example, the nature of ante-bellum slavery was challenged, but not thwarted by the state's aggressive stance against communism. Foner's father and uncle, historians at City College, New York, were both ejected from lectureships in the early 1940s on account of their membership of the Communist Party.[18] The political shifts of the 1950s and 1960s have also occasioned a subsequent distancing of academic history from orthodox communist ideology. The trend has accelerated since 1989 and the fall of Eastern European communism.

Paradoxically, this 'distancing' has also promoted, at various junctures, a different kind of 'engagement' with Marxism. 'History from below' revolted both against the crudely economic Marxism of historians standing in the tradition of the Social Democratic mainstream, and against the near-exclusive emphasis on the Party as the sole guarantor of revolutionary success characteristic of communist historiography. To quote one such example, Hilton's discussion of the Peasants' Revolt of 1381 attempted to place the peasantry of pre-industrial society, and notably of medieval society, alongside the industrial proletariat of the modern era, as the necessary base for social movement. In order to do so, Hilton examined in depth the social structure of the revolt of 1381, including detailed prosopographical analysis of its participants, an approach aimed at establishing the class basis of the movement and the collective endeavour to improve the condition of that class.[19] This more empathetic engagement with past societies – a desire to describe the lives of working men and women, slaves, peasant rebels – was, in no small part, an outcome of the unease and disappointment of Marxist intellectuals with the communist experiment in the 1950s and the growth of the New Left in the 1960s.[20] Furthermore, from the late 1960s and into the 1970s and 1980s, the rise of other new and potent 'socio-political movements', notably, the energetic development of women's and peace movements in the West, has also occasioned a distancing of academic history from communist ideology.

Earlier generations of Marxist historians had been far more closely influenced in their work by the demands of abiding political imperatives. In the West, Marxist historians who were members of the Communist Party had, in certain measure, been constrained by the expectations of the Party. As Hobsbawm records, for example, the members of the Historians' Group of the CP set about, in the late 1940s, preparing a series of volumes on the history of the British labour movement which were intended to meet the needs of readers in the trades unions and in adult education.[21] Ultimately, propinquity to the designs of the Party leadership created insurmountable tensions for academic historians operating within the Party, 'since', as Hobsbawm also writes, 'the issue of Stalin was literally one of history'.[22] When, in 1956, both the professional conscience of the historian and sympathy for the working class ran up against the demands of loyalty to the Party, the result was the decimation of the Historians' Group of the Communist Party.

In the Eastern Bloc, Party and state politics made far greater demands on historians. Stalin's intervention, in 1931, in a dispute over the history of Bolshevism, made concrete the themes of future Russian historiography under communism.[23] But those themes had already emerged in the decade after the Revolution, when the work of an earlier generation of Russian historians was employed to provide historical foundation to a Marxist-Leninist schema. Under Stalin such collaboration between old and new historism was rejected, and those historians who represented a bourgeois historiography were purged. Iggers has suggested that, despite a posited uniformity of conceptual programme within dictatorships which subscribed to Marxism-Leninism, room for manoeuvre and intellectual independence were not necessarily as restricted as might, *prima facie*, be supposed.[24] Yet it is certainly the case that, under early 1930s Stalinism, even those historians who had been in the vanguard of strict Marxist accounts of the Russian past were vulnerable. Pokrovsky, whose *Brief History of Russia*, written in 1920, applied an orthodox Marxist materialism, was a key figure in the early establishment of a post-Revolutionary academy but, by the early 1930s, his Marxism was forced to give way to Stalinism, just as the paradigm of proletarianism replaced that of economic determinism.[25]

In ways that were hardly dissimilar, the leadership of the German Communist Party, in 1945, set about a programmatic reinterpretation of history aimed at explaining away the rise of fascism and extolling the positive aspects of the German past, including a rich heritage of democracy and revolution. The role of the party and the state in facilitating this education extended to the establishment of research institutes in Berlin and the convening of writing teams of historians who were to be employed in the preparation of Marxist-Leninist surveys of German history and of labour in Germany. By then, with the gradual establishment of a one-party dictatorship, came the Stalinisation of East Germany, the renunciation of a 'German road to socialism' and also a purge of the academy, with non-Marxists replaced by Marxist-Leninist historians, some of whom had been hastily equipped with the necessary skills. Further, a Council for History was established by the Socialist Unity Party, the successor of the German Communist Party, in order to provide historians with a direction to their work which best met the needs of the country.[26]

While, however, the approach and commitment of Marxist historians were forged in the fire of 'politics' on a variety of levels, Marxist historians, rather like the subjects of which they often wrote, were, of course, not simply 'sackfuls of potatoes', acted upon but incapable of acting. Their approach was collective, sometimes overtly so: part of an enterprise intended to meet the expectations of discrete agendas. Rather than bringing Marxism to their history they typically brought their history to Marxism. Allied to the sense that Marxist theoretical writing offered a vital explanatory model, there existed the conviction amongst Marxist historians that a historical narrative which asked the right questions and approached the appropriate topics would help service their political ends.[27]

By the early 1950s, these convictions also extended into engagements with non-Marxist historians, dialogues which proved highly productive for the discipline. As we have noted, the work of some of the earliest Marxist historians, in the Eastern Bloc and in the West, necessarily drew upon the labour of present and previous generations of non-Marxists. In the decades after the Second World War, the extension of Marxism was also dependent upon the cross-fertilisation of Marxist and non-Marxist perspectives upon the past. The emergence of the journal *Past and Present* in 1952 occurred, for example, at the initiative of members of the Historians' Group of the Communist Party; but the journal was not published by the group and neither was its editorial board populated entirely by Marxists. Instead, the journal arose from engagement between historians, Marxist and non-Marxist, who sought to proceed beyond a traditionalist conception of the past and its study. While such collective endeavour served to direct the next generation to themes and potential areas of research, areas that would attract those working within and beyond Marxist traditions, it also prompted further discussion with regard to the application of Marxist theory and, indeed, the very nature of the historical endeavour.

Hilton, in his introduction to *The Transition from Feudalism to Capitalism*, offers an angry denunciation of the nineteenth-century historical tradition. In language that speaks of a persistent frustration with the approach to the past of what he saw as the 'establishment', he writes,

What is preferred in the British academic tradition, at any rate since the end of the nineteenth century, is exact and detailed scholarship directed towards the amassing of verifiable data. The training of the historian does not lie in the discussion of hypotheses by which significant historical devlopments can be explained, still less in the attempt to penetrate to the essence or 'prime mover' of socio-political formations.[28]

If we allow British Marxism to stand as our example of a Marxist historiography, then we cannot but be struck by the way in which it demands broad conceptions of the past and even when dealing with the minutiae of historical research. This feature is also reflected, albeit with some variety, in other national examples of the Marxist tradition. At its core is a restatement of the form and nature of historical agency, an explicit rejection of an earlier teleology which, as has already been discussed in this volume, sat at the heart of the nineteenth-century historiographical tradition. With no little glee, Hobsbawm records how, in meeting the great *Annaliste* historian Fernand Braudel in 1950 for the first time, Braudel, a truly international figure, demanded to know who this Namier, of whom his English colleagues were speaking, actually was. For Hobsbawm, this was confirmation that an ' "old-fashioned" politico-constitutional or narrative history' (represented here by Professor Lewis Namier, a historian who had developed a prosopographical approach to Parliamentary history), and which Marxists were reacting against, had been sidelined.[29] In its place came an historical approach that was theoretically charged and which depended upon political passions that extended far beyond the archive and the lecture theatre. While the continued contribution of Marxist historiography has been curtailed by an inevitable proximity to political (un)fashion, its insistence upon theory and upon the essentiality of exploring history from below mean that the legacy of Marxist historiography remains a vital one.

Notes

1   E. Hobsbawm, 'What Do Historians Owe to Karl Marx?', in *idem*, *On History*, London, Weidenfeld and Nicolson, 1997, p. 147.
2   E. Breisach, *Historiography. Ancient, Medieval and Modern*, Chicago, University of Chicago Press, 1983, p. 298.
3   Though they also, of course, brought their own novelties; see, for a recent short discussion of Trotsky's contribution, M. Perry, *Marxism and History*, Basingstoke, Palgrave, 2002, pp. 66–72.
4   And this despite Marx's own denial, for Eastern Europe, of a model of historical materialism which posits the emergence of capitalist production and a process of expropriation, T. Shanin (ed.) *Late Marx and the Russian Road. Marx and 'the Peripheries of Capitalism'*, London, Routledge and Kegan Paul, 1983, pp. 105, 124, quoting draft replies to Vera Zasulich.
5   E. A. Kosminsky, *Studies in the Agrarian History of England in the Thirteenth Century*, Oxford, Blackwell, 1956.
6   *Ibid.*, pp. vi–vii.
7   *Ibid.*, p. vi.

8 For Greece, see E. Gazzi, *Scientific National History. The Greek Case in Comparative Perspective (1850–1920)*, Frankfurt, Peter Lang, 2000, p. 133.

9 But see the comments of Hilton regarding the cool reception of Maurice Dobb's *Studies in the Development of Capitalism* (1946), R. H. Hilton, 'Introduction', *The Transition from Feudalism to Capitalism*, London, Verso, 1976, p. 10.

10 Hobsbawm, 'What Do Historians Owe to Karl Marx?', p. 156.

11 *The Transition from Feudalism to Capitalism*, London, Verso, 1976.

12 T. H. Aston and C. H. E. Philpin (eds) *The Brenner Debate: Agrarian Class Structure and Economic Development in Pre-Industrial Europe*, Cambridge, Cambridge University Press, 1985. On 'history from below', see, for instance, the discussion by Jim Sharpe, 'History from Below', in P. Burke (ed.) *New Perspectives on Historical Writing*, Cambridge, Polity, 1991.

13 J. W. Scott, *Gender and the Politics of History*, New York, Columbia University Press, 1988; A. Clark, *The Struggle for the Breeches: Gender and the Making of the British Working Class*, Berkeley, University of California Press, 1995. See also T. Koditschek, 'The Gendering of the British Working Class', *Gender and History*, 1997, vol. 9.

14 E. Hobsbawm, 'The Historians' Group of the Communist Party', in M. Cornforth (ed.) *Rebels and their Causes. Essays in Honour of A. L. Morton*, London, Lawrence and Wishart, 1978, p. 26.

15 R. Samuel, 'British Marxist Historians I', *New Left Review*, 1980, vol. 120, pp. 41–2.

16 G. Eley, *Forging Democracy. The History of the Left in Europe, 1850–2000*, Oxford, Oxford University Press, 2002, p. 266, where he notes that Popular Frontism prompted, in Britain, work on Chartism and the Levellers. See also Samuel, 'British Marxist Historians I', p. 41. C. Hill, *The English Revolution*, London, Lawrence and Wishart, 1940; *idem*, 'From Lollards to Levellers', in Cornforth (ed.) *Rebels and their Causes*. Note also, for example, R. H. Hilton, 'Peasant Movements in Medieval England', *Economic History Review*, 1949, 2nd series, vol. 2.

17 Samuel, 'British Marxist Historians I', p. 27.

18 E. Foner, *Who Owns History? Rethinking the Past in a Changing World*, New York, Hill and Wang, 2002, pp. 4, 6. See also above, pp. 112–13 (Chapter 7).

19 R. H. Hilton, *Bond Men Made Free. Medieval Peasant Movements and the English Rising of 1381*, London and New York, Methuen, 1973; for a modernist's example of the same approach, see E. Acton, *Rethinking the Russian Revolution*, London, Edward Arnold, 1990.

20 See, for instance, R. Johnson, 'Edward Thompson, Eugene Genovese, and Socialist-humanist History', *History Workshop Journal*, 1978, vol. 6.

21 Hobsbawm, 'Historians' Group', pp. 28–9.

22 *Ibid.*, p. 41.

23 Breisach, *Historiography*, p. 351.

24 G. G. Iggers, *Historiography in the Twentieth Century: From Scientific Objectivity to the Postmodern Challenge*, London, Wesleyan University Press, 1997, p. 83.

25 B. Williams, 'Soviet Historians and the Rediscovery of the Soviet Past', in W. Lamont (ed.) *Historical Controversies and Historians*, London, UCL Press, 1998, pp. 227–8.

26 A. Dorpalen, *German History in Marxist Perspective. The East German Approach*, London, Tauris, 1985, pp. 46–54.

27 Thus, for instance, Hobsbawm, 'What Do Historians Owe to Karl Marx?', pp. 142–3,

> Even by the modest standards of the human and social sciences, history was ... an extremely, one might say a deliberately, backward discipline. Its contributions [*sic*] to the understanding of human society, past and present, was negligible and accidental. Since an understanding of society requires an

understanding of history, alternative and more fruitful ways of exploring the human past had, sooner or later, to be found.

28 Hilton, 'Introduction', *Transition from Feudalism to Capitalism*, p. 10.
29 Hobsbawm, 'Historians' Group', p. 38. For Braudel, see also above, pp. 84–6.

Further reading

There is, of course, a vast corpus of texts written on Marxism and its relationship to history. Recent contributions include S. H. Rigby, *Marxism and History. A Critical Introduction*, Manchester, Manchester University Press, 2nd edn, 1998; M. Perry, *Marxism and History*, Basingstoke, Palgrave, 2002; E. Hobsbawm, 'What Do Historians Owe to Karl Marx?', in *idem, On History*, London, Weidenfeld and Nicolson, 1997, pp. 66–72. Other recent short and accessible overviews include G. Eley, 'Marxist Historiography', in S. Berger, H. Feldner and K. Passmore (eds) *Writing History. Theory and Practice*, London, Arnold, 2003, pp. 63–82; S. H. Rigby, 'Marxist Historiography', in M. Bentley (ed.) *Companion to Historiography*, London, Routledge, pp. 889–928.

For examples of national studies of Marxist historiography, both in the East and in the West, see, for instance, E. Gazzi, *Scientific National History. The Greek Case in Comparative Perspective (1850–1920)*, Frankfurt, Peter Lang, 2000; B. Williams, 'Soviet Historians and the Rediscovery of the Soviet Past', in W. Lamont (ed.) *Historical Controversies and Historians*, London, UCL Press, 1998; A. Dorpalen, *German History in Marxist Perspective. The East German Approach*, London, Tauris, 1985.

On the development of British Marxist history, see R. Samuel, 'British Marxist Historians I', *New Left Review*, 1980, vol. 120; H. J. Kaye, *The British Marxist Historians. An Introductory Analysis*, Basingstoke, Macmillan, 1995, introduction; for an insider view of a key institutional foundation of that development, E. Hobsbawm, 'The Historians' Group of the Communist Party', in M. Cornforth (ed.) *Rebels and Their Causes. Essays in Honour of A. L. Morton*, London, Lawrence and Wishart, 1978.

The development of socialist-humanist history in the West, from the 1960s, and the adoption of 'history from below', is epitomised in the work of E. P. Thompson and, most particularly, his *The Making of the English Working Class*, Harmondsworth, Penguin, 1968. For some responses to the agenda established by Thompson, see J. W. Scott, *Gender and the Politics of History*, New York, Columbia University Press, 1988; A. Clark, *The Struggle for the Breeches: Gender and the Making of the British Working Class*, Berkeley, University of California Press, 1995. See also T. Koditschek, 'The Gendering of the British Working Class', *Gender and History*, 1997, vol. 9; and for an assessment of Thompson and socialist-humanist history, R. Johnson, 'Edward Thompson, Eugene Genovese, and Socialist-humanist History', *History Workshop Journal*, 1978, vol. 6. For a general discussion of 'history from below', see also J. Sharpe,

'History from Below', in P. Burke (ed.) *New Perspectives on Historical Writing*, Cambridge, Polity, 1991.

Prior to the departure of socialist humanism, a more direct engagement with classical Marxism and the materialist conception of history is strongly evident in British Marxism. Central works here include Maurice Dobb's *Studies in the Development of Capitalism*, London, Routledge, 1946; and elements of the subsequent debate gathered in *The Transition from Feudalism to Capitalism*, London, Verso, 1976. The persistence of that perspective is evident in the later debate on transition, T. H. Aston and C. H. E. Philpin (eds) *The Brenner Debate: Agrarian Class Structure and Economic Development in Pre-Industrial Europe*, Cambridge, Cambridge University Press, 1985. The force of a Marxist perspective remains evident in historical writing and model building; for a recent overview of its relative contribution, from a particular perspective, see J. Hatcher and M. Bailey, *Modelling the Middle Ages*, Cambridge, Cambridge University Press, 2002, ch. 3.

Chapter 13

Women's history and gender history

Michael Roberts

Women's History as an organised field of study is a legacy of the 1960s, when an emerging liberation movement began seeking explanations for women's oppression, an oppression which was manifest even within the campaigns for civil rights and against war in Indo-China. It was not inevitable that liberation should involve a return to the past. After all, in the United States the suffocating pressures on married women which Betty Friedan described in *The Feminine Mystique* (1963) were largely the outcome of a very recent period of post-war affluence, and its 'ferocious pursuit of private domesticity'.[1] When forty-three year old Gerda Lerner went to graduate school at Columbia in 1963 she found some of the women students more hostile than were the men to her 'constantly "harping" on women'.[2] In Britain even at the very end of the 1960s it was hardly self-evident to Sheila Rowbotham that 'women's lives mattered, or that what women have done has shaped this century'.[3]

Women were driven towards the past as a way of understanding how women's access to higher education had stirred ambitions, but thwarted expectations: Friedan's bombshell had been based on interviews she conducted with fellow Smith College graduate housewives. When Lerner offered her first course in Women's History whilst still an undergraduate in New York in 1962, she could not raise the minimum ten-student enrolment. As well as indifference there was incredulity. The first Women's Liberation conference in Britain was convened in reaction against the 1969 'History Workshop' at Ruskin college, Oxford, where proposals for a separate meeting of those interested in 'women's history' had initially been met with laughter.[4] As demos and teach-ins proliferated around the world, however, history seemed to be in the making, and 'great men' were no longer the only ones making it. Even so, 'Bewilderment and mystery surrounded the birth of women's liberation',[5] as questions were being posed which 'we could not find answered in books'.[6]

When in 1971 Joan Kelly was asked to contribute a lecture on women to a new syllabus Gerda Lerner was organising, she replied that 'since I was in Renaissance history, there was nothing much I could offer about women'. It took the determined Lerner four hours of conversation to convince Kelly otherwise. After a weekend's reflection, Kelly was converted. As she recalled not long before her death in 1982,

> The change I went through was kaleidoscopic. I had not read a new book. I did not stumble upon a new archive. No fresh piece of information was added to everything I knew. But I knew now that the entire picture I had held of the Renaissance was partial, distorted, limited, and deeply flawed.[7]

She compared the revelation to Leonardo's imagining our looking at the earth from the moon. The article which Kelly eventually contributed to the published version of this new syllabus asked 'Did Women Have a Renaissance?'[8] It suggested in its very title just how fundamentally the new approach might re-shape established notions of periodization in Western historiography: had great periods of change for men simply passed women by? In its conclusion the article also showed how present concerns might lead to reinterpretations of the past, as Kelly's Renaissance grew to resemble Betty Friedan's America:

> All the advances of Renaissance Italy, its protocapitalist economy, its states, and its humanistic culture, worked to mold the noblewoman into an aesthetic object: decorous, chaste, and doubly dependent on her husband as well as on her prince.[9]

Similar revisions have followed, notably Lyndal Roper's reinterpretation of the Reformation through its impact on women in *The Holy Household* (1989). Sometimes the 'female world' has been viewed more positively.[10] But a view of the sexes as living in more or less 'separate spheres' has proved controversial, for its Whiggish sense of chronology, its tendency to concentrate on the lives of middle-class women, and its indifference to the relational character of the experience of both sexes. Natalie Davis argued in 1975 that 'we should be interested in the history of both women and men ... we should not be working only on the subjected sex any more than the historian of class can focus entirely on peasants'.[11] The first experiments in women's history often derived their explanatory forms from currently influential mainstream models, adopting these as they emulated professional historical practice. 'Separate spheres' offered an elaboration of, and substitute for, the existing class framework of analysis. Judith Bennett has recalled how her generation of women were also inclined to emphasise evidence for *change* and *variety* in the past, in reaction against the essentialist accounts of women as witches or healers with which they had grown up. The emphasis on long-term *continuity*, which Kelly's paper foreshadowed, took some time to develop.

The earliest ventures in women's history often celebrated the process of discovery itself, seeking to help women who had been 'hidden' become 'visible'.[12] The collaborative basis of the work was explicit in the collections of articles through which it was published, and in writers' acknowledgements (though Mitchell's key article from 1966 achieved wide circulation through pirated editions).[13] The personal and the public were mixed, as in the early work of Denise Riley, who explored the history of wartime nurseries as a way of thinking through for herself, as a single parent, how best to campaign for child-care provision in the 1970s.[14] By the time Rowbotham was introducing her own synthesis of women's history to an American audience in 1974, she identified two broad approaches to the subject: one, defiantly popular, romantically identifying with women in the past; and the other a 'quiet burrowing, yet to see the light of day, of innumerable lonely women' in the archives. The first way risked overidentification with the subject matter and 'becoming impatient with the time it takes to do careful research'. Yet by the second 'we might find ourselves creating just another academic subject'.[15] How could passion and rigour be combined?

To conventional minds, moreover, concentration on women and their interests seemed to narrow or lower the historian's sights. Gerda Lerner was advised to advance her career by presenting herself as 'a social historian and a specialist in reform history' rather than as a historian of women, but she refused.[16] Mary Beard had observed how 'Equal education for which women have clamoured has merely meant the extension to women of men's education in their own history and judgements of themselves'.[17] At various points from the later nineteenth century historians had illuminated women's political subordination, economic position, and 'domestic' responsibilities.[18] Nor had women been entirely neglected during the 1950s.[19] But these initiatives had never coalesced into a lasting presence in the academy, or on the bookshelves. After the 1960s this was all to change, and the novelty lay less in doing women's history *per se*, than in the implications of its being done regularly, by many people, in a concerted fashion. To the extent that it also entailed an *interdisciplinary* approach, and often an innovative approach to source materials, the study of women's history found itself moving to the centre of contemporary intellectual concerns.

At the same time its development varied geographically. In the United States a concerted campaign to give women a larger place in the historical profession gelled with empirical research on the political culture of the maturing early nineteenth-century republic, for example in writings by Barbara Welter and Gerda Lerner.[20] By the 1960s the proportion of Ph.D.s awarded to women had actually fallen since before 1939 from 15 per cent to 10 per cent,[21] and even at the end of the decade the ten most-regarded research departments in history employed no women full professors, and only four associates or assistants. Within the American Historical Association, the Berkshire Conference, founded in 1930 to counter the isolation which women experienced in an academic world defined by male sociability, was dedicated from 1972 to the pursuit of women's history, and measures were taken to monitor the recruitment of women to academic posts.[22] The proportion of women graduating with Ph.D.s in history rose through 16 per cent in the early 1970s to 38 per cent by 1988, and though women still supplied only 12 per cent of faculty as a whole, they were by then figuring in the most prominent positions in the profession.[23]

Professionalisation provided some security both for the long-term future of women's history as a subject of study, and for some of those able to commit themselves to it (current estimates suggest that an average of 11.3 years are required after graduation to obtain a doctorate in the United States).[24] The price paid was the assimilation of the field to existing disciplinary structures, at a time when the relationship between varieties of feminist theory and the practice of research remained fluid. Fortunately this allowed scope for heated debate about the competing paradigms within which women's history as a putative 'normal science' should best be undertaken in the decade after 1985. One of the reasons Joan Scott's pivotal discussion of *gender* proved so unsettling then was its appearance as the lead article in the *American Historical Review*,[25] signalling both the *presence* of women at the heart of the academy and their possible transformation and *displacement*.

In the UK it was to take twenty years to achieve this kind of institutional impact, and women's *history* remains peripheral to many feminists' vision.[26] Very important contributions to the development of historical writing were made meanwhile by women such as Averil Cameron, Jose Harris, Barbara Harvey, Margaret Spufford, Joan Thirsk and Dorothy Thompson, but without concentrating specifically on women's history. Headway was also made more informally by History Workshop, and through the growing enthusiasm for social history.[27] During the later 1920s the Economic History Society had drawn on networks of women historians in schools and university extension classes, and in 1927 one-fifth of its 500 members were women, the same proportion of the regular teaching staff at the LSE when Alice Clark studied there as a mature student before the First World War.[28] But the contribution of this generation had been largely forgotten by the 1960s.[29] Contributions to the *Economic History Review* from women comprised little more than 6 per cent of the total before the 1980s, growing to almost 14 per cent in the 1990s.[30] The society's women's committee which was to run annual work-shops was established in 1988, and the sub-title of the *Review* was formally extended to embrace social history in 1991. A separate nation-wide Women's History Network was set up in 1991. By late 2001 women held the chief offices of all three leading UK historians' associations. But in the early days women's history in the UK owed much more, even through contesting its premises, to socialism.

Judith Mitchell's 1966 essay 'Women: The Longest Revolution' provided the first analytical framework, examining the interplay between production, reproduction, sex and childrearing:

> The variations of woman's condition throughout history will be the result of different combinations of these elements – much as Marx's analysis of the economy in *Precapitalist Economic Formations* is an account of the

different combinations of the factors of production, not a linear narrative of economic development.

This was the 'younger' Marx, as edited two years previously by Sheila Rowbotham's graduate supervisor Eric Hobsbawm. Mitchell saw her combined elements as constituting a specific 'structure', in keeping with contemporary thinking, whilst her title pointed to a third key New Left influence in the work of Raymond Williams.[31] The combination of elements was creative and provocative. As Sheila Rowbotham recalls, women with children 'were our equivalent of the Marxist proletariat'.[32] Mitchell herself, in the powerfully analytical book in which she re-published the article in 1971, sought to resolve the tension between the categories of class and gender through a unified 'politics of oppression'.[33]

The New Zealander Mitchell was also insistent in distinguishing the Women's Liberation Movement, as an international phenomenon, from 'its historical predecessors', seeing the suffrage movement as more insular, and thus a weak precedent in the popular imagination: 'women went wild before, so they are again. It's only a flash in the pan!'[34] In 1970 Mitchell gave up her lectureship in English to write and train as a psychoanalyst, a move from a social towards a very much more personal sense of history. A counter-impulse came from the left of the labour movement. A 1968 campaign to extend workers' control over factory production saw the publication of a historical compendium of earlier twentieth-century writings on the subject.[35] The same year saw the reprinting of Alice Clark's *Working Life of Women in the Seventeenth Century*, originally published in 1919, and in 1969 followed a reprint of Ivy Pinchbeck's *Women Workers and the Industrial Revolution 1750–1850* (1930). The inclusion of a talk on the history of women's factory work at the 1969 Ruskin History Workshop led indirectly to plans for the first Women's Liberation conference for the following February. Women continued to play a key role in the History Workshop movement, including the journal launched in 1976, though dissatisfaction with the limitations of Marxist analysis by 1982 saw 'feminist' joining the word 'socialist' on the masthead. Whilst it lasted, however, the combination of interests sustained fruitful work, on both sides of the Atlantic. Joan Scott and Louise Tilly's *Women, Work and the Family* (1978) attempted a synthesis of Marxist and feminist approaches to the impact of industrialisation; whilst Barbara Taylor's *Eve and the New Jerusalem* (1979) showed the Owenite socialists to have come closest to a gender-aware critique of emerging industrial capitalism. This work has more recently been taken further by Anna Clark's *The Struggle for the Breeches* (Berkeley CA, 1995), and Deborah Valenze in *The First Industrial Woman* (Oxford, 1995).

The links with a wider political movement, though problematic in several respects, were probably crucial in the UK experience, given how small a proportion of the population had access to higher education in the 1960s. This context sustained the plausibility of a class analysis of women's as well as men's

experience well into the 1970s. There was a corresponding resistence to a sepa-
ratist women's history, Rowbotham insisting in 1974 that this 'can actually
restrict the radical implications of a feminist approach to the past', risked
putting it in the hands of women who were not feminists, and reducing 'human
consciousness to biology in a deterministic manner, forgetting that a man
writing history can be transformed by the existence of a feminist movement'.[36]
The same broad sense of possibility led to her suspicions of 'patriarchy' as a way
of characterising the long-standing dominant male order. For her it implied 'a
structure which is fixed, rather than the kaleidoscope of forms within which
women and men have encountered each other'.[37] But there remained the need
for positive discrimination in the appointment of women to teaching posts for
an *organised* exploration of women's past experience. Rowbotham's earliest
publications included the pioneering synthesis, *Hidden from History*, and a
separately published critical bibliography of existing work on women in the
past. Serious, critical work seemed all the more necessary given the sweeping
treatment of historical experience in the founding texts of the women's movement.[38]

In retrospect, the progress made during the 1970s and 1980s appears quite
uneven. Only a handful of the 750 journals searched for the first major analysis
of the periodical literature in 1992 were specifically devoted to the history of
women. The earliest British journal with a major commitment to the field was
founded in 1976, just a year after *Signs* in the United States. Only once the
challenge of 'gender' had become substantial were more journals added, the
Journal of Women's History (1986) in the United States, and in Britain *Gender
and History* (1989) and, in reaction to the turn to gender, *Women's History
Review* (1992). Even in 1992, mainstream historical journals in the UK were
devoting barely one-tenth of their pages to women's history.[39] In France,
meanwhile, where formal attention to women's history came relatively late,
nevertheless over the period 1970–82 some 18.5 per cent of articles in *Annales*
were written by women, a proportion equivalent to women's presence in the
profession, though concentration specifically on women's history was very
much more limited.[40]

Whatever its implications for chronology, women's history did not overturn
the broad pattern of historical research in practice. In 5,500 articles published
in the 1980s alone, the history of the historian's own culture, and of more
recent periods, figured most often. Likewise, more than two-thirds of the paper
proposals to the Berkshire Conferences in the 1980s and 1990s dealt with US
history. Publication on British women's history down to 1992 yielded 588
items on the medieval period, 974 on the early modern period, and 1,632 on
the period after 1800. The most popular (or most accessibly researched) themes
were those connected with politics, power, and work in the modern period;
politics and power in the early modern period; followed by the place of women
in the family after 1800. As the site of economic and micropolitical activity in
pre-industrial societies, the family attracted most interest from medievalists. At

the Berkshire conference in 1999 there were over 200 presentations on twen-tieth-century topics, a further 100 dealing with the nineteenth century, and not many more than fifty on the period 1500–1800. Only seven dealt with any period before 1500.[41] This concentration may have been exaggerated by the chosen conference theme, but also reflects the way in which a history broad-ened to embrace post-colonial and post-Soviet experience contributes to a shift in the centre of gravity in historical studies generally.[42]

Women's history has thus shaped, and been shaped by, changing views of the purpose of historical writing as a whole. Subjects explored primarily through conventional empirical research, such as the history of pre-industrial women's work, have contributed to the re-thinking of chronology both over the long term, and of such break points as the 'Industrial Revolution'. A different approach has been taken by examining spheres where women's influence had been assumed to be at its least, as with Amy Erickson's *Women and Property in Early Modern England* (1993). The exploration of European medieval women's experience has seen distinct national interpretative approaches develop, as well as a growing awareness of geographical variation within the over-arching cate-gory 'Christendom, and between varieties of heresy. Studies of medieval writing are showing how women as patrons and readers influenced authors and shaped the text'.[43] To the idea of 'difference' has thus been added what Natalie Zemon Davis has termed 'mixture'. At the same time, a multicultural approach has reinterpreted the history of the USA in terms of different regional perspectives on gender, from the Northeast, the Southeast and the West.[44] Europe has been similarly reconceptualised as the domain not so much of families, as of single women, a provocative reversal of the hitherto dominant paradigm of household demography.[45]

Interest in differences *between* women as well as from men flourished during the 1980s when historians increasingly wrote of such distinctions as reflecting a socially constructed (rather than biologically determined) gender identity. This allowed topics from the pioneering 1970s, such as the importance of 'experi-ence', to be revisited in the light of new insights born of the linguistic turn, alongside a new subject, the body. Excellent studies on this basis by Caroline Walker Bynum, Lyndal Roper and Miri Rubin have made us view medieval and early modern culture anew. The term gender itself aroused disquiet by seeming to weaken the claims of women as an organised political movement, though work on the body has shown how these can be redefined in terms of a situated subjectivity. The same goes for men. David Halperin suggested that 1992 might be celebrated not as the five hundredth anniversary of Columbus' discovery of America, but as the centenary of an invention of Charles Gilbert Chaddock, the man whom the *Oxford English Dictionary* credits with introducing the term 'homo-sexuality' into the language. Joanna Bourke has used an interest in expe-rience and emotion as a way of exploring and re-defining the traditional terrain of men's History par excellence, warfare, in *An Intimate History of Killing* (2000). The interplay between bodily experience, sexual orientation and gender identity has recently been taken to new heights of subtlety in Laura Gowing's *Common Bodies: Women, Touch and Power in Seventeenth-Century England* (2003).

Studies of masculinity are flourishing, but the extent to which History as a project remains 'male' in its overall conception is unresolved. Bonnie Smith has shown how firmly professional historiography was shaped by the habits and assumptions of men in the nineteenth century, and we have learnt how the achievements of Eileen Power and Lucie Varga were underplayed after their deaths in the 1940s.[46] Joan Thirsk writes ruefully of how women who prove themselves good editors 'may never emerge from that role'.[47] Even where women hold their ground professionally against men, moreover, Luce Irigaray suggests we should still distinguish between the sex of the writer and the gender of what is written: most women do men's writing for them, for example by striving to maintain a measured authorial voice.[48] When Sheila Rowbotham complained that 'aspirations for happiness or fantasies of transgression are much harder to chart historically than rates of pay',[49] her critics worried about a drift to the irrational.[50] Whether the pressures of professionalisation have thwarted the development of a more expressive, experimental historiography by women, however, is doubtful given the evidence of Carolyn Steedman's *Landscape for a Good Woman* (1986), which blends biography, story-telling and history, and Jill Liddington's *Female Fortune* (1998), an extended commentary on the diaries of Lesbian landowner and scholar Anne Lister; or Denise Riley's notorious *'Am I That Name?'* (1988), an essay subtly combining poststructuralism with a poet's sensibility.

It seems likely that a more experimental mode of historical writing will be required of all of us to do justice to experience of time in an increasingly interconnected world. The first women's history seminar in China was held at Tianjin Normal University in August (1999), and in the same year the Center for Gender Studies of the European Humanities University sponsored a conference in Minsk, Belorus, on 'Writing Women's History and the History of Gender in Countries in Transition'. 'Gender' sometimes proves to be a strategically more useful category for such work than 'women', though it can also squeeze women back to the margins.[51] But the first ventures from the West to engage with this huge landscape have been disappointingly prosaic.[52] Part of the problem is simply the accumulation of detail, which in the West is now so great that the evolution of women's history has itself become a historical phenomenon, something from which we need to stand back to fully appreciate. A genuinely integrated *world* history presents a prospect immeasurably more complex. Natalie Davis has shown how this task might be handled through interlocking geographies and biographies in *Women on the Margins* (1995).

We can end with three examples which weave in concentric circles a framework of interpretation around early modern European experiences of gender. Cynthia Herrup has re-told the story of the trial and execution of the Earl of

Castlehaven in 1631 for abetting the rape of his wife and committing sodomy with his servants. Carefully reconstituting not only 'the events' but also the degrees of freedom with which seventeenth-century people were able to articulate their experience, she reflects, in turn, on the degrees of freedom available to the modern historian and to her audience when they come to imagine and interpret such experiences. Sara Mendelson and Patricia Crawford, working by email on different continents, have constructed a surpassing synthesis of what we can now know about Castlehaven's society and contemporaries, a work which addresses the history of the whole of society, not as a context within which women lived, but as a cultural world whose shape they were participants in designing. Olwen Hufton has achieved something similar on a European scale, again imaginatively seizing the opportunity of crafting a work from a woman's point of view by organising her immense materials around the simple, yet infinitely variable, stages of the life cycle. Avoiding a false resolution of the tensions between women's and gender history, between subjectivity and objectivity; all these works give us ways of thinking about gendered experience in time which must be lastingly fruitful.

Notes

1 Friedan's data comes from S. M. Evans, *Born for Liberty: A History of Women in America*, New York, Free Press, 1989, p. 237.
2 G. Lerner, 'Autobiographical Notes, by way of an Introduction', in *The Majority Finds Its Past: Placing Women in History*, New York, Oxford University Press, 1979, p. xx.
3 S. Rowbotham, *A Century of Women: The History of Women in Britain and the United States*, New York, Viking, 1997, p. 3.
4 J. Alberti, *Gender and the Historian*, Harlow, Longman, 2002, p. 29 quoting Sally Alexander.
5 S. Rowbotham, *Woman's Consciousness, Man's World*, Harmondsworth, Penguin, 1973, p. ix. The bulk of this work, originally part of *Women, Resistance and Revolution*, London, Allen Lane, 1972 was written in mid-1971: p. vii.
6 Rowbotham, *A Century of Women*, p. 4.
7 J. Kelly, *Women, History, and Theory*, Chicago, University of Chicago Press, 1984, p. xiii.
8 R. Bridenthal and C. Koonz (eds) *Becoming Visible: Women in European History*, Boston MA, Houghton Mifflin, 1977, pp. ix, 161.
9 *Ibid.*, p. 161.
10 C. Smith-Rosenberg, 'The Female World of Love and Ritual: Relations between Women in Nineteenth-century America', *Signs*, 1975, vol. 1:i, pp. 1–29.
11 N. Z. Davis, ' "Women's History" in Transition: The European Case', *Feminist Studies*, 1976, vol. 3, p. 90.
12 S. Rowbotham, *Hidden from History: 300 Years of Women's Oppression and the Fight Against It*, London, Pluto Press, 1973; Bridenthal and Koonz, *Becoming Visible*.
13 J. Mitchell, *Women: The Longest Revolution: Essays on Feminism, Literature and Psychoanalysis*, London, Virago, 1984, p. 17.
14 D. Riley, 'Reflections in the Archive?', *History Workshop Journal*, 1997, vol. 44, p. 238.

15 S. Rowbotham, *Dreams and Dilemmas: Collected Writings*, London, Virago, 1983, p. 177.

16 G. Lerner, *The Majority Finds Its Past: Placing Women in History*, New York, Oxford University Press, 1979, p. xxiv.

17 Quoted in Lerner, *Majority*, p. xxii.

18 B. G. Smith, *The Gender of History: Men, Women, and Historical Practice*, Cambridge MA, Harvard University Press, 1998, chs 1–3. For earlier periods see N. Z. Davis, 'Gender and Genre: Women as Historical Writers, 1400–1820', in P. Labalme (ed.) *Beyond their Sex: Learned Women of the European Past*, New York, New York University Press, 1980, pp. 153–83; J. Thirsk, 'Introduction' to M. Prior (ed.) *Women in English Society 1500–1800*, London, Methuen, 1985; M. Berg, *A Woman in History: Eileen Power, 1889–1940*, Cambridge, Cambridge University Press, 1996.

19 The history of ideas gave an even earlier impulse: A. L. Gabriel, 'The Educational Ideas of Christine de Pisan', *Journal of the History of Ideas*, 1955, vol. 16, pp. 3–21; K. Thomas, 'The Double Standard', *Journal of the History of Ideas*, 1959, vol. 20, pp. 195–216; G. J. Barker-Benfield, *The Horrors of the Half-Known Life*, 1974, 2nd edn, London, Routledge, 2000, pp. xi–ii, summarises work on American women's history being done by male historians in the 1950s and early 1960s.

20 B. Welter, 'The Cult of True Womanhood 1800–1860', *American Quarterly*, 1966, vol. 18; G. Lerner, 'The Lady and the Mill Girl: Changes in the Status of Women in the Age of Jackson', *Midcontinent American Studies Journal*, 1969, vol. 10.

21 C. Farnham, 'Foreword', in G. V. Fischer, *Journal of Women's History Guide to Periodical Literature*, Bloomington IN, Indiana University Press, 1992, p. 2.

22 J. W. Scott, 'The Problem of Invisibility' in S. Jay Kleinberg (ed.) *Retrieving Women's History: Changing Perceptions of the Role of Women in Politics and Society*, London and Paris, Berg/Unesco 1988, p. 9. An International Federation for Research in Women's History was established in 1987 and its first conference in Madrid in 1990 marked a similar global landmark.

23 Farnham, 'Foreword', p. 5.

24 R. B. Townsend, 'On the Plateau's Edge? Dramatic Growth of History PhDs in the 1990s Appears to Be Slowing', *American Historical Association. Perspectives Online*, January 2002, vol. 40:1.

25 J. Scott, 'Gender: A Useful Category of Historical Analysis', *American Historical Review*, 91, 1986, pp. 1053–75.

26 Virtually no treatment in S. Jackson and J. Jones (eds) *Contemporary Feminist Theories*, Edinburgh, Edinburgh University Press, 1998, for example.

27 Harold Perkin was appointed to the first full chair in social history at Lancaster in 1967. The journal *Social History* was established in 1975 and the Social History Society in 1976.

28 A. Erickson, 'Introduction' to A. Clark, *Working Life of Women in the Seventeenth Century*, 1919, reprinted London, Routledge and Kegan Paul, 1982, p. xii, noting 22 per cent for the 1895–1932 period as a whole.

29 Berg, *A Woman in History*, p. 167.

30 E. A. Wrigley, 'The *Review* during the last 50 years', p. 19 at http://www.ehs.org.uk/.

31 J. Mitchell, 'Women: The Longest Revolution', *New Left Review*, 1966, vol. 40; R. Williams, *The Long Revolution*, London and New York, Columbia University Press, 1961.

32 S. Rowbotham, *Promise of a Dream: Remembering the Sixties*, London, Allen Lane, 2000, p. 214.

33 J. Mitchell, *Women's Estate*, Harmondsworth, Pelican Books, 1971, Preface.

34 *Ibid.*, p. 11.

35 K. Coates and T. Topham (eds) *Workers' Control*, London, Panther, 1970.

36 Rowbotham, *Dreams and Dilemmas*, pp. 177–8.

37 *Ibid.*, p. 209.

38 See the works by Greer, Figes and Millett subjected to a Marxist historical critique by Branca Margas in *New Left Review*, 1970, vol. 66, and Anna Davin, 'Women and History' in M. Wandor (ed.) *The Body Politic: Women's Liberation in Britain, 1969–72*, London, Stage One, 1972.

39 Fischer, *Guide to Periodical Literature*, p. 9.

40 A. Farge, 'Method and Effects of Women's History', in A. Farge (ed.) *Writing Women's History*, Oxford, Blackwell, 1992, French edn 1984, p. 16.

41 Calculated by author from web catalogue.

42 The theme chosen for the celebration of Women's History Month in 2002 was a rousingly patriotic one: 'Women Sustaining the American Spirit'.

43 M. Rubin, 'A Decade of Studying Medieval Women, 1987–1997', *History Workshop Journal*, 1998, vol. 46, p. 230.

44 V. L. Ruiz and E. C. DuBois (eds) *Unequal Sisters: A Multi-Cultural Reader in US Women's History*, New York, 1990, 2nd edn, London, Routledge, 1994, a collection of thirty-six articles and four bibliographies, on African American, Asian American, Latina, and Native American women, more than half the articles dealing with women of colour.

45 J. M. Bennett and A. M. Froide (eds) *Singlewomen in the European Past 1250–1800*, Philadelphia, University of Pennsylvania Press, 1999.

46 Berg, *A Woman in History*, p. 257; P. Schottler, *Lucie Varga: Les autorités invisibles. Une historienne autrichiennes aux annales dans les années trente*, Paris, Le Cerf, 1991; idem, 'Lucie Varga: A Central European Refugee in the Circle of the French "Annales", 1934–1941', *History Workshop Journal*, 1992, vol. 33, pp. 100–20; cf. N. Z. Davis, 'Women and the World of the Annales', *History Workshop Journal*, 1992, vol. 33, pp. 121–37.

47 Thirsk, 'Introduction', p. 4. Thirsk's achievements include editing the massive *Agrarian History of England and Wales*.

48 T. Moi, *Sexual/Textual Politics: Feminist Literary Theory*, London, Routledge, 1985, p. 108. M. E. Wiesner-Hanks, *Gender in History*, Oxford, Blackwell, 2001.

49 Rowbotham, *A Century of Women*, p. 538.

50 J. R. Richards, *The Sceptical Feminist*, Harmondsworth, Penguin, 1980, p. 33 accusing Rowbotham of irrationalism.

51 A. Marwick, *The New Nature of History: Knowledge, Evidence, Language*, Basingstoke, Palgrave, 2001, (five references in index to ' "gender", gender roles, "gender theory"', four references to 'women, history of (feminist history)', including brief critiques of three recent works by women historians); J. H. Arnold, *History: A Very Short Introduction*, Oxford, Oxford University Press, 2000, index: 'gender' (nine page references, none for 'women'); L. Jordanova, *History in Practice*, London, Arnold, 2000, index: 'gender' (seven page references), 'women's history' (nine references); A. Green and K. Troup, *The Houses of History: A Critical Reader in Twentieth-century History and Theory*, Manchester, Manchester University Press, 1999, index: 'women's history see gender history' (one chapter of twelve).

52 P. Stearns, *Gender in World History*, London, Routledge, 2000; Wiesner-Hanks, *Gender in History*.

Further reading

That this field has come of age is demonstrated by a crop of book-length studies of its evolution. J. P. Zinsser, *History and Feminism*, New York, Twayne

Publishers, 1993 concentrates on the period since the 1960s, whilst B. G. Smith, *The Gender of History: Men, Women and Historical Practice*, Cambridge MA, Harvard University Press, 1998, is fascinating on the gendering of the historical profession from its inception in the nineteenth century. Both P. N. Stearns, *Gender in World History*, London, Routledge, 2000, and M. E. Wiesner-Hanks, *Gender in History*, Oxford, Blackwell, 2001, survey the impressive if sometimes awkward emancipation of women's history from single national agendas. J. Alberti, *Gender and the Historian*, Harlow, Longman, 2002 confirms that 'gender' has become the category of choice for many younger historians. Sometimes cutting-edge study of the body and sexual orientation is still framed by a national context, as in T. Hitchcock, *English Sexualities 1700–1800*, Basingstoke, Macmillan, 1997. The interest in gender and sexuality makes it all the more important to register the vital contributions made earlier by historians of women *per se*. These include S. Rowbotham, *Hidden from History: 300 Years of Women's Oppression and the Fight Against It*, London, Pluto Press, 1973; R. Bridenthal and C. Koonz (eds) *Becoming Visible: Women in European History*, Boston MA, Houghton Mifflin, 1977; G. Lerner, *The Majority Finds its Past: Placing Women in History*, New York, Oxford University Press, 1979. A. Farge (ed.) *Writing Women's History*, Oxford, Blackwell, 1992 (first French edn 1984) and S. J. Kleinberg (ed.) *Retrieving Women's History: Changing Perceptions of the Role of Women in Politics and Society*, London and Paris, Berg/Unesco, 1988. The role of an individual article in launching a whole new range of possible interpretations is well captured in Joan Kelly's 'Did Women Have a Renaissance?', in J. Kelly, *Women, History and Theory*, Chicago, University of Chicago Press, 1984, and in J. W. Scott, 'Gender: A Useful Category of Historical Analysis', *American Historical Review*, vol. 91, 1986, reprinted in *Gender and the Politics of History*, revised edn, New York, Columbia University Press, 1999. Relatively few women historians have as yet been given full-length biographical treatment. One of the best so far is M. Berg, *A Woman in History: Eileen Power, 1889–1940*, Cambridge, Cambridge University Press, 1996.

Chapter 14

History, identity and ethnicity

John Davidson

It is one of the clichés of historiographical discussion that individuals and societies use the past in order to sustain current identities. The founders of modern historiography took it for granted that the focus of identity was the nation-state, whether conceived in *volkisch* terms or as the construct of heroic founding fathers, as in the case of the USA or post-revolutionary France. In recent times many very different sorts of groups have demanded their own history and joined E. P. Thompson's stockingers in search of emancipation from the 'vast condescension of posterity'. The first challenges to the statist view came from those who argued on behalf of non-elite groups within the nation-state: the working class, women, immigrants. More recently some have sought to dismantle the entire paradigm and the grand narratives it sustained. Those developments are the product of the interplay between shifts in social and critical theory, often mediated through closely related disciplines, and changes in the wider political, social and cultural context. The increase since *c.*1970 in the attention paid by historians and others to questions to do with ethnicity and identity demonstrates the interaction of context and theory particularly neatly. The persistence, indeed resurgence, of communal and linguistic divisions in the postcolonial states, the emergence of new and remembered nationalisms in Eastern Europe after 1989, the reassertion of regional/national identities in Western Europe, the increased significance of religious identities as in the Balkans, the Islamic world and Ulster, the impact of immigration on Western Europe and North America, have all brought old certainties into question. In particular, they challenge the implicit prediction of earlier modernisation theory that older, traditional, customary identities and loyalties would fade away under the impact of an increasingly powerful and global modernity of which the nation-state was a major agent. From the early 1980s onwards, French social and critical theory, particularly that of Foucault, together with Edward Said's *Orientalism*, had a major impact on a range of disciplines: on literary theory and anthropology, and especially on the emerging disciplines of cultural studies and postcolonial studies, but also on sociology, political science and history.[1] The emphasis placed by Foucault on the role of powerful interested elites in structuring the idea of nation, and the enthusiasm of Said's followers for unmasking the 'discourse of colonialism' deflected attention from the nation-state towards alternative, subaltern, diasporic identities.

The concepts 'identity' and 'ethnicity' are problematic; both words have complex etymologies and variable current usage. The root meaning of identity, from Latin *idem*, is sameness; the word retains that meaning in its adjectival form, 'identical'. The word passed into academic usage in the mid-twentieth century via psychology and in particular through the work of Erik Erikson.[2] As used by Erikson, identity is essentially individual, a consistent core of selfhood that develops over the course of the life cycle. For others, especially sociologists, identity is about affinity, entailing membership of a commonality of, for example, class or gender or nation. In both senses identity is about difference as well as about sameness. The root of ethnic/ethnicity is Greek *ethnos* meaning people or nation. In New Testament Greek *ethnos* meant the heathen, the 'other', a direct translation of Hebrew *goyim*. The English word 'ethnic' was first used to mean 'heathen'. In the nineteenth century, at a point at which a biological account of racial divisions, including those between Celt, Saxon and Slav, was almost universally accepted, 'ethnic' referred to race. As the biological account of human variation weakened its hold in the early twentieth century, 'ethnic' and 'ethnic groups' came to refer more to language and to culture, though it was still in some versions to do with descent. The use of 'ethnicity' as a sociological category to parallel those of age, gender, religion or class dates from studies of American urban life in the early 1940s by W. Lloyd Warner and others, building on older traditions going back to Horace Kallen and Robert Park. After 1945, and particularly after *c*.1970, the concept was widely used by writers on nationalism, by anthropologists and by postcolonial critics. Much effort has been devoted to finding a precise definition of what constitutes an *ethnie* – the French noun is increasingly substituted for the English 'ethnic group'. Definitions vary in complexity and precision. The key common elements are that the 'sense of people-hood' that is at the core of ethnicity constitutes a self-aware iteration of identity on the part of the 'people' involved, that it is so recognised by their neighbours, and that the core defining criteria are linguistic and cultural.

The word and the concept escaped from the academy into journalistic and popular usage, though in rather different ways in the USA and Britain. In the USA, particularly after 1970, 'ethnics' meant in effect 'white, non Anglo-Saxon urban working-class'. In Britain 'ethnic', usually used as an adjective modifying 'minority', carries the sub-text 'being people of colour'. In both cases the popular usage points up a confusion between the notion of ethnicity and that of race. Recent work, particularly in genetics, has restored biology to a major role in the discussion of human difference. Few academics believe that 'race' provides a useful category within which to describe that difference: biological difference within 'races' is as great as differences between 'races'. Despite that, belief in the social significance of biological difference survives in the popular, public sphere. Moreover, race exists as a socially constructed reality. In varying degrees in different places perceived physical differences, overwhelmingly those of skin colour, are hugely significant in affecting attitudes and in structuring society.

A major division of view that underlies much recent discussion of collective identities, particularly ethnicity, but also, in slightly different form, nationality, is that between primordialism and constructivism (sometimes also called circumstantialism or instrumentalism). Primordialists hold that identities are deeply rooted in history, to do with descent, language and culture. Earlier writers operating within racist assumptions were primordialists by definition. More recent primordialists, for example Clifford Geertz and Edward Shils, argued that ethnic attachments are so rooted in perceived common descent, and in shared language, territory, custom and religion as to have 'an ineffable, and at times overpowering coerciveness in and of themselves'.[3] Constructivists, by contrast, argue that nations in the modern sense are the product of the Enlightenment and the revolutions of the late eighteenth century, and that ethnic identities, and many other features of recent social life, were 'constructed' by a series of intellectual and social developments, 'invented' or 'imagined' by elites, to meet a variety of social and political ends. In recent discussion constructivist views, in a variety of rather different versions, have been dominant. Some, for example Adrian Hastings and Anthony Smith, press a modified primordialism, particularly by insisting on the deep historical roots of identities of various sorts and by stressing the significance of the primordialist convictions, sometimes murderously maintained, of ethnic actors themselves. These points could be developed over a range of issues, notably that of nationalism. Here they will be considered in relation to the historiography of immigration and ethnicity in the United States of America and of tribe and tribalism in Africa.

In the USA the conversation within the academy has both affected and reflected developments in the wider public sphere. Despite the strong sense of exceptionalism, of unified difference from European experience, that has characterised many Americans' sense of themselves, American society has always been culturally diverse. Native Americans preceded immigrants from Europe by many centuries. African-American forced immigration dates back almost to the beginning of European settlement. Both were excluded from the master narrative of American identity until the late twentieth century. In the seventeenth and eighteenth centuries a range of peoples from northern Europe arrived to supplement though not to overwhelm the British founders. Expansion to the south and west incorporated earlier French and Spanish settlements within the United States. Immigration from all sources declined in the post-revolutionary period, but revived again in the mid-nineteenth century and continued in ever-greater diversity up to 1924. In the late nineteenth century the increased number of new immigrants and the growing proportion of those arriving from eastern and southern Europe occasioned fierce controversy. In 1924, the Johnson-Reed Act sharply reduced immigration and sought, on eugenic and racialist arguments, to exclude groups thought less desirable. From the mid-1920s to the mid-1960s immigration was of little importance either demographically or politically. In 1965 the Hart-Cellar Immigration Act modified the discriminatory element in the quota system. Immigration increased significantly: at the 2000 census 10 per cent of the population were returned as foreign-born, as compared with a high of 14.7 per cent in 1910 and a low of 4.7 per cent in 1970. New immigrants came overwhelmingly from Latin America and the Caribbean, from Asia and, once again, though in smaller numbers, from Africa. The shifting pattern of immigration, and the terms of the associated public debates, from mid-nineteenth-century nativism to late twentieth-century multiculturalism, strongly affected historians' treatment of the issues involved.

The establishment of academic history in the United States during the late nineteenth century coincided with the height of the immigration wave and with the first years of public controversy about the place of immigrants in American life. Early academic history, representing as it did the dominant Anglo-Saxon elite, in its personnel and outlook, ignored immigration and immigrants. The new progressive historians of the early twentieth century broadened their range of interests to include social history, but had little to say directly about immigration.[4] Early interest in the history of immigrant communities was mainly amateur and filiopietistic, evidence of a concern to celebrate rather than to analyse the contribution of the immigrant to American life. Academic interest was confined to economics and sociology, both much more open than was history to recruiting descendants of immigrants to the academic profession. Academic historians' earliest interest in immigration derived from Frederick Jackson Turner's emphasis on the role of the frontier, and concentrated on the German and other Northern European farming communities of the Midwest. Between the mid-1920s and the mid-1960s, when immigration was reduced to a trickle, a strong patriotic Americanism was forged in the international conflicts of the twentieth century. At the same time 'race' came to be constructed as essentially about colour, about the difference between African-Americans and everybody else, and the notion of a single 'Caucasian' race replaced the nineteenth-century racial distinctions of Celt, Slav and Saxon. In response to these shifts, historians of immigration sought to provide a strongly assimilationist account. In *The Uprooted*, Oscar Handlin, himself the son of Jewish immigrants, summed up what was then the dominant view. As Handlin famously wrote; 'Once I thought to write a history of the immigrants in America. Then I discovered that the immigrants *were* American history'.[5] His account records the process of Americanisation, of the operation of the melting pot – that metaphor of amalgamation that goes back to Crèvecoeur in the eighteenth century and was given wide currency by Zangwill's 1908 play. Handlin and others of his generation took it as a given that that process was inevitable and inexorable. Handlin believed the outcome was a positive one, providing the children of immigrants with the 'birthright of individuality' that fitted them for citizenship of a civic nation founded on individual rights. For all that, many immigrants, in Handlin's account coming mainly from European peasant backgrounds, achieved their new identity at considerable cost in the trauma and alienation of the fracturing of older, primordial, rural attachments.

In the 1960s the political and intellectual consensus that had characterised the United States since 1945 came under challenge. The major new factor was the emergence of the Civil Rights movement, quickly followed by the sharper challenge of Black Power. The need to accommodate African-American experience in the understanding of the American past challenged assimilationist assumptions. The bitter disputes about Vietnam called in question the moral force of the distinctive American identity that was the grounding of the assimilationist account. The reaction of working-class, white, non Anglo-Saxon groups, particularly Italians, Poles and Slavs, hostile to the student culture of the 1960s, and fearful of the competition of African-Americans, confirmed a pluralistic account of American identity. This view was given polemical historical expression in Michael Novak's *The Rise of the Unmeltable Ethnics*.[6] The melting pot might have operated in some of the ways argued for in the older accounts; what was now in question was the shape and authority of the mould.

The shift in emphasis away from the dominant assimilationist view is first detectable among social scientists, most importantly in Glazer and Moynihan's *Beyond the Melting Pot*, which sought to demonstrate how ethnic identities were maintained and indeed reconstructed by the circumstances of urban life.[7] In 1964 Rudolph Vecoli, building on recent work by Frank Thistlethwaite, threw down the first direct challenge by an historian to the Handlin view.[8] In the decades which followed an increasing range of new work on immigration and ethnicity – part of a much larger shift from political to social and intellectual history – broadened the account. The new view, given a general statement in 1985 by John Bodnar, held that assimilation was a myth. The melting pot had not worked. Immigrants had maintained their own cultures and their own identities, and had often continued contact with the old country. Ethnicities were developed and re-imagined in the new context, notably in creating single German and Italian American identities out of earlier divided regional loyalties. Immigrants had contributed to American life not by assimilating to the dominant Anglo-Saxon norm, but rather by challenging it, thus helping to produce the rich multicultural society of the contemporary United States.[9] The domain of ethnic history was extended to include not only greater attention to the origins of the newer waves of immigrants from Asia and Latin America, but also to encompass African-American and Native-American history, hitherto sidelined as minor sub-fields. Historians of labour and the working class also responded to new emphases.[10] The emphasis on the importance of ethnicity was strengthened by the impact of the culturally diverse immigration of the last quarter of the twentieth century, and by the significance of multiculturalism within public debate on, for example, education. That went together in timing and in intellectual emphasis with the increased impact, particularly in anthropology and literature, of discourse theory and of postmodernism more generally. Much work on ethnicity was undertaken by anthropologists, and by scholars of literature, notably Werner Sollors, that in turn fed into the work of historians.

It is clear that in the early twenty-first century the balance of public debate between emphasis on multiculturalism and emphasis on the peculiarities of American identity will again shift in response to resurgent American patriotism. Moves towards renewed restriction on immigration began in the 1980s and have intensified. But the increased size of the Hispanic and Asian-American communities, together with the growing proportion of marriages contracted across the broad ethno-racial lines, will continue to call in question the clarity of American notions of 'ethnicity' and 'race' and sustain an emphasis on cultural complexity. The impact on historiography of an enhanced awareness of changing and variable identities and of the broader, even global, contexts of migration seems likely to be an enduring one. To take two examples from among many possibilities: studies by M. A. Gomez and Jon Gjerde provide accounts of the process of change in the New World rooted in an understanding of the diversity of the cultures brought from the Old in ways which will permanently affect historians' understanding.[11]

Questions of identity and ethnicity play an even more central part in the historiography of colonial Africa than they do in that of the USA. The African case points up the question of 'colonial discourse' and displays a sharp difference of view between primordialists and constructivists. The assertion of European colonial control in tropical Africa at the end of the nineteenth century entailed the creation of a body of colonial knowledge, an 'Africanist discourse', put together in a rather haphazard way from the accounts of travellers, missionaries, traders, administrators, anthropologists, and, though this was little recognised at the time, by Africans themselves. A key concept in the organisation of this knowledge, and one that cast a long shadow over outsiders' views of Africa, and over Africans' ideas about themselves, was the notion of 'tribe'. The idea of tribe neatly combined two of the principal requirements of a justifying theory for the establishment of colonial rule. It provided a system of classification within which knowledge could be organised, peoples identified, maps drawn and administrative structures imposed. Moreover, since the dominant, evolutionist theory of the time placed 'tribal societies' low on the ladder of human development, it seemed inevitable, and right, that they should fall under the control of developed Western states. The dominance of structural functionalism in the anthropology of the colonial period maintained the key importance of clearly bounded tribal groups as the unit of analysis. As late as the 1960s, neat maps of the distribution of tribes continued to be produced, on a continent-wide scale, as, for example, in the work of G. P. Murdock and, on a national basis, in the 1960 census of Ghana.[12] The salience of intra-African competition along 'tribal' lines in the immediate post-independence period and later, engaged the interest of the political scientists in questions of ethnicity;

Crawford Young's *Politics in the Congo* was particularly prescient.[13] The language of 'tribe', 'tribal' and 'tribalism' maintains a journalistic and popular currency. But it has come increasingly to be questioned by academics and particularly by historians.

Late nineteenth-century African intellectuals on the Gold Coast and in Lagos understood very well the significance of identities other than tribal ones.[14] Drawing on E. W. Blyden they were conscious of a West African, even a pan-African, identity, while Gold Coast lawyer journalists such as Mensah Sarbah and J. E. Caseley-Hayford stressed the significance of a broad Akan identity common to the peoples of the central and southern Gold Coast, despite the sharp political divisions between Fante and Asante. Some colonial anthropologists outside the academic mainstream explored the complex, multilingual, multi-ethnic structure of pre-colonial states. But it was the development in the 1960s of a richer historiography of the continent that cast widespread doubt on the salience of 'tribes'. New research showed that in many small-scale African societies, as well as in the great states, multilingualism was common, and that boundaries between communities were shifting and porous. Trading networks linked elite groups over long distances and across political and cultural divisions. Religious cults drew multilingual, culturally mixed groups of adherents from a wide area, for example to the great oracle at Aro-Chuku in Eastern Nigeria and to the seat of the Mwari cult in Zimbabwe. Even the clans and lineages central to the kinship-centred anthropologists' account of African society came to be understood as ideological as much as sociological constructs. Kinship rules, particularly relating to residence, were often very loosely observed. Clientship, slavery and other forms of subordination played as significant a part as kinship in the recruitment of domestic groups and political alliances. The Niger Delta canoe houses (the basis of the African firms involved in the slave and palm oil trade) and the early Cape farming households (out of which the Cape Coloured community developed) cited by Ranger are no doubt extreme cases, but the features they demonstrate were very much more general.[15] In the 1970s two articles, one by a historian and the other by a historically minded anthropologist, explicitly problematised the notion of 'tribe'.[16] Both dealt with East African examples and argued that tribal classifications hitherto taken as given were actually constructed in the course of the imposition of British colonial control. Thus, in late-nineteenth-century Tanzania, 'Nyamwesi' and 'Sukumu' were labels adopted by incomers for the 'people of the west' and the 'people of the north'. That division elided with an ecological frontier, tsetse/non-tsetse, and was confirmed by colonial administrative structures. Thus Nyamwesi and Sukumu became 'tribes'. The area of Western Kenya also provides many illustrations of administrative, political and infrastructural considerations overriding the cultural and linguistic affinities central to any primordial notion of community in the construction of what became the ethnic groups of colonial and postcolonial Kenya.

In 1983 Terence Ranger made the general case for colonial 'invention' in a much-cited essay in the influential collection, *The Invention of Tradition*.

Ranger argued that 'What were called customary law, customary land-rights, customary political structure and so on, were in fact all invented by colonial codification'.[17] He acknowledged that invention involved Africans as well as Europeans, and stressed the use by colonial chiefs of the new structures to further the interests of elders *vis-à-vis* women and young men. Much subsequent work, particularly in Eastern and Southern Africa, has built on and modified what Ranger acknowledged to be a preliminary sketch. Leroy Vail's *The Creation of Tribalism in Southern Africa*, gave wider currency to the idea of 'invention', as did a growing body of work on the Zulu.[18]

As research deepened and extended into new areas, the rather stark formulations of the first unpicking of the colonial discourse of tribalism came to be modified and in some measure contested. Ranger's own views shifted substantially, as he made plain in a series of later articles.[19] He himself, along with many others, concentrated on rendering the account of the process of ethnogenesis more sophisticated by emphasising the importance of missionaries, particularly in the development of written versions of African languages and, thereby, in the creation of a literate monolingualism alongside the older, flexible, oral multilingualism. That new and powerful language, associated with access to the colonial institutions of church and state, could and often did become the basis of a sharper, more clearly bounded ethnicity. But the process of producing a written language depended on Africans as interpreters, assistants, catechists and teachers. And the extent to which the written language took local root and became a vehicle of a Christian religious life and of many other things, depended entirely on the degree to which those Africans, and the wider communities of which they became leaders, adopted it as their own. Ranger has thus come to prefer Benedict Anderson's concept of 'imagined community' to convey the complex and complicit nature of the new identities. Colonial rulers may have drawn the boundaries and appointed the first colonial chiefs. But Africans wrote the 'traditional' histories, codified 'tribal' customs, and later used these 'imagined' ethnic identities as an instrument with which to contest colonial authority.

Others, seeking to maintain a modified primordialist case, have argued that new identities built not only on modern African agency but also on pre-existing social and cultural patterns. 'Unless [invented tradition] makes genuine contact with people's actual experience, that is with a history that happened, it is not likely to be effective'.[20] Historians of West Africa, where areas such as Asante and Yoruba have long, continuous and complex histories, made those points particularly strongly. Modern Yoruba is very clearly an 'imagined' identity, sustained in large part by the circumstances of political competition within Nigeria since 1945. But it has deep roots in elements of shared culture, closely related language and a tradition of common origin that characterised the peoples who lived in the separate states of what became Western Nigeria. The assertion of a common identity, and the development of a language within which to articulate that identity, are comparatively modern. Yoruba were first spoken of as a single entity in exile in Sierra Leone, where some had been settled in the course of British attempts to suppress the slave trade. There other people called them 'Aku', a named derived from their conventional greeting. It was Christian 'Aku' (and their missionary associates) who returned to their homeland and completed the 'imagining' of Yoruba identity. 'Yoruba' the Hausa name for Oyo, the dominant, northern state of what became Western Nigeria, was used by Samuel Crowther, later to be the first African Anglican bishop, in the title of his *Vocabulary of the Yoruba Language* (1843) to refer to the language of Oyo. That language was adopted by the Church Missionary Society as the 'standard' language into which the Bible was translated and which became the written and to some extent the spoken language of the pan-Yoruba elite. In the course of the second half of the nineteenth century, before the imposition of British colonial rule, that elite, comprising mainly clergy and teachers, developed the notion of a Yoruba identity that encompassed loyalty to the individual states, Oyo, Egba, Ijebu, and so on. That identity was given its historical charter by Samuel Johnson's *History of the Yorubas*, completed in 1897, though not published until 1921. In the twentieth century consciousness of being Yoruba spread more broadly in the population, including Muslims, and came to be a major factor in political mobilisation.

Whatever its origins, ethnicity has come to be a powerful and often violently divisive factor, sometimes confirming other solidarities, for example religion, as in some parts of Nigeria, sometimes cutting across them, as in Rwanda. Whether in Africa or in the USA, ethnicity will continue to be a significant concern in academic analysis and in the real world. Perhaps, as Adrian Hastings has suggested, religious identities will figure more significantly in academic analysis, as increasingly they do in the politics of many parts of the world.[21] But everywhere understanding requires an historical context. What Peel argues for Yoruba holds more generally: 'only in a historical analysis can we see ... ethnicity for what it is: a process or a project rather than a structure'.[22]

Notes

1   E. W. Said, *Orientalism*, London, Routledge and Kegan Paul, 1978. The critical literature is extensive. For two recent critiques from historians see J. M. Mackenzie, *Orientalism, History, Theory and the Arts*, Manchester, Manchester University Press, 1995; and D. A. Washbrook, 'Orients and Occidents: Colonial Discourse Theory and the Historiography of the British Empire', in R. W. Winks (ed.) *The Oxford History of the British Empire: Volume 5. Historiography*, Oxford, Oxford University Press, 1999.

2   E. H. Erikson, *Childhood and Society*, New York, Norton, 1950.

3   C. Geertz, 'The Integrative Revolution: Primordial Sentiments and Civil Politics in the New States', in C. Geertz (ed.) *Old Societies and New States: The Quest for Modernity in Asia and Africa*, New York, The Free Press of Glencoe, 1963, reprinted in C. Geertz, *The Interpretation of Cultures*, New York, Basic Books, 1973, p. 259.

4   See above, pp. 110–11, 114.

5 O. Handlin, *The Uprooted: The Epic Story of the Great Migrations that Made the American People*, Boston MA, Little Brown, 1951, p. 3.
6 M. Novak, *The Rise of the Unmeltable Ethnics*, New York, Macmillan, 1971.
7 N. Glazer and D. P. Moynihan, *Beyond the Melting Pot: The Negroes, Puerto Ricans, Jews, Italians and Irish of New York City*, Cambridge MA, MIT Press, 1963.
8 R. J. Vecoli, '*Contadini* in Chicago: A Critique of *The Uprooted*', *Journal of American History*, 1964, vol. 51, pp. 404–17.
9 J. E. Bodnar, *The Transplanted: A History of Immigrants in Urban America*, Bloomington, University of Indiana Press, 1985.
10 D. R. Roediger, *The Wages of Whiteness: Race and the Making of the American Working Class, 1776–1863*, London, Verso, 1991.
11 M. A. Gomez, *Exchanging our Country Marks: The Transformation of African Identities in the Colonial and Ante Bellum South*, Chapel Hill, University of North Carolina Press, 1998; J. Gjerde, *The Minds of the West: Ethnocultural Evolution in the Rural Mid West, 1830–1917*, Chapel Hill, University of North Carolina Press, 1997.
12 For the former, see G. P. Murdock, *Africa: Its Peoples and their Cultural History*, New York, McGraw Hill, 1959.
13 C. Young, *Politics in the Congo: Decolonization and Independence*, Princeton, Princeton University Press, 1965.
14 C. Lentz and P. Nugent, 'Ethnicity in Ghana: A Comparative Perspective', in C. Lenz and P. Nugent (eds) *Ethnicity in Ghana: The Limits of Invention*, Basingstoke, Macmillan, 2000, pp. 7–8.
15 T. Ranger, 'The Nature of Ethnicity: Lessons from Africa', in E. Mortimer (ed.) *People, Nation and State: The Meaning of Ethnicity and Nationalism*, London, Tauris, 1999, p. 18.
16 A. W. Southall, 'The Illusion of Tribe', in Peter C. W. Gutkind (ed.) *The Passing of Tribal Man in Africa*, Leiden, Brill, 1970; J. Lonsdale, 'When Did the Gussi (or Any Other Group) Become a Tribe', *Kenya Historical Review*, 1977, vol. 5.
17 T. Ranger, 'The Invention of Tradition in Colonial Africa', in E. Hobsbawm and T. Ranger (eds) *The Invention of Tradition*, Cambridge, Cambridge University Press, 1983, p. 250.
18 L. Vail, *The Creation of Tribalism in Southern Africa*, London, James Currey, 1989.
19 T. Ranger, 'The Invention of Tradition Revisited', in T. O. Ranger and O. Vaughan (eds) *Legitimacy and the State in Twentieth Century Africa*, Basingstoke, Macmillan, 1993; Ranger, 'The Nature of Ethnicity: Lessons from Africa'; T. Ranger, 'Concluding Comments', in P. Yeros (ed.) *Ethnicity and Nationalism in Africa: Constructivist Reflections and Contemporary Politics*, Basingstoke, Macmillan, 1999.
20 J. D. Y. Peel, 'The Cultural Work of Yoruba Ethnogenesis', in E. Tonkin, M. McDonald and M. Chapman (eds) *History and Ethnicity*, London, Routledge, 1989, p. 200.
21 A. Hastings, *Nationhood, Ethnicity, Religion and Nationalism*, Cambridge, Cambridge University Press, pp. 1–2 and ch. 8 *passim*.
22 Peel, 'Cultural Work of Yoruba Ethnogenesis', p. 200.

Further reading

Issues of ethnicity and identity have been of concern to students of sociology and cultural studies as well as to those of history and anthropology. Two rather different readers give a good sense of the range of issues discussed. W. Sollors (ed.) *Theories of Ethnicity: A Classic Reader*, Basingstoke, Macmillan, 1996, is good on questions of definition and of theory and draws most of its illustrative material from the experience of the United States. J. Hutchinson and A. D. Smith (eds) *Ethnicity*, Oxford, Oxford University Press, 1996, ranges much more widely geographically and thematically. Recent surveys of the issues from within the disciplines of history, politics and anthropology are: A. Hastings, *The Construction of Nationhood: Ethnicity, Religion and Nationalism*, Cambridge, Cambridge University Press, 1997; E. Mortimer, *People, Nation and State: The Meaning of Ethnicity and Nationalism*, London, Tauris, 1999; A. D. Smith, *The Nation in History: Historiographical Debates about Ethnicity and Nationalism*, Oxford, Polity Press, 2000; and M. Banks, *Ethnicity: Anthropological Constructions*, London, Routledge, 1996.

The literature on the issues of race, immigration and ethnicity in the history of the United States is immense. Only a few leads can be provided to recent relevant material, all in their turn fully provided with references. D. R. Gabaccia, *Immigration and American Diversity: A Concise Social and Cultural History*, Oxford, Blackwell, 2002; and J. Gjerde, *Major Problems in American Immigration and Ethnic History: Documents and Essays*, Boston and New York, Houghton Mifflin, 1998, provide useful introductions. The best brief account of the historiography is P. Gleason, 'Crèvecoeur's Question: Historical Writing on Immigration, Ethnicity and National Identity', in A. Moelo and G. S. Wood (eds) *Imagined Histories: American Historians Interpret the Past*, Princeton, Princeton University Press, 1998, pp. 120–43. Among many recent works M. F. Jacobson, *Whiteness of a Different Color: European Immigrants and the Alchemy of Race*, Cambridge MA, Harvard University Press, 1998, is particularly interesting in providing an account of shifting definitions of the idea of race in the nineteenth century. D. A. Hollinger, *Postethnic America: Beyond Multiculturalism*, 2nd edn, New York, Basic Books, 2000, gives a useful, polemical, introduction to more recent debates.

The literature on the African issues is also substantial. F. Cooper, *Africa since 1940: The Past of the Present*, Cambridge, Cambridge University Press, 2002, gives an introduction to recent events. P. Yeros (ed.) *Ethnicity and Nationalism in Africa: Constructivist Reflections and Contemporary Politics*, Basingstoke, Macmillan, 1999, deals directly with a number of the issues. T. Ranger, 'The Invention of Tradition in Colonial Africa', in E. Hobsbawm and T. Ranger (eds) *The Invention of Tradition*, Cambridge, Cambridge University Press, 1983, pp. 211–62, is the key article. C. Lentz and P. Nugent (eds) *Ethnicity in Ghana: The Limits of Invention*, Basingstoke, MacMillan, 2000, includes a range of chapters on a country where ethnicity matters, but has had a less corrosive impact than elsewhere. J. D. Y. Peel, *Religious Encounter and the Making of the Yoruba*, Bloomington, Indiana University Press, 2000, gives the definitive account of that important Nigerian case.

Chapter 15

Historians and the 'new' British history

Paul O'Leary

It is rare for newspaper editorials to notice, let alone take issue with, the work of academic historians. So it was worthy of note when the London *Times* took advantage of the publication of a government-funded report on muticulturalism to attack revisionist interpretations of British history. In an editorial entitled 'Nation and Race' on 12 October 2000, the newspaper disagreed vehemently with a loosely connected group of historians whose work has come to be known as the 'new British history'. In particular, *The Times* singled out writers like Linda Colley, whose work on the 'invention' of Britishness as an official ideology in the eighteenth century was seen as part of an uncongenial re-interpretation of the national past. Special criticism was reserved for her emphasis on the constructed nature of British national identity. *The Times* judged this kind of historical writing to be part of an insidious trend which could only serve to undermine confidence in a British identity rooted in what it believed to be a longer and more durable past. The idea that the constituent nations of the United Kingdom might have forged a common identity partly out of self-interest (and thus, implicitly, might withdraw from it in the light of changing self-interest) caused the newspaper particular offence.

What was more surprising than the editorial's disagreement with this approach to British history was the claim that it lacked originality. According to the editorial, the 'plural nature of our past' was well known. In reality, however, an emphasis on national diversity and cultural plurality has been a relatively recent development in academic writing about British history, and one that has yet to receive universal assent in the profession. It is precisely this novelty that has led to the epithet 'new' being associated with the writings of historians who, in their different ways, emphasise the importance of understanding the interaction between the different national groupings of the British Isles. Their work challenges the assumptions underpinning the separate historiographical traditions of England, Scotland, Ireland and Wales, and stands in opposition to the dominant anglocentric trend in history writing among those who have claimed to write the history of Britain as a whole.

Historiographical traditions

In some ways, this re-appraisal of 'the national past' strikes at the dominant traditions of writing British history that were established when history became an academic discipline in the nineteenth century. At that time, the adoption of a critical historical method coincided with a conviction that the nation was the only proper unit of enquiry. This paradigm was translated into British academia in a very particular manner. A 'Whig' interpretation of history whose characteristics were pride in English liberties and a belief in the superiority of centralised English institutions, such as the monarchy, Parliament and the Church of England, meant that an impetus was given to the study of English constitutional history as the driving narrative of the state. To a large extent, the histories of the other nations of the British Isles were treated as separate entities, relevant only in so far as they impinged on the development of England. Rather than an attempt to fashion a history of the British Isles, or even merely the island of Britain, in terms of their cultural and national diversity, the emphasis was placed on the success story of the rise of English institutions and culture. The distinctive historical experiences of Scotland and Wales – let alone Ireland – were considered to be marginal if not irrelevant to British history. The result was that four separate historiographical traditions eventually became entrenched in the universities: those of Ireland, Scotland and Wales, and an English tradition that sometimes became elided with 'British' history. Each tradition developed its own journals, debates and discussions.

By the 1970s, however, changing political and intellectual circumstances conspired to produce both a reappraisal of the anglocentric interpretation of the British past and a critique of the separate national historiographical traditions of the British Isles. This development reflected changes in the nature of British society in the second half of the twentieth century. The rise of Scottish and Welsh nationalisms in the 1960s and the ensuing debate on devolution in the 1970s raised important questions about the structure of the British state, as did the onset of civil unrest in Northern Ireland and the abolition of that province's parliament. The end of empire, the attenuation of links with former colonies and the increasing integration of the United Kingdom into European economic and administrative structures has been another strand in this fundamental re-orientation. Against this background, it would have been surprising had British historians not begun to re-think the history of national identity and the British state.

It was in this context that J. G. A. Pocock made his 'plea for a new subject', that is the re-interpretation of British history in terms of its cultural and national diversity. Writing in 1975, he asserted that British history should properly denote the 'plural history of a group of cultures situated along an Anglo-Celtic frontier and marked by an increasing English political and cultural domination'. According to this view, an adequate understanding of developments in and across Britain and Ireland could not be accommodated in the nation-centred narratives of English, Scottish, Irish and Welsh history. This new perspective on the past required new terminology. In an attempt to coin a term that avoided the 'British Isles' – a term often offensive to Irish sensibilities – Pocock suggested a neutral geographical term for the collection of islands located off the northwest coast of continental Europe which included Britain and Ireland: the Atlantic archipelago.[1]

Thus, Pocock's terminology emphasised the Atlantic dimension to British history. For him, this meant paying proper attention to the settler colonies of North America, of that part of the continent that became the United States and of Canada, which remained a British outpost where the conflict of cultures went on as it had been shaped in the British Isles. In the context of its time, with the United Kingdom turning away from its former colonies and towards a closer, albeit fractious, relationship with continental Europe, this assertion of the Atlantic context of British history has attracted some criticism. For historians like Raphael Samuel, the term 'the Atlantic archipelago' has 'a subtly, and no doubt unconscious, anti-European bias'.[2] Partly for this reason and partly for reasons of intelligibility, most historians have steered clear of the term, although it does occur sporadically in the historiography.

Raphael Samuel highlights Pocock's New Zealand origins (his seminal article originated as a public lecture in that country) and the importance of the United Kingdom joining what was then called the European Economic Community for the weakening of relationships with former colonies. Pocock appeared to provide some justification for this view when he used a galactic metaphor to explain his reasons for demanding a re-think of the way in which the British past is depicted:

> The British star cluster is at present in a highly dispersed condition, various parts of it feeling the attraction of adjacent galaxies; the central giant has cooled, shrunk, and moved away, and the inhabitants of its crust seemed more than ever disposed to deny that the rest of us ever existed. Since it no longer emits those radiations we felt bound to convert into paradigms, we are free and indeed necessitated to construct cosmologies of our own.[3]

The passage reveals a great deal about the impulses behind this seminal article. The 'adjacent galaxies' in this passage is an oblique reference to continental Europe; the 'we' are New Zealanders and, by implication, other peoples of the former empire; the new 'cosmologies' meanwhile indicates different ways of configuring a national past. Thus the new British history was conceived of as a way of fashioning a history for the changing times. It recognised the tiredness of existing narratives of British history in the face of challenges from more exciting perspectives on the past, but it insisted that there remained a valid problematic to be tackled which previous historians had failed to address.

The proposal for a new field of study encountered hostility in some quarters and indifference in others and was slow in getting off the ground. When Pocock returned to the topic in 1982 he subtitled his article 'In Search of the

Unknown Subject'. Initially, it appeared as though there were few enthusiasts for re-thinking the parameters of British history. To some extent, the gap was filled by ambitious sociological interpretations of the growth of the British state, the most influential example of which is Michael Hechter's *Internal Colonialism: The Celtic Fringe in British National Development, 1536–1966* (1975), a book which achieved a certain vogue in the late 1970s as the debate about Scottish and Welsh devolution intensified. Hechter's work filled a gap left by historians' reluctance to address the problem of British state development in such a way as to make later developments intelligible.

As late as 1988 – long after Pocock's original clarion call – R. R. Davies warned that although the new vision of British history had been 'much in the air of late', it had 'not in truth arrived'. His sober assessment was that historians' rhetoric about taking full cognisance of the national diversity that existed in the British Isles had outpaced their achievements in both teaching and research. The new British history still had a somewhat chimerical existence.[4] However, in spite of this justifiable pessimism about the limited achievements of the new approach to British history by that date, the late 1980s can be seen in retrospect as a crucial period for the development of this perspective on the past.

Davies' comments appeared in a seminal book of essays which applied the paradigm of the new British history (or simply 'British history', as Davies described it) to the period 1100–1400. The book was not alone. Several detailed studies of particular periods of history as well as an attempt at essaying an overarching interpretation of the new history appeared in a rush. The same year that Davies warned of the limitations of practical achievements saw the publication of Keith Robbins' analysis of the tensions between national integration and diversity in nineteenth-century Britain, while the following year Robin Frame's study of the political development of the British Isles in the period 1100–1400 appeared. As well as these detailed studies of particular periods, the late 1980s saw the publication of Hugh Kearney's landmark book, *The British Isles: A History of Four Nations* (1989), a study which sought to chart the plurality of cultures and their interaction over a long chronological span.

Since the late 1980s even greater strides have been taken in giving this approach to British history a more substantive reality, so much so that by the mid-1990s Pocock could make the confident claim that the new field was 'well enough established to have both its paradigms and its critics'.[5] His self-proclaimed 'unknown subject' of 1982 was now more widely recognised. But if we are to apply the concept of paradigms to this field of enquiry, it remains in some important ways an incomplete or flawed paradigm. While the new British history has made some important inroads in historical research and thinking, it remains somewhat marginal to certain periods of history. Moreover, there are fundamental disagreements about what exactly should constitute the new history's most appropriate object of enquiry.

Defining the object of inquiry

One early attempt at fleshing out a distinctive approach to the history of the British Isles was contributed by Hugh Kearney, who described his approach as that of 'four nations history'. Paradoxically, this entailed a rejection of the nation as a unit of historical analysis. He saw greater merit in starting with the British Isles as a geographical unit, that is adopting a unit of analysis comparable to the Danube valley or the Iberian peninsula, 'in which various cultures struggled for supremacy or survival over a thousand years and more'.[6] This approach is less concerned with tracking the continuities in the histories of the English, Irish, Scottish, or Welsh peoples than it is with complex interactions between the cultures and sub-cultures of the British Isles. Kearney emphasises the Britain-wide nature of phenomena such as the Norman invasion, the Reformation and the Industrial Revolution, and argues that such phenomena cannot be fully understood within the parameters of the separate histories of the constituent nations of the British Isles. There is a feel of the holistic approach of the *Annales* to this interpretation, with culture being defined as comprising lifestyle, religion, customs and attitudes. Kearney has summed up his approach in terms of a difference between emphasising the particularities of the four nations and stressing what they have in common. Taking up this theme, Raphael Samuel saw 'four nations history' as a means of challenging the grand narratives and traditional chronologies of British history:

> Britannic or 'archipelago' history invites us to jettison our conventional notions of period (what does 'early modern' mean to the Blasket Islands, or 'Tudor and Stuarts' in the Trossachs?). It also positively requires us to experiment with new time-frames.[7]

In practice, few historians have attempted to emulate Kearney's initiative by developing further such an interpretation of the British Isles.

Other historians have focused their attention on specific periods and problematics. In his essay 'In Praise of British History', R. R. Davies set out a clear conception of how the new approach might change historians' perceptions of the medieval period. He outlined the areas in which a British approach could shed new light on familiar topics and trends, such as connections between members of the aristocracy that transcended national boundaries and the waves of English colonisation through the islands. He argued that taking a British Isles approach to such questions promised to illuminate common themes that previously had been investigated predominantly within the confines of separate English, Scottish, Irish and Welsh historiographical traditions. More controversially, Davies asserted that a degree of anglocentricity in British history was inevitable because of the fact of English political, economic and cultural hegemony in the British Isles during the last millennium. However, he also insisted that the British Isles is not the only or necessarily a more appropriate unit of analysis for some historical enquiries than England, Ireland, Scotland and Wales.

Moreover, in expressing his enthusiasm for British history he was wary of imposing a 'specious uniformity' on the diversity within the British Isles, and recommended the adoption of comparative approaches to the histories of the different nations of the islands.

By contrast, some historians of later periods have argued for a tightly defined problematic, preferring to see the process of state formation as the fulcrum of British history. The early modernist Steven G. Ellis summed up this approach in his statement that 'British history ... ought properly to refer to the whole process of state-building in the archipelago'.[8] He sees this process as 'a continuum of success and failure, ranging from southern England, through northern England and Wales, to Scotland, Northern Ireland, and at the opposite extreme the present Republic of Ireland'. After the consolidation of the English realm, the key dates in this development are 1536 (the so-called Act of Union between England and Wales), 1541 (the creation of the Kingdom of Ireland), 1603 (the Union of Crowns) and 1707 (the Anglo-Scottish Act of Union). Other developments were less successful, such as the Cromwellian Union of 1654 and the Act of Union with Ireland of 1800. In his view, the apparent exception of the Republic of Ireland to the success story of the onward march of English institutions merely proves the rule, because it is no less British in its cultural, administrative and legal traditions.

While R. R. Davies saw the addition of the British dimension to the medieval past as complementing the labours of historians who worked within their national traditions, others were more dismissive of the different historiographical traditions of the British Isles. Steven G. Ellis has taken a robust attitude towards nation-centred history, and contrasts 'nationalist history', by which he means those historiographical traditions concerned with the rise of the separate nations of the British Isles, with attempts to write the history of the state. He protests that nation-centred approaches reflect modern ideas of nationhood and modern boundaries, as opposed to the changing state boundaries of the past, and thus historians who write the histories of the constituent nations of the British Isles are engaging in an anachronistic exercise. Some historians have adopted a more conciliatory tone. For example, while sharing an interest in the enterprise of writing the history of state building, John Morrill has been less abrasive in his criticisms of the different national traditions of historical writing within the United Kingdom. He has written that in addition to the histories of England, Scotland, Ireland and Wales, there is a British history that examines the interactions between the component parts of the archipelago, emphasising that there are some stubborn questions that can only be satisfactorily addressed by this second approach.

In practice, many exponents of the new British history have contributed to the histories of the individual nations as well as the history of state-building. One area where this has been most obvious is the question of nationality. Pocock identified nationality as one of the central methodological problems of the new field. In his 'Plea for a New Subject' he was careful to point out that

'The fact of a hegemony does not alter the fact of a plurality, any more than the history of a frontier amounts to a denial that there is history beyond the advancing frontier'. Thus the question of what kind of collective political identity was developed to accompany the new state requires a consideration not only of the creation of a British identity, but also entails some reflection on the persistence of other national identities in the British Isles. How this relationship has been characterised by historians has varied from period to period.

Britishness as a unifying political identity is a relatively recent construct and one which was initially more prevalent among the ruling classes than among the mass of the people until the nineteenth century. Consequently, there is a strong impression that a definitive sense of Britishness was lacking before the eighteenth century. For some historians of the modern period, it is the integration of the separate nationalities of Britain to form a common identity that has been the dominant feature of national identity in Britain. The crucial difference of opinion on this subject is that between Linda Colley and Keith Robbins. In her study of the 'forging' of the British nation after the Act of Union of 1707, Colley has argued that Britishness provided an umbrella identity under which the distinct peoples of the island could shelter without sacrificing their own identities. Thus, from this perspective, an involvement in Britain and attachment to a capacious Britishness did not entail an erosion of other identities. By contrast, Keith Robbins has persuasively argued that the development of a British identity during the nineteenth century involved a 'blending', implying the partial erosion or pooling of the separate identities. In some ways, these views simply reflect the different extent to which a sense of national identity was mobilised in European society as a whole in the two periods discussed. In other ways, however, they reflect different approaches to historiography: the one allowing for a complementarity between Britishness and the subordinate nationalities of the United Kingdom as distinct entities, the other emphasising that a British identity involved the creation of a hybrid identity.

Critics of the 'new' history

In a review of progress in implementing his vision of British history, Pocock observed in 1995 that the 'new' history has not been without its critics. Criticisms focus on four main areas. The first important criticism draws attention to the way in which much of what has been written under this banner concentrates on high politics and the state. For example, Raphael Samuel complained that it tended to repackage old approaches to historical writing in new clothes. He argued that in practice it is often 'top-down, even, after a fashion, drum-and-trumpet history', in which historical agency resides among the powerful and privileged. He complained that 'the people, whether in the form of "nationalities", "peasantries" or the men who took the King's Shilling, are a more or less inert backdrop'.[9] His is not the only dissenting voice. Others have expressed their unease, protesting that the new history's concentration on high politics has tended to widen the existing gap between political history on the one hand, and economic and social history on the other. Indeed, few historians have followed Kearney in shifting away from state-centred history, although a recent collection of essays edited by S. J. Connolly (1999) gave as much, if not more attention to the social, economic and cultural history of the four nations of the British Isles as it did to high politics.

The second major criticism of the new British history is the charge that it is not new enough, that in practice its central problematics are determined by the concerns of what happened in England's history. One Scottish historian has gone so far as to claim that it could turn out to be 'a poisoned chalice' because 'the nagging doubt persists that even with the best will in the world ... the emergence of British History looks like a reincarnation of the history of the English state'.[10] This judgment was based on a fear that rather than the recognition of the plurality of the history of the British Isles, the central problematic remained the rise of English domination over those territories, thus continuing to marginalise the distinctive historical experience of the Scots, the Welsh and the Irish. Some support for this scepticism was inadvertently provided by the editor of the collection of essays in which the comments appeared. In that book, Ronald G. Asch decided to concentrate on the three nations of England, Scotland and Ireland and omit Wales on the basis that 'during the period under discussion here [1600–1920] no Welsh Covenanters, Jacobites or Confederates ever threatened to invade England, let alone succeeded in doing so'. His claim that British history should be more than 'enriched English history' was hardly borne out by this comment.[11] A suspicion that many exponents of the new history are more concerned with similarities than differences receives some support from this statement.

The third criticism, voiced most forcefully by Nicholas Canny, maintains that a focus on the British Isles implies an integrity for this unit of study 'probably in excess of anything that ever existed'.[12] This has, in his view, the unfortunate effect of distracting attention from the connections between the different communities of the British Isles and the European continent. Although the two approaches are not necessarily incompatible, a concentration on the similarities between the different cultures of the British Isles has tended to downplay external connections that do not fit this framework.

Perhaps the most important criticisms of the new paradigm have come from some Irish historians, sceptical of what they perceive as an attempt to re-assert at the level of historical research the unity of a past that has been rejected at the political level. This fourth criticism goes to the heart of the new approach to the history of the British Isles. The rejection of the British state by a majority of the Irish makes the notion of a single narrative history of the British Isles particularly problematic. Even when one considers the only period when the British Isles were ruled by the same government, the years from 1801 to 1922, advocates of the new British history, like Keith Robbins, David Cannadine and Linda Colley, have rejected the appropriateness of dealing with Irish experiences within their paradigm. In spite of the fact that Ulster was home to the most militantly British people in the kingdom, few historians have been willing to incorporate this experience in their treatment of Britishness in Britain itself. Moreover, the *a priori* exclusion of Catholic Ireland from the analysis of Britishness can be interpreted as presenting a more optimistic interpretation of the British state in this period than might emerge from a consideration of the failure to integrate the majority of the Irish.

In some ways, however, it is the habit of the majority of historians simply to ignore the implications of the new British history that should cause its practitioners the greatest concern. If some historians of Ireland, Scotland and Wales have expressed their doubts about the pretensions of the new history, Steven G. Ellis admits that the welcome of English historians for the removal of southeast England from the centre stage has been 'less than wholehearted', while as late as 1995 John Morrill could aver that 'The English have to overcome their indifference to what is happening elsewhere in the archipelago'.[13]

In addition to these criticisms and the indifference of some historians, it should be pointed out that the success of the new British history has been more pronounced in relation to some periods than others. In broad terms, it has been more attractive to historians of pre-industrial periods than to those of the nineteenth and twentieth centuries. One reason for this can be found in a tendency to see the state-building project as being substantially complete by the eighteenth century, after which class identities rather than national particularities have been assumed to have greater salience. Perhaps the dominance of Anglo-Marxism in the writing of the social history of the industrial revolution since 1945 is partly responsible for this; for these historians, the mobilisation of class identities in the first class society has been the priority.

This issue is compounded by the changing demographic balance of the United Kingdom in the nineteenth century. In 1841, 55.7 per cent of the United Kingdom population lived in England, whereas by 1901 this proportion had increased to 73.6 per cent, and would increase again during the twentieth century. If Ireland is excluded from the equation, then the numerical dominance of England is even greater. Against this background, historians schooled in a statistics-based discipline of the 1960s and 1970s might see the non-dominant national groupings as marginal to a history dominated by England. What these statistics do reveal, however, is that much more needs to be said about the problematic relationship of Englishness to Britishness in this debate. In a real sense, the United Kingdom was unlike other composite states of Europe, such as Austria-Hungary, because of the overwhelming numerical dominance of a single national grouping within its boundaries.

In the light of this chronological imbalance in the take-up of the new British history, it is easier to accuse proponents of the approach of subscribing to a teleological version of the creation of the United Kingdom, 'inevitably' resulting in the successful integration of the nineteenth century and the emergence of an integrated class-based society. However, accounts of nineteenth-century Britain, like that of Keith Robbins, which demonstrate that the themes of both integration and diversity continued to have salience during the nineteenth century, remain thin on the ground.

There are some signs that this state of affairs might be changing. In the second half of the 1990s the tone of contributions to debates was more questioning of the success story of the British state, more interrogative in their approach. In the light of political devolution in the United Kingdom a new tone of uncertainty began to tinge discussions of British history. The perceived indifference of the Conservative governments of 1979–97 to Scotland and Wales occasioned a questioning of centralised structures of government and eventually precipitated the constitutional reforms of the Labour government of 1997–2001. Perhaps the titles of historical studies like *Uniting the Kingdom?* (1995), *Kingdoms United?* (1998) and *A Disunited Kingdom?* (1999) reflect a growing sense that the direction of British state development in the present may be changing and that such changes could presage a new emphasis on diversity and plurality in our understanding of the past. It is possible that historians will consider more carefully the part of Pocock's original formulation of British history which stressed both English dominance and plurality. In future, historians must be alive to alternative trajectories in British history, ones that did not necessarily lead to greater centralisation and integration. Such an approach might have the additional benefit of making it easier to discuss the complex and changing relationships between Ireland and the different parts of Britain as an integral part of British history.

Conclusion

It is now possible to design and teach courses that draw on the research produced by practitioners of the new British history. However, it would be erroneous to believe that an anglocentric approach has been completely displaced. In the field of modern political history in particular, there is still a tendency to write the history of political institutions as though they were of significance to England alone. For most historians, getting to grips with the plurality of the history of the British Isles entails moving beyond familiar historiographical trends and re-thinking established chronologies.

One potential consequence of current political developments is that this flurry of interest in how the different national groupings of the British Isles have interacted with each other over the centuries will be superseded by a return to self-contained national histories of the constituent countries of the archipelago. After all, such histories continue to flourish, in spite of the increasing interest in the new British history. However, even this would require a reassessment of what constitutes English history as an entity separate from the wider British polity, especially in the modern period, and would necessitate a more reflective approach to the development of English national identity and its relationship to Britishness. What is undeniable, however, is that attempts to reconfigure the historiography of the British Isles are the result of a continuing dialogue between historians and the assumptions which informed historical writing when history became an academic discipline in the nineteenth century. They are also intimately bound up with changing perceptions in the present. Whether the new British history survives the centrifugal impulses of current political change remains to be seen.

Notes

1 J. G. A. Pocock, 'British History: A Plea for a New Subject', *Journal of Modern History*, 1975, vol. 47, pp. 601–28.
2 R. Samuel, 'Four Nations History' in *idem, Island Stories: Unravelling Britain*, London, Verso, 1998, p. 26.
3 Pocock, 'British History: A Plea for a New Subject', p. 621.
4 R. R. Davies, 'In Praise of British History', in *idem* (ed.) *The British Isles, 1100–1500*, Edinburgh, John Donald, 1988, p. 9.
5 J. G. A. Pocock, 'Contingency, Identity, Sovereignty', in A. Grant and K. J. Stringer (eds) *Uniting the Kingdom? The Making of British History*, London, Routledge, 1995, p. 292.
6 H. Kearney, *The British Isles: A History of Four Nations*, Cambridge, Cambridge University Press, 1989, p. 286.
7 Samuel, 'Four Nations History', p. 29.
8 S. G. Ellis, 'Introduction: The Concept of British History', in S. G. Ellis and S. Barber (eds) *Conquest and Union: Fashioning a British State*, London, Longman, 1995, p. 4.
9 Samuel, 'Four Nations History', pp. 32–3.
10 K. M. Brown, 'British History: A Sceptical Comment', in R. G. Asch (ed.) *Three Nations – A Common History? England, Scotland, Ireland and British History* c.*1600–1920*, Bochum, Universitäts Verlag, 1993, p. 117.
11 R. G. Asch, 'Obscured in Whiskey, Mist and Misery: The Role of Scotland and Ireland in British History' in Asch (ed.) *Three Nations*, pp. 15–16, 17.
12 N. Canny, 'Irish, Scottish and Welsh Responses to Centralisation, c.1530–c.1640: A Comparative Perspective', in Grant and Stringer (eds) *Uniting the Kingdom?*, pp. 147–8.
13 Ellis, 'Introduction', p. 7; J. Morrill, 'The Fashioning of Britain', in Ellis and Barber (eds) *Conquest and Union*, p. 39.

Further reading

A key article in the development of the new British history is J. G. A. Pocock, 'British History: A Plea for a New Subject', *Journal of Modern History*, 1975, vol. 47, pp. 601–28. Pocock elaborated his argument in 'The Limits and Divisions of British History: In Search of an Unknown Subject', *American Historical Review*, 1982, vol. 87, pp. 311–36.

A number of historians have reflected on what should be the proper scope and subject matter of British history, such as R. R. Davies, 'In Praise of British History', in R. R. Davies (ed.) *The British Isles, 1100–1500*, Edinburgh, John Donald, 1988, pp. 9–26. H. Kearney, *The British Isles: A History of Four Nations*, Cambridge, Cambridge University Press, 1989, argues in favour of 'culture' as the central issue of concern, whereas S. G. Ellis stresses the centrality of state-building as the appropriate focus in his 'Introduction: the Concept of British History', in S. G. Ellis and S. Barber (eds) *Conquest and Union: Fashioning a British State*, London, 1995, pp. 1–7. A similar focus can be found in B. Bradshaw and J. Morrill (eds) *The British Problem c.1534–1707: State Formation in the Atlantic Archipelago*, London, Macmillan, 1996; and Glenn Burgess (ed.) *The New British History: Founding a Modern State, 1630–1715*, London, I. B. Tauris, 1999.

National identity is given prominence in B. Bradshaw and P. Roberts (eds) *British Consciousness and Identity: the Making of Britain, 1533–1707*, Cambridge, Cambridge University Press, 1988, while the multinational character of the United Kingdom is stressed in L. Brockliss and D. Eastwood (eds) *A Union of Multiple Identities: the British Isles c.1750–1850*, Manchester, Manchester University Press, 1997. The interaction between different nationalities is the focus of Keith Robbins, 'Core and Periphery in Modern British History', *Proceedings of the British Academy*, 1984, vol. LXX, pp. 275–97. One historian has located the rise of the new British history in the context of 'history from below': see 'Introduction', S. J. Connolly (ed.) *Kingdoms United? Great Britain and Ireland since 1500: Integration and Diversity*, Dublin, Four Courts Press, 1998, pp. 9–12. The Atlantic dimension to British history is explored in a group of articles in the *American Historical Review*, 1999, vol. 104, pp. 426–500.

A number of monographs have applied these insights to specific periods: R. Frame, *The Political Development of the British Isles, 1100–1400*, Oxford, Oxford University Press, 1989; R. R. Davies, *Domination and Conquest: the Experience of Ireland, Scotland and Wales, 1093–1343*, Cambridge, Cambridge University Press, 1990; L. Colley, *Britons: Forging the Nation, 1707–1837*, London, Yale University Press, 1992; K. Robbins, *Nineteenth-Century Britain: Integration and Diversity*, Oxford, Oxford University Press, 1988; R. Weight, *Patriots: National Identity in Britain, 1940–2000*, London, Macmillan, 2002. A student text on the modern period is C. Kinealy, *A Disunited Kingdom? England, Ireland, Scotland and Wales, 1800–1949*, Cambridge, Cambridge University Press, 1999.

For critical perspectives, see: R. Samuel, 'Four Nations History', in his *Island Stories: Unravelling Britain*, London, Verso, 1998, pp. 21–40; N. Canny, 'Irish, Scottish and Welsh Responses to Centralisation, *c.*1530–1640: A Comparative Perspective', in A. Grant and K. Stringer (eds) *Uniting the Kingdom? The Making of British History*, London, Routledge, 1995, pp. 147–69; T. Claydon, 'Problems with the British Problem', *Parliamentary History*, vol. 16, 1997, pp. 221–7. D. Cannadine claims that the British perspective has greater relevance to some periods than others in his 'British History as a "New" Subject: Politics, Perspectives and Prospects', in A. Grant and K. Stringer (eds) *Uniting the Kingdom? The Making of British History*, London, Routledge, 1995, pp. 12–28.

Chapter 16

Postmodernism and the linguistic turn

Michael Roberts

The term 'postmodern' was used from the 1930s onwards to define a style, in particular a turn away from the sleek lines of the formerly dominant 'international style' in architecture. Modernism had flourished between the wars, when a commitment to the use of new techniques and materials to meet mass housing needs made older building styles seem redundant, and elevated machine-made architecture into an aesthetic principle. Its adaptation to the needs of a resurgent corporate economy after the war stirred a reaction. The new postmodern approach drew on the mounting jumble of images thrown up by contemporary consumer affluence, on the discordant juxtaposition of older with newer signs and symbols. An early treatise on the new style, Robert Venturi's aptly titled *Complexity and Contradiction in Architecture* (1966) celebrated 'messy vitality over obvious unity'. Postmodern architects enjoyed placing emphasis on the *facade* of a building, rather than on its *structure*, and on using historical allusions in fragments and details in the design.[1] Sociologists like Daniel Bell meanwhile were studying 'Post-Industrial Society ... a society which has passed from a goods-producing stage, to a service society'. In the same year, 1959, C. Wright Mills pondered Western man's dwindling concern as 'a cheerful and willing robot' for freedom and reason in the 'post-modern period'.[2] Fascination with the world of advertising and with built-in obsolescence were further stimuli, as was their rejection in the counter-cultural 'happenings' of the 1960s. The new thinking abandoned the totalising approach associated with Marxism in Jean-François Lyotard's *The Postmodern Condition* (1979). Jean Baudrillard ironically reinvented Western historical development as a sequence of 'orders of appearance', an age of production currently giving way to one of simulation.[3] So 'postmodernity' came into fashion, naming our present epoch.

Sustained discussion of the subject only gathered pace in the 1980s, as confidence in the manageability of world financial markets reeled under the impact of the two oil shocks of 1973 and 1979. These made more widely plausible philosophical doubts about the certainty of 'Western' scientific knowledge which had been growing since the 1950s. By separating the structure, purpose and appearance of buildings, postmodernist architects seemed to be matching the uncoupling of 'reality' and our linguistic means of access to it which disciplines from maths to anthropology had embraced in the name of 'structuralism' and its successors.

Structuralism substituted for the organic or mechanical approaches of earlier social science a *linguistic* model. This viewed society as a self-regulating and closed system, but the emphasis shifted from the functional or structural stability of the system to the transformations between its component parts of which the system was capable. Versions of such an approach could be found in the linguistics of de Saussure, the anthropology of Mauss, the philosophy of the later Wittgenstein, the deep structures of grammar associated with Noam Chomsky, and there was a parallel development in the philosophy of science, where Kuhn's 'paradigm shift' provided an account of such structural transformation.[4] The erosion of interest in relations between language and the real world was disguised by broadening the concept of language into 'culture' as a whole: the striptease acts and wrestling matches studied by Roland Barthes in *Mythologies* (Paris 1957; English translation New York, 1972).

The reaction against the rigidity of structuralism which Barthes amongst others pioneered also took its character from the centrality of *language* in human experience. But whereas structuralists had emphasised the underlying orderliness of linguistic systems, poststructuralists began to concentrate on language's unstable habit of slipping beyond the grip of intended or assumed meanings. Language was found to be the plaything of social convention, psychological pressures and political power, and the scholar's principal task became less explanation and the search for the causes of events, than to catalogue and interpret meanings. The effect in many disciplines has been to abandon the governing paradigm of the physical sciences for a model in which hypothesis-testing, experimentation and proof have been replaced by interpretation and communication between the participants of a culture, as both the principal subject matter, and the prevailing scholarly activities. When Daniel Dennett came to publish his best-guess account of the workings of human consciousness in 1991 he found that he had been beaten to it, by a novelist's satire of 'semiotic materialism': as he conceded, both he and the fictional protagonist Robyn 'think alike – and of course we are *both*, by our own accounts, fictional characters of a sort, though of a slightly different sort'.[5] This is the sea-change in our outlook which has come to be known as the 'linguistic turn'.[6]

The linguistic turn contributes to postmodernity by redefining the basis of our knowledge of 'the real world'. As never-perfect users of language our best reaction to a world constituted in its image may be ironical, our response to the grand narratives of Western civilisation and progress one of incredulity. The relationship of both texts and buildings to their creators' intentions, and their users' needs, is more complicated, messy and unpredictable than had seemed the case for modernists. This being the case we can learn from deconstruction, the critical procedure evolved by poststructuralists to unpick the illusory unity of a text to reveal what its composition had suppressed or displaced.

Deconstruction reached the height of its influence in transatlantic criticism around the time Lyotard was diagnosing the postmodern condition in 1979, before withering after news of Paul de Man's youthful anti-Semitic writings began to emerge late in 1987. By that stage, Gertrude Himmelfarb was gloomily anticipating the application of deconstruction in history.[7]

Self-conscious applications of poststructuralist techniques to historical work were thus quite late to develop, but postmodernity had already been shaping the character of historical writing in other ways. The idea of a *post*modern epoch, by detaching the present from the 'modern' epoch which began with the European Discoveries and the consolidation of the 'Western' cultural tradition during the Renaissance and Reformation makes possible a history of the world in which Western dominance ceases to appear inevitable, a world of several 'centres' and no periphery. This idea was already familiar in several guises from the work of Spengler, Toynbee, Butterfield, and after the war, Geoffrey Barraclough who argued in 1955 that extensive historical research had 'shattered' and 'discarded' such a framework.[8] But serious attention to the history of the world at large was not given until the decade after 1974 in work by Fernand Braudel, William McNeil, John Roberts, Immanuel Wallerstein and Eric Wolf. The same period saw Edward Said's *Orientalism* (1978), which demonstrated both what non-historians drawing on Foucault might have to offer, and historians' own complicity in the construction of an imperialist tradition. An appetite for de-centering within the UK itself was also kindled, after the October 1974 general election left a Labour government needing alliances with Scots and Welsh nationalists as its majority dwindled to nothing by the end of 1976.[9]

A de-centred approach could also be found in a more subtle sense in the interrogation of the categories through which history had hitherto been understood. In the 1950s Keith Thomas anticipated the deconstruction of male privilege in his lectures at Oxford on the Double Standard.[10] In the early 1960s his willingness to seek contrasts and parallels with Shakespeare's England in the findings of anthropologists from late nineteenth and early twentieth-century Africa was deemed professionally irresponsible. The comparative approach freed the historian from being confined to the study of unique and particular historical events, whose meaning could only be read back from the present latest stage in the chronological sequence. Comparison required interpretation of ways in which the ingredients of human societies were capable of transformation, across space as well as through time. The popularity of social history during the later 1960s and 1970s thus inadvertently laid the basis for the de-centering of national histories and the 'Western' tradition, by providing subject matter which was susceptible to ever more centrifugal analysis.

At first social history was written in aggregated forms; social structure, the crowd and classes taking the place of the individual actors in the history of high politics. But by taking the words and gestures of the crowd seriously historians forced themselves to invent new ways of organising their material, and of recognising differences within it. The 'making' of the English working class as described by E. P. Thompson was in part a process of linguistic elaboration, of clubs, associations, pass-words as well as self-recognition. Richard Cobb's study of the People's Armies of revolutionary France offered 'example piled upon example, quotation upon quotation, lists of names, occupations, places, responses, situations'.[11] As the multifariousness of social history increased, alternatives to the organising idea of social *structure* were found in the past historical situation itself, often paradoxically joining categories which had become separate in modern times, as in the celebrated essay by Natalie Zemon Davis on 'The Rites of Violence'. Even Lawrence Stone's massively sociological treatment of the Elizabethan nobility (*The Crisis of the Aristocracy, 1558–1641*, 1965) had included an almost dramaturgical analysis of their participation in street violence.

Stone's masterpiece was reissued to a wider audience in abridged form, as was his next book *The Family, Sex and Marriage in England 1500–1800* (1977), as though there was some difficulty in reconciling the scale of the sociologically inspired projects undertaken in the 1960s with the new interest in history's social drama. Indeed, the essay re-emerged as a leading vehicle for the new approach, allowing a more personal, exploratory treatment of a particular theme. The anthropologist Clifford Geertz's seminal *The Interpretation of Cultures* (1973) was composed in this way, as was Natalie Zemon Davis' first book (*Society and Culture in Early Modern France*, 1975), and Robert Darnton's *The Great Cat Massacre*, to which Geertz contributed through shared teaching with Darnton at Princeton after 1972. Edward Thompson sponsored an equally influential set of approaches to the history of crime and disorder in *Albion's Fatal Tree* (1975). All of these works organised themselves around a pregnant theme or episode and combined this with an explicit, often experimental attitude to its interpretation. Geertz's notion of 'thick description', and his explication of the Balinese cock-fight, have served a figurative function in this respect, signalling a method where, because of the heterogeneity of the instances explored, there can be no common procedure.

The close study of particular episodes drew historians closer to the individual biographies of ordinary people, though these could often only be recovered by indirect means, for instance through the narrative momentum of their appearances before a court. Historians with long-standing interests in literary sources helped pioneer the approach, as in Christopher Hill's essays, and parts of a book like *The World Turned Upside Down* (1972), or in Edward Thompson's *Whigs and Hunters* (1975). Thus whilst the 1970s were at first dominated by the variety and brilliance of work conceived in large-scale sociological or Marxist terms,[12] the latter was soon eclipsed as a point of reference by work on a smaller scale but greater depth from Emmanuel Le Roy Ladurie (*Montaillou*, 1975 and 1978 in English) and Carlo Ginzburg (*The Cheese and the Worms*, 1976, English trans. 1980).[13]

Evidence of a more self-conscious turn towards symbolic interpretation was summarised by Lawrence Stone at the end of the decade. Stone announced a more complex, two-way traffic between the quantifiable factors beloved of 1960s social historians (demography, prices, food supply, etc.) and 'the culture of the group, and even the will of the individual, [which] are potentially at least as important causal agents of change as the impersonal forces of material output and demographic growth'.[14] He recognised how the new tendency risked producing a history of fascinating but atypical and sensational stories, and worried with what skills historians might be trained to negotiate these rapids in the future: 'In the ancient arts of rhetoric? In textual criticism? In semiotics? In symbolic anthropology? In psychology?'

Stone's questions, and his rather nervous single reference to Hayden White's *Metahistory* (1973), indicated that the discipline was at something of a cross-roads. Stone was writing at the height of the influence of poststructuralism in literary criticism, and White's work exposed the deep-seated figurative character of historical writing. At the same time, another current with claims to the historical method was emerging in the form of cultural materialism, crystallised in the United States through Stephen Greenblatt's *Renaissance Self-Fashioning* (Chicago, 1980), and drawing inspiration from Geertz's 'thick description'.[15] The work of Carlo Ginzburg, and of Natalie Zemon Davies in *The Return of Martin Guerre* (1983) shared common ground with the New Historicism in brilliantly mobilising the technical intricacies of interpretation to involve the reader, and draw repeated parallels between the choices available to historical actors and to present-day historians and their audience.[16] By making the act of interpretation more overt, and open to the reader, historians tacitly narrowed the distance between the professional and the 'ordinary' person. At the same time, how the reality effect was achieved, and which chunks of history came to be subjected to interpretation, became more public questions, as their equivalents were in other disciplines. Clifford Geertz observed of anthropology in 1983 that 'Attention to how it gets its effects and what those are, to anthropology on the page, is no longer a side issue, dwarfed by problems of method and issues of theory'.[17] The opening up of such questions to scrutiny promised to enrich the reader's experience, but threatened professional authority at a time when governments, pressure groups and rival academic fields were competing for authority over the historian's terrain. As an overtly 'postmodern' approach to historical writing laid siege to the practice of 'normal science' in the field, controversy erupted.

Yet much that was to be debated was not new. Hayden White had discovered through his early work on Croce in the 1950s how professional history, having laid claim to the study of the entirety of human experience through time, yet positioning itself *between* art and science, could lay *full* claim to neither way of knowing.[18] His subsequent work, notably an essay from 1966 on 'The Burden of History', went on to deconstruct the claims made for the certainty of historical knowledge since the nineteenth century. The American early modernist J. H. Hexter had also insisted in 1961 that

A good part of the troubles of the historian results from the way people use words. The people whose writings are the main contemporary sources of information about the period which concerns the historian often used words carelessly. So do many of the historians who have written about that period – any period whatever.[19]

Hexter prompted a review from J. G. A. Pocock calling for more attention to the historian's language, not so much its logic and verifiability as 'language as a social instrument and thought as social behaviour'.[20] Hexter went on to attempt a systematic defence of narrative against both relativistic and law-based claims to knowledge in 'The Rhetoric of History' in 1967.[21] By the time White presented his own approach in book-length form he was drawing on the work of Roland Barthes, whose *Michelet par lui-même* (1954) had been followed by an attempt to decode 'The Discourse of History' (1967), as well as on work by Lévi-Strauss, Foucault, and the Canadian critic Northrop Frye. Frye's interesting work applied a Blakean vision of biblical figuration to the study of all forms of writing, and thus provided a way of revisiting the Crocean observation about history's anomalous position between other 'forms' of knowledge. In 1969 the historian Richard Berkhofer Jr began a long project into 'how best to present history in the light of modernist fictional techniques'.[22] These developments were paralleled in the philosophy of science by the recognition that observational reports are dependent on the theoretical context in which they are made, and ultimately by Paul Feyerabend's calls for the dissolution of the philosophy of science into the wider study of cultural history,[23] But with the lunar landing of 1969 'normal science' could afford to continue untroubled, whilst for the moment a broadly realistic social history flourished on the campuses.

Historical writing had retained its commitment to realist prose well into the twentieth century, long after modernist prose of the kind written by James Joyce had moved beyond so straightforward a relation between fiction and reality.[24] Postmodern writers like Don DeLillo indeed often compose what Linda Hutcheon has called 'historiographic metafiction', in which historically validated 'facts' are redeployed fictionally, rather as Theodore Zeldin invents conversations with Newton in his journey to paradise, in *Happiness*.[25] The potentially fictional character of the historian's writing has been further exposed from another direction since 1967 by the insights of Jacques Derrida, in suggesting how professionally written histories rely on the privileged 'Western' categories of perfect presence, proximity and plenitude. Historians have committed themselves to telling the history of *entire* nations, telling it 'as it *really* was' (von Ranke), their ever-expanding *completeness* of factual detail '*telling* in the end' (Bury). At the same time, modernist histories are haunted by the sheer multifariousness of empirical data as the subject-matter of history has expanded, by the barely glimpsed foreignness of Eric Wolf's 'People Without History', the multiple ways for men and women of being 'as it really was', and by the increasing hopelessness, as the quantity of work mounts up, of an eventual single synthesis. The sense of historical progress which has underpinned the discipline of history appears from this viewpoint as a form of false consciousness, a mis-directed assertion of the human will, concealing from us the actually more complex situation of the human species in relation to time. This is a very difficult perception to absorb, so 'natural' has the notion of linear historical time come to seem in our culture.

That difficulty explains, in turn, why historians themselves have contributed so little to debates about postmodernity. The postmodern obliterates the secure linear relation between present and past upon which conventional historical interpretation (Stone's search for 'causal agents of change') depends. Historians have increasingly preferred to reinterpret the past itself in the light of the linguistic turn, rather than to theorise about the sand upon which their edifices are built.[26] Interest in the history of mentalities, of literacy and reading practices has expanded. The consumption of commodities has tended to replace labour and production as a focus for study, whilst the culture and words of the workers themselves have been deconstructed by Stedman-Jones, Rancière, Biernacki and others. After Foucault, the human body has been anatomised afresh as but one space of culture. Meanwhile, interests and approaches formerly associated with medievalists and early modernists have been transferred to later periods, in the work of Alain Corbin on the nineteenth century for example, and as Umberto Eco playfully points out, the 'post-modern' has come to seem more 'medieval'.[27]

By the spring of 1988, postmodernism in architecture had become a part of history according to the *New York Times*,[28] just as the hegemony of deconstruction was unravelling in the wake of Paul de Man's compromised reputation. History of a recognisable sort had re-started, and historians worried at being left behind.[29] The political scientist Francis Fukuyama's detection of 'the end of history'[30] was rapidly overtaken by the renewed flow of historical events, opening access to new sources, and a host of new political and ethical problems in the so-called 'societies of transition'.[31] It was time for the relation of post-modernity and history to become itself a historical subject,[32] stimulated in part by curriculum reform,[33] and partly by the sheer 'overproduction' of historical works.[34]

When, therefore, more than twenty years after his celebration of 'the revival of narrative', Lawrence Stone announced in 1991 a 'crisis of self-confidence' in the historical profession brought about by an excessive application of deconstruction, cultural anthropology and the New Historicism, the first thing that shocked respondents was the *tone* of Stone's allegations.[35] In a clarification he explained his concern to deny 'the extreme position that there is no reality outside language', and to identify a breakpoint beyond which 'fact and fiction become indistinguishable from one another'. Such a view 'makes entirely nugatory the dirty and tedious archival work of the historian to dig "facts" out of texts'. That even as brilliant a historian as Simon Schama had chosen the 'deliberate obliteration of the difference between archival fact and pure fiction in his book *Dead Certainties*' seemed particularly worrying.

A decade or more on, Stone's own words enact the very linguistic phenomenon he sought to deny. As against the irresponsible airiness of linguistic construction, the historian 'digs' facts with hard labour out of the archive. So endowed with value, 'archival fact' stands at the opposite extreme from 'pure' fiction. What Stone denies is 'that there is no reality out there which is anything but a subjective creation of the historian'. Literally speaking, as is widely agreed, there *is* in fact no past 'out there' with which we can come into contact, but the emptiness of Stone's claim is filled out with the figure of the creative but stereotypically (feminine?) 'subjective' historian. The fear of creativity, of subjectivity, in handling the traces of the past which do survive with us in the present conceals an awkwardness in the historian's relationship with a potential audience, a reluctance to acknowledge their shared humanity, and the likely fragility of their grasp upon the world's meaning.[36]

These are exactly the issues explored in Natalie Zemon Davis's *The Gift in Sixteenth-century France* (2001), which began life as an engaged response to Reaganite economics, another way of looking at commodities as expressions of affinity, of shared interests and understandings. Even the form of this book has been prepared to appeal as a gift, a modern replica of the gift-books about whom Davis writes so sensitively. This is creative history, openly subjective in its inspiration, imaginatively forging a common ground between the remnants of the sixteenth-century past and the books we hold in our hands today. The ventriloquism is not of course an entirely novel device: Christopher Hill fused predestinarian Puritanism and Marxist dialectic half a century ago, persuading us to think as one whilst mentally inhabiting the other. It is also capable of startling revelations. Caroline Steedman's *Dust* (2001) starts from Derrida's metaphorical representation of the Western yearning for origins as a kind of fever, and cleverly recovers a material history of historical research in which the industrial diseases of nineteenth-century artisans, Michelet's breathing in of the dust of the archives, and the modern historian's own bodily discomforts figure as the components of a craft constantly in motion between present and past, between metaphor and epidemiology.[37]

Work of this kind produces a richer, more multi-faceted, access to 'the past' than the barricaded fortresses of so many 'normal' works of history, whose plausibility is called into doubt as soon as the 'reality' of an actual past is questioned. At its most effective the postmodernist historical work occupies an intellectual space between past and present, a basis for the thinking through of how what might have actually happened might have affected our present selves. The distance between past and present is not blurred by its narrowing, but sharpened as historians increasingly use visual images and reproductions of source materials to concretise differences and similarities.[38] The apparatus of scholarship has itself been laid open in this way,[39] as well as the discovery of 'facts',[40] and alternative forms of representation sampled.[41] Denying the obviousness of the fit between prose and history can pay dividends.[42] Sometimes it is a visual image that underpins 'the historian's claim to be an authentic witness and, consequently, a serious analyst'.[43] Historians who have adopted fictionalising devices in their written work, like Natalie Davis and Simon Schama, also work well with visual materials and new media.

The confusion of work and leisure which the student's use of a computer entails is allowing historians to burst the self-imposed bounds of a genre founded over a century ago. Historians have always been purveyors of 'virtual' truth, opening a window on to an actually non-existent past, but today they can do so with a clearer conscience. When Hayden White says of the Holocaust that 'there are no grounds to be found in the historical record itself for preferring one way of construing its meaning over another',[44] he points to our moral obligation to use that record, through discussion in courts of law if need be, to establish meaning for ourselves.[45] There are many signs that this is happening. The work of Michael Kammen reflectively revisits such themes as American exceptionalism, the historian's personal role, cultural and political shapings of history, and the role of collective memory.[46] A de-centred, postmodern standpoint equips us to breathe fresh life into the study of periods or civilisations most subject to the modern West's condescension.[47] But the West itself can be turned on its head as well, as by Roy Porter's clever application of Baudrillard's description of 'the world of objects' as 'a world of *general hysteria*' to the early eighteenth-century writings of Bernard Mandeville, demonstrating just how early so-called 'postmodern' characteristics appeared, and how fundamental the irrational has always been to the nature of capitalism.[48] Or the canons of the West can be re-read from afar.[49]

Finally, to the South Seas with Greg Dening, whose 'ethnographic history' is 'an attempt to represent the past as it was actually experienced in such a way that we understand both its ordered and its disordered natures'.[50] Revisiting the mutiny on the *Bounty*, Dening draws on the theatre as metaphor for a space within which both he, his audience, and his protagonist can be temporarily housed in a multi-layered interpretative performance. The 'theatricality' of the historian's stance is linked to the various past representations of the mutiny, including those on film, and like Prospero, Dening even transmutes the remoteness of the inaccessible past: 'The Bounty and what happened on her and around her is now transformed into texts – logs, journals, court transcriptions, newspaper pieces'.[51]

Aware that what he is doing may be dismissed as 'claptrap', Dening restores an eighteenth-century meaning to the term, noting both the truth-telling capacity of the dramatic stage and the blinkeredness of the Enlightenment's ethnographic gaze. The book also explores the symbolic violence of the ship's punishments, Bligh's 'bad language', and the untranslatable vocabulary with which Polynesian 'natives' encountered the European 'strangers'. Endnotes offer not so much citations of authority as a running commentary on the text, and its role as an ethnography of history and the act of remembering, completed amidst bicentennial celebrations.[52] Dening's ambitions for his students match those for the book, a more effective and sensitive use of language to make what sense we can of what the past has left us:

> I want them to be ethnographic – to describe with the carefulness and realism of a poem what they observe of the past in the signs that the past has left ... [to] represent human agency in the way in which it happens, mysteriously combining the totally particular and the universal.

Notes

1 D. Ghirardo, *Architecture After Modernism*, New York, Thames and Hudson, 1996, pp. 7–40. M. A. Rose, *The Post-Modern and the Post-Industrial: A Critical Analysis*, Cambridge, Cambridge University Press, 1991, offers the most useful conspectus of the many uses of these terms.

2 C. Wright Mills, *The Sociological Imagination*, Harmondsworth, Penguin, 1959, p. 184.

3 Jean-François Lyotard, *The Postmodern Condition: A Report on Knowledge*, Manchester, Manchester University Press, 1984 (French edn 1979); Jean Baudrillard, *The Mirror of Production*, St Louis, Telos Press, 1975; and *Simulation*, New York, Semiotext(e), 1983.

4 J. L. Austin, *How To Do Things with Words*, Oxford, Oxford University Press, 1962, 2nd edn, 1975; T. Kuhn, *The Structure of Scientific Revolutions*, Chicago, University of Chicago Press, 1962.

5 D. C. Dennett, *Consciousness Explained*, Harmondsworth, Penguin, 1991, referring to David Lodge, *Nice Work*, 1988.

6 R. Rorty (ed.) *The Linguistic Turn: Recent Essays in Philosophical Method*, Chicago, University of Chicago Press, 1967.

7 D. Lehman, *Signs of the Times: Deconstruction and the Fall of Paul de Man*, New York, Simon and Schuster/Poseidon, 1991; G. Himmelfarb, *On Looking into the Abyss*, New York, Alfred A. Knopf, 1994, p. xiii.

8 G. Barraclough, *History in a Changing World*, Oxford, Blackwell, 1955, pp. 31–2.

9 J. G. A. Pocock, 'British History: A Plea for a New Subject', *Journal of Modern History*, 1975, vol. 47; T. Nairn, *The Break-Up of Britain: Crisis and Neo-Nationalism*, London, New Left Books, 1977. The *Past and Present* conference on 'The Invention of Tradition' was held in London in 1977. See E. Hobsbawm and T. Ranger (eds) *The Invention of Tradition*, Cambridge, Cambridge University Press, 1983.

10 K. Thomas, 'The Double Standard', *Journal of the History of Ideas*, 1959, vol. 20, pp. 195–216.

11 R. Cobb, *The People's Armies*, New Haven, Yale University Press, 1987, 1st French edn, Paris, 2 vols, 1961/1963, p. xiii.

12 R. Fogel and S. Engerman, *Time on the Cross*, London, Wildwood House, 1974; I. Wallerstein, *The Modern World System*, New York and London, Academic Press, 1974–80; the translation of F. Braudel's *The Mediterranean and the Mediterranean World in the Age of Philip II*, London, Collins, 1972–3; Moses Finley's *The Ancient Economy*, London, Chatto and Windus, 1973; Perry Anderson's *Passages from Antiquity to Feudalism*, London, New Left Books, 1977, and *Lineages of the Absolutist State*, London, New Left Books, 1979.

13 Cf. also J. Barrell, *The Dark Side of the Landscape: The Rural Poor in English Painting, 1730–1848*, Cambridge, Cambridge University Press, 1980; W. Sewell Jr,

Work and Revolution in France: The Language of Labor from the Old Regime to 1848, Cambridge, Cambridge University Press, 1980; Natalie Zemon Davis, *The Return of Martin Guerre*, Cambridge MA, Harvard University Press, 1983.

14 Lawrence Stone, 'The Revival of Narrative: Reflections on a New Old History', in his *The Past and the Present*, London, Routledge and Kegan Paul, 1981, p. 80; first published in *Past and Present*, 1979, vol. 85.

15 H. Aram Veeser (ed.) *The New Historicism*, London, Routledge, 1989, pp. xi–xiii.

16 Christopher Hill used a similar approach in his mordant post-Thatcher, *The Experience of Defeat: Milton and some Contemporaries*, London, Faber, 1984.

17 C. Geertz, *Works and Lives*, Stanford CA, Stanford University Press, 1988, p. 149.

18 C. Antoni, *From History to Sociology*, translated and introduced by H. White, Detroit, Wayne State University Press, 1959.

19 J. H. Hexter, *Reappraisals in History*, London, Longmans, 1961, p. 187.

20 *History and Theory*, 1964, vol. 3, p. 121.

21 *History and Theory*, 1967, vol. 6, pp. 3–13, subsequently greatly expanded in *International Encyclopaedia of the Social Sciences*, 1968, vol. 6, pp. 368–94, and in *Doing History*, London, Allen and Unwin, 1971, where the story of the article's evolution is told at pp. 2–4. R. T. Vann commends Hexter's prescience but emphasises the isolation of his position in 'Turning Linguistic: History and Theory in *History and Theory*, 1960–1975', in F. Ankersmit and H. Keller (eds) *A New Philosophy of History*, Chicago, University of Chicago Press, 1995, p. 56.

22 R. F. Berkhofer Jr, *Beyond the Great Story: History as Text and Discourse*, Cambridge MA, Harvard University Press, 1995.

23 P. K. Feyerabend, 'Philosophy of Science: A Subject with a Great Past', in R. Struewer (ed.) *Historical and Philosophical Perspectives on Science*, Minneapolis, University of Minnesota Press, 1970; *Against Method*, London, New Left Books, 1975.

24 E. D. Ermarth, *The English Novel in History 1840–1895*, London, Routledge, 1997, brilliantly explores how Victorian novelists contributed to an expanding sense of experience taking place serially, 'in' History.

25 T. Zeldin, *Happiness*, London, Collins Harvill, 1988; L. Hutcheon, *A Poetics of Postmodernism: History, Theory, Fiction*, London, Routledge and Kegan Paul, 1988.

26 G. Stedman Jones, *Languages of Class*, Cambridge, Cambridge University Press, 1983; S. Bann, *The Clothing of Clio*, Cambridge, Cambridge University Press, 1984. W. A. Reddy, *The Rise of Market Culture*, Cambridge, Cambridge University Press, 1984; P. Corrigan and D. Sayer, *The Great Arch: English State Formation as Cultural Revolution*, Oxford, Blackwell, 1985; A. Appadurai (ed.) *The Social Life of Things: Commodities in Cultural Perspective*, Cambridge, Cambridge University Press, 1986; N. Z. Davis, *Fiction in the Archives: Pardon Tales and Their Tellers in Sixteenth-century France*, Cambridge, Polity, 1987; P. Burke and R. Porter (eds) *The Social History of Language*, Cambridge, Cambridge University Press, 1987; R. Chartier, *Cultural History: Between Practices and Representations*, Ithaca NY, Cornell University Press, 1988; A. Marwick, *Beauty in History*, London, Thames and Hudson, 1988; L. Hunt (ed.) *The New Cultural History*, Berkeley, University of California Press, 1989; P. Ariès and G. Duby (eds) *A History of Private Life*, 5 vols, Cambridge MA, Harvard University Press, 1989–92; C. Ginzburg, *Myths, Emblems, Clues*, London, Radius, 1990; J. Bossy, *Giordano Bruno and the Embassy Affair*, New Haven, Yale University Press, 1991, a true detective story self-consciously written in the context of debates about 'discourse'; C. Walker Bynum, *Fragmentation and Redemption: Essays on Gender and the Human Body in Medieval Religion*, New York, Zone Books, 1991, presented as history in the 'comic mode'; J. Bremmer and H. Roodenburg (eds) *A Cultural History of Gesture*, Ithaca NY, Cornell University Press, 1991; S. Schama, *Dead Certainties (Unwarranted Speculations)*, New York,

Alfred A. Knopf, 1991; P. Burke and R. Porter (eds) *Language, Self, and Society: A Social History of Language*, Cambridge, Cambridge University Press, 1991; P. Corfield (ed.) *Language, History and Class*, Oxford, Blackwell, 1991; P. Joyce, *Visions of the People: Industrial England and the Question of Class 1848–1914*, Cambridge, Cambridge University Press, 1991; *idem, Democratic Subjects: The Self and the Social in Nineteenth-century England*, Cambridge, Cambridge University Press, 1994; S. Lubar and W. David Kingery (eds) *History from Things: Essays on Material Culture*, Washington DC, Smithsonian Institution Press, 1993; J. Demos, *Unredeemed Captive: A Family Story from Early America*, New York, Alfred A. Knopf, 1995; C. Kudlick, *Cholera in Post-revolutionary France: A Cultural History*, Berkeley, University Presses of California, Columbia and Princeton, 1996; D. Purkiss, *The Witch in History: Early Modern and Twentieth-century Representations*, London, Routledge, 1996.

27 U. Eco, 'The Return of the Middle Ages' in *idem, Travels in Hyper-Reality*, New York, Harcourt Brace, 1986, p. 62.

28 D. Harvey, *The Condition of Postmodernity*, Oxford, 1989, p. 356.

29 See discussion of the *Annales* editorials, above p. 87.

30 Fukuyama's essay was originally published in *The National Interest*, summer 1989.

31 Orlando Figes, *A People's Tragedy: The Russian Revolution 1891–1917*, London, Viking, 1996, was written out of such newly opened archives.

32 D. Attridge, G. Bennington and R. Young (eds) *Post-structuralism and the Question of History*, Cambridge, Cambridge University Press, 1987; B. D. Palmer, *Descent into Discourse: The Reification of Language and the Writing of Social History*, Philadelphia PA, Temple University Press, 1990.

33 For issues raised by the National Curriculum, which was introduced by the Education Reform Act of 1988, see K. Jenkins and P. Brickley, ' "A" Level History: From "Skillology" to Methodology', *Teaching History*, October 1986, vol. 46, pp. 3–7; *idem*, ' "A" Level History: On Historical Facts and Other Problems', *Teaching History*, July 1988, vol. 52, pp. 19–24; *idem*, 'Empathy and the Flintstones (GCSE in History)', *Times Educational Supplement*, 13 May 1988, p. A25. Discussion, 27 May 1988, p. A25.

34 F. Ankersmit, 'Historiography and Postmodernism', *History and Theory*, vol. 28:2, 1989, reprinted in K. Jenkins (ed.) *The Postmodern History Reader*, London, Routledge, 1997, p. 279.

35 L. Stone, 'History and Postmodernism', *Past and Present*, 1992, vol. 135, reprinted in Jenkins, *Reader*, p. 257. The original article from 1991, and replies, are reprinted at pp. 242–54.

36 For a slightly different deconstruction of Stone's style from the 1950s see A. Easthope, *Englishness and National Culture*, London, Routledge, 1999, pp. 145–51.

37 C. Steedman, *Dust*, Manchester, Manchester University Press, 2001. Cf. *American Historical Review*, December 2001, vol. 106:5, p. 1744; cf. J. A. Amato, *Dust: A History of the Small and the Invisible*, Berkeley, University of California Press, 2000.

38 Compare the presentation of original marks and signatures in D. Hay, P. Linebaugh and E. P. Thompson (eds) *Albion's Fatal Tree*, Harmondsworth, Penguin, 1975; and A. Macfarlane, *The Justice and the Mare's Ale*, Oxford, Blackwell, 1981.

39 A. Manguel, *A History of Reading*, New York, Viking, 1996; H. Petroski, *The Book on the Shelf*, New York, Alfred A. Knopf, 1999; A. Grafton, *The Footnote: A Curious History*, Cambridge MA, Harvard University Press, 1997.

40 S. Shapin, *The Social History of Truth*, Chicago, University of Chicago Press, 1994; M. Poovey, *A History of the Modern Fact*, Chicago, University of Chicago Press, 1998.

41 R. Samuel, *Theatres of Memory, i. Past and Present in Contemporary Culture*, London, Verso, 1994.

42 Compare Gabrielle Spiegel's empirical work on thirteenth-century French historiography and the relation of prose and ideology: *Romancing the Past: The Rise of Vernacular Prose Historiography in Thirteenth-century France*, Berkeley, University of California Press, 1993.

43 S. Bann, *Under the Sign: John Bargrave as Collector, Traveler, and Witness*, Ann Arbor, University of Michigan Press, 1994, p. 123.

44 H. White, 'The Politics of Historical Interpretation', 1982, quoted by Saul Friedlander in his *Probing the Limits of Representation: Nazism and the 'Final Solution'*, Cambridge MA, Harvard University Press, 1992, reprinted in Jenkins, *Reader*, p. 389.

45 Friedlander (ed.) *Probing the Limits of Representation*; R. J. Bernstein, *The New Constellation: The Ethical-political Horizons of Modernity/Postmodernity*, Cambridge MA, MIT Press, 1992; D. Lipstadt, *Denying the Holocaust: The Growing Assault on Truth and Memory*, New York, Free Press, 1993.

46 M. Kammen, *In the Past Lane: Historical Perspectives on American Culture*, Oxford, Oxford University Press, 1997.

47 M. Bernal, *Black Athena*, New Brunswick NJ, Rutgers University Press, 2 vols, 1987/1991; A. Frantzen, *The Desire for Origins*, New Brunswick NJ, Rutgers University Press, 1990; O. Giollain, *Locating Irish Folklore*, Cork, Cork University Press, 2000, p. 182.

48 R. Porter, 'Baudrillard: History, Hysteria and Consumption', in C. Rojek and B. S. Turner (eds) *Forget Baudrillard?*, London, Routledge, 1993, p. 2.

49 C. Ginzburg, *No Island Is an Island: Four Glances at English Literature in a World Perspective*, New York, Columbia University Press, 2000; S. Federici (ed.) *Enduring Western Civilization: The Construction of the Concept of Western Civilization and its 'Others'*, Westport CT, Greenwood Press, 1995.

50 G. Dening, *Mr Bligh's Bad Language: Passion, Power and Theatre on the Bounty*, Cambridge, Cambridge University Press, 1992, p. 5.

51 *Ibid.*, p. 376.

52 *Ibid.*, pp. 378–9.

Further reading

The roots of what has come to be called a 'postmodern' approach to history can be traced to Hayden White's deconstruction of nineteenth-century historians in *Metahistory*, Baltimore, Johns Hopkins University Press, 1973, and to J-F. Lyotard's post-'68 manifesto, *The Postmodern Condition*, Manchester, Manchester University Press, 1984 (1st French edn Paris, 1979). In terms of the dissemination of 'postmodern' ideas, in the UK Keith Jenkins began a sequence of polemical studies with *Re-thinking History*, London, Routledge, 1991; *On 'What is History?' From Carr and Elton to Rorty and White*, London, Routledge, 1995; *Why History? Ethics and Postmodernity*, London, Routledge, 1999; and *Refiguring History*, London, Routledge, 2002. Jenkins has also edited an invaluable collection of extracts, *The Postmodern History Reader*, London, Routledge, 1997; and with Alan Munslow, *The Nature of History Reader*, London, Routledge, 2003. For his part Munslow has been instrumental in establishing the journal *Rethinking History* and has also published *Deconstructing History*, London, Routledge, 1997; and *The Routledge Companion to Historical Studies*, London, Routledge, 2000. On an international scale, F. Ankersmit and H.

Kellner (eds) *A New Philosophy of History*, London, Reaktion Books, 1995, is a varied collection of very high quality, devoted to the impact of the linguistic turn. R. M. Burns and H. Rayment-Pickard (eds) *Philosophies of History From Enlightenment to Postmodernity*, Oxford, Blackwell, 2000, provides the primary sources with which to locate postmodern scepticism in a historical context stretching back to David Hume. Critical responses to postmodern approaches have come from many directions, in the UK from R. J. Evans, *In Defence of History*, London, Granta Books, 1997 (revised edn 2001); and Arthur Marwick, *The New Nature of History: Knowledge, Evidence, Language*, Basingstoke, Palgrave, 2001; and from the USA in E. Fox-Genovese and E. Lasch-Quin (eds) *Reconstructing History: The Emergence of a New Historical Society*, New York and London, Routledge, 1999.

Part V

Beyond the academy

In this final part of the volume, four historians explore the relationship between history as it is taught in universities, and practiced within the academy, and history 'beyond the academy'. 'Beyond the academy' – in other words all that lies beyond the university – clearly offers a near infinite range of possibilities. In this part, the four chapters present examinations of very particular aspects of what lurks 'beyond'. But, in their exploration of film, popular culture, 'amateur history' and heritage, these chapters stand as case-studies and ways into other approaches to historical study and a broad interest in the past which survives and often thrives beyond the history faculty.

The four contributors to Part V adopt distinct approaches to their task. Peter Miskell offers an analysis of the manner in which film and the study of history have come together. He discusses ways in which historians and film-makers have employed or contemplated the employment of film as both a medium for the portrayal of the past and a source for the study of the past. As historians test the methodology of their discipline, the possibilities of film, both as source and as mode of expression are, he argues, increasingly likely to be realised. For Miskell, the extent to which historians have engaged with film-making is a litmus test of the potential of the discipline to reflect upon its own claims to represent the past in ways that are objective and truthful. The very nature of film, as an alternative mode of presenting the past, presents historians with a challenge to their hegemony. Some, relatively few, historians have embraced that challenge and work closely with film-makers; others have not been inclined to seek out such opportunities. While Miskell argues that the film-makers' view of the past is no more or less valid than that of the historian, he also suggests that the use of film as a source for the historian reflects, and may have encouraged, a willingness of historians to employ material other than the most traditional. If film opened up opportunities for social and political historians, or at least for those of the last century, it was also a product of 'popular culture'. The extent to which the media, and in particular television's documentary histories, inform and infect the teaching and writing of history is an issue currently debated within the academy.[1] But what such debates reflect is an awareness of the truism that history, even academic history, is not and cannot be separated from its cultural context.

Gareth Williams' chapter on 'popular culture' examines that immediate relationship between the 'popular' and the work of the historian. In contrast to the chapter by Miskell, with its focus upon the impact of 'popular culture' on the subject of history more generally, Williams' piece has more to say on the historiography of 'popular culture' *per se*. He notes that it was long into the second half of the twentieth century before historians turned their attention to sport as a valid subject of study. Though this historiographical development is explicable in terms of the expansion and diversification of new social history, it also, as Williams reminds us, reflects the development of forms of 'popular culture'. Where would the historian of rugby be without the game and its pervasiveness? How would the historian of rugby cope without the intellectual apparatus, the evidential awareness, the approach to the subject of study of his or her discipline? It is from the marriage of the 'popular' and the 'academic' that the historian of popular culture was born. But what also of the ways in which 'popular culture' provided not only the subject matter of history, but also its motive force? Are historians encouraged to work in certain areas more than others because that which is popular conditions their sense of appropriateness? Do they mould their approach to accommodate the more typical, and perhaps thereby lose sight of the nuanced? Will historians abandon rigour in order to entertain? While some historians clearly express concern that a broadly based popular culture presents such challenges not only to historians but also to their students ('students who have watched too much television history expect to be told stories rather than acquire the skills of the historian'[2]), there are others who see in the outlets for 'popular culture' opportunities for dialogue and the nurturing of the study of the past.

As Bill Rubinstein's chapter on 'amateur historians' illustrates, there is a vibrant audience for the work of historians, but an audience that is not just content to sit and listen, watch, or read, but also to participate. Audience participation implies that the main figures on the stage are somehow different, and in some cases this is clearly the case. There is a meeting of amateur and academic history, as Rubinstein points out, in local history societies and through other collective endeavours. While academic and amateur historians share elements of approach to the past, including the initial definition of their chosen topic, it is the wider contextualisation, the engagement with the historiography, and the application of the rules of engagement with the sources, that separate much academic from much non-academic history. Academic historians, where they have particular theses to develop, have tended to employ amateur historians as data gatherers more than as intellectual partners in the pursuit of answers to historical questions.[3] But, as often as not, historians do not work with large teams of researchers, academic or otherwise, and the close active collaboration of academic and amateur (outside of the classroom) is relatively rare. Instead, 'amateur' historians, as Rubinstein also shows, have ploughed their own distinctive furrows, and in fields where historians have seldom toiled. The difference that Rubinstein invites us to consider between, for instance, the work of the amateur historian of 'Jack the Ripper' and that of the academic addressing the murders in the East End of London resides in the calculation of what can be constructed from the historical material that is available. Most academic historians would not pursue the identity of the Ripper because they recognise that the historical material does not sustain that endeavour; amateur historians make other choices and take other directions. A possible reason why the respective approaches remain at such variance relates to a calculation of ultimate success and a comprehension of the terms of that success: for the academic historian, plausibility in the light of the rules of evidence, for the amateur, enjoyment of the pursuit, a pursuit that can be as relentless as it can be unthinking.[4] But it would be deeply inappropriate to suggest that academic history was or is necessarily of a higher calibre than 'amateur' history. However, unless academic historians are simply prejudiced against amateurs' work, they will – quite properly – judge it by the same criteria as 'good' academic history: consistent and appropriate in its use of historical sources, sensibly structured and robust in the presentation of argument, suitably engaged with the relevant secondary literature, and so on. There is less sense, despite Miskell's suggestion in his chapter, that the work of film-makers has encouraged historians to rethink their approach to the past, or that amateur historians, through their method, have caused academic historians to reassess how they study the past.

While 'method' may not have been challenged in ways that are fundamental by the work and interest of historians 'beyond the academy', it is certainly possible to conceive of ways in which demand may have effected the choices of academic historians. In particular, as Susan Davies indicates in her chapter on heritage and history, the organised and increasingly structured 'past' that is defined as 'heritage' depends upon an educative process. For those who are to be employed as the guardians of heritage, for those who are to instruct those guardians and for a wider public who need to understand the value of their historical legacy and to desire its preservation, there is need of education and training. Where, as in the case of heritage in the West, the state supports such initiatives, then historians within the academy find themselves encouraged to think of tailoring their teaching and, since teaching and research are inseparable, their research. Thus the expectations of external bodies, including the perceived expectations of a wider public, influence the work of academic historians. We will return, in the conclusion, to the ways in which historians are subject to the power of others, but Davies' chapter, written from the perspective of an historian who is also an archivist, offers an example of the ways in which historians' work can be conditioned to meet demands which do not reside within the discipline. Again, there is no sense that these expectations will affect the nature of the discipline, except and in so far as they help determine its content. However, at a remove, the work of historians, presented through the cipher of the heritage industry, may well appear distinct from that presented in more traditional scholarly form. In that respect, the heritage industry, and the advisory or educative work of the historian located within it, returns us to issues of 'popular culture' and its potential impact upon history within the academy.

Notes

1   See, for instance, *History Today*, August 2003, p. 55.
2   *Ibid.*
3   See, for instance, E. A. Wrigley and R. Schofield, *The Population History of England, 1541–1871. A Reconstruction*, Cambridge, Cambridge University Press, 1989, pp. xxxv–vi, 490–2. This volume is dedicated to the 'local population historians of England'; it was the work of 'several hundred men, women and schoolchildren', as Wrigley and Schofield fully acknowledge, that provided the aggregate data of baptisms, burials and marriages which facilitated this highly sophisticated demographic survey.
4   See, for instance, P. Cornwell, *Portrait of a Killer. Jack the Ripper – Case Closed*, New York, Putnam, 2002.

Chapter 17

Historians and film

Peter Miskell

> Let's be blunt and admit it: historical films trouble and disturb professional historians – have troubled and disturbed historians for a long time.[1]

In an examination of the relationship between professional history and versions of the past created and presented outside of the academy, film must be a prime candidate for our attention. The cinema has not only provided an outlet for those unconnected with academia to exhibit publicly their own versions of the past, it allows history to be presented, and consumed, in a form entirely new to the twentieth century.[2] Moreover, the immense international popularity of the movies has meant that history as seen on the screen has reached a far wider audience than the writing of professional historians. This chapter will not engage in a detailed theoretical discussion on the subject of whether academic historians have any more right than film makers to claim that their work provides a valid interpretation of the past. The intention here is to offer a survey of the changing relationship of historians to film throughout the twentieth century. It will question why 'historical films have troubled and disturbed professional historians'. To what extent have their attitudes to history presented on screen developed over the course of the twentieth century? Has the popularity of historical film actually had an effect on the way in which professional historians themselves present their work? These questions will be examined from the perspective of historians working in Britain and North America, and the main focus will be on their attitude to commercial feature films.

Film as a medium for historical expression

It is possible to identify three distinct approaches to the subject of film and history. First, there is the study of the development of film as an industry, art form or cultural institution in the twentieth century. Second, films can be studied as historical documents or 'texts' which provide a valuable insight into the societies which made and watched them. Third, film can be treated seriously in its own right as a medium for presenting versions of the past. As Robert Rosenstone points out, 'The two most popular of these [the first two] are well within the boundaries of traditional historical practice' but the third is 'far more radical in its implications'.[3]

In Britain, it was in the 1960s that film history came to be regarded as a legitimate area of historical research. This was a period when something of a paradigm shift occurred within the profession as traditional boundaries of historical research were pushed back. Not only were new fields of historical study opened up (such as womens' history, labour history, the history of ethnic minorities or of popular culture), new sources were also sought out (novels, popular magazines, and non-written sources such as cartoons or advertising posters). Film history was a beneficiary of both of these developments. The history of the cinema, as a social/cultural institution and as an industry, can certainly be seen as yet one more aspect of social history opened up as a result of the changes of the 1960s. In addition, film was also one of the previously neglected non-written sources which helped shed new light on societies of the past. The importance of film as a new source (the second of the approaches to film history outlined above) was taken up by a number of historians in the 1960s and 1970s. Their work will not be discussed in detail here, but they included Anthony Aldgate, Nicholas Pronay and K. R. M. Short.[4] Numerous others have followed in their wake. Those interested in examining new fields of historical research, rather than new sources, took rather longer to turn their attention to the cinema. By the 1980s, however, Jeffrey Richards, Michael Chanan, Margaret Dickenson and Sarah Street were among those producing work in this area.[5]

This still leaves us with the third approach to film history: the use of film as a medium for historical expression. The changes in the historical profession in the 1960s may have altered attitudes to what constituted historical research, but they did little to alter the way in which history was presented. Films made *in* the past had come to be regarded as useful historical documents, but films *of* the past were still treated with suspicion as secondary interpretations of historical events. Historical films, it was felt, taught much about the societies that produced and watched them, but very little about the periods they sought to portray. Hence Pierre Sorlin's comment, in 1980, that 'when professional historians wonder about the mistakes made in an historical film, they are worrying about a meaningless question'.[6] In order for this thinking to change – for the third of the approaches to film and history to become accepted – a further paradigm shift needed to occur within the profession. This is why Rosenstone has described it as being 'radical in its implications'. Before exploring the question of whether or not this paradigm shift has actually occurred, however, something should be said about traditional attitudes to historical films.

Complaints by professional historians about the accuracy of historical films date from the period when the cinema first emerged as an influential medium of mass popular entertainment, and have been voiced at regular intervals ever since. Academic historians have certainly been protective of their territory, yet their attitude to film has not been unanimously hostile. As early as 1927 one contributor to the British journal *History* expressed his puzzlement as to why, at the annual meeting of the Historical Association the previous year, 'there was a good deal of prejudice against any attempt to use moving pictures in the teaching of history'.

> We expect the teacher to make history live by vivid descriptions. We praise realistic historical writing. The Historical Association even countenances historical novels. Pictures, too, are tolerated ... But let the pictures move, and for many it at once ceases to be historically satisfactory.[7]

This particular commentator may have felt that his views were out of step with those of the Historical Association, but there is evidence to suggest that in the first half of the twentieth century the actual medium of film itself was quite widely accepted as a potentially useful means of portraying past events.

The cinema, as Michael Chanan has cogently argued, was not invented with a clear purpose in mind. Films, though immediately popular with audiences in fairground booths or as part of music hall entertainment, were not initially thought of as a new medium of mass entertainment. Many of the pioneers who struggled to perfect a means of projecting moving images in the nineteenth century, such as Janssen, Muybridge and Marey, were more interested in furthering scientific knowledge than appealing to a mass audience.[8] As the commercial appeal of the movies became ever more apparent over the following decades, with audiences in their millions flocking to specially designed cinemas in search of an evening's entertainment, the educational or scientific value of the film became somewhat obscured, but it was not lost altogether.

It was the use of film as an educational tool that the above-mentioned contributor to *History* had in mind when he argued that historians should treat the medium more seriously. (He had just returned from Canada where he 'had been lecturing on General Wolfe for the Order of the Daughters of the British Empire', with the aid of 'a moving picture illustrating the conquest of Canada by the British'.)[9] Another history teacher argued in *Sight and Sound* (a publication of the British Film Institute) that two short animated films, *The Development of the English Railways* and *The Expansion of Germany 1870–1914*, would be of invaluable assistance to teachers in the classroom. His argument being that they 'not only combined the virtues of the atlas and the black board, but also overcame what they lacked because of their static properties'.[10]

It seems that the idea of using film as a means of presenting the past was not in itself such a radical concept. What has so troubled professional historians was not so much the medium of film, but the way in which the films themselves were made and consumed. There are three observations which can be made here about the way historical films have been viewed by those within the academy for much of the twentieth century. First, it was quite possible for film to be regarded as a novel way of teaching history to schoolchildren that might encourage them to develop a deeper interest in the subject, but it was not thought that historical films had anything to teach professional historians. Second, films shown in a classroom environment with a teacher present to ensure that children interpreted its message 'correctly', could not be compared to historical epics viewed by audiences in their thousands at commercial cinemas. Third, films which had been made under the guidance of professional historians were not the same as those produced as entertainment for the masses by commercial film studios. Given that the vast majority of films were produced as entertainment and watched in commercial cinemas, it is unsurprising that academic historians distanced themselves from the versions of history usually presented on screen. When they did acknowledge historical feature films at all, it was usually so that factual inaccuracies could be pointed out.

Sue Harper has documented in some detail the interventions of the Historical Association in the making of historical feature films in Britain in the 1930s and 1940s. The Association, she points out, 'was organised for the teachers of history. ... Those at the centre were eminent figures such as professors; those on the periphery were teachers or local historians'. One professor with an interest in film was F. J. C. Hearnshaw, who held a chair at the University of London, and who was president of the Association in the mid-1930s. Harper refers to a letter he wrote to *The Times* in 1936, and the passage is worth quoting here because it seems to encapsulate the attitude to film not only of the Historical Association but of the academic community of historians more generally.

> He argued that historical film was poised between 'meticulous accuracy' and 'dramatic intensity'. He said that it was handicapped by its need for a story and by the limitations of the audience, and considered it impossible to reform their taste for inaccuracy; the only hope lay with educational films, and even they were 'too imaginative, doubtfully accurate and too colourful'. He insisted on a rigid categorisation of discourses, implying that no one could watch a feature film and expect to learn good history.[11]

Historical feature films, according to this view, were inferior to intellectual history because their concern with escapist entertainment rendered them incapable of sticking to the truth. But was it really truth itself that professional historians were so keen to protect, or their control over what was deemed to be true?

Control of the media for historical expression

> Question: Why do historians distrust the historical film? The overt answers: Films are inaccurate. They distort the past. They fictionalise, trivialise, and romanticise people, events, and movements. They falsify history.
>
> The covert answers: Film is out of the control of historians. Film shows we do not own the past. Film creates a historical world with which books cannot

compete, at least for popularity. Film is a disturbing symbol of an increasingly post-literate world (in which people can read but won't).[12]

The first part of this chapter argued that changes within the historical profession in Britain in the 1960s led to the development of new studies of film and history, but did little to alter the deep seated suspicion of the historical film. In this section it will be argued that pressures from outside the history profession, and indeed outside the academy, have led a number of historians to treat the history presented on screen more seriously.

The postmodernist challenge to the pursuit of history is dealt with in more detail elsewhere in this volume.[13] For the purposes of this chapter, however, it is necessary to re-emphasise one of the key features of it. At the risk of over-simplification, the case will be put very briefly here. At its core is the assertion that there is no such thing as historical truth. The task of the historian is not to uncover a single ('true') version of past events that constitutes 'history'. On the contrary, the studies of the past that historians undertake are fundamentally influenced by the political/intellectual perspective from which they write. History, therefore, is 'created' to suit the needs of those who wish to use it; it is not something 'out there' waiting to be discovered. With this being so, it is impossible to argue that any one historical account is more truthful or reliable than another: it may be believed by more people, but this is not the same thing. Historians, therefore, cannot claim any exclusive right to ownership of the past. Their views are, in fact, no more valid than those of anyone else – including film makers.

This is a line of argument which academic historians often find uncomfortable, but it is one which they can do little to refute. Few would disagree that absolute historical truth is unattainable, and that any historical account is a creation of its author and therefore shaped by his or her beliefs. (The more time one spends engaged in archival research the more apparent this becomes: our decisions about which documents are interesting or relevant cannot be made impartially, even if we do try to be objective in the way we use them.) Since the 1960s historians have often been quite open about the political standpoint from which they have written. Marxist or feminist historians, for instance, have sometimes seemed as interested in pointing out how more established versions of history have themselves been shaped by the specific interests of those by (and for) whom they were written – usually middle-class white males – as they have been in explaining the past 'as it really was'.

Yet while there is a broad acceptance among historians about the slipperiness of the concept of historical truth, and that facts are there to be interpreted in different ways, most find it difficult to accept that *all* historical accounts are equally valid. Our decisions as to which versions of history are most reliable may be based on our own political, cultural or moral beliefs, but this does not mean that the distinctions are unimportant. Historians, it could be said, have maintained the right to question and to challenge versions of the past. Yet while it is widely assumed that no account can be called 'true', some accounts can be more 'truthful' than others.

Professional historians, then, have come to accept that they do not hold a patent on the past. They are no longer in a position to argue that they alone have the right to manufacture and distribute versions of historical events. The history teacher who toured Canada with a film of General Wolfe in the 1920s, confidently argued that 'it was a good and accurate film' because it was 'made under the close supervision of learned historians'.[14] Such a view would have been out of place by the end of the twentieth century. The same could be said of the thoughts expressed by Louis Gottschalk, of the University of Chicago, in a letter to MGM studios in 1935: 'No picture of a historical nature ought to be offered to the public' he opined, 'until a reputable historian has had a chance to criticise it'.[15] Gottschalk's suggestion, of course, was not taken up and, unable to control the versions of history that made it onto the big screen, academic historians were usually dismissive of their value. By the end of the twentieth century, however, as the pursuit of historical truth was called into question, the historical value of feature films also came to be re-assessed.

The idea that feature films provide an equally valid interpretation of the past as academic history is by no means a dominant belief within the profession, but it is a view that has gained increasing credence in recent years. Tony Barta observed in 1998 that 'It was a relatively straight forward matter some years ago for historians to criticise the misrepresentations of dramatised versions of the past'. By the end of the 1990s, however, he considered the idea that film 'was more the creature of historical pressures than academic history' as being merely 'a delusion still to be found in some corners of the academy'.[16] Barta may have somewhat overstated the extent to which opinion has actually shifted, but the general trend is certainly clear enough. 'Thirty years ago', Robert Rosenstone wrote in 1995, 'the idea that historical film might be worthy of attention as a medium for seriously representing the past was unthinkable'.[17] Yet by the 1990s periodicals such as the *American Historical Review* and the *Journal of American History*, as well as bodies such as the American Historical Association and the Organisation of American Historians, were treating historical feature films seriously. Far from dismissing 'history by Hollywood', scholars such as Rosenstone, Robert Brent Toplin and Natalie Zemon Davis were addressing it as a subject in its own right.

There has been some movement in this direction in Britain too. It is not unusual for university students to be shown feature films, as well as given lectures, by their history tutors. Historical films are often discussed thoughtfully in publications such as *History Today*, and academic books have also begun to appear on the subject of historical feature films.[18] It is also worth mentioning that the *Historical Journal of Film, Radio and Television* was established in Britain in 1980, although it has since relocated to the United States.

Professional historians, clearly, have come to accept that the versions of the past presented in feature films cannot be ignored. But to what extent has the actual practice of academic historians been influenced by commercial film-making?

The historical film and the professional historian

For much of the twentieth century feature films were regarded as being unreliable as history precisely because the process of making a film was so far removed from the act of compiling a more reputable (written) historical account. There can certainly be little doubt that the demands of working in the medium of film require quite different skills from those needed to write a book. Film makers need to be adept at handling a multitude of practical problems which arise on a daily basis: shooting schedules, working with actors, editing and continuity, sound, scenery, studio politics and even the weather. To a much greater extent than academic historians, film makers need to be managers of people. This, in addition to the rather more obvious point that film makers need to express their ideas visually, means that professional historians are not usually well suited to making historical films.

Academic historians and film makers clearly work in different media and have quite different skills. This is not to say that they do not face similar problems, however, or that the purpose of their work is necessarily so different. Both film makers and academics are in a position to influence the way in which society thinks about the past. Neither can claim that the versions of history they present are absolutely true, and both have to face similar methodological problems: what to do about gaps in the evidence, what to leave out, how to decide what is the most important message to get across, and what the audience will actually want to see/read. The way in which these problems have been overcome, however, has usually varied between those working through film and those using the printed word.

Film makers often need to invent situations, characters and dialogue in order to provide their historical characters with a personality. Moreover, if narrative coherence and dramatic intensity are to be achieved, then some degree of artistic license needs to be permitted with regard to historical evidence. For instance, it is often necessary to simplify events, or to combine numerous historical figures into a few central characters in order to express the film's theme more clearly and powerfully. Such historical 'inaccuracies' would usually be criticised in a book, but should they be held against a film? Robert Rosenstone, for one, thinks not, arguing that 'on the screen, history must be fictional in order to be true'. According to Rosenstone, historians must come to terms with invention if they are to come to terms with historical films. This does not mean that they must abandon the notion of historical truth altogether. It means that they must accept that historical truth is *created by*, rather than *mirrored in*, accounts of the past. The way in which a 'truthful' historical account is presented on screen is necessarily different from the way written historical texts are created. What becomes important is not so much the factual details themselves, but the meaning imparted by the film – the message it sends to viewers and the historical authenticity of that message. Robert Brent Toplin puts it thus:

> I suggest that both praise and criticism are essential in judging the work of cinematic historians. ... it does not help simply to chastise cinematic historians, expecting them to operate under the most exacting standards of scholarship regarding the presentation of evidence. At the same time we need to be aware of the dangers of too much tolerance. Artistic creativity can be abused.[19]

By accepting the validity of historical film, and therefore accepting that others outside the academy might have something useful and interesting to say about the past, professional historians have, in effect, begun to extend the boundaries of what might be called the practice of history. As far as the feature film is concerned, the role of the historian is not just to create versions of the past, but to criticise and analyse them. The intention being to ensure that the interpretations of the past provided by those outside the academy are consistent with information and evidence available to those within it. In this sense the role of professional historian becomes as much that of cultural critic as archival researcher. It is not surprising, therefore, that it has tended to be those historians most interested in culture, symbolism and perception who have been most interested in exploring the possibilities of historical film making.

One historian who has done more than most to engage with film makers is Natalie Zemon Davis. Davis conceptualises her role as being that of a conversationalist, engaged in an ongoing dialogue not only with her historical sources, but also other scholars and with the consumers of history. The task of the historian, as Davis sees it, is not just to inform, but to listen. In her work on early modern Europe she has made every effort to listen to stories of previously neglected historical characters (nuns, beggars, men dressed in women's clothing), and has also been prepared to listen to contributions made to the historical 'conversation' by those outside the academy – notably film makers. Davis makes no claim for academic history being more reliable or authentic than filmed versions of the past. Historians, she argues, are better able to 'tell about the past' than to 're-create' or 'represent' it. Her message to film makers (delivered in a lecture to the American Film Institute) was not to produce pictures that were more accurate or authentic, but to allow greater scope for complexity, ambiguity and for alternative interpretations of the events depicted. Film makers, she argued, should have recourse to the equivalent of terms like 'perhaps' or 'may have been', and went on to cite several examples of how this had been (or could be) achieved.[20]

For historians such as Davis, dialogue with film makers is an important part of the process by which versions of the past are created and made publicly available. In her case 'dialogue' has taken the form of acting as historical consultant on the film *Le retour de Martin Guerre*, and in addressing the American Film Institute. Davis has not attempted to become a film maker herself but, like Rosenstone and Toplin, she does regard criticism of historical films and engagement with their makers to be a part of the practice of history.

As the legitimacy of non-written versions of the past has come to be accepted by at least some within the profession, we also find that increasing numbers of historians are seeking to present their work on screen as well as in print. Historians might not have become feature film makers, but in the UK at least, they are among the most sought after (and in some cases handsomely remunerated) presenters of television programmes. The likes of Simon Schama and David Starkey are more widely known for their television programmes than for their books. There is nothing new about historical documentaries appearing on television, or indeed in historians using television to reach a wider public. Yet whereas, say, A. J. P. Taylor used television in the 1960s to give a series of lectures on the history of warfare, the programmes written and fronted by Schama and Starkey contain a much wider range of visual imagery, including reconstructions of historical events and, just to bring the story full circle, excerpts from historical feature films. These are not simply cases of historians providing talking heads for television documentaries, these are historians who are choosing to present their work on screen as well as in print, knowing it will be the screen version on which they are judged by the vast majority of their audience.

In many respects the practice of history has remained unchanged for most of the twentieth century. History continues to be predominantly (though by no means entirely) a literary discipline, historians continue to rely on archival records as the basis for their research (though the range of evidence used has increased significantly), and the majority of historians continue to conduct research alone (or with the aid of a small number of research assistants). It would be difficult to argue that film makers have caused a radical change in the way most historians go about their work. This examination of the evolving relationship between professional historians and historical films, however, has attempted to illustrate some of the ways in which the practice of history has developed over the last century.

The reluctance of historians to accept the validity of filmed versions of the past for much of the twentieth century has reflected a more general discomfort with the idea that anyone outside the history profession was in a position to comment knowledgeably on the past. As long as historians hold to the view that their task is to uncover some kind of objective historical truth (however incomplete) there is a reluctance to accept that anyone outside the profession (much less the academy) is qualified to embark on such an undertaking. Where historians are prepared to argue that notions such as 'truth' and 'objectivity' are problematic, and that there can be many valid interpretations of the past, it becomes, for them, far easier to reject the notion that good history has to be academic history. The willingness of historians to accept that accounts of the past produced by non-academics can be both valid and valuable is largely, therefore, a consequence of developments that have taken place within the academy itself. By extending this recognition to historical films, historians are also conceding that good history does not even need to be written history. This is a very recent development, and potentially a highly significant one. Already we have seen some historians become much more actively engaged in discussions and collaborations with film makers; we have also seen a number of historians seeking to present their work on television as well as in print. The fundamental principles of historical research may not have altered significantly, but the way in which this research is presented, and the range of secondary sources to which historians refer, show signs of becoming even more diverse.

Notes

1   R. A. Rosenstone, *Visions of the Past: The Challenge of Film to Our Idea of History*, Cambridge MA, Harvard University Press, 1995, p. 45.
2   The cinematograph was, in fact, invented at the end of the nineteenth century, but the first historical feature films did not emerge until the second decade of the twentieth century.
3   Rosenstone, *Visions of the Past*, p. 3.
4   A. Aldgate, *Cinema and History: British Newsreels and the Spanish Civil War*, London, Scolar Press, 1979; N. Pronay, 'British Newsreels in the 1930s. 1: Audiences and Producers', *History*, 1971, vol. 56, pp. 411–18; *idem*, 'British Newsreels in the 1930s. 2: Their Policies and Impact', *History*, 1972, vol. 57, pp. 63–72; K. R. M. Short (ed.) *Feature Films as History*, London, Croom Helm, 1981.
5   J. Richards, *The Age of the Dream Palace: Cinema and Society in Britain 1930–1939*, London, Routledge and Kegan Paul, 1984; M. Chanan, *The Dream That Kicks: The Prehistory and Early Years of the Cinema in Britain*, London, Routledge, 1980, 2nd edn 1996; M. Dickinson and S. Street, *Cinema and State: The Film Industry and the British Government, 1927–1984*, London, BFI, 1985.
6   P. Sorlin, *The Film in History: Restaging the Past*, Oxford, Blackwell, 1980, p. 21.
7   W. T. Waugh, 'History in Moving Pictures', *History*, 1927, vol. 15, pp. 326–7.
8   Chanan, *The Dream that Kicks*; see also R. Armes, *Film and Reality: An Historical Survey*, Harmondsworth, Penguin, 1974, pp. 17–21.
9   Waugh, 'History in Moving Pictures', p. 324.
10   F. Wilkinson, 'New History Films', *Sight and Sound*, 1936, vol. 5, p. 100.
11   S. Harper, *Picturing the Past: The Rise and Fall of the British Costume Film*, London, BFI, 1994, p. 65.
12   Rosenstone, *Visions of the Past*, p. 46.
13   See above, Chapters 11 and 16.
14   Waugh, 'History in Moving Pictures', p. 324.
15   Rosenstone, *Visions of the Past*, pp. 45–6.
16   T. Barta (ed.) *Screening the Past: Film and the Representation of History*, Westport CT and London, Praeger, 1998, p. ix.
17   Rosenstone, *Visions of the Past*, p. 2.
18   For example Harper, *Picturing the Past*; Barta (ed.) *Screening the Past*; Rosenstone, *Visions of the Past*; M. Landy (ed.) *The Historical Film: History and Memory in Media*, London, Athlone Press, 2001; A. Kuhn and J. Stacey (eds) *Screen Histories: A Screen Reader*, Oxford, Oxford University Press, 1998.

19 R. B. Toplin, *History by Hollywood: The Use and Abuse of the American Past*, Chicago, University of Illinois Press, 1996, p. 2.
20 N. Z. Davis, ' "Any Resemblance to Persons Living or Dead": Film and the Challenge of Authenticity', *The Yale Review*, 198, vol. 76, pp. 457–82.

Further reading

The first attempts by professional historians working in Britain seriously to examine films as historical documents began in the late 1960s, and initially attention was focused mainly on 'factual' films such as newsreels and documentaries. For example N. Pronay, 'British Newsreels in the 1930s', *History*, 1971, vol. 56, pp. 411–18, and in *History*, 1972, vol. 57, pp. 63–72; also A. Aldgate, *Cinema and History: British Newsreels and the Spanish Civil War*, London, Scolar Press, 1979. By the beginning of the 1980s a body of literature was beginning to emerge in the US and the UK which dealt with commercial feature films as important historical documents. For example, P. Smith (ed.) *The Historian and Film*, Cambridge, Cambridge University Press, 1976; P. Sorlin, *The Film in History: Restaging the Past*, Oxford, Blackwell, 1980; K. R. M. Short (ed.) *Feature Films as History*, London, Croom Helm, 1981; R. Sklar, *Movie-Made America*, New York, Vintage Books, 1975; L. May, *Screening out the Past: The Birth of Mass Culture and the Motion Picture Industry*, Oxford, Oxford University Press, 1980. The growing interest of historians in feature films is neatly summarised in the opening chapter of A. Aldgate and J. Richards, *Best of British: Cinema and Society in Britain from 1930 to the Present*, London, I. B. Tauris, 1999 edn.

S. Harper, *Picturing the Past: The Rise and Fall of the British Costume Film*, London, BFI, 1994, shows how historical feature films made in Britain in the 1930s and 1940s were regarded by professional historians at that time, though her primary concern is the context in which feature films were created rather than the events or societies the films depicted. Early examples of academic historians beginning to engage with the feature film as a medium for interpreting and presenting historical events include: N. Z. Davis, ' "Any Resemblance to Persons Living or Dead": Film and the Challenge of Authenticity', *The Yale Review*, 1987, vol. 76, pp. 457–82. Since the mid-1990s a number of books have been produced by professional historians in the US and the UK (some of whom have worked as 'historical consultants' on commercial films) which have reflected thoughtfully on the representations of history provided on cinema screens: R. A. Rosenstone, *Visions of the Past: The Challenge of Film to Our Idea of History*, Cambridge MA, Harvard University Press, 1995; R. B. Toplin, *History by Hollywood: The Use and Abuse of the American Past*, Chicago, University of Illinois Press, 1996; T. Barta (ed.) *Screening the Past: Film and the Representation of History*, Westport CT and London, Praeger, 1998; M. Landy (ed.) *The Historical Film: History and Memory in Media*, London, Athlone, 2001.

As well as those within the history profession itself, there are also scholars in the field of media studies who have shown an interest in cinematic representations of the past. For example, G. Nowell-Smith, 'On History and the Cinema', *Screen*, 1990, vol. 31, pp. 160–71; A. Kuhn and J. Stacey (eds) *Screen Histories: A Screen Reader*, Oxford, Oxford University Press, 1998.

Chapter 18

Popular culture and the historians

Gareth Williams

Popular culture is easier to explore, or deplore, than to define, and decoupling its two constituent elements does not help the task of definition, for neither enjoys an agreed definitional status.

At the most recognisable level, *culture* is what the cultured do, enjoying, appreciating and practising artistic, musical and literary works. On the other hand the 'whole way of life' concept derived from anthropology makes culture virtually synonymous with society: as E. B. Tylor expressed it in 1871, 'that complex which includes knowledge, belief, art, morals, law, custom and any other capabilities and habits acquired by man as a member of society', or what the cultural theorist Stuart Hall has called 'the lived practices that enable a society, group or class to experience, define, interpret and make sense of its conditions of existence'.[1]

A culture that embraces the whole community must presumably be *popular*, though to Peter Burke, a specialist in early modern Europe, popular culture is the culture of the people who are not elites.[2] Raymond Williams, without whose observation about culture no discussion of popular culture can safely proceed – that it is simultaneously 'ordinary' and 'one of the two or three most complicated words in the English language' – saw *popular* as denoting 'low' or 'base' as early as the sixteenth century, the shift to the more modern meaning of 'widely-favoured' (tinged with 'a sense of calculation') having occurred by the nineteenth.[3] On this reading popular culture is subtly defined not by the people themselves but by others, and implies inferiority, an interpretation that has persuaded a whole generation of historians in the last quarter of the twentieth century to see the history of popular culture as the history of attempts to change it.

The difficulty here is that a history of popular culture that approaches it through the censorious eyes of its policemen shows the people as not so much *doing* as having things *done to* them: a way of life becomes a way of struggle. This conflictual approach is formulated, again by Stuart Hall who shares it, as 'a continuing tension' that is essential to the definition of popular culture, 'one of the sites where [the] struggle for and against a culture of the powerful is engaged'.[4] Hall is in the company of historians like Peter Bailey, Raphael

Samuel, Gareth Stedman Jones, Stephen and Eileen Yeo, and above all Edward Thompson, who uses metaphors not only of conflict but of warfare, of a cultural war zone with its battles for territory and counter-offensives; certainly more fields of struggle and contestation than of praise and celebration.[5]

It is important, however, as Peter Burke has cautioned us, to be aware of the substantial overlap between elite/dominant/learned culture and popular/ dominated/illiterate culture, and that often a two-way traffic can be discerned. Saints' days, parish wakes, carnivals and pre-industrial calendar festivities were not merely opportunities for letting off steam, they were actively sanctioned and sponsored by the gentry. Moreover, shaming rituals like charivaris, skimming- tons and rough ridings were permitted to emerge unscathed from campaigns to reform popular culture because that culture's active manifestations actually endorsed a patriarchal society. Early modernists point out how these shame- sanctions complemented those officially handed down by the courts because they subscribed to concepts and symbols expressed in the inversions and binary opposites which Stuart Clark has shown to be among the organising intellectual assumptions of the period.[6]

Yet the history of popular culture, though it can be defined by symbolic opposites, does not *have* to be conceived in oppositional terms. Richard Suggett, while entirely agreeing that popular culture has to be 'firmly grounded in the experience of social relations', shows how little pressure towards the reform of popular culture in eighteenth-century Wales came from the usual villains, the gentry and clergy, because they recognised the social pay-off to accrue from tolerating and patronising the characteristic popular activities of the Vale of Glamorgan. Suggett shows that popular cultural pastimes could be as much integrative as conflictual, with some festivities concerned with differentia- tion *between* groups and others with the structuring of relationships *within* them. He makes his case by drawing out the contrasting significances between patronal feast day celebration (the *gwyl mabsant*) which was an expression of the antagonistic competitive nature of inter-parochial relationships, and festivals like carnivals which expressed the internal ordering or re-ordering of social relation- ships *within* a group.[7]

The distinction derived from Matthew Arnold between an elevating high culture and a debasing mass culture lends itself to many parallel forms of expres- sion: high and low, respectable and rough, patrician and plebeian, polite and vulgar, elite and popular, dominant and dominated, a game for antonym anoraks where the second element in the combination is always pejorative, and the ordinary people seen as victims denied an active role in making their own culture. Edward Thompson's sturdy eighteenth-century plebeians, though, are far from deferential; popular – a term he never uses, preferring 'plebeian' – culture is to him a site of resistance to those in whose interests the Industrial Revolution was made.

Another Thompson arrives at the same conclusion from a different direction. In reviewing the devices of social control by which the great unwashed of nineteenth-century Britain were policed, Michael Thompson demands that we 'give due weight to the autonomous development of working-class culture': the working class generated their own values and attitudes – in sum their own cultural response – to meet the requirements of industrial society. 'It is indeed', writes *this* Thompson, 'unwarrantably condescending to the humble and anonymous masses to suppose that they were incapable of cultural development except as a result of instruction or coercion from outside'. People, however humble and unprivileged, did not need to be instructed about cleanliness or have the importance of family life drummed into them. The working class were not puppets dancing at the end of bourgeois strings; to the contrary, Thompson muses, in so far as the middle class adapted and modified what the working class desired, some aspects of popular culture might have been suggested by the working class to the bourgeoisie.[8]

This might well have been the case with what in the nineteenth century became the organised, codified sports of football, cricket and boxing, as the surprising yet relatively recent upsurge in the history of sport suggests.[9] The surprise lies in the recentness not the topic: historians have been slow to appreciate the significance of Anna Karenina's husband's observation that 'sport has a deep value and as is always the case we see only its superficial aspect'.[10] As the twentieth century unfolded sport became a commercial phenomenon, a signifier of gender, nationality and ethnicity, and increasingly global. But if sport was everywhere, its serious scholars were nowhere. When in the 1960s the anthropologist Max Gluckman took his Manchester University students to Old Trafford it was to watch the crowd, not the football. As late as 1971 Eugen Weber noted that 'grandfather clocks, balloons and potatoes have benefited from historical studies that games and sports still lack'.[11]

That lack was about to be remedied. The 1960s had seen social history begin to acquire a new legitimacy. Christopher Hill, Eric Hobsbawm and Edward Thompson blazed the trail, and other pathfinders began to open up tracts of unexplored, often previously invisible, territory. At the same time a new wave of cultural criticism, conceived within a broadly Marxist theory and influenced by the work of Richard Hoggart and Raymond Williams, saw a British sociology of leisure emerge. Sport, like popular culture generally, would eventually find its historians (and its sociologists), especially among those of a Marxist hue – a somewhat unexpected development given that historians of the working class had generally shown themselves to be more at home with work than pleasure, with Black Friday than Sheffield Wednesday.[12] Sports history was moving away from the antiquarian, the commemorative and the statistical to explore 'the ways in which sport was historically constituted and shaped by socio-economic, political and ideological forces'.[13] In the 1970s and early 1980s a generation exposed to the mass coverage of sports on television wrote the first serious historical studies of horse-racing, English soccer and Welsh rugby.[14] The crucial paradigm-shifter was Tony Mason, whose *Association Football and English Society 1863–1915*, published in 1980, penetrated hitherto no-go areas like the background and living standards of the players, the composition of the crowds who idolised and vilified them, and the economic structure of the clubs: in other words who played, who watched and who controlled the people's game. With its clear sense on the one hand of the organic relationship between sport and wider social questions, and on the other of the tensions and pleasures intrinsic to its pursuit as a social activity, Mason opened the floodgates to a shoal of studies written by historians who were clearly waving not drowning in the sea of mass-mediated popular culture which saturated virtually every aspect of their daily existence.[15] The historians and sociologists who launched and kept afloat the new journals of popular culture and sports history thereby became subsumed within the popular culture whose study they themselves were defining and legitimising.

The extent of this literature can be gauged from R. W. Cox's bibliographical guides, especially his *Sport in Britain: A Bibliography of Historical Publications* (1991) and its regular update in *The Sports Historian*, the journal of the British Society of Sports History (founded in 1983), one of the new breed of serials like *The International Journal of the History of Sport* (1984–) that has counterparts in the USA (*Journal of Sport History*, 1984–), Canada (*The Canadian Journal of the History of Sport*, 1986–), Australia (*Sporting Traditions*, 1984–) and, outside the English-speaking world, France (*Sport Histoire*, 1988–). During the 1990s the Frank Cass publishing house has built up an impressive sports history catalogue, and Manchester University Press has both an *International Studies in the History of Sport* series edited by J. A. Mangan, and a series of *Studies in Popular Culture* under the editorship of Jeffrey Richards. An example of the media utilising to its benefit popular culture's newfound friends in the academy occurred when historians scripted, advised and made frequent appearances on the well received BBC2 series *The Union Game* which sought 'to stitch social history and sporting activity into a whole' and was screened to coincide with the Rugby World Cup in Cardiff in late 1999.[16] Elsewhere, dedicated museums and heritage centres began to give increasing prominence to leisure and recreational life while institutions that once would have found the artefacts of sport irredeemably vulgar also responded to the new cultural climate. Christie's held its first auction of sporting memorabilia in 1995, and between October 1998 and January 1999 the National Portrait Gallery mounted an exhibition of British Sporting Heroes. It was accompanied by a handsomely illustrated volume combining celebration and analysis by Richard Holt,[17] one of the foremost practitioners of sports history world-wide, and a member of De Montfort University's pioneering International Centre for History and Culture; significantly his *Sport and the British: A Modern History* (1989) made its first appearance in OUP's *Studies in Social History* under the rigorous general editorship of Keith Thomas, himself once a member of the Barry Grammar School cricket First Eleven.

If the embrace of the popular by universities and their presses, prestigious sales-rooms and publishing houses was relatively new, a definition of culture that accommodated it could already be found in equally unlikely places. The first eight of T. S. Eliot's thirteen 'characteristic ... interests of a people' were sporting: 'Derby Day, Henley Regatta, Cowes, the Twelfth of August, a cup final, the dog races, the pin table, [and] the dart board', as well as 'Wensleydale cheese, boiled cabbage cut into sections, beetroot in vinegar, nineteenth century Gothic churches, and the music of Elgar'.[18] Cricket on the village green fortified by warm beer and visions of old maids bicycling to church through the morning mist may have constituted prime minister John Major's sense of English culture, but the man who was about to supplant him made the point more succinctly when he told the Football Association on the occasion of Stanley Matthews' eightieth birthday that Matthews was 'a culture in himself', the embodiment of sporting values whose apparent decline the speaker, Tony Blair, regretted.[19] But the historian Mason had already provided a sharper historical appraisal of Sir Stan that eschewed nostalgia or belief in a golden age.[20]

Work on the social history of rugby football in Wales is a notable case of all history as contemporary history and of a popular culture imposing its own agendas on its historians, for it was not difficult for graduates of the postwar generation enthusiastic about sport, privileged by educational opportunity and excited by the new social history to be intrigued by its development in an industrial society like South Wales over the previous hundred years, and which in this particular case seemed to have reached its dazzling apotheosis in the pyrotechnic artistry of Gareth Edwards, Gerald Davies, Barry John and other wizards of Welsh rugby's 'golden era' of the 1970s.[21] The subsequent collapse of the Welsh rugby narrative in an incoherent morass of undignified wrangles over television rights and professionalism suggested, since it coincided with the sudden deindustrialisation of their country,[22] the classic postmodernist condition. As Jeffrey Hill points out, a postmodern history of sport will have to focus, as the best sports history always has done, on what sporting heroes 'mean' to their public in terms of the emotional capital invested in them by their adoring public, and how a star, a performance, a following, a funeral,[23] can be read as texts where a variety of competing and inter-connecting discourses can be played out, 'cultural artefacts over which meaning is contested'.[24] For while it could be claimed that this is merely to follow fashions in literary theory, it is the historian's obligation to be aware of the specific *historical* context in which the reading is taking place.[25] What the public gets – what is mediated to the public, as opposed to what the public wants – is where any deconstruction of a popular cultural hero like the sports star must surely begin.

We are back to mediation, which has a crucial role to play, to take a non-sporting example, in the early twentieth-century 'revival' of English folk song. The collecting and saving of English folk songs in the late nineteenth century by antiquarian clergymen like the Reverends John Broadwood and Sabine Baring-Gould involved seeking out old country singers in pubs, workhouses and almshouses. Many singers were shy about these songs and reluctant about singing them to strangers, especially when they were in clerical garb and accompanied by the squire. Often what the visitors were offered was not a genuine folksong but a schoolroom memory. Baring-Gould succumbed to the desire to improve the ballads according to the literary and musical criteria of the time and contemporary notions of decency. A further complication arose when Cecil Sharp's interest in publishing his discoveries led him to the reasonable belief that songs could only live and be meaningful if memorised and sung, and he saw schools as commercially his main market as well as being the best hope for preservation. This entailed tidying the words up for school consumption, bowdlerising them and arranging the music for piano. Thus folksong became a fabrication, 'fakesong', scarcely the organic, authentic, genuinely spontaneous creation of the people it purported to be.[26]

Mediation presents problems for the stark binary model of high and low, respectable and rough cultural opposites. A particular difficulty for disciples of Gramsci is the little space a bipolar representation allows for 'negotiation', a subtle process whereby the working class are persuaded rather than coerced into apparently voluntarily adopting middle-class values like playing by the rules, or indeed the notion of amateur sport itself. Assimilated and reinterpreted, they become integrated into working-class traditions, and hegemony is achieved by a ready acceptance of bourgeois values; sport then becomes part of a wider cultural process that makes the workers submissive to hierarchy whilst unthinkingly accepting the competitive principle. This view refuses to see ordinary people as always being moulded, repressed and reformed; what it does see is the active production of culture as above its passive consumption. Ignoring the elements of integration as well as resistance, and seeing the population at large as consumers who merely appropriate what is on offer, is to deny them any creative function, when in fact appropriation and selection can themselves be a creative process. It is, then, too defeatist to see sport or music-making – say the emergence of brass bands and choral singing in nineteenth-century industrial communities in England and Wales[27] – as a culture of consolation embraced by the powerless, the subordinate, the underprivileged and the repressed. John Fiske goes further by giving a subtle spin to Gramscian hegemony in his proposal that popular culture is made by subordinate groups apparently in their own interest from resources provided by a social system that actually disempowers them: thus, today's satellite TV dishes, designer clothes, video games and mobile phones are avidly pursued by the working class to the economic benefit of those above.[28]

Of course, these objects of conspicuous consumption are hardly 'traditional', another word fraught with danger for the historian. Popular culture is constantly remaking itself. Traditional customs, sports and rituals, after their demise, Mark Twain-like, had been announced in the early nineteenth century, had a remarkable capacity for survival, though not necessarily in precisely the same form but with adaptations and adjustments to new constraints and pressures. We have been well advised 'to be sensitive to possible changes in context and content and not confuse the apparent continuity in form with a continuity of function and meaning'.[29] We have always to be on our guard against claims that a particular custom had been practised this way since time immemorial or that any particular custom was on its last legs. The past is a soft target for sentimentality and it is just as easy to envelop the industrial working-class community in the cosy shawl of warm communal fellowship and neighbourliness as to conjure up a supposed rural arcadia, both perspectives preferring to ignore evidence of the violence, abuse, neglect and exploitation that too often characterised the world we have lost.

A 'traditional' popular culture of maypoles, cakes and ale obituarised in the early nineteenth century is also at odds with the accumulated studies of the last two decades regarding the commercialisation of leisure in seventeenth- and eighteenth-century England. It is easily thirty years since J. H. Plumb drew attention to this phenomenon, citing a gentry who sought to encourage, promote and profit from horse-racing, prize-fighting and cricket, sports that were already drawing large numbers of spectators.[30] What we have since learned about the pre-industrial 'urban renaissance' has added a gloss to this picture.[31]

As for popular recreations, the pioneering work of Robert Malcolmson has stood the test of time less well.[32] The anthropologically derived insights he brought to bear on the social function of a rich calendar of holidays, games and general pastimes certainly shed further light on the canvas of a thriving eighteenth-century rural culture. Where doubt arises is in his readiness to subscribe to the vacuum theory of leisure: that between 1780 and 1830 the combined forces of enclosing landlords, evangelical reformers and the demands of a new labour discipline marked the end of such recreations as the old game of football, along with bloodsports and 'traditional' pastimes in general. Whether recreational life was so dramatically transformed is open to question, for custom is tenacious and there is little evidence for the reform of popular culture having had much influence on eighteenth-century Glamorgan where, as we have seen, patronal festivities, including maypoles, bandy-ball, bull-baiting and fist-fighting continued to enjoy the enthusiastic sponsorship of the local rulers. What happened to rituals like the *twmpath* (folk-dancing), *ceffyl pren* (skimmington) and *cwrw bach* (shebeens) was their shift from the Vale of Glamorgan to the rough environment of the iron-making uplands, where they were taken up with renewed vigour. Merthyr Tydfil's notorious criminal quarter, 'China', was pure Beggar's Opera, where pastimes as diverse as foot-racing and the Mari Lwyd (the grey mare, a wassailing custom) entered on a new lease of life.[33]

Here we are once again compelled to face the difficulty inherent in the use of the heavily freighted term 'traditional society'. For one thing the industrial revolution was not a great disjunction between early modern and modern. Traditional is not a synonym for changeless, and in any case rarely extends further back than three generations. It is doubtful whether any society has known a period before change began. Our historical sense demands that we pause before signing up to a Merrie England (or Wales) of festive frolics, warm, unsophisticated and unchanging, if only because the highly capitalistic nature of an English countryside penetrated by commercial relationships from at least the sixteenth century is accepted by most early modernists. Idealising the cheery, organised popular culture of a golden pre-industrial age peopled by mute inglo-rious Miltons is to polarise, after the fashion of F. R. Leavis, Denys Thompson and the Scrutinisers of the 1930s, a spontaneous and active 'folk' at one end and a dulled, passive audience inertly soaking up modern mass culture at the other. The only sensible conclusion must be that there never was a traditional popular culture, since, being a social product, like society itself, it is always changing.

While Malcolmson's account of an enforced reconstruction of recreational life meshed with the pessimistic interpretation of the social consequences of the industrial revolution by his mentor, Edward Thompson, it was also going against the grain of Thompson's insistence on the capacity of ordinary people to make and re-make their own culture. Hugh Cunningham, by insisting on the working class's ability to think and act for itself (and confessing to his unease at finding himself thereby thrust into the 'unwelcome embrace' of the optimist school of historians) cannot accept that there *was*, by 1850, a vacuum in popular recreations.[34] Age-old sports and pastimes like Fifth of November cele-brations may have acquired new meanings – we recall Tim Harris' point about confusing continuity of form and function – but the rise of industrial society did not sign their death warrant either. Quite the reverse, since new economic conditions provided new opportunities and a reshaped environment for their continuance: the advent of the railways provided yet larger audiences for public hangings, seaside excursions became literally more common, and the Turf was transformed from being the preserve of the Quality and the Fancy to becoming a regular spectator sport. And as horse-racing was diffused downwards, other sports like pugilism and cricket moved socially upwards: what were once class-specific activities were by the mid-nineteenth century well on the way to becoming the entertainments of the masses, for there were now more people to participate and watch, and better means of transport to get them there. The railways ensured not the strangulation of custom but its survival. The Lancashire wakes were revitalised and community identity reinforced when the railways transported whole streets in Oldham to adjacent boarding houses in Blackpool run by people from their own town.[35]

Those 'traditional' dispensers of sociability, the brewers and publicans, to whom popular amusements had long been an opportunity for commercial advantage, agreeably personified this type of pre-industrial continuity. It is unsurprising that in the nineteenth-century many of them diversified into managing circuses, movable theatres and the music hall, for these were the insti-tutional expressions of a carnival culture, profane, playful, sensual, liberating and often offensive, implicitly challenging a repressive and disciplinary social order. If it is the generosity and spontaneity of popular culture that predisposes historians to speak appreciatively of it, it is an appreciation derived from

Bakhtin's study of Rabelais and from Ginzburg's hapless Menocchio, an hitherto obscure miller – rational, anti-clerical and cussed – from the Friuli in northeast Italy who fell foul of the Inquisition in 1599 and whose scandalous ideas show a striking convergence with those of the more educated intellectual groups of his day. There are traces in Menocchio's robust irreverence of the anarchic, carnivalesque bawdy world of Breughel as well as Rabelais, which prompts the thought that European high culture of the sixteenth century might have had popular roots, and that what we are actually observing here is that two-way cultural exchange that Bakhtin calls 'circularity', a reciprocal relationship between the dominant and subordinate classes of pre-industrial Europe.[36]

Finally, why are we ready to be so appreciative of past activities whose present-day equivalents provide embarrassment if not downright hostility? It is relatively easy to applaud what is safely distanced from us in the past, and the German Reformation scholar Gerald Strauss, concerned that to extol popular culture 'exalts the commonplace [and] legitimises a know-nothing counter-culturalism', admits to reservations about conferring on the popular cultural activities of the past a dignity, weight and significance that we would deny equivalent activities in our own day. Are all these carnival pranks, village feuds and charivaris, he asks, 'those more or less identical specimens of adolescent rowdyism, urban rioting ... and peasant pig-headedness really worth the heavy hermeneutics lavished on them?'[37] The answer must be that any approach, any technique that contributes to recovering the lives of those lost to history, the powerless, the submerged, the marginalised and the forgotten, is its own justification.

Notes

1 Both quoted in T. Eagleton, *The Idea of Culture*, Oxford, Blackwell, 2000, p. 34.
2 P. Burke, *Popular Culture in Early Modern Europe*, London, Temple Smith, 1978.
3 R. Williams, *Keywords: A Vocabulary of Culture and Society*, London, Fontana, 1976, p. 76.
4 S. Hall, 'Notes on Deconstructing the Popular', in R. Samuel (ed.) *People's History and Socialist Theory*, London, Routledge and Kegan Paul, 1981, pp. 235, 239.
5 P. Burke, 'Revolution in Popular Culture', in R. Porter and M. Teich (eds) *Revolution in History*, Cambridge, Cambridge University Press, 1986, pp. 212, 223 n. 28.
6 S. Clark, *Thinking With Demons: The Idea of Witchcraft in Early Modern Europe*, Oxford, Clarendon Press, 1997, pp. 38–42.
7 R. Suggett, 'Festivals and Social Structure in Early Modern Wales', *Past and Present*, 1996, vol. 152, pp. 108–9.
8 F. M. L. Thompson, 'Social Control in Victorian Britain', *Economic History Review*, 1981, vol. 34, pp. 189–208.
9 For a useful overview see N. Tranter, *Sport, Economy and Society in Britain 1750–1914*, Cambridge, Cambridge University Press, 1998, pp. 13–31.
10 L. Tolstoy, *Anna Karenina*, ch. 28.
11 E. Weber, 'Gymnastics and Sport in *fin-de-siècle* France', *American Historical Review*, 1971, vol. 76, p. 70.
12 K. O. Morgan in the *Times Literary Supplement*, 13 February 1981, p. 157.

13 S. G. Jones, *Sport, Politics and the Working Class*, Manchester, Manchester University Press, 1988, p. 2.

14 W. Vamplew, *The Turf. A Social and Economic History of Horse Racing*, London, Allen Lane, 1976; T. Mason, *Association Football and English Society 1863–1915*, Brighton, Harvester Press, 1980; D. Smith and G. Williams, *Fields of Praise*, Cardiff, University of Wales Press, 1980.

15 See the appreciation by Richard Holt and others in *The Sports Historian*, May 2002, vol. 22:1, a special edition entitled *Sporting Lives: Essays in History and Biography presented to Tony Mason*.

16 D. Smith, 'Introduction', in S. Smith, *The Union Game: A Rugby History*, London, BBC Consumer Publishing, 1999, p. 8.

17 Richard Holt, 'Introduction', pp. 10–25, in *The Book of British Sporting Heroes*, London, National Portrait Gallery, 1998, compiled by James Huntington-Whiteley.

18 T. S. Eliot, *Notes Towards a Definition of Culture*, London, Faber and Faber, 1948, p. 31.

19 M. Polley, *Moving the Goalposts: A History of Sport and Society since 1945*, London, Routledge, 1998, p. 1.

20 T. Mason, 'Stanley Matthews', in R. Holt (ed.) *Sport and the Working Class in Modern Britain*, Manchester, Manchester University Press, 1990, pp. 159–78.

21 Smith and Williams, *Fields of Praise*, pp. 407–58.

22 D. Smith and G. Williams, 'Beyond the Fields of Praise', in H. Richards, P. Stead and G. Williams (eds) *More Heart and Soul – The Character of Welsh Rugby*, Cardiff, University of Wales Press, 2000, pp. 205–32.

23 See the description of the funeral of the boxer Jim Driscoll in P. O'Leary, *Immigration and Integration: The Irish in Wales 1789–1922*, Cardiff, University of Wales Press, 2000, pp. 1–2.

24 J. Hill, 'Reading the Stars: A Post-Modernist Approach to Sports History', *The Sports Historian*, 1994, vol. 14, pp. 45–55.

25 *Ibid.*, p. 54.

26 D. Harker, *Fakesong: The Manufacture of British 'Folksong' from 1700 to the Present Day*, Milton Keynes, Open University Press, 1990.

27 D. Russell, *Popular Music in England 1840–1914: A Social History*, Manchester, Manchester University Press, 1987; G. Williams, *Valleys of Song: Music and Society in Wales 1840–1914*, Cardiff, University of Wales Press, 1998.

28 J. Fiske, *Understanding Popular Culture*, London, Routledge, 1982, pp. 1–2.

29 T. Harris, 'Problematising Popular Culture', in T. Harris (ed.) *Popular Culture in England c.1500–1850*, London, Macmillan, 1995, pp. 1–27, quotation at p. 23.

30 J. H. Plumb, *The Commercialisation of Leisure in Eighteenth Century England*, Reading, University of Reading Press, 1973.

31 P. Borsay, *The English Urban Renaissance: Culture and Society in the Provincial Town*, Oxford, Oxford University Press, 1989.

32 R. W. Malcolmson, *Popular Recreations in English Society 1700–1850*, Cambridge, Cambridge University Press, 1973.

33 Gwyn A. Williams in Glanmor Williams (ed.) *Merthyr Politics*, Cardiff, University of Wales Press, 1966, pp. 17–18.

34 H. Cunningham, *Leisure in the Industrial Revolution: c.1780–c.1880*, New York, St Martin's Press, 1980, p. 9.

35 R. Poole and J. K. Walton, 'The Lancashire Wakes in Nineteenth Century England', in R. D. Storch (ed.) *Popular Culture and Custom in Nineteenth Century England*, New York, St Martin's Press, 1982, pp. 100–24.

36 M. Bakhtin, *Rabelais and His World*, English translation by Hélène Iswolsky, Cambridge MA, MIT Press, 1968; C. Ginzburg, *The Cheese and the Worms: The*

Cosmos of a Sixteenth-century Miller, English translation by John and Anne Tedeschi, London, Routledge and Kegan Paul, 1980.
37 G. Strauss, 'The Dilemma of Popular History', *Past and Present*, 1991, vol. 132, pp. 130–49, quotation at p. 138.

Further reading

Historians have preferred to engage with the practice of popular culture rather than its theory, but two useful guides to theoretical approaches are J. Fiske, *Understanding Popular Culture*, London, Routledge, 1991; and J. Storey, *An Introductory Guide to Cultural Theory and Popular Culture*, London, Harvester Wheatsheaf, 1993. A valuable historiographical review tracing historians' deployment of the concept of popular culture since the 1970s, when it first entered their lexicon, is E. Griffin, 'Popular Culture in Industrialising England', *Historical Journal*, 2002, vol. 45, pp. 619–35.

The most illuminating explorations of popular culture in early modern society *c*.1500–1800, remain the magisterial works of K. Thomas, *Religion and the Decline of Magic: Studies in Popular Beliefs in Sixteenth and Seventeenth Century England*, London, Weidenfeld and Nicolson, 1971 (now regularly reprinted by Penguin) and P. Burke, *Popular Culture in Early Modern Europe*, London, Temple Smith, 1976. Burke's further reflections on the historiography of this theme are to be found in his essay 'Revolution in popular culture', in R. Porter and M. Teich (eds) *Revolution in History*, Cambridge, Cambridge University Press, 1986. Inevitably influenced by Thomas and Burke – hardly a crime – are the contributors to T. Harris (ed.) *Popular Culture in England c.1500–1850*, London, Macmillan, 1995; and B. Reay, *Popular Cultures in England 1550–1750*, London, Longman, 1998. For sheer intellectual dynamism combined with stylistic verve, E. P. Thompson's essays *Customs in Common*, London, Penguin, 1993, are required reading.

For the industrial period the thoroughfare has become as crowded as a Lowry canvas. A wide-ranging reader is B. Waites, T. Bennett and G. Martin (eds) *Popular Culture: Past and Present*, London, Croom Helm with the Open University, 1983; while the notion that the history of popular culture is mostly the history of attempts to control it underlies the by now classic collections of E. Yeo and S. Yeo (eds) *Popular Culture and Class Conflict 1590–1914*, Hassocks, Brighton, 1983; A. P. Donajgrodski (ed.) *Social Control in Nineteenth-century Britain*, London, Croom Helm, 1977; and R. Storch (ed.) *Popular Culture and Custom in Nineteenth-century England*, London, Croom Helm, 1982. J. M. Golby and A. M. Purdue, *Popular Culture in England 1750–1900*, London, Batsford, 1984, revised edn 1999, argue zestfully against the notion of industrialisation and urbanisation as a watershed for popular culture and emphasise the importance of continuity from the pre-industrial era. The rationalisation of working-class recreation is the theme of P. Bailey, *Leisure and Class in Victorian England*, Methuen, revised edn 1987, and the music hall his focus in *Politics and Performance in the Victorian City*, Cambridge,

Cambridge University Press, 1998. Knotty but rewarding are G. Stedman Jones, *Languages of Class: Studies in English Working Class History*, Cambridge, Cambridge University Press, 1983; and P. Joyce, *Visions of the People*, Cambridge, Cambridge University Press, 1991, especially Part iii, 'Custom, History, Language: Popular Culture and the Social Order'. A range of topics from sport and the cinema to smoking and the seaside are explored in two enterprising monograph series published by Manchester University Press, *Studies in Popular Culture* (ed. Jeffrey Richards) and *International Studies in the History of Sport* (ed. J. A. Mangan), while these and other popular cultural pursuits are given a suggestive postmodern inflection in J. Hill, *Sport, Leisure and Culture in Twentieth Century Britain*, Basingstoke, Palgrave, 2002. Newcomers to the field, having consulted R. Williams, *Keywords*, London, Collins, 1976, for contested definitions of 'popular' and 'culture', will find an original reading of the master's thought in D. Williams (ed.) *Who Speaks for Wales? Nation, Culture, Identity: Raymond Williams*, Cardiff, University of Wales Press, 2003.

Chapter 19

History and 'amateur' history

William D. Rubinstein

Beyond the type of history practised and engaged in by university academics there is a vast other-world of amateur, antiquarian, popular, and public historians who are almost invariably ignored by university historians, just as these outsiders ignore the academics. In number, they surely dwarf the university contingent by many orders of magnitude. In the year 2000, for instance, there were about 2,900 university lecturers in history in the United Kingdom. By contrast, the monthly British magazine *History Today*, a valuable, well illustrated journal of popular history, sells 30,000 copies per issue. The great majority of these must be purchased by ordinary members of the reading public who are keenly interested in history but have little or no connection with, or understanding of, academic history or historians. The aim of this essay is to survey some of the most popular varieties of non-academic history, examining what they have in common with academic history as this is pursued by university academics, but also how they differ. One such field, that of museum or heritage studies (and the work of professional archivists) is deliberately not examined here, as it is an established profession of its own closely akin to the work of academic historians and normally requiring a post-tertiary degree in history or a related subject.[1] Most or all of the areas discussed here are dominated by the non-professional historian – often, indeed, by persons wholly lacking in formal university training in history.

Unquestionably the most important single area of 'history beyond the university' is family history or genealogy, a subject pursued by literally hundreds of thousands of people around the world, and one with an elaborate infrastructure of institutions, data banks, internet sites, and dedicated journals and societies. Family history must, in fact, be vastly greater in size than the whole enterprise of academic historiography. Family history normally concerns an attempt to build up one's own family tree (or the family tree of a close relative), identifying as many of one's ancestors as possible, or a closely related enterprise. (There are, for instance, many so-called 'Single Name Societies', devoted to researching the histories of everyone named Brown, Esterhazy, Blair, Hague, or any other name.) Family historiography's *raison d'être* is the unquestionably true axiom that every single human being, without exception, has two parents, four grandparents, eight great-grandparents, and so on *ad infinitum*, a truth which holds equally well for those in the highest places or the lowest. Although modern genealogical research began among the aristocracy and the wealthy classes, who in Britain often attempted to show their descent from the Norman nobility, paradoxically the fact that every single person has the same number of ancestors has meant that genealogical research has become a popular mass pursuit. In Britain, parish registers recording most births, marriages and deaths exist dating back to the time of Henry VIII, while the civil registration of all births, marriages and deaths dates from 1837. Indexes with tens of millions of names can be consulted in London. Other countries have similar records, many of which have been collected by the Mormons (the Church of Jesus Christ of the Latter Day Saints) which retroactively baptises the ancestors of its members (including those converted to Mormonism from other religions). An enormous industry of genealogical research and family history has thus grown up, expanding exponentially during the past generation. The Society of Genealogists, the main English family history body, with an extensive headquarters and library near the Barbican in London, currently has nearly 15,000 members. Writers and publishers have not been slow to spot this as a growth area. The Society of Genealogists produces a 'bookshelf catalogue' of works available for sale to its members which currently lists about 1,500 items. These include not merely general works about family history but highly specific and particular works, such as a thirty-three volume series of 'London Apprentices', giving the names of boy apprentices to the City of London's livery companies between 1600 and 1800, or the twenty-five volumes of muster rolls of country militias in 1781–2. Increasingly, computers have inevitably been enlisted as an aid to genealogists, with more than thirty genealogy software packages advertised for sale. The aim of all this, for most genealogists and family historians, is to build up as comprehensive a picture of their own ancestry as possible. Although few genealogists are academically trained historians, they are engaging in *bona-fide* historical research, and it is worth comparing what they do to what the academic historian is normally attempting to do.

To a remarkable extent, the intellectual format of questions addressed by family historians is similar to those addressed by academic historians. The family historian begins by posing a factual certainty such as 'I have sixteen great-great-grandparents', and then asks 'who were they?' Much in what academic historians habitually do when they are engaged in research and writing is very similar. For instance, one might proceed from the factual certainty that Winston Churchill became British Prime Minister in May 1940, replacing Neville Chamberlain, to ask 'why was this?' The question of 'why' in this case (and in virtually all other cases addressed by the academic historian) is much more complex, subtle and multi-faceted than the question addressed by the family historian, but they are, essentially, logically very similar. In this case, the historian examining the replacement of Chamberlain by Churchill would certainly have to examine public opinion, press opinion, the feelings of backbenchers in the ruling Conservative party and the views of the opposition Labour party, and so on, as well, of course, as the perspective of Chamberlain, Churchill, and other Cabinet and front bench leaders, and the deteriorating military situation. The historian would also certainly wish to explain why Churchill became prime minister rather than his rival Lord Halifax, which would entail an examination of, for instance, the role of King George VI, who actually chose Churchill. Nevertheless, despite the seeming complexity of the task, what the academic historian attempts to do here is similar to what the family historian does, in being finite in its goals, definite in its aims, and requiring pertinent and relevant evidence and information. It does, however, differ from what the family historian is attempting to do in some clear-cut ways. Most strikingly, it has no absolutely right or wrong answer as such, and many well qualified and expert historians have given markedly different accounts of this event, some emphasising one factor (say the celebrated debates in the House of Commons after the German conquest of Norway) and some very different factors (for instance Chamberlain's poor health, or shifts in Labour party opinion). In contrast, there are sixteen great-great-grandparents to be identified, and once that is done, the task is definitely completed and all that there is to be known is known, barring only the discovery of some wholly unexpected new evidence, for instance that one great-grandparent was in fact fathered on the wrong side of the blanket by someone else. Although the family historian's task can be completed, the academic historian's never really is, with new works written all the time on familiar events which examine them with fresh eyes and, surprisingly often, new evidence. In the example just mentioned, for instance, it seems a virtual certainty that over the next forty years several, perhaps many, new works by academic historians examining Churchill's coming to power will be written, all of which will claim to have something new to say.

To be sure, there are issues examined by academic historians which are much more complicated than the answers sought by family historians, especially for events in pre-modern times. (Was Latin a vernacular language in Roman or pre-Roman Britain? What languages were spoken in Britain in 2000BC?) Even in modern times, some very important historical questions cannot satisfactorily be answered, given the evidence which exists. (When and why did Hitler decide to kill the Jews? Did President Franklin Roosevelt know of Japan's impending attack on Pearl Harbor ahead of time?) Some historical questions are so speculative that academic historians have steered clear of them entirely, leaving the field to 'amateur' researchers and inquirers. (Did Lee Harvey Oswald act alone? Who was 'the man in the iron mask'?) Some fields of history are *a priori* more complicated than are tackled by family historians, for instance econometric-oriented economic history, which requires a highly technical knowledge of economic theory and sophisticated mathematical techniques. Nevertheless, even in these areas there are surprising parallels. While some questions in family history are probably unanswerable in most cases (who was my grandmother's great-great-grandmother?), approximate answers, probably accurate to within a certain margin of error, can be advanced. For instance, one can be fairly certain that one's grandmother's great-great-grandmother came from Staffordshire and was born around 1790, and one can be absolutely certain that she was not born in China or Ethiopia or in Buckingham Palace. The family historian must also sift through conflicting evidence in almost precisely the same manner as the academic historian must weigh evidence and arrive at the best interpretation of the sources, for instance in deciding which man (if any) named 'Clarkson', given a choice of three men of that name appearing in an eighteenth-century parish register, was one's actual ancestor. The family historian must also avoid wishful thinking in dealing with the evidence, for instance in postulating a family relationship between one's ancestor and a gentry family of the same name living nearby. This was very often actually done in family trees prepared for late nineteenth-century business and professional families in Britain keen to show the early high status of their ancestors. Many families whose genealogies appear in *Burke's Landed Gentry* and similar works have what is known in the trade as 'the slide', whereby a member of a well born or gentry family is grafted onto the family tree with a statement such as 'known to be living in the vicinity' or 'very likely the ancestor of'. Academic historians have been known to shade evidence in order to demonstrate the accuracy of their interpretations, in similar ways, for instance giving manifestly greater weight to a statement or remark made in the past than is objectively deserved. (This is very different from actually inventing evidence, which would mark the historian out as a fraud and a charlatan.)

There are, therefore, very many ways in which what the family historian and the academic historian do are extremely similar, even identical, especially in the investigatory process both undertake. Where they part company, however, is in the sophistication with which they pursue their aims. The family historian is only concerned with building up a factual account of his or her family tree, pushing it as far back as possible and tracing as many branches as possible. Some full-scale family histories, especially those compiled in the recent past, are much more sophisticated, attempting to link the evolution of a family to socio-economic conditions and the political background of the time, employing letters, diaries and general histories to this end. Some, indeed, do not differ in any real way from a family biography written by an academic historian, say of a prominent business dynasty. Nevertheless, there are almost always perceptible differences. Academic historians normally proceed, as it were, the other way round, placing a specific subject in the wider context of a national history or the events of a particular historical period: the wider history is always there as the fundamental context. Academic historians typically employ a much greater variety of both primary and secondary evidence drawn from many more sources of differing types. The background context against which a family historian writes tends to be more two-dimensional, with only the large events of history, such as major wars, drawn in. Until very recently, family historians often deliberately eschewed any hint of sexual, financial, or political impropriety in accounts of their family's history, and often dwelled excessively on any direct connection with the famous or powerful. Nevertheless, having said all this, it must also be said that academic history and family history are probably much more alike than many academic historians would credit, especially in the more sophisticated narrative-cum-genealogical histories which are now fairly common. Academic historians might, indeed, do well to turn to these where they exist, as an untapped source of some utility.

To the 'person in the street', the very notion of history may well be rather different from what is probably the case among academic historians. University lecturers customarily conceptualise history in terms of broad periods, whose bench-marks and dividing lines consist of major wars, revolutions, plagues, conquests, depressions, and so on, but whose substance consists of fundamental political, economic, social and religious factors which bring about significant change. Thus, to most academic historians the 1789 French Revolution was indeed of the greatest importance, but because (to many, but not all such historians) it marked the overthrow of the feudal aristocracy by the bourgeoisie in France, and then elsewhere in continental Europe. Academic historians would search for its underlying causes in broader social and economic causes, such as resentment at the excessive French tax burden, from which the aristocracy was exempted, the impact of the radical ideas of the *philosophes*, or the example of the American Revolution a few years earlier. It is not a patronising stereotype to contrast the academic's view of the 1789 Revolution with that of the 'person in the street', for whom the French Revolution was the Reign of Terror and Marie Antoinette being led to the guillotine. For the average person interested in history, the major events of the past are the most colourful, the most murderous, and the most mysterious. Indeed, a world of historical writing by 'amateur historians' exists which is observed from afar, but otherwise virtually unknown, to academic historians. Such subjects as the fate of the Little Princes in the Tower (were they murdered by Richard III, Henry VII, or no one?), the actual author of Shakespeare's plays, the true identity of 'Jack the Ripper', whether one or more of the Czar's family survived the Bolshevik slaughter in 1918, and if Lee Harvey Oswald acted alone when President Kennedy was assassinated in 1963, are well known stocks-in-trade of this genre of amateur historiography. More books have probably been written on these subjects than on most recognisably serious topics about historical events. For instance, in the decade 1990–9 alone no fewer than thirty-nine books were written on 'Jack the Ripper' (the incredibly brutal murderer of five prostitutes in London's East End in 1888, whose identity remains unknown), most of which offered a new theory as to who he actually was. It is entirely possible that, apart from the two world wars, there is no other topic in British history about which thirty-nine books were written in the decade 1990–9. Probably hundreds of books and articles have been written about President Kennedy's assassination in 1963, most taking issue with the accepted view, arrived at by the officially appointed Warren Commission in 1964, that Lee Harvey Oswald, an unstable twenty-four year old ex-US Marine turned Marxist, acted alone. Indeed, no book about Kennedy's assassination has ever been written by an academic historian, all of the vast number of books on this event being the work of non-academic historians (including journalists, lawyers, doctors, and engineers) who have taken a profound interest in this subject. The most important book which defends the verdict of the Warren Commission, Gerald Posner's *Case Closed* (1992), was also written by a lawyer. Many of these topics arouse an extraordinary degree of interest among the 'amateur historians' who passionately pursue them, inspiring clubs and societies with dozens and in some cases hundreds of members. Occasionally, rival societies are formed between whom little love is lost, for instance those devoted to the respective claims of Sir Francis Bacon and the Earl of Oxford as the actual author of Shakespeare's plays. The Cloak and Dagger Club, devoted exclusively to studying 'Jack the Ripper', has nearly 300 members, many of whom certainly had little formal education but who devotedly study and explore the Ripper murders with considerable erudition. The Cloak and Dagger Club publishes a bimonthly journal, *The Ripperologist*, devoted to the Ripper case. Remarkably, four other journals devoted exclusively to the Ripper case are also published in Britain, America and Australia.

The intellectual process undertaken by the amateur historian in considering a favourite historical issue such as the true identity of Shakespeare or the actual assassin of JFK, is obviously similar, broadly speaking, to that of the academic historian, although there are typically, notable differences. Theoretically, the academic historian begins a research project with no preconceptions as to the conclusion he or she will reach; the conclusions are inferences from the evidence, with the wider the range of historical evidence, the more well-founded the inferences. Of course most historical outcomes and events are known to the historian beforehand: the historian who, say, is investigating why Pearl Harbor was bombed in December 1941 will know *ipso facto* that it was bombed, and his historical endeavour is to determine why. Of course, too, historians invariably bring an enormous range of preconceptions with them to any research, as well as a range of relevant subjects at which they have greater or lesser competence (for instance, in the Pearl Harbor example, a diplomatic historian would probably be less sensitive to relevant technological developments in weaponry than a military historian, etc.). While some classical problems of amateur historiography are like this, others are not. Most of the amateur historiography of President Kennedy's assassination, for instance, begins with the presupposition that Lee Harvey Oswald did *not* act alone (or did not commit the crime at all); i.e. a presupposition at variance with the official conclusion of the US Government's Warren Report that he killed Kennedy alone and was not part of a conspiracy. Similarly, amateur historians writing on the true identity of Shakespeare begin by denying that the man William Shakespeare (1564–1616), who was born and died in Stratford, actually wrote the plays attributed to him. If they believed that the Stratford man actually wrote the plays, there would be no 'Shakespeare problem' to solve! Some well known amateur historical subjects are different. No one knows, for instance, who 'Jack the Ripper' actually was, so there is no official position to contradict. Most amateur historians who have intensively studied the 'Ripper' question believe, however, that they have probably discovered the actual identity of the Ripper, or at least that their solution is superior to that suggested by other amateur historians. Beyond such relatively mainstream subjects of amateur historiography there is also an ever-growing number of more *outré* subjects for the amateur historian, often involving 'ancient mysteries', which can be found in any large bookshop by the dozen. Such matters as the true nature of the Great Pyramids, whether Jesus survived the Crucifixion, the origins of the Knights Templar and the Freemasons, the identity of King Arthur, and the Shroud of Turin have been the subject of innumerable recent books, many intelligent and intriguing, many the opposite. Well beyond even this is the underworld of occultry, UFOs, unexplained phenomena and the like, which often impinges on the extreme edge of historical mysteries.

This consideration suggests some other important conclusions about the typical efforts of 'amateur historians'. Many, especially those treating one of the classical puzzles, certainly are engaged in doing so because they think that they, and perhaps they alone, are clever enough to solve the persistent riddle, or to penetrate the smokescreen of dissimulation erected by the government or 'accepted opinion'. Superficially, this is different from the motivation of academic historians, whose considered views may well echo 'accepted opinion' and who are ready to acknowledge outstanding scholarship in previous historians. Nevertheless, there are also similarities: most academic historians constantly search for new interpretations and, indeed, new paradigms for our understanding of past events. By and large, professional esteem (and university promotion) comes to those academic historians who are the most original in their interpretations, although originality must always be founded in solid research and is rarely uncontested by other historians.

Very often, however, the 'amateur historian' is distinguishable by his lack of convincing background knowledge of the event he is surveying, and by a decontextualisation of that event from the wider sweep of its contemporary world. Indeed, a naive decontextualisation and lack of searching background knowledge is often among the tell-tale signs of the 'amateur historian'. It has been repeatedly pointed out, for instance, that historians who believe that Shakespeare's plays were written by someone else are positing a far-reaching conspiracy among the government and leading intellectuals of Elizabethan England which is very difficult (though not, perhaps, impossible) to credit. No convincing evidence for any such conspiracy to conceal the identity of the actual authorship of Shakespeare's plays has ever been found among any of the thousands of documents which survive from the period. The academic historian of Elizabethan England, in contrast, would proceed the other way round, by studying the documents and then drawing inferences about Shakespeare, which points overwhelmingly to the Stratford man having written the plays, despite his apparently meagre education. This naivety and decontextualisation probably most distinguishes 'amateur' from academic historiography.

To a considerable extent, this observation is also true (though increasingly less so) for local historiography, another enormous field of history which, until recently, has been relatively absent from the agenda of the academic historian. Virtually every community in the Western world, and certainly in the English-speaking world, has acquired its local historians. In nineteenth-century England these were often local vicars, men with both learning and time on their hands, who collected the stuff of antiquarian history – local lore, the inscriptions on old buildings and artefacts, entries in parish documents, etc. – and compiled and published these in histories of a town, a county, or a geographical area. Of course these remain valuable, and would be used by today's academic historian in writing a more sophisticated history of that place. Often, however, some of the main ingredients which today's historians would probably wish to include in a sophisticated history are absent, especially the social and economic background of the community and virtually anything concerned with the poor, the working classes, women, and other groups not in the 'establishment' of the day. Old-fashioned antiquarian local histories also tend to minimise local conflicts and disputes based in socio-economic or ethnic factors, and to protect the reputations of well known leading local families. Nevertheless, local historiography does normally provide a firm and valuable basis for more sophisticated histories which should, perhaps, be better known to today's graduate students and researchers, whose iconoclasm and search for conflict based in socio-economic and other factors may have gone too far in the other direction. It should also be noted that long-standing local historical societies exist in most communities in the English-speaking world, as they do for many other local or national institutions, for instance religious or military bodies. These often present a range of speakers and papers, and publish journals which, again, are not always sufficiently well known to academic historians. What is remarkable is just how many of these efforts are entirely maintained by non-academic historians with a keen and continuing, though often unsophisticated and untrained, interest in history, at least of familiar things. It is also the case that over the past forty years or so academic historians have increasingly moved into the field of local history, with journals of local or institutional history now increasingly including essays and research by academic historians. Indeed, the journals of local and institutional historical societies are among the only places where the work of academic and non-academic historians coexist, happily or not. Many British universities present courses in local history, which of course feeds into the world of the archivist and museum and heritage studies that is increasingly popular and visible. Again, this is one area where the two types of historian can apparently live together.[2]

Rather closer to the normal sphere of academic history are commissioned histories, usually of business, societies, or local governments, normally to commemorate the centenary of the body or another important anniversary.

Invitations to historians to write such commissioned histories are often advertised in quality newspapers, and the successful applicant (or applicants, since
sometimes a group will apply) is decided after an interviewing process. In some
countries, because of the paucity of tenured academic jobs in history, the
writing of commissioned histories has become a recognised sub-discipline of the
profession, its practitioners known as 'public historians'. Pay for commissioned
histories is often substantial, and represents an increasingly recognised way of
undertaking satisfying research and writing for historians unable to find a
teaching job, or not wishing to pursue an academic career. The disadvantages of
the 'public historian' are also obvious, especially the hand-to-mouth existence
without guarantee of future employment. As well, the relationship of the historian to the commissioning body is fraught with potential difficulties. Most
commissioning institutions will want to see their history presented as a hagio-
graphical success story, with failures, let alone scandals, if they are presented at
all, discussed only for events in the distant past. The obligation of any historian
always to tell the truth is thus potentially compromised in the most basic way.
Publication, even if a contract is signed and payment made, is still a voluntary
act of the commissioning body. Some commissioned histories of business enterprise which were researched and actually written were never published because
the author was rather too frank about the entrepreneurial deficiencies of their
recent leaders. There is an opposite danger as well, that of the historian undertaking an institutional history almost automatically tending to 'go native' (as
the phrase goes), presenting a history from the viewpoint of the commissioning
body rather than a 'warts and all' objective account. Very few historians who
have free access to confidential records and have met regularly with an institution's senior personnel can resist this danger, which applies, of course, to many
other types of histories, especially to biographers, who often almost necessarily
become defenders of their subject, and certainly empathise with him or her,
except when the subject is an infamous villain.

Many published histories are what might be termed 'popular histories', of
which various types exist. Recently, accounts of an eighteenth-century Duchess
of Devonshire and of the Battle of Stalingrad by 'popular historians' have
become unlikely best-sellers in Britain, while authors of popular histories like
Lady Antonia Fraser are among the most famous of recent historians. To the
informed general public, indeed, non-academic historians like Philip Ziegler are
vastly better known than 99 per cent of academic historians. The very image in
the informed popular mind of what the historian does and how he or she writes
is almost certainly formed to a far greater extent by writers of this kind than by
academic historians authoring scholarly monographs, which remain virtually
unknown to the vast majority of people.

There is, thus, a vast demand by the public for history which is not being
satisfied by the academic historian and his or her craft. To a considerable extent,
non-academic historians obey the same canons of evidence and procedural
methodologies as do academic historians, although they differ in some salient

respects. It would do the academic historian no harm at all to become better acquainted with this vast world, of which, too often, she or he knows so little.

Notes

1   See also below, p. 287.
2   See also below, pp. 287–8.

Further reading

Among the many guides on the sources and techniques of the family-tree researcher, see D. Hay, *The Oxford Guide to Family History*, Oxford and New York, Oxford University Press, 1993; S. Fowler, *The Public Record Office Introduction to the Joys of Family History*, Richmond, PRO, 2001. The opening of a gulf between academic and amateur historians is widely recognised, but rarely analysed or even commented on in print. For recent attempts to do so, see W. D. Rubinstein, 'Oswald Shoots JFK', *History Today*, 1999, vol. 49:10, pp. 15–21; *idem*, 'The Hunt for Jack the Ripper', *History Today*, 2000, vol. 50:5, pp. 10–19. The divergences concern more than just techniques of research and communication: they are about choice of subject, motive, taste and purpose. On the problem in general, see F. Fernández-Armesto, 'Epilogue: What is History Now?', in D. Cannadine (ed.) *What is History Now?*, Basingstoke, Palgrave Macmillan, 2002, pp. 148–61; and P. Mandler, *History and National Life*, London, Profile, 2002. Both provide insightful comment on the explosion of popular interest in 'family history' (more properly called genealogical research) and its relative neglect by academic historians. In fact, that neglect has never been absolute. For an exemplary instance of the uses to which academic historians may put the research of amateur genealogy, see E. A. Wrigley and R. S. Schofield, *The Population History of England and Wales, 1541–1871: A Reconstruction*, Cambridge, Cambridge University Press, 1981. The four-volume series, *Studying Family and Community History: The Nineteenth and Twentieth Centuries*, Oxford, Blackwell and New York, Cambridge University Press, 1994, explores ways in which amateur genealogical research on the one hand and academic history and the social sciences on the other can complement each other, and includes useful bibliographies. So, too, does David Hey (ed.) *The Oxford Companion to Local and Family History*, Oxford and New York, Oxford University Press, 1996. These two fields often go together, and for the local just as for the 'family' historian, intimacy is part of the attraction. For a vigorous discussion, especially of how theory developed by practitioners of the 'new cultural history' can help rescue local history from the dead end of antiquarianism, see J. A. Amato, *Rethinking Home: A Case for Writing Local History*, Berkeley, Los Angeles and London, University of California Press, 2002. In Britain, the journal *Amateur Historian*, published from 1952 to 1967, set out to combine the two tastes before re-inventing itself as *The Local Historian*.

Curiously, even in its first guise, the journal gave no space to amateur historiography conceived on a grander scale. National and international histories, histories of the military and wars, were held to be inappropriate, perhaps even to be matters beyond the capacity of the amateur. Yet, in Britain in the course of the twentieth century, amateur and professional historiography did not generally diverge in their choice of subject-matter. Amateur historians like Arthur Bryant or Winston Churchill who did write on 'big' subjects were often more widely read than professionals. The university-trained historian who outsold all others, G. M. Trevelyan, had turned his back on his teachers and their view that good history was 'scientific', reverting instead to his own 'family tradition' (Lord Macaulay was his great uncle) of writing history in a 'Whiggish' and literary mode and producing much of his best-selling work in the course of a self-imposed exile – lasting almost a quarter of a century – from the university system. See D. Cannadine, *G. M. Trevelyan: A Life in History*, London, HarperCollins, 1992.

Chapter 20

History and heritage

Susan Davies

The term 'heritage' refers us to something that is inherited, either by individuals or collectively. It is a broad term, widely accepted both in Britain and internationally, and derived from the Latin *heres*, meaning an 'heir', and various associated words relating to inheritance and things that can be inherited. Among the definitions in the *Oxford English Dictionary* is the following: 'That which comes from the circumstances of birth; an inherited lot or portion; the condition or state transmitted from ancestors'. This suggests a breadth of meaning that some regard as unsatisfactorily vague, preferring, for example, 'cultural assets' as a more specific term. A recent report by English Heritage, *The Power of Place* (December 2000), suggests 'the historic environment' as a preferred term. Yet neither of these is as generous in meaning or concept as 'heritage'.

Although 'heritage', in terms of definition, is the subject of debate, there is general agreement that it relates to the past and must therefore share a close relationship with history. Yet, heritage raises fundamental questions for historians that are not as obvious to other disciplines or to the population at large. What, for instance, is the role of factual, source-based evidence which is interpreted and presented according to scholarly principles, and how far should/may the historian's principles and practices be adapted to the commercial and popular pressures of the heritage industry? Moreover, dealing with the past is not necessarily a simple matter for the historian operating within the academic tradition, because opinions vary on the nature and ownership of the past and, of course, on how accurately we can interpret evidence.

Lowenthal helps to clarify the relationship between history and heritage, by identifying three principal 'modes of access' to the past: namely memory, history and 'relics'.[1] These are defined in the following ways. Memory is essentially personal, largely unverifiable, and naturally limited in span; it gives us appreciation of the past, familiarity, participation and pride, also the wish to belong and to know our roots. History offers 'shared data and conclusions for public scrutiny', is potentially immortal in print but is inevitably subjective and shaped by hindsight; it contributes the framework of context through the collection of data, evaluation of evidence and structured interpretation. Relics, defined as surviving physical remains of all kinds (buildings, artefacts, and the like), always produce an emotional response, whether favourable or unfavourable; they provide a focus for the same feelings and needs as those inspired by memory, together with senses of time and time-lessness. These 'modes of access' to the past are, in fact, the key contributors to heritage consciousness in our modern developed society, and the link with history is similarly indicated in a very different text, the European Convention on the Protection of the Archaeological Heritage (the 1992 'Valetta Convention') in which the first aim is 'to protect the archaeological heritage as a source of the European collective memory and as an instrument for historical and scientific study'. The connection between history and heritage is thus fundamental and inextricable. Not only do today's concepts of heritage require a retrospective contextual framework for meaningful appreciation, but this need will grow as time moves on in order to present (and re-present) historical information in a way that will be relevant to future audiences. This is already reflected in opinion at policy and strategic level in the heritage industry, which suggests that sound historical scholarship is *essential* to all worthwhile and successful ventures, both for establishing validity and authenticity and for contributing to public knowledge. Yet history does not enjoy a monopoly over heritage.

There are many contributory influences to the evolution of a concept of heritage. Some are broad and pervasive, such as movements of national consciousness and identity and developments in historical and cultural under-standing, while others are more specific, represented by events, institutions and genres that have added to cumulative development. The French Revolution, for example, focused minds on change and awareness of what had been lost in the turmoil. Civil war in 1640s England triggered searches for historical precedent. More recently, the collapse of historic landed estates in twentieth-century Britain and reconstruction in Europe after World War II had similar effects. So, times of crisis, change and conflict have all raised consciousness of the past, feelings of loss and a desire for continuity of the familiar.

The 'age' of countries is certainly a relevant factor in the evolution of this sense of heritage, especially the length of occupation by particular peoples. In the USA, for example, one kind of heritage goes back to colonisation from Europe, but an older heritage of an earlier population extends beyond that. Many of today's US citizens have family roots in Europe, so traditions were transplanted across the Atlantic. Heritage consciousness is strong in the USA and manifest in the quality of museums, care of historic buildings and enthusiasm for visiting the countries of origin. Yet appropriate representation of the older indigenous population and of the place of slavery has been difficult to achieve, raising the full range of ethical and historical sensitivities that challenge the heritage business today – none more difficult than the anti-Semitic and Holocaust issues of more recent history.

The direct involvement of the state in the creation and preservation of a 'heritage' appeared earliest in Western Europe, and dates back to the eighteenth century. But different patterns emerged. In Germany responsibility has been largely devolved, while in France it is more centred upon Paris. In Britain the framework has developed piecemeal through a variety of legislation, agencies and bodies, some state funded and some with charitable or independent status, such as the National Trust. In relatively recent years, international bodies such as UNESCO have added a global dimension by raising heritage awareness and monitoring relevant issues. A scheme for designating 'World Heritage Sites' is in place, represented in Wales, for example, by Edward I's castles in the north and, since 1999, by the historic industrial landscape at Blaenavon in Gwent. There are no financial benefits, but visitor attraction is enhanced and protection secured against damaging change or development. Other international bodies, such as ICOM, the International Council of Museums, serve more specific needs, including disaster recovery. Yet nothing could prevent the recent destruction in Afghanistan of the Buddhas of Bamiyan, giant statues demolished because of what they represented in religious terms to those in power. So local priorities vary, and while more developed countries can be expected to treat their 'heritage' in a way that befits 'civilised' society, under-developed areas respond to prevailing circumstances and must focus on human survival.

Having outlined the concept of heritage and its connection with history, we will turn to the factors and influences that shape the heritage industry today.

The physical manifestations of heritage are found in diverse settings, some in museums and historic buildings or in protected landscapes, but others outside formal care. The industry now includes heritage centres that hold no original material, relying on modern technology and the 'virtual' experience, with strong emphasis on interpretation. Such diversity results in 'untidy' arrangements for responsibility by both central and local government. Heritage does not fit naturally into one administrative 'box' and is commonly linked with culture or leisure pursuits. Although specific aspects, for instance, ancient monuments, are most obviously categorised as 'heritage', it is often difficult to determine where responsibility should lie. Archives, for example, often described as the documentary heritage, are difficult to locate within this administrative schema because they serve a dual purpose, sharing their cultural and historical importance with a powerful evidential role in the legal sense. Any legislative or statutory base for heritage has in most cases grown in an unstructured way, differing between countries. Devolution of government in Wales, Scotland and Northern Ireland has added further variety and a different pace of development, since new administrations rarely perceive heritage as a top priority.

Professional standards of care, both national and international, constitute the principal quality controls for the industry. They may be specific, for instance rules for cataloguing which facilitate electronic data exchange or prescribed conditions for care of materials, or much more comprehensive, like the Museums and Galleries Registration Scheme in Britain. The standards must be met in order to qualify for a 'registration' or 'approval' process, and may govern eligibility for financial aid. While this pattern is not entirely satisfactory, it works reasonably well in practice. Indeed, it is inconceivable that the diverse interests within the heritage field could be constrained more tightly by regulation, and there will always be those who operate outside formal systems. Various statutory and other measures provide protection for aspects of heritage, whether for ancient monuments and sites, landscapes, buildings or artefacts. They are too complex to consider here, and tend to be specific to subject and circumstances, such as arrangements to encourage the reporting of archaeological finds, which are increasingly discovered by metal detectorists and are at risk of being removed from their archaeological context without systematic recording. These currently operate under a 'portable antiquities' scheme in Britain, while international controls use the same description in providing protection against illicit trade.

Of particular significance in the present context is a range of controlling influences that have had notable effects on the heritage business since the 1980s, broadly categorised as financial, commercial, technical and socio-political. While each is individually significant, they combine in a powerful mix that affects the way in which the industry functions.

Financial issues range from shortage of money to the complex requirements of competitive funding schemes that now provide the best prospect of additional finance, thus creating a 'bidding culture'. Heritage interests have always struggled for financial support, whatever their organisational status. In Britain, for example, there are national museums that are largely dependent on government 'grant in aid', state-supported 'umbrella organisations' and independent chartered bodies, alongside local authority establishments or privately run, perhaps charitably funded, operations from the smallest special-interest museum to a huge body like the National Trust. None are fully funded for their needs and many are dependent for survival on donations and/or admission charges, voluntary effort and fund raising. New opportunities for additional financial support have emerged during the last 10–15 years, but they are not accessible to all and come with 'strings attached'. For instance, government policy has favoured competitive 'challenge' funding on particular themes, with emphasis on raising standards and supplying perceived needs. Similar European initiatives emphasise inter-regional partnerships. Since 1994, the Heritage Lottery Fund (HLF) has made a substantial contribution to the industry, heritage being one of the National Lottery's designated good causes. Large grants have supported high-profile building and expansion projects, such as the recent redevelopment of the central courtyard at the British Museum to improve the visitor experience, and small projects have benefited in an unprecedented way. The public profile of heritage has also risen, although not without controversy over the relative merits of the various 'deserving causes', as reflected by the press.

While such opportunities are welcome, they have affected the overall balance of the heritage industry. For example, HLF grants are primarily restricted to capital expenditure, and they require matching funds and evidence that planned developments are sustainable. Many deserving cases are too poor to participate, but others move forward, thus widening the gaps in comparative development through inequality of opportunity. Core functions, such as a museum curator's day-to-day care and research of collections, or a conservator's increasingly sophisticated scientific techniques for preservation and conservation, are not usually eligible for grant aid, so the system cannot help those whose most urgent need is for daily operational support. At the same time, the competitive bidding process demands skill in business planning and project management and time to complete application procedures, thus distracting attention from specialist functions and from the wider issues of strategic planning which are more difficult to sustain in a project-focused environment. Furthermore, success in gaining a grant does not guarantee success of the project, and examples of failure to meet targets highlight the difficulty – even impossibility – of quantifying the 'attraction' element of heritage developments. Changes in public policy may also cause difficulty, where, for example, admission charges have been included in financial projections but government policy promotes free admission. These concerns may seem far removed from historical scholarship, but they are part of the daily experience of those who work in the heritage business.

Financial and commercial pressures are closely related in terms of the need to generate income, balance budgets, seek funding opportunities and remain viable. But increased expectation that business principles and systems should be applied to all organisations, especially those that are publicly or charitably funded, has created added burdens for the heritage industry. It must now produce measurable outputs in terms of statistics and 'performance-indicators', and offer cost effectiveness and value for money, all of which demand business acumen and a competitive spirit. Heritage attractions must therefore compete with each other for visitor attention as well as with all other popular destinations and pursuits, including theme parks.

Perhaps the most difficult influence to quantify is the impact of computer technology on the heritage business, where it is used not only for presentation and interpretation and for management, but also for creating surrogate copies of fragile materials as part of preservation measures and/or access initiatives. The advance of digitised images and 'virtual reality' in the early 1990s initially raised concerns that the 'virtual' experience would make the 'actual' obsolete. Experience is proving otherwise: it seems that people are encouraged by the virtual to visit the actual, but only when the first experience is good in terms of quality and interpretative information. Public expectation is thus growing in sophistication, and heritage attractions must be prepared for visitors who arrive well informed about what they want to see and with specific expectations of how they expect to see it. This increasingly critical audience has impacted powerfully upon standards of presentation and interpretation, in that visitors who have used computer technology to examine artefacts that are expertly presented in digital media, with excellent explanatory text, are unlikely to be impressed by an object in an aging glass case with a tired-looking label! So, heritage attractions are now expected to have up-to-date technical facilities, but there are also implications for academic scholarship. Since the success of the virtual experience, in particular, is dependent upon appropriate levels of inter-pretation in order to be meaningful, the role of specialist/academic knowledge becomes increasingly important, but it must now work alongside skill in tech-nical presentation with mutual respect if it is to function to best effect.

Of course, the internet has transformed access to information in the heritage world and is often used as a starting point, whether for basic information, such as the location of organisations and explanatory information, or for specialised purposes such as identifying reference details and even placing reservation or copy orders online, or perhaps downloading suitably prepared teaching mate-rials. There are also 'gateways' to special interest areas, digital art galleries, virtual tours of historic sites and an infinite variety of introductions to sources on particular themes. The BBC's website is just one example that offers particu-larly good guidance relating to history and heritage and, in this case, is linked to broadcast programmes, but similar examples are available world-wide. Yet, these advantages of new technology must be balanced with elements of risk. All internet material shares the inherent weakness of lack of control over the quality of information, apart from the reputation of the provider. The heritage industry is vulnerable to inaccurate or biased information, and the fact that website success is characterised by visual impact and arresting information may exert inappropriate influence on the choice of content.

The current political agenda in Britain is impacting significantly on the heritage industry through measures to combat social exclusion and extend access to learning. This is seen in reports and policy documents such as *Centres for Social Change: Museums, Libraries and Archives for All* (DCMS 2000) and *The Learning Power of Museums* (DCMS and DfEE 2000), and various publica-tions by Resource: The Council for Museums, Archives and Libraries, which was established in 2000 as a new, central strategic and advisory body.[2] Socio-political priorities are thus made clear, with the effect that policy and strategy in the heritage industry are being shaped by government tenets which organisa-tions are expected to match in their operations and priorities. While the use of heritage concepts in socio-political thinking is not new, its profile as an instru-ment for delivering government policy for social change at the beginning of the twenty-first century is unusually high. Current debates can be followed in the reports and policy documents produced by or for government departments and public bodies, and available on their websites.

New emphasis on the educational potential of the heritage industry is less surprising, given the 'education for all' aspirations of the Victorian founders of some of our oldest and largest museums and a long tradition of educational 'outreach'. In recent years the needs of the National Curriculum (NC) have figured prominently, but efforts are now being adapted to meet government policies on lifelong learning. Inherent diversity enables the industry to support a very wide range of curricular and other learning needs across the disciplines, but history is commonly the central focus.

In practice, the heritage business today is all about introducing and explaining the past, and preserving it in order to inform the present and future. It therefore acts as a shop window for history, which has powerful influence through popular appeal; it also offers boundless opportunities to introduce new audiences to historical scholarship in a context that encourages them to explore further. In no other line of work is the challenge to the historian's skill and adaptability greater, or his/her contribution to popular understanding more crucial. Yet, how is the interaction and synergy of history with heritage best achieved?

This chapter has argued that historical knowledge and frameworks hold a central and inextricable position in heritage concepts and enterprises; it follows that historians should and must contribute. Indeed, most historians would accept the principle that historical scholarship should underpin the heritage industry by providing historical information and lending authenticity to the factual knowledge and its interpretation. Three practical routes for productive partnership suggest themselves, namely working with the industry, or within it, and supporting the industry's historical training needs. But what are the specific challenges and implications? Some are fundamental while others are more circumstantial.

The current operational environment of the heritage industry raises fundamental issues for history as a discipline. Historians generally dislike constraints that channel historical effort in the service of projects, because popularly defined or themed projects may not allow the intellectual freedom that the academy defends. In particular, the 'management' world of project timescales and competitive challenges may interfere with maintaining detachment, objectivity and other principles of academic history. Historians naturally prefer to set research parameters according to academic judgment and identifiable research needs, and strive to resist distraction or distortion by external influences. The breadth of the heritage industry is also problematic, in that it includes some activities and pursuits that are less well founded in historical evidence or of a more controversial nature, such as popular medieval banquets and other re-creations. While there is no wish to cast doubt on the research accuracy or attention to detail of those who seek to recreate the skills and activities of past times for personal and shared interest, historians must question how far such re-creations, out of context, are connected with the reality of the original. Such are the issues that shape the historian's biggest dilemma vis-à-vis the heritage industry: how far can/should historical integrity be defended in the face of commercial and popular pressures?

Heritage also provides an outlet for the employment of historians and for the dissemination of their work but in both respects the historian may be constrained by the expectations of the industry. Opportunities for involvement by historians with or within the heritage industry are many and varied. Making the fruits of scholarly historical research available or acting in an advisory capacity are established options, while conducting specific, project-led research and assisting in interpretation of the outcomes is equally valuable and more direct. Employment within the industry is perhaps the most direct contribution of all. Indeed, historical skills may be specifically required, as in more specialised work in the heritage field, such as the care and recording of historic buildings.

Providing for the historical training needs of the heritage industry has implications for the skills base of both university teachers and students. Addressing the teaching and learning requirements of, for instance, local history involves far more than simply finding space in the curriculum. For a variety of reasons, the majority of school leavers today have focused on modern history, and many university courses do the same, while declining linguistic skills cause difficulty in coping with the demands of archaic English, Latin, and other European languages. At the same time, and for similar reasons of social and educational change, the public today has less knowledge of historical frameworks and is less well equipped to deal with archaic language and concepts than was the case until perhaps the 1970s. The heritage industry must therefore provide increased explanation and interpretation in a format that appeals to contemporary understanding and experience, but which also supplies the depth and accuracy of concept that is essential to awakening interest.

Skills necessary to the heritage industry and readily appreciated by historians require the application of theoretical knowledge to a variety of practical circumstances, e.g. interpreting artefacts, buildings, landscape, archives, images, etc., for public benefit and adapting information for education and explanation at different levels. Of course, such skills cannot be fully comprehended within a three-year degree course, and some elements are more usually offered at postgraduate level. Yet students and teachers should be aware of these needs and of strategies for gaining skill. For example, those who wish to become archivists, and will need Latin for reading pre-eighteenth-century documents, frequently take short courses after graduating in order to start the necessary learning process before undertaking advanced vocational training.

No immediate solutions are available for the local history skills shortage, but it is worth noting that not only those who work in the heritage industry require training of this kind; others share this need for working with the industry in delivering educational provision, to say nothing about the needs of dedicated family historians who tackle very difficult archival sources in their researches. The NC has placed local history requirements on both primary and secondary pupils, and therefore on teachers. In Wales, the upper primary level focuses on the Victorians and on a local study, also requiring pupils to experience quantitative work. Lack of suitable teaching resources prompted the county archives service in Powys to develop the web-based Powys Digital History; this presents archival information (including statistics), maps and images relating to communities in Powys in Victorian times, all carefully selected and commented upon in order to provide raw data for use in fulfilment of the NC requirements.[3] Such careful choice of material with essential but minimal explanation without bias, and visual presentation that uses a typeface that will assist slow learners as well as the more capable readers, has resulted in a most attractive and popular website of wide appeal in a heritage context, far beyond the initial target audience. Good material, carefully considered, interpreted and presented is the key to success, and this is, in fact, the principal success factor in the interaction between history and heritage in practical terms.

This chapter therefore concludes with a confident assertion that historians can share their highest aspirations with the heritage industry without compromise, since the high quality of work that is essential to awakening historical interest and fostering scholarship is equally important to the popular success of heritage activities. Historical training and skill is thus being extended to new purposes and in new media in a demand-led environment. Surely this must be supported by the best historical efforts and by the will to succeed in collaborative effort?

Notes

1   D. Lowenthal, *The Past Is a Foreign Country*, Cambridge, Cambridge University Press, 1985, pp. xxii–iii.
2   In spring 2004 Resource changed its name to MLA: the Museums, Libraries and Archives Council.
3   Website: http://history.powys.org.uk (at the time of writing).

Further reading

This is a complex subject area for which to provide an introductory bibliography, because so many works are relevant in one way or another: these include many that focus primarily on historical perspectives, others that look more closely at the raison d'être of the modern heritage 'business', and a third category that charts the development of particular institutions which also happen to have played a major role in the relationship between history and heritage. Moreover, by today, much relevant information is to be found through regular reading of professional journals, such as the *Museums Journal* (published by the Museums Association in the UK), and also in policy documents and reports published by government in the broad culture and heritage context. Just as important, is the need to take note of press and other media reports that reflect popular concepts of heritage and blurred distinctions between heritage and history.

Many readers benefit from starting with David Lowenthal's books as noted below, but the following categorised works all provide useful starting points. The first six, in no particular order, consider the directions in which concepts and representations of heritage have moved in the late twentieth century and the connection with views of history: J. Arnold, K. Davies and S. Ditchfield, *History and Heritage: Consuming the Past in Contemporary Culture*, Shaftesbury, Donhead, 1998; D. Lowenthal, *The Heritage Crusade and the Spoils of History*, Cambridge, Cambridge University Press, 1998; R. Hewison, *The Heritage Industry: Britain in a Climate of Decline*, London, Methuen, 1987; P. Wright, *On Living in an Old Country: The National Past in Contemporary Britain*, London, Verso, 1985; K. Walsh, *The Representation of the Past: Museums and Heritage in the Post Modern World*, London, Routledge, 1992; and T. Bennett, *The Birth of the Museum: History, Theory, Politics*, London, Routledge, 1995.

Next are three works of wider scope and more subtle appeal, in that they explore human perceptions of the past and the strength of historical and heritage concepts within human experience: D. Lowenthal, *The Past is a Foreign Country*, Cambridge, Cambridge University Press, 1985; R. Samuel, *Theatres of Memory I: Past and Present in Contemporary Culture*, London, Verso, 1995; and S. Schama, *Landscape and Memory*, London, Fontana, 1996.

Finally, there are various works on the intellectual and cultural impact of museums, which are relevant in the present context, notably those by Eilean Hooper-Greenhill (for example, *Museums and the Shaping of Knowledge*, London, Routledge, 1992; and *Museums and the Interpretation of Visual Culture*, London, Routledge, 2000), while two very different works will serve to represent the role of institutions and organisations in maintaining active links between history and heritage over long periods of time: E. Miller, *That Noble Cabinet: A History of the British Museum*, London, Cox and Wyman, 1973; and J. Jenkins and P. James, *From Acorn to Oak Tree: The Growth of the National Trust 1895–1994*, London, Macmillan, 1994.

Conclusion

History and power

Peter Lambert and Phillipp Schofield

At either side of the turn of the millennium, it was and is becoming common to cast doubt on the place of history in contemporary society. Thus Eric Hobsbawm has lamented the fact (as he saw it) that 'Most young men and women at the century's end grow up in a sort of permanent present lacking any organic relation to the public past of the times they live in'.[1] Yet whatever vacuum the lack of an *organic* relation to the public past may have left has been filled to overflowing. 'Consciousness of history', Richard Evans notes, 'is all-pervasive at the start of the twenty-first century'.[2] Contributions to Part V of this volume have discussed some of the areas in which public fascination about the past has increased exponentially. The increase in private research on family trees, for instance, owes nothing to professional historians and everything to 'popular taste and demand'. In public record offices, professional historians rub shoulders with amateur genealogists all the time, but intellectual contact between them is rare.[3] Professional historians have been more involved in and responsive to television history and the heritage industry, but their contributions have hardly been decisive. The development of these public spheres of history has brought no crumbs of comfort to those academic historians who see them only as waste-products of the problem Hobsbawm had highlighted, and one can hear complaints that it 'has at times verged on collective hysteria, more befitting teenage crowds at rock concerts than well-mannered urban philistines and restrained semi-intellectuals'.[4]

Academic historians have succeeded in forging a collective identity as members of a profession. It is not, however, a profession comparable to that (say) of doctors or dentists, who enjoy a near-monopoly on practice. Anyone can set up as 'an historian' and more and more people in fact do so; no qualifications are necessary. Many academic historians feel themselves to be 'a beleaguered species'. The 'lowering of the historian's status and prestige is synchronic to' the myriad forms and mass appeal of 'today's media-driven historical culture'. Powerless to defend their domain against this surge of extra-academic intruders, historians cannot even take refuge in university safe-havens. In Part IV, we addressed a variety of instances of contact between history and other disciplines. A common thread among them is the willingness of many historians, once history had rid itself of youthful insecurities as to its own identity and become firmly established, to exchange ideas with scholars in other fields. Now, however, the insecurities are welling up again, and former trading-partners in interdisciplinarity are accused of having turned pirate. 'In academe, history is up for grabs, and it has again become an open field for plunder and a target for colonialism for literary scholars, sociologists, political scientists, anthropologists and psychoanalysts'.[5]

Of course, academic historians have not simply resigned themselves to defeat and quit the field. But how have they responded, or should they respond? By redoubling efforts, some elder statesmen among them have argued, and by ensuring that the histories they make address the wider public. 'Today is the great age of historical mythology', Hobsbawm argues, and it is that fact that makes 'defence of history by its professionals ... more urgent in politics than ever. We are needed'.[6]

An alternative strategy, and one of which many historians have availed themselves, is to swim with the tide of the heritage industry. They argue that, since academic historians are after all an integral part of the societies in which they work, they are also party to those societies' 'historical cultures'.[7] The French historian Pierre Nora gathered an impressive team of colleagues who set out to identify the 'sites' of French national memory.[8] In some respects, Nora acknowledged, they were returning to a nineteenth-century agenda. Indeed, although they proposed 'to define France as a reality that is entirely symbolic', they treated France as an enclosed space. And so, very much in the manner of nineteenth-century nationalist historiography, they reified France and 'its national roots' after all. The overall impression they created was not of a critical attempt to lay bare the invented or imagined qualities of French national identity so much as of nostalgic celebration and commemoration of those very qualities. Thus national memory had become not only the subject of their work but also the object of their cultural desires. 'Less interested in "what actually happened" than in its perpetual reuse and misuse', they tended to erode or at least to demote the significance of the distinction between fact and fiction. What *did* interest them was the matter of documenting and encouraging the 'return to our collective heritage'.[9]

Nora, noting France's 'threatened countryside, lost traditions, wrecked way of life', was responding to what Hobsbawm had called the loss of 'organic relation to the public past'. For Nora, the widespread and 'deep consciousness' of loss makes writing the history of national memory the sole possible means whereby historians may come to terms with loss itself, for

> only such a history, at once scholarly and accessible to the wider public, is capable of responding to the needs of the moment, of reconciling, in France and perhaps elsewhere as well, the requirements of science with the demands of conscience.[10]

Internationally, a host of emulators, publishing similarly monumental volumes, have taken up Nora's suggestion, so that there are now Dutch, Italian, Austrian, German and US works employing Nora's sensibilities and broad schema and (to varying degrees) replicating his nostalgic patriotism.[11] Heritage, in many ways a response to fears generated by 'globalisation', has reached global proportions; a heritage-orientated historiography is racing to catch up.

The elision of fact and fiction has become more frequent in the aftermath of the 'linguistic turn'. In some of its extreme manifestations, there appears to be nothing left to be unearthed beneath layers of memory or beyond the texts, images, and other 'sites' on and around which memories accumulate.[12] Postmodernists will, of course, insist that there is no recoverable past in any case. New cultural historians ask 'not only "How it really was" but rather "How was it for him, or her, or them?" '.[13] But historians of national memory may incline to dispense with discovering 'what actually happened' for more specific reasons. They may find themselves so caught up in the articulation of identity that realities which are not merely symbolic can pass them by. Above all, they are trapped by the self-referential logic of their own enterprise for, as Linda Colley has pointed out, 'We cannot tell the truth about a piece of patriotic mythology because to do so would be meaningless'. The 'cynicism' or 'despair in the face of the past' that memory-histories may therefore provoke among their readers are, Colley also reminds us, not in the least necessary: there is no shortage of areas in which historians can tell truths and make verifiable statements about the past.[14]

For most academic historians, striving to do so remains definitive. In this, as also in the critical use of sources as the means of establishing verifiability and in the insistence on a distinction in principle between history and antiquarianism, a conception of 'what history is' has remained strikingly persistent. On these counts at least, professional historians in the twenty-first century can still recognise their strong disciplinary family resemblance to nineteenth-century professional historians. They are lines of continuity in historiography that have survived successive and robust challenges to virtually all the other assumptions underpinning the discipline as it had existed around 1900. They still provide historians with a kind of code of professional conduct, establishing normative behaviour. But we measure that persistence, we record its survival, and we explain its limits, in the challenges it faces, in the relationship of the discipline to power that its practitioners enjoy and the power that others hold over it.

Historians are influenced by the distribution of power in both past and present. The creation, survival and accessibility of the sources from which they work are outcomes and expressions of power-relations. Inevitably, the sources available to the researcher will provide a finite number of windows onto the past. Historians of literate elites will generally have an easier time finding sources than historians of the illiterate, the poor, or the oppressed. Which windows should historians choose to look through, from what angle, with what focus? What should they elect to describe, and how? Addressing these questions, fundamental to any historian's work, involves choices which are conditioned by the operation of power in the present. The dissemination of patronage and imposition of censorship, the policies of regimes, the educational and social backgrounds of historians themselves, the technical and material resources at their disposal, intellectual taste and fashion: all conspire to influence the ways in which histories are made. All these variables are indicative of ways in which historians and their work are themselves subject to the very processes they research and write about.

Power, by whom, why, and how effectively it is exercised and contested, are vital concerns, therefore, for historians. They are implicated in the concerns of power in three ways. First, power furnishes historians with their subject matter. Second, historians are subject to the exercise of power by others. Third, in varying degrees they themselves wield power through the histories they produce. How much room for manoeuvre is available to historians as they negotiate the rapids of power?

To paraphrase Karl Marx: historians make histories, but not under conditions of their own choosing. What historians do is conditioned by powers to which the historian is subject. For academic historians, a paradigmatic concept of what constitutes *good* history serves to guide and to constrain practice. *Good* history, according to this view, emerges from interaction between the historian's politically or morally derived questions and hypotheses and the evidence she or he then encounters. Historians should thus always be prepared to jettison preconceptions if the evidence tends to contradict them. They must either modify or surrender views which prove incompatible with the evidence. And, at least for the purposes of the work in hand, they must be prepared to do so even when those are the very views which had attracted them to a particular subject in the first place. Of course, they are at liberty simply to give up on a project altogether. If, however, they should maintain prejudices that fly in the face of the available evidence, do so persistently, publicly and in print, they risk being unmasked as bad historians or as no kind of historians at all, but ideologues and propagandists.

The distinction is not merely an ideal one. Historical sources may be capable of various interpretations, but there are clear limits to the variety of interpretations that can legitimately be put on them. Where historians find themselves up against the limits of interpretability, they may succumb to temptations. They may disregard sources that do not fit their arguments or quote selectively from them. In the worst of cases, they may alter the meaning of documents by excising key words or phrases, may wilfully misread them and substitute one word for another with a quite different meaning, or simply add words which the originals did not contain. The eclectic emphasis on such evidence as fits an historian's argument is widespread. There is nothing intrinsically improper about it. Its persuasiveness as a strategy is dependent on historians' arguing for the superior significance of the sources they stress by using the tried and tested techniques of source-criticism. In other words, a range of sources will be compared to rank them within a hierarchy of significance and reliability. The practise of leaving out inconvenient evidence altogether is also common, but less so – if only because it is obviously vulnerable to correction.

Sins of omission may, however, be more common in some kinds of history than in others – and less easy to correct. Philip L. Cantelon complains that there is systematic neglect of work commissioned by businesses or government agencies and undertaken by historians whose skills are available for hire on an open market. It is 'to the detriment of the entire profession'. Cantelon argues that academic historians turn a blind eye because they assume that historians who have been hired have sold their souls in the process. This, Cantelon points out, assumes a community of interest between an employer who wants, and an employee who is prepared to deliver not history, but propaganda. Instead of dismissing it out of hand, academic historians should judge 'public' historical scholarship with exactly the same critical engagement as they would bring to any university-based work.[15]

There are ethical considerations here. Historians who depend entirely on income generated by private industrial or governmental contracts will necessarily find themselves in a position of greater susceptibility to influence than will historians whose academic liberty is defended and whose livelihood is dependent largely on their peers' esteem.[16] Some kinds of 'public' history are more likely to allow vested interests to intrude than others. The position of someone like Richard J. Evans, whose duty as an expert witness in the Irving trial, an event to which we shall return below, was to the court and not to the defence which had hired him, is unlike that of the historian working for a business, on its history. Businesses may not always hire historians for political reasons. But sometimes they emphatically do. The proliferation of legal claims for compensation and restitution against companies which had flourished under conditions of dictatorship and, for instance, used slave labour in the process, has resulted in a number of company-commissioned histories. Threats of litigation would have to be countered, or their likely cost assessed, if the enterprises concerned were to continue to be able to attract investment. Not 'public', but university historians were most often involved here. Volkswagen, for instance, turned to Hans Mommsen, an historian with an international reputation, to write a history of the company in the Third Reich. Mommsen, a left-leaning historian, was hired also because it seemed unlikely that he would be suspected of any pro-business bias, and highly improbable that he should have entertained any desire to produce apologias for Nazi policies. Nevertheless, when he published his findings,[17] they met with a mixed reception. Mommsen was held by some experts and other observers to have at least underplayed the Volkswagen concern's dependency on and brutal exploitation of forced labour.[18] But how was the impression that the work was suspiciously convenient for Volkswagen to be dispelled? The problem arises whenever historians have enjoyed privileged access to sources. This puts Cantelon's plea that the scholarly work of the hired historian be read like any other work of professional historical scholarship into a different light. Where historians' references to documents in private archives cannot (at least for the foreseeable future) be checked by their colleagues, they must expect their work to be approached with more than usual scepticism. The track record of 'official' historians enjoying privileged access to state documents suggests that the scepticism is healthy. Between the two world wars, the 'coloured books' of edited collections of documents which governments had published in order to propagate their foreign policies, and which were riddled with error and invention, gave way to scholarly editions of foreign ministries' documents on the origins of the First World War. Though a material as well as technical improvement on the practices of the compilers of 'coloured books', the work of professional historians was nevertheless often infected by apologist motives. In Germany, the principal editor misleadingly proclaimed his independent status when he was in fact intimately bound to the Foreign Ministry bureaucracy. He excised politically awkward passages and marginalia from documents. He pre-empted the censorship regime which oversaw his work, and sometimes outdid the censors in his zeal. In Britain, the editors allowed themselves to be hoodwinked by civil servants who concealed politically sensitive material from them. In a sense, because they appeared to conform to scholarly standards and since they depended for their persuasiveness on their editors' reputations, these monumental editions of sources were thus even more pernicious than 'coloured books'. The demands of patriotism and scholarly objectivity had come into conflict to a far greater degree than ever before 1914, and the former had overridden the latter.[19]

Historians do, of course, exercise a measure of power themselves, on occasion in the employment of the historical methodological paradigm; sometimes in the face of it. Under some conditions, they can help undermine democracies. They can legitimate dictatorships and aid in the pursuit of criminal undertakings. But they can also contribute to the development of a sense of civic responsibility and of active citizenship. As we have seen, Germany from the 1920s to the 1970s affords evidence of the historical profession playing each of these roles in succession.[20] Historians' work can inform policy decisions and can inspire individuals or movements. Sometimes, their scholarship can lead individual historians directly into political careers; sometimes – even in the same society but at another date – a serious engagement with history can be incompatible with involvement in formal politics.

Most professional historians, whether they admit it or not, set out with some sort of political agenda, or at least with a moral standpoint which influences their work and has a bearing on politics. Partisanship may, of course, cloud judgments. Equally, strong motivations and sympathies may stimulate research. In a pluralist society or academic culture, this accounts for the enormous range of generic species of historical research interests and perspectives. It also clearly raises choices about the ways in which the historian goes about her or his work.

Mangling documents by leaving words out or misreading them is something scarcely any historian could confidently assert she or he has never done. But the vast majority of such errors are caused by human frailties ranging from occasional carelessness, through stress and tiredness, to imagining that words you hoped or expected to find were actually on the page before you. The phenomenon of 'historians' programmatically changing meanings is far less frequently to be encountered. Fabrications of evidence occur more rarely still. Both are fundamentally at odds with ground-rules historians first established for their discipline in the nineteenth century and according to which the community of professional historians has policed itself ever since. Nationalist historians in the era of history's professionalisation may have had a habit of papering over gaps in their histories of the development of nation-states with tenuous arguments and leaps of the imagination disguised in sobre, steady prose. But they did not plug gaps by falling back on myth or manufacturing fake sources. On the contrary, professional historians across Europe played a significant role in exposing fabrications. Confident in both their nationalism and their integrity as scholars, they reasoned that manifest falsehoods could furnish no secure basis for either.

The choice of how to employ the paradigm also resides with historians. From time to time, it is employed as a weapon of assault. Just occasionally, a professional historian working with documents which *are* generally accessible, is found to have played fast and loose with sources. David Abraham's study of big business relations with Nazism in the Weimar Republic was found to have contained passages in which evidence was manipulated in order both to exaggerate the scale of business donations to the Nazis, and to suggest these had occurred much earlier than in fact they actually had. Neither his widely acknowledged theoretical sophistication, nor the fact that his errors occurred in the context of a broader argument which challenged crude perceptions of the Nazis as constituting no more than the hired thugs of capitalism, nor even his preparedness to admit to and rectify a host of individual factual errors, saved him. His career as an academic historian was abruptly terminated. Whether or not the punishment was proportionate to the offence, the point is that Abraham's mistakes and distortions were brought to light rapidly and comprehensively.[21] By contrast, decades were to pass before the dubious practices of various 'official' historians' editorial work on the origins of the First World War were exposed. Abraham's errors left no traces in subsequent historiography; by contrast, the interwar 'official' historians' efforts did lasting damage. They had helped generate a vast body of secondary literature. Inevitably, it reflected the catalogue of deficiencies in the published collections of documents.

And it is not only academic historians who have wielded the weapon of the shared historical paradigm with force. In a recent court case in Britain, David Irving, author of a number of books on the Second World War, was found by the trial judge to have constructed arguments which tended 'to exonerate the Nazis for the appalling atrocities which they inflicted on the Jews' on the basis of 'unfounded assertions' and a propensity, 'where he deems it necessary, to manipulate the historical record in order to make it conform with his political beliefs'. As Richard J. Evans, Professor of Modern History at Cambridge University, and other expert witnesses had shown in the course of the trial, Irving had persistently and speciously denigrated evidence that undermined his case while he had depended on evidence he knew to be fabricated. Irving had prided himself on being an 'independent historian' who considered himself 'reputable' precisely because he was neither a university-trained nor a university-employed historian. Therefore he did not have to worry over the opinions of what he claimed was a corrupt establishment. Most professional historians ignored his work in their turn. Thoroughgoing examination of Irving's work, and the resultant exposure of its inventions and distortions, were by-products of a rare instance of mutual contact. The American historian Deborah Lipstadt had alleged that Irving was a holocaust denier; Irving had threatened her and her publisher with a law suit alleging defamation; Lipstadt and her publisher stood by what she had written. There are three important consequences. First, we now know in great detail about the breaches of the rules of evidence to which professional historians should adhere which were committed by Irving. Second, historians' rules of evidence proved essentially compatible with those applied in a court of law. Third, and as a direct result, it remains possible for academic historians to call writers who are well informed about the Holocaust and nevertheless deny that it happened by their right name: liars.[22]

Such is the force of a nineteenth-century historical tradition which, although subject to inordinate and discrete pressures in the succeeding century, appears to have gained more power than it has lost. How far its norms and standards extend beyond the academy remains an urgent question. There is even more at stake here than securing against posthumous insults to the victims of genocide and grotesque affronts to the memories of its survivors. Because they can inspire people to act, stories about the past can be dangerous. Linda Colley, writing in 1991, alerted us both to the tangibility and scale of the danger and to the commensurate obligations laid on academic historians. In the twentieth century,

> Millions of men and women have died because they or others have believed fabrications about the past fed them by politicians, by journalists, by fanatics – and by bad historians as well. If historians have any public function at all, and they should have, it is to point out that the past cannot be entirely mocked: that some truths can be ascertained amidst the myths, the memories, and the doubts. If they fail to do this, they deserve nothing better than … to be hounded from the shelter of academe and buried in unknown graves.[23]

Notes

1   E. Hobsbawm, *Age of Extremes: The Short Twentieth Century 1914–1991*, London, Michael Joseph, 1994, p. 3.

2   R. J. Evans, 'Prologue: What Is History? – Now', in D. Cannadine (ed.) *What Is History Now?*, Basingstoke, Palgrave Macmillan, 2002, pp. 1–18; p. 10.

3   Cf. F. Fernández-Armesto, 'Epilogue: What Is History *Now*?', in *ibid.*, pp. 148–61; p. 158.

4   M. Confino, 'Some Random Thoughts on History's Recent Past', *History and Memory*, 2000, vol. 12, pp. 29–51; pp. 50–1.

5   Confino, 'Random Thoughts', p. 29.

6   Hobsbawm, *Interesting Times: A Twentieth-Century Life*, London, Allen Lane, 2002, p. 296.

7   See e.g. K. Füßmann, H. T. Grütter and J. Rüsen (eds) *Historische Faszination. Geschichtskultur heute*, Cologne, Böhlau, 1994.

8   P. Nora (ed.) *Les lieux de mémoire*, 7 vols, Paris, Gallimard, 1984–92.

9   P. Nora, 'From *Lieux de mémoire* to *Realms of Memory*', Preface to *idem* (ed.) *Realms of Memory vol. 1: Conflicts and Divisions*, New York, Columbia University Press, 1996, pp. xxiii–xxiv.

10   Nora, 'From *Lieux de mémoire*', p. xxiv.

11   For useful discussion and further references, see R. Koshar, Review Article: 'Where Does German Memory Lie?', *Central European History*, 2003, vol. 36, pp. 435–45; E. François and H. Schulze, 'Einleitung', in *idem* (eds) *Deutsche Erinnerungsorte*, Munich, C. H. Beck, 2001, pp. 9–24 and 674 n. 23.

12   Cf. S. Schama, *Dead Certainties (Unwarranted speculations)*, London, Granta, 1991.

13   M. Rubin, 'What is Cultural History Now?', in D. Cannadine, *What is History Now?*, pp. 80–94; p. 81.

14   L. Colley, 'Fabricating the Past', *Times Literary Supplement*, no. 4602 (14 June 1991) p. 5.

15   Philip L. Cantelon, 'As a Business: Hired, Not Bought', in J. B. Gardner and P. S. LaPaglia (eds) *Public History: Essays from the Field*, Malabar FL, Krieger, 1999, pp. 385–95.

16   These issues are usefully addressed in J. Revel and G. Levi (eds) *Political Uses of the Past: The Recent Mediterranean Experience*, London and Portland OR, Frank Cass, 2002.

17   Hans Mommsen with Manfred Grieger, *Das Volkswagenwerk und seine Arbeiter im Dritten Reich*, Düsseldorf, ECON, 1997.

18   For a brief discussion, see R. J. Evans, *Telling Lies About Hitler. The Holocaust, History and the David Irving Trial*, London, Verso, 2002, p. 240.

19   K. Wilson (ed.) *Forging the Collective Memory. Government and International Historians through Two World Wars*, Oxford, Berghahn, 1996; S. Zala, *Geschichte unter der Schere politischer Zensur. Amtliche Aktensammlungen im internationalen Vergleich*, Munich, Oldenbourg, 2001; P. Lambert, 'Friedrich Thimme, G. P. Gooch and the Publication of Documents on the Origins of the First World War: Patriotism, Academic Liberty and a Search for Anglo-German Understanding, 1920–1938', in S. Berger, P. Lambert and P. Schumann (eds) *Historikerdialoge. Geschichte, Mythos und Gedächtnis im deutsch-britischen kulturellen Austausch 1750–2000*, Göttingen, Vandenhoeck & Ruprecht, 2003, pp. 275–308.

20   See above, Chapter 6.

21   See R. J. Evans, *In Defence of History*, London, Granta, 1997, pp. 116–24.

22   R. J. Evans, *Telling Lies About Hitler*.

23   L. Colley, 'Fabricating the Past'.

Index

Abraham, D. 296
Abrams, P. 146
Abse, L. 130
academic liberty 3, 11–12, 14, 40, 41, 44–5, 46, 48, 83, 110, 294
Achebe, C. 167
Acton, J. E. E. D. 31–3, 46
Adams, C. K. 22
Adams, G. B. 34
Adams, H. B. 21, 33, 49
Adler, A. 130
agency, problem of 2, 46, 51, 94, 98–9, 103, 114, 115, 176, 211; *see also* causation; 'history from below'
Aldgate, A. 246
Alltagsgeschichte 87, 170
amateur historians and amateur historiography 3, 15–17, 20, 22, 26, 30, 31–2, 44, 72, 79, 113, 130, 241, 243 n. 3, 242–3, 269–7, 290, 297; amateur historical societies 30–31, 274, 276; *see also* professionalisation of history; public interest in history
American Film Institute 252
Anderson, B. 211
Anderson, P. 146
Andrews, C. 21
Annales School 62–3, 78–88, 94, 97, 123, 125–7, 142, 152, 155, 156, 165, 176, 219; *see also* journals
anthropology 257, 259; and history 84–5, 112, 115, 122–3, 144, 150–61, 229, 230, 231, 263; and sociology 141; cultural 152, 233; 'historical turn' in 157; physical 151; *see also* ethnography
anti-modernism and history 15, 97
antiquarianism 26, 117, 259, 261, 276,

278, 292; *see also* amateur historians and amateur historiography
archival research 28, 29–30, 34, 56, 162, 194, 233–4; and fieldwork 156, 157, 294–5
archives 9, 14, 16, 28, 29–30, 32, 38, 43, 80, 158, 234, 253, 270, 282, 287–8, 290, 294, 296
Arnold, M. 258
Asch, R. G. 222
Ashley, W. J. 47, 66–7, 70
Aubin, H. 94–5

Bailey, P. 257–8
Bailyn, B. 118
Bakhtin, M. 265
Baring-Gould, S. 261, 262
Barraclough, G. 129–30, 142, 147, 229
Barta, T. 249
Barth, J.
Barthes, R. 87, 156, 228, 232
Barton, J. 114
Baudrillard, J. 227, 235
Beard, C. 49–52
Beard, M. 194
Becker, C. 49, 51
Beesly, E. S. 18
Behar, R. 157
Bell, D. 227
Below, G. von 13, 28, 41–2
Belsey, C. 164
Bender, T. 116–18
Benjamin, W. 163
Bennett, J. 193
Berghofer, R. Jr 232
Bergson, H. 80–1
Berr, H. 80
Beveridge, W. 73